HOLT McDOUGAL LITERA

Adapted Interactive Reader Teacher's Edition

GRADE 9

a division of Houghton Mifflin Harcourt

Printed in the U.S.A.

ISBN-13 978-0-547-61954-5

1 2 3 4 5 6 7 8 9 10 0982 18 17 16 15 14 13 12 11

4500295307 ^ B C D E F G

TABLE OF CONTENTS

The **Essential Course of Study** designates an effective and efficient choice of selections for mastery of Reading Literature and Informational Text Standards.

SKILLS STRAND	Text Analysis	Reading
UNIT 1		
The Most Dangerous Game	Conflict	Visualize
The Gift of the Magi	Irony	Predict
Horse of the Century		Synthesize
The Raven/Incident in a Rose	Narrative Poetry	Reading Poetry
UNIT 2		
The Necklace	Character Motivation	Make Inferences
from *I Know Why the Caged Bird Sings*	Characterization in Autobiography	Analyze Perspectives
from *Rosa Parks/Rosa*	Characterization Across Genres	Set a Purpose for Reading
UNIT 3		
A Christmas Memory	Details of Setting	Analyze Imagery
Through the Tunnel	Setting as Symbol	Analyze Details
The Cask of Amontillado	Mood	Paraphrase
from *A Walk in the Woods*	Setting and Mood	Identify Author's Perspective
Wilderness Letter		Read Primary Sources
UNIT 4		
The Scarlet Ibis	Symbol	Make Inferences About Characters
Poem on Returning to Dwell in the Country/My Heart Leaps Up/The Sun	Universal Theme	Reading Poetry for Theme
Two Kinds/Rice and Rose Bowl Blues	Theme Across Genres	Set a Purpose for Reading
UNIT 5		
Who Killed the Iceman?/Skeletal Sculptures	Text Features	Take Notes
The Lost Boys	Author's Purpose	Interpret Graphic Aids
Consumer Documents	Consumer Documents	Adjust Reading Rate

SKILLS STRAND	Text Analysis	Reading
UNIT 6		
I Have a Dream	Argument	Understand Rhetorical Devices
Testimony Before the Senate	Persuasive Techniques	Summarize
How Private Is Your Private Life?/The Privacy Debate: One Size Doesn't Fit All	Fact and Opinion	Recognize Bias
UNIT 7		
Spring is like a perhaps hand/Elegy for the Giant Tortoises/Today	Diction	Paraphrase
UNIT 8		
Where Have You Gone, Charming Billy?/ Tim O'Brien: The Naked Soldier	Realism	Analyze Sequence
A Few Words	Tone	Paraphrase
The Sneeze from *The Good Doctor*	Farce	Visualize
UNIT 9		
from *Angela's Ashes*	Memoir	Use Allusions to Make Inferences
American History	Influence of Author's Background	Connect
Special Report	Controlling Idea	
UNIT 10		
from *The Tragedy of Romeo and Juliet*	Shakespearean Drama	Reading Shakespearean Drama
Great Movies: Romeo and Juliet		Analyze a Critical Review
UNIT 11		
The Cyclops from the *Odyssey*	Epic Hero	Reading an Epic

How to Use the Student Book

Academic Vocabulary for Unit 1

You will see these Academic Vocabulary words as you work through this book. You will also be asked to use them as you write and talk about the selections in this unit.

Analyze (AN uh lyz) is a verb that means *to examine something by looking critically or closely at it.*
After I read a story, I like to **analyze** the plot.

Why might a sports team analyze one of its videotaped games? ________

Element (EL uh muhnt) is a noun that means *a needed or basic part of something.*
An interesting setting is one **element** of a good story.

Name one element of a good class discussion: ________

Infer (in FER) is a verb that means *to make a reasonable guess based on clues or facts.*
Based on Susan's frown, I **infer** that she did not like my answer.

What might you infer if you saw a "Road Closed" sign? ________

Sequence (SEE kwuhns) is a noun that means *the order in which one thing follows another.*
The directions include a **sequence** of steps for setting the clock.

What is the sequence of steps for making your favorite snack? ________

Structure (STRUK chuhr) is a noun that means *something made of parts put together or the way something is put together.*
The **structure** of a story's plot can add to its suspense.

Describe the structure of your school building: ________

ACADEMIC VOCABULARY 3

Academic Vocabulary for the Unit

Academic vocabulary is the language your students use to talk and write about the subjects they are studying, including math, science, social studies, and language arts. Understanding and using academic vocabulary correctly will help them succeed in their classes and on tests.

Each unit in this book introduces five academic vocabulary words. They will practice each word on this page by writing a sentence about their lives using the word. They will also have a chance to study these words in more depth later in the unit.

Before Reading

The Necklace

Based on the short story by Guy de Maupassant

How important is STATUS?

What happens when people place too much importance on status, or the standing they have in a group? In "The Necklace," you'll meet Madame Loisel, a woman whose desire for status costs her more than she bargains for.

TURN AND TALK With a partner, discuss how status is determined at your school. Then, add at least three of these things to the list at left. After you've finished your list, discuss with a partner whether you think the things on the list *should* determine status.

Things That Determine Status

1. *stylish clothes*
2. *athletic ability*
3. ________
4. ________
5. ________

Text Analysis: Character Motivation

Motivation (MOH tuh VAY shuhn) is the reason behind someone's action. Motivation makes a person or character act in a certain way. In the chart below, a person's action is described in the left column. A possible motivation is in the right. In each of the last three rows, write down a possible reason for Ryan's action.

ACTION	MOTIVATION
Ignoring her pain, the runner sprints to the finish line.	*The runner wants to win the race.*
Serena secretly watches Justin in class all day.	*Serena has a crush on Justin.*
Ryan misses a friend's party to work on his science project.	
Ryan borrows money to buy new shoes.	
While at a coffee shop, Ryan shouts at one of his friends.	

As you read "The Necklace," you will consider what Madame Loisel's actions tell you about her motivation.

72 ADAPTED INTERACTIVE READER / UNIT 2: CHARACTERIZATION AND POINT OF VIEW

Before Reading

The Before Reading pages will prepare your students to read the selection. Here they can preview the skills and vocabulary they will need as they read.

Big Question

This activity will get your students thinking about a real-life question the selection addresses, and how that question connects to what is important to them. Sometimes they will work in a group or with a partner to complete this activity. After reading, they will return to this activity.

Text Analysis

This section presents a brief, easy-to-understand lesson that introduces an important text element and explains what students should look for in the selection as they read.

Reading Skill: Make Inferences

Sometimes writers tell you directly what a character is like. At other times, they will give clues. Using these clues, you can make an **inference** (IN fuhr uhns), or logical guess, about what the character is like. As you read, you will make inferences about the story by adding what you know from your own experience to these clues. Notice how a reader might make an inference in the chart below.

Clue from Story	My Experience	Inference
Mr. Loisel says, "We must replace the necklace." (line 70)	When I broke my friend's MP3 player, my mom made me work to replace it.	Mr. Loisel is honest and careful to do the right thing.

Vocabulary in Context

Note: Words are listed in the order in which they appear in the story.

Prospects (PROS pektz) is a noun meaning *chances of success.*
*Madame Loisel's **prospects** for obtaining wealth were limited.*

Pauper (PAW puhr) is a noun that means *a very poor person.*
*Mathilde thought her clothes made her look like a **pauper.***

Adulation (aj uh LAY shuhn) is a noun that means *too much praise.*
*The partygoers expressed **adulation** for Madame Loisel.*

Aghast (uh GAST) is an adjective that means *shocked or horrified.*
*Loisel was **aghast** when he heard that the necklace was lost.*

Askew (uh SKYOO) is an adjective meaning *crooked or leaning to one side.*
*Mathilde straightened the slightly **askew** necklace.*

Vocabulary Practice

Review the words and sample sentences above. Then, with a partner, discuss possible answers to each of the following questions. Use each boldface word at least once in your discussion.

1. How is a **prospect** different from a hope?
2. How is a **pauper** different from a beggar?
3. Why is respect better than **adulation**?
4. How is **aghast** different from surprised?
5. What is the difference between **askew** and messy?

THE NECKLACE 73

Reading Skill or Strategy

This lesson presents a reading skill or strategy that will help your students' reading comprehension. They will learn why this skill is important, and how it can help them become betters readers. A graphic organizer will help students put the strategy into practice.

Vocabulary in Context

Through this feature students will be introduced to key Vocabulary words in the selection. Each entry gives the pronunciation and definition as well as an example sentence.

Vocabulary Practice

This activity gives students a chance to practice the selection Vocabulary words.

Monitor Your Comprehension

SET A PURPOSE FOR READING
Read this story to find out how a borrowed necklace changes a woman's life.

BACKGROUND At the time of this story, France had three classes of society—upper, middle, and lower. A man could become rich enough to move into a higher class, but a woman had to marry to get into a higher class. To do that, her family had to pay a dowry (DOW ree)—money or property—to her new husband.

VOCABULARY
The word **prospects** (PROS pektz) is a noun meaning *chances of success.*

MAKE INFERENCES
Underline words and phrases in lines 5–10 that describe how Mathilde Loisel looks. Then, circle words and phrases in the same lines that describe her emotions. Make an inference about what kind of person she is.

Mathilde was a pretty, charming, middle-class girl. She had no dowry—no money from her family to take to her marriage. She also had few prospects of meeting a rich man, so she married a clerk in the Ministry of Education.

She dressed plainly, and she was unhappy that she couldn't afford fine clothes. She daydreamed about being rich.

Her husband would say, "Ah! A good stew! There's nothing I like better." But she dreamed of fancy dinner parties.

She had no evening clothes or jewelry, yet she wanted them and felt she should have them. She needed to be charming.

One evening her husband handed her an envelope. Excited, she opened it and found an invitation to a grand party at a **mansion**, the huge home of a government official.

She tossed it aside.

VISUAL VOCABULARY
A **mansion** is a very large and fancy home.

74 ADAPTED INTERACTIVE READER / UNIT 2: CHARACTERIZATION AND POINT OF VIEW

Adapted Readings

Most of the selections in this book have been adapted, or retold, to make the text more accessible for struggling readers. That is, the selection vocabulary and sentence structure have been simplified. In the process of adapting these selections, great care has been taken to maintain the selection flavor and tone.

Set a Purpose for Reading

This feature gives students a reason for reading the selection.

Background

This paragraph gives students helpful information about the selection they are about to read. They may learn more about the author; the time period the selection was written; or other facts that will help them better understand the selection.

Text Analysis or Reading Skill or Strategy

Notes in the margin help your students identify and analyze the text element or reading skill they learned about on the Before Reading pages.

Visual Vocabulary

This feature uses pictures to help students understand a word's meaning.

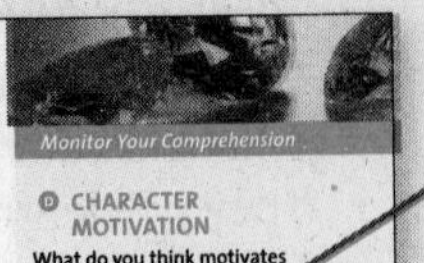

Her husband came in around seven. He'd had no luck.

By the end of the week, they had given up all hope. Loisel looked five years older. He said, "We must replace the necklace."

They found a necklace exactly like the first. It cost forty thousand francs, but they could get it for thirty-six.

IN OTHER WORDS At home, Mathilde realizes that she has lost her friend's necklace. She and Loisel look for it everywhere. They can't find it, so they decide to buy a matching necklace. The new necklace will cost thirty-six thousand francs.

Loisel had eighteen thousand francs he had inherited from his father. He borrowed the rest. He got a thousand francs from one, four hundred from another—a hundred here, sixty there. He signed notes and made deals with loan sharks.[3] ⊙

When Madame Loisel returned the necklace, her friend said coldly, "You should have returned it sooner."

Madame Forestier didn't open the case.

Madame Loisel bravely faced being poor. That debt had to be paid, and she would pay it. She let her maid go, and she and her husband moved to a cheap attic apartment. ⊙

She cooked and did housework. She scrubbed the laundry, took out the garbage, carried up water, and dressed like a peasant. She watched every coin she spent. She bargained for food with the fruit dealer and the grocer, and they insulted her.

Her husband worked evenings as a bookkeeper and at night, he copied documents for very little pay.

This lasted for ten years.

Finally, all the debts and interest were paid.

Madame Loisel looked old now. Sometimes she'd remember when she had been so admired. Now her hair was messy, her skirts askew her hands red, and her voice shrill.

What if she hadn't lost the necklace? Who knows? How little there is between joy and misery! PAUSE & REFLECT

⊙ CHARACTER MOTIVATION
What do you think motivates the Loisels to go into such great debt?

⊙ LANGUAGE COACH
"She let her maid go" (line 81) is an idiom, an expression that is not meant to be taken literally. In this idiom, to "let someone go" means *to end a job*. The maid was not trapped and freed; the Loisels ended her job with them because they could not afford to pay her.

VOCABULARY
The word askew (uh SKYOO) is an adjective meaning *crooked or leaning to one side.*

PAUSE & REFLECT
With a partner, discuss what you think the Loisels' life would have been like if they hadn't lost the necklace.

3. **loan sharks:** People who lend money by requiring that borrowers pay a very large amount of money in addition to repaying the amount of the loan.

THE NECKLACE 77

In Other Words

These summaries help students understand what they have just read.

Language Coach

These notes will help your students master the finer points of the English language.

Vocabulary words

The Vocabulary words introduced on the Before Reading page are defined in the side column and appear underlined in blue within the selection.

Pause & Reflect

These notes appear at key points throughout the selection. Pause & Reflect questions give students a chance to think about what they have just read.

After Reading

Text Analysis: Character Motivation

Consider what you know about each character's feelings and goals. Review the actions listed in the left column of the chart below. In the right column, write down the motivation for each action. One motivation has been filled in for you.

Action	Motivation
Mathilde Loisel is upset because she does not have any jewelry to wear to the party. (lines 38–39)	*Mathilde wants to be well dressed so that others will admire and praise her.*
Mathilde looks at herself in the mirror one last time. (lines 59–60)	
Mathilde's husband searches everywhere for the lost necklace. (lines 64–68)	
The Loisels go into debt to pay for the new necklace. (lines 74–76)	
Madame Forestier is angry because Mathilde does not return the necklace immediately. (lines 77–79)	

How have Mathilde's motivations led her and her husband into difficulties? Write your answer on the lines below.

THE NECKLACE 79

After Reading

After Reading pages feature graphic organizers. Students will use them to review the skills they have practiced throughout the selection.

Text Analysis

Here students can review the text element they have been practicing throughout the selection.

After Reading

Reading Skill: Make Inferences

In the story, we learn a lot about the Loisels, but we don't know very much about Madame Forestier. Look back through the story to find three details about Madame Forestier and record them below. Then use the clues and your own knowledge to make an inference about her.

Clues from the Story
1. ______
2. ______

↓

My Experience
1. ______
2. ______

↓

Inference
______

How important is **STATUS?**

Do you think popularity, or status, is an important thing to have or pursue? Why or why not?

______

Vocabulary Practice

With a partner, discuss why each statement below is true or false. Use each Vocabulary word once in your discussion.

1. If you have **prospects** of wealth, you believe you will be a **pauper.**
2. If someone heaps **adulation** on you, you must have done something well.
3. If you are **aghast** about something, you are not surprised at all.
4. If a picture is **askew**, it is perfectly straight.

80 ADAPTED INTERACTIVE READER / UNIT 2: CHARACTERIZATION AND POINT OF VIEW

Reading Skill or Reading Strategy

The Reading Skill or Strategy activity follows up on the skill students used to understand the text.

Big Question

Here's a chance for students to think again about the Big Question they examined before reading. It offers your students an opportunity to consider whether their thoughts have changed now that they have read the selection.

Vocabulary Practice

This activity gives students an opportunity to practice the selection Vocabulary words.

Academic Vocabulary in Speaking

The word **complex** (kuhm PLEKS) means *made up of two or more parts.*
Richard could not find all the pieces for the **complex** tool.
Complex can also mean *not simple.*
That story is very **complex** and confusing.

The word **evaluate** (ih VAL yoo ayt) means *to judge the value or importance of something.*
The store owner wants to **evaluate** my collection of baseball cards to see how much they are worth.

TURN AND TALK In "The Necklace," you learned about characters with **complex** motivations. With a partner, **evaluate** your own motivations for achieving a goal. Be sure to use **complex** and **evaluate** in your discussion.

Assessment Practice

DIRECTIONS Use "The Necklace" to answer questions 1–4.

1 Madame Loisel is unhappy at the beginning of the story because —
- (A) she wishes she were pretty and charming
- (B) she does not like her husband
- (C) she wishes she had wealth and luxuries
- (D) she does not like housework

2 What is Madame Loisel's motivation for borrowing the necklace from her friend?
- (A) She wants to appear elegant and well dressed at the party.
- (B) She wants to add glamour to the old dress she has to wear.
- (C) She likes her friend's jewelry better than her own.
- (D) She does not want to appear too dressed up at the party.

3 What inference can you make about why the Loisels are so willing to replace the necklace?
- (A) They are embarrassed by the situation.
- (B) They want everyone to think highly of them.
- (C) They are trying to trick Madame Forestier.
- (D) They want to keep the necklace for themselves.

4 What unexpected plot twist occurs at the end of the story?
- (A) Madame Forestier learns that the Loisels have been paying off a debt.
- (B) Monsieur Loisel goes into debt to pay off the necklace.
- (C) Madame Loisel learns that the necklace she borrowed was fake.
- (D) Madame Forestier immediately recognizes Madame Loisel.

THE NECKLACE 81

Academic Vocabulary

In this activity, students use the Academic Vocabulary words for the unit in a speaking or writing activity about the selection.

Assessment Practice

Finally, after each selection, multiple-choice questions assess your students' knowledge of the selection and the skill taught with it.

UNIT 1 The Plot Thickens

NARRATIVE STRUCTURE

Be sure to read the Text Analysis Workshop on pp. 28–35 in *Holt McDougal Literature.*

Academic Vocabulary for Unit 1

You will see these Academic Vocabulary words as you work through this book. You will also be asked to use them as you write and talk about the selections in this unit.

Analyze (AN uh lyz) is a verb that means *to examine something by looking critically or closely at it.*

After I read a story, I like to **analyze** the plot.

Why might a sports team **analyze** one of its videotaped games? ________

Answers will vary.

Element (EL uh muhnt) is a noun that means *a needed or basic part of something.*

An interesting setting is one **element** of a good story.

Name one **element** of a good class discussion: ________

Answers will vary.

Infer (in FER) is a verb that means *to make a reasonable guess based on clues or facts.*

Based on Susan's frown, I **infer** that she did not like my answer.

What might you **infer** if you saw a "Road Closed" sign? ________

Answers will vary.

Sequence (SEE kwuhns) is a noun that means *the order in which one thing follows another.*

The directions include a **sequence** of steps for setting the clock.

What is the **sequence** of steps for making your favorite snack? ________

Answers will vary.

Structure (STRUK chuhr) is a noun that means *something made of parts put together or the way something is put together.*

The **structure** of a story's plot can add to its suspense.

Describe the **structure** of your school building: ________

Answers will vary.

The Most Dangerous Game

Short story by Richard Connell

What does it take to be a SURVIVOR?

In a test of survival, what traits, or qualities, help a person succeed? In "The Most Dangerous Game," you'll find out if one man has what it takes to face terrible danger and overcome it.

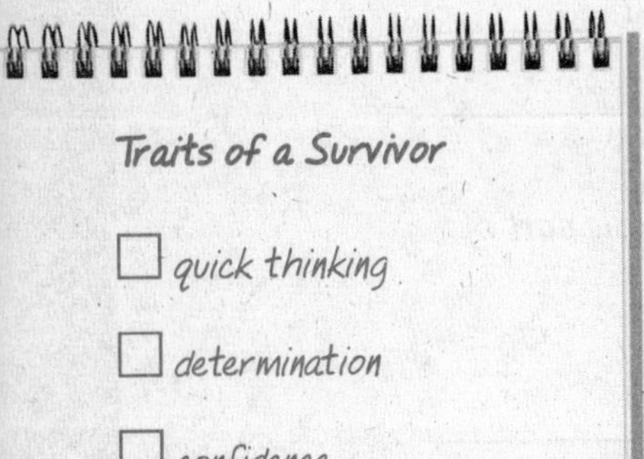

Traits of a Survivor
quick thinking
determination
confidence
willingness to take risks
intelligence
experience
imagination
sharp senses
calmness
physical strength

TURN AND TALK All of the traits listed on the left might be useful in a dangerous situation. But which one is the most important? Number the list of traits from 1 to 10, with 1 being the most important and 10 being the least. Then share the reasons for your opinions with a partner. ***Answers will vary.***

Text Analysis: Conflict

Plot is the series of events that make up a story. At the heart of any plot is **conflict,** the main character's struggles with someone or something else. Conflict fits into basic plot structure as shown in the diagram below.

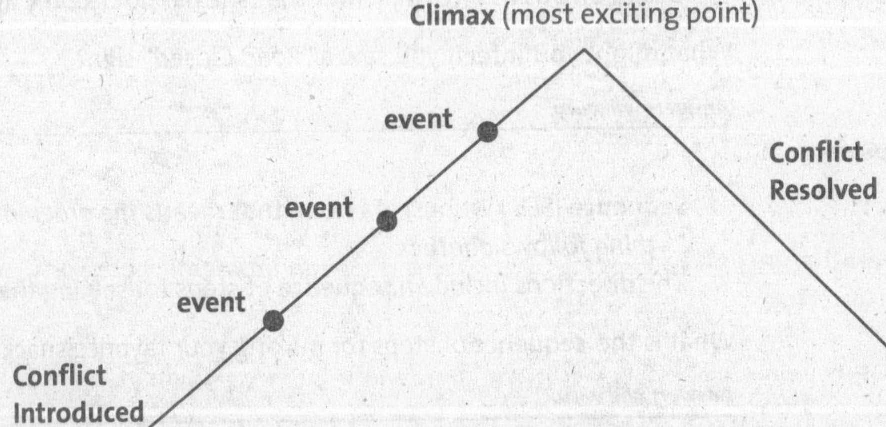

Sometimes, however, plot events are not as **linear**—occurring one after another in time—as this diagram might suggest. **Non-linear plot development** can increase **suspense,** the reader's sense of anxiety or worry, as the conflict builds. Nonlinear plot development includes the use of

- **foreshadowing:** hints at what is coming in the story
- **flashbacks:** a look at events before the story started
- **flash-forwards:** sudden jumps forward in time

Reading Strategy: Visualize

Good readers use a writer's words to **visualize,** or form images of the story's setting, characters, and events. By paying attention to the details the writer includes, you can form mental pictures, almost as if you were watching a movie. To visualize a story:

- pay special attention to descriptions and word choices
- look for **sensory details,** details that appeal to one or more of your senses—sight, hearing, touch, smell, or taste
- reread long descriptions to catch details you may have missed

As you read, you will use a chart like the one below to record story details that help you visualize.

Details from Story	What I Visualize
Dank tropical night . . . thick warm blackness	*The Dark heavy air is almost like a blanket.*

Vocabulary in Context

Note: Words are listed in the order in which they appear in the story.

Disarming (dis AHR ming) is an adjective that means *removing dislike or suspicion.*
At first, Rainsford finds General Zaroff's manners **disarming.**

Condone (kuhn DOHN) is a verb that means *to forgive or overlook.*
Rainsford cannot **condone** horrible deeds.

Imperative (im PAIR uh tiv) is an adjective that means *absolutely necessary.*
Rainsford knows that escape is **imperative** if he is to survive.

Uncanny (uhn KAN ee) is an adjective that means *far beyond what is normal.*
Zaroff's amazing ability to keep finding Rainsford is **uncanny.**

Vocabulary Practice

Review the words and sample sentences above. Then, tell whether each statement below is true or false by writing either "T" or "F."

1. ___T___ Food and water are **imperative** for survival.
2. ___F___ The police **condone** crimes such as burglary.
3. ___F___ A person's sense of smell is **uncanny** if it is about average.
4. ___T___ A friendly greeting might be **disarming**

SET A PURPOSE FOR READING
Read this story to find out what one hunter thinks is the most dangerous game.

The Most Dangerous Game

Short story by
RICHARD CONNELL

BACKGROUND This story is about two men who hunt only for sport—for the fun of it, not for food. They especially enjoy killing large or dangerous animals. The word "game" can have two meanings for these hunters—a playful contest and their prey, or the animals they hunt. As the story begins, one of the two men is aboard a boat. He and another passenger are discussing a mysterious island nearby.

Ⓐ **CONFLICT**
Foreshadowing is the use of clues to hint at what's to come. Circle the words in lines 1–6 that foreshadow a possible **conflict**, or problem, in the story.

"Off there to the right—somewhere—is a large island," said Whitney. "It's rather a mystery—"

"What island is it?" Rainsford asked.

"The old charts call it 'Ship-Trap Island,'" Whitney replied. "A suggestive name, isn't it? Sailors have a curious dread of the place. I don't know why. Some superstition—" Ⓐ

"Can't see it," remarked Rainsford, trying to peer through the dank tropical night that was palpable as it pressed its thick warm blackness in upon the yacht.

"You've good eyes," said Whitney, with a laugh, "and I've seen you pick off a moose moving in the brown fall bush at four hundred yards, but even you can't see four miles or so through a moonless Caribbean night."

"Nor four yards," admitted Rainsford. "Ugh! It's like moist black velvet."

"It will be light enough in Rio,"[1] promised Whitney. "We should make it in a few days. I hope the jaguar guns have come from Purdey's.[2] We should have some good hunting up the Amazon. Great sport, hunting."

"The best sport in the world," agreed Rainsford.

"For the hunter," amended Whitney. "Not for the jaguar."

"Don't talk rot, Whitney," said Rainsford. "You're a big-game hunter, not a philosopher. Who cares how a jaguar feels?"

"Perhaps the jaguar does," observed Whitney.

"Bah! They've no understanding." (B)

"Even so, I rather think they understand one thing—fear. The fear of pain and the fear of death."

"Nonsense," laughed Rainsford. "This hot weather is making you soft, Whitney. Be a realist. The world is made up of two classes—the hunters and the huntees. Luckily, you and I are hunters. Do you think we've passed that island yet?"

"I can't tell in the dark. I hope so."

"Why?" asked Rainsford.

"The place has a reputation—a bad one."

"Cannibals?" suggested Rainsford.

"Hardly. Even cannibals wouldn't live in such a Godforsaken place. But it's gotten into sailor lore, somehow. Didn't you notice that the crew's nerves seemed a bit jumpy today?"

"They were a bit strange, now you mention it. Even Captain Nielsen—"

"Yes, even that tough-minded old Swede, who'd go up to the devil himself and ask him for a light. Those fishy blue eyes held a look I never saw there before. All I could get out of him was: 'This place has an evil name among seafaring men, sir.' Then he said to me, very gravely: 'Don't you feel anything?'—as if the air about us was actually poisonous. Now, you mustn't laugh when I tell you this—I did feel something like a sudden chill. **PAUSE & REFLECT**

1. **Rio:** Rio de Janeiro (REE oh day zhuh NAIR oh): a city on the coast of Brazil.
2. **Purdey's:** a British company that made hunting equipment.

(B) CONFLICT

Reread lines 20–25. In your own words, describe the **conflict,** or disagreement, between Rainsford and Whitney.

Possible answer: Rainsford and Whitney disagree about what hunted animals may or may not feel.

PAUSE & REFLECT

The author has given you important information about the **setting,** where the story takes place. With a partner, discuss what you have learned about Ship-Trap Island.

Students should discuss that the island is located in the Caribbean Sea (line 13). The island frightens the sailors and is difficult to see because it is a moonless night.

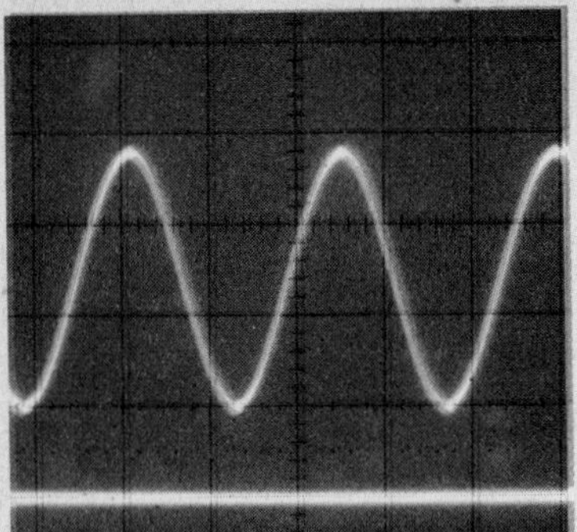

VISUAL VOCABULARY

A **wavelength** (WAYV lengkth) is the distance between the peaks, or tops, of waves. Sound, light, and other types of energy travel in waves.

"There was no breeze. The sea was as flat as a plate-glass window. We were drawing near the island then. What I felt was a—a mental chill; a sort of sudden dread."

"Pure imagination," said Rainsford. "One superstitious sailor can taint the whole ship's company with his fear."

"Maybe. But sometimes I think sailors have an extra sense that tells them when they are in danger. Sometimes I think evil is a tangible[3] thing—with **wavelengths**, just as sound and light have. An evil place can, so to speak, broadcast vibrations of evil. Anyhow, I'm glad we're getting out of this zone. Well, I think I'll turn in now, Rainsford."

"I'm not sleepy," said Rainsford. "I'm going to smoke another pipe up on the afterdeck."

"Good night, then, Rainsford. See you at breakfast."

"Right. Good night, Whitney."

IN OTHER WORDS Whitney and Rainsford are on a ship traveling to a hunting trip in South America. Whitney has heard from the sailors that an island in the distance is evil. He has a bad feeling about it. Rainsford insists that there is no reason to worry.

There was no sound in the night as Rainsford sat there but the muffled throb of the engine that drove the yacht swiftly through the darkness, and the swish and ripple of the wash of the propeller.

Rainsford, reclining in a steamer chair, indolently puffed on his favorite brier.[4] The sensuous drowsiness of the night was on him. "It's so dark," he thought, "that I could sleep without closing my eyes; the night would be my eyelids—"

An abrupt sound startled him. Off to the right he heard it, and his ears, expert in such matters, could not be mistaken. Again he heard the sound, and again. Somewhere, off in the blackness, someone had fired a gun three times. (C)

Rainsford sprang up and moved quickly to the rail, mystified. He strained his eyes in the direction from which the reports had

(C) VISUALIZE

Reread lines 67–74. Underline the details that appeal to your senses. To which senses do the details you underlined appeal?

Possible answer: The details appeal to the following senses: smell, sight, and hearing.

---

3. **tangible** (TAN juh buhl): able to be touched or felt.
4. **indolently** (IN duh luhnt lee) . . . **brier** (BRY er): lazily smoked a tobacco pipe made from the root of a brier bush.

come, but it was like trying to see through a blanket. He leaped upon the rail and balanced himself there, to get greater elevation; his pipe, striking a rope, was knocked from his mouth. He lunged for it; a short, hoarse cry came from his lips as he realized he had reached too far and had lost his balance. The cry was pinched off short as the blood-warm waters of the Caribbean Sea closed over his head.

IN OTHER WORDS Rainsford hears gunshots. He moves to the edge of the ship to see more and falls overboard.

► What causes Rainsford to fall from the ship? Underline the details of his fall.

He struggled up to the surface and tried to cry out, but the wash from the speeding yacht slapped him in the face, and the salt water in his open mouth made him gag and strangle. Desperately he struck out with strong strokes after the receding lights of the yacht, but he stopped before he had swum fifty feet. A certain cool-headedness had come to him; it was not the first time he had been in a tight place. There was a chance that his cries could be heard by someone aboard the yacht, but that chance was slender and grew more slender as the yacht raced on. He wrestled himself out of his clothes and shouted with all his power. The lights of the yacht became faint and ever-vanishing fireflies; then they were blotted out entirely by the night. D

Rainsford remembered the shots. They had come from the right, and doggedly he swam in that direction, swimming with slow, deliberate strokes, conserving his strength. For a seemingly endless time he fought the sea. He began to count his strokes; he could do possibly a hundred more and then—

Rainsford heard a sound. It came out of the darkness, a high, screaming sound, the sound of an animal in an extremity of anguish and terror.

He did not recognize the animal that made the sound; he did not try to; with fresh vitality he swam toward the sound.

D CONFLICT

An **internal conflict** is created when a character struggles with something *inside*—within his or her own heart or mind. An **external conflict** occurs when an *outside* force prevents the character from reaching a goal. Describe the conflict Rainsford now faces. Is the conflict internal or external?

Possible answer: The conflict is external. Rainsford has to fight for survival in the sea by swimming ashore.

Monitor Your Comprehension

He heard it again; then it was cut short by another noise, crisp, staccato.

"Pistol shot," muttered Rainsford, swimming on.

Ten minutes of determined effort brought another sound to his ears—the most welcome he had ever heard—the muttering and growling of the sea breaking on a rocky shore. He was almost on the rocks before he saw them; on a night less calm he would have been shattered against them. With his remaining strength he dragged himself from the swirling waters. Jagged crags appeared to jut up into the opaqueness[5]; he forced himself upward, hand over hand. Gasping, his hands raw, he reached a flat place at the top. Dense jungle came down to the very edge of the cliffs. What perils that tangle of trees and underbrush might hold for him did not concern Rainsford just then. All he knew was that he was safe from his enemy, the sea, and that utter weariness was on him. He flung himself down at the jungle edge and tumbled headlong into the deepest sleep of his life. E

E VISUALIZE

Underline the details in this paragraph that help you visualize the scene.

When he opened his eyes, he knew from the position of the sun that it was late in the afternoon. Sleep had given him new vigor; a sharp hunger was picking at him. He looked about him, almost cheerfully.

"Where there are pistol shots, there are men. Where there are men, there is food," he thought. But what kind of men, he wondered, in so forbidding a place? An unbroken front of snarled and ragged jungle fringed the shore. **PAUSE & REFLECT**

PAUSE & REFLECT

Why does Rainsford ask himself "what kind of men" live on the island?

Possible answer: Rainsford asks what kind of men live on the island because of its unwelcoming landscapes of dense jungle and steep cliffs.

He saw no sign of a trail through the closely knit web of weeds and trees; it was easier to go along the shore, and Rainsford floundered along by the water. Not far from where he had landed, he stopped.

Some wounded thing, by the evidence a large animal, had thrashed about in the underbrush; the jungle weeds were crushed down, and the moss was lacerated; one patch of weeds was stained crimson. A small, glittering object not far away caught Rainsford's eye, and he picked it up. It was an empty cartridge.

5. **opaqueness** (oh PAYK nis): here, darkness. Something opaque does not let light pass through.

"A twenty-two," he remarked. "That's odd. It must have been a fairly large animal, too. The hunter had his nerve with him to tackle it with a light gun. It's clear that the brute put up a fight. I suppose the first three shots I heard was when the hunter flushed his quarry[6] and wounded it. The last shot was when he trailed it here and finished it." F

He examined the ground closely and found what he had hoped to find—the print of hunting boots. They pointed along the cliff in the direction he had been going. Eagerly he hurried along, now slipping on a rotten log or a loose stone, but making headway; night was beginning to settle down on the island.

IN OTHER WORDS As Rainsford swims, he hears an animal's scream and another gunshot. Finally, he reaches land. He discovers that it is a jungle and finds clues that the noises he heard were the end of a hunt. He also finds footprints and follows them along the island.

Bleak darkness was blacking out the sea and jungle when Rainsford sighted the lights. He came upon them as he turned a crook in the coastline, and his first thought was that he had come upon a village, for there were many lights. But as he forged along, he saw to his great astonishment that all the lights were in one enormous building—a lofty structure with pointed towers plunging upward into the gloom. His eyes made out the shadowy outlines of a palatial château; it was set on a high bluff, and on three sides of it cliffs dived down to where the sea licked greedy lips in the shadows. G

"Mirage," thought Rainsford. But it was no mirage, he found, when he opened the tall spiked iron gate. The stone steps were real enough; the massive door with a leering **gargoyle** for a knocker was real enough; yet about it all hung an air of unreality.

He lifted the knocker, and it creaked up stiffly as if it had never before been used. He let it fall, and it startled him with its booming loudness. He thought he heard steps within; the door remained closed. Again Rainsford lifted the heavy knocker and let

6. **quarry** (KWAWR ee): the object of a hunt; prey.

Monitor Your Comprehension

F VISUALIZE

Reread lines 131–145. Then fill out the rest of the chart below. In the second box, answer the following question: How do you picture the hunt that Rainsford imagines?

Details from Story
Web of plants, crushed weeds, . . . *a large animal, had thrashed about in the underbrush; "one patch of weeds was stained crimson"*

↓

What I Visualize
I picture a vicious animal in a dense forest . . . *Possible answer: A hunter shoots at the bushes to get the animal to come out in the open. The hunter kills the animal.*

G LANGUAGE COACH

A château (line 158) is a large, often castle-like country house. This type of house is most common in France and other parts of Europe. The word *château* (sha TOH) comes to English directly from French and can be traced to an older word meaning "castle."

VISUAL VOCABULARY

A **gargoyle** (GAHR goyl) is a strange-looking creature used to decorate parts of buildings, often the spouts that drain rainwater from roofs. The gargoyle Rainsford sees is a door knocker.

Monitor Your Comprehension

it fall. The door opened then, opened as suddenly as if it were on a spring, and Rainsford stood blinking in the river of glaring gold light that poured out. The first thing Rainsford's eyes discerned was the largest man Rainsford had ever seen—a gigantic creature, solidly made and black-bearded to the waist. In his hand the man held a long-barreled revolver, and he was pointing it straight at Rainsford's heart.

Out of the snarl of beard two small eyes regarded Rainsford.

"Don't be alarmed," said Rainsford, with a smile which he hoped was **disarming**. "I'm no robber. I fell off a yacht. My name is Sanger Rainsford of New York City."

The menacing look in the eyes did not change. The revolver pointed as rigidly as if the giant were a statue. He gave no sign that he understood Rainsford's words, or that he had even heard them. He was dressed in uniform, a black uniform trimmed with gray astrakhan.[7]

"I'm Sanger Rainsford of New York," Rainsford began again. "I fell off a yacht. I am hungry."

The man's only answer was to raise with his thumb the hammer of his revolver. Then Rainsford saw the man's free hand go to his forehead in a military salute, and he saw him click his heels together and stand at attention. Another man was coming down the broad marble steps, an erect, slender man in evening clothes. He advanced to Rainsford and held out his hand.

In a cultivated[8] voice marked by a slight accent that gave it added precision and deliberateness, he said: "It is a very great pleasure and honor to welcome Mr. Sanger Rainsford, the celebrated hunter, to my home."

Automatically Rainsford shook the man's hand.

"I've read your book about hunting snow leopards in Tibet,[9] you see," explained the man. "I am General Zaroff."

Rainsford's first impression was that the man was singularly handsome; his second was that there was an original, almost bizarre quality about the general's face. He was a tall man past

VOCABULARY

The word **disarming** (dis AHR ming) is an adjective that means *removing dislike or suspicion.*

Underline the details that tell you Rainsford's words and actions don't succeed at being *disarming*.

7. **astrakhan** (AS truh kan): a fur made from the curly, wavy wool of young lambs from Astrakhan (a city of southwest Russia).
8. **cultivated** (KUHL tuh vay tid): showing good education and proper manners.
9. **Tibet** (tuh BET): a region in central Asia.

middle age, for his hair was a vivid white; but his thick eyebrows and pointed military moustache were as black as the night from which Rainsford had come. His eyes, too, were black and very bright. He had high cheekbones, a sharp-cut nose, a spare, dark face, the face of a man used to giving orders, the face of an aristocrat. Turning to the giant in uniform, the general made a sign. The giant put away his pistol, saluted, withdrew. (H)

"Ivan is an incredibly strong fellow," remarked the general, "but he has the misfortune to be deaf and dumb. A simple fellow, but, I'm afraid, like all his race, a bit of a savage."

"Is he Russian?"

"He is a Cossack,"[10] said the general, and his smile showed red lips and pointed teeth. "So am I.

IN OTHER WORDS Rainsford reaches a large building. He knocks at the door and is met by a giant man with a gun. Before the giant can shoot, an elegant man stops him, introduces himself as General Zaroff, and welcomes Rainsford.

"Come," he said, "we shouldn't be chatting here. We can talk later. Now you want clothes, food, rest. You shall have them. This is a most restful spot."

Ivan had reappeared, and the general spoke to him with lips that moved but gave forth no sound.

"Follow Ivan, if you please, Mr. Rainsford," said the general. "I was about to have my dinner when you came. I'll wait for you. You'll find that my clothes will fit you, I think."

It was to a huge, beam-ceilinged bedroom with a canopied bed big enough for six men that Rainsford followed the silent giant. Ivan laid out an evening suit, and Rainsford, as he put it on, noticed that it came from a London tailor who ordinarily cut and sewed for none below the rank of duke.

The dining room to which Ivan conducted him was in many ways remarkable. There was a medieval magnificence about it; it suggested a baronial hall of feudal times with its oaken panels, its

10. **Cossack** (KOS ak): a member of a southern Russian people. Many Cossacks served as horseman under the Russian tsars (zars), or emperors, and were famous for their fierceness in battle.

Monitor Your Comprehension

(H) VISUALIZE
You've just read a detailed description of General Zaroff. Visualize him based on this description. What does the way he looks lead you to believe about what kind of person he is?

Possible answer: The description of General Zaroff makes me believe that he is a tall, handsome, intelligent, older military leader.

high ceiling, its vast refectory table where two score men could sit down to eat. About the hall were the mounted heads of many animals—lions, tigers, elephants, moose, bears; larger or more perfect specimens Rainsford had never seen. At the great table the general was sitting, alone.

"You'll have a cocktail, Mr. Rainsford," he suggested. The cocktail was surpassingly good; and, Rainsford noted, the table appointments were of the finest—the linen, the crystal, the silver, the china.

They were eating *borsch,* the rich red soup with whipped cream so dear to Russian palates. Half apologetically General Zaroff said: "We do our best to preserve the amenities[11] of civilization here. Please forgive any lapses. We are well off the beaten track, you know. Do you think the champagne has suffered from its long ocean trip?"

"Not in the least," declared Rainsford. He was finding the general a most thoughtful and affable[12] host, a true cosmopolite.[13] But there was one small trait of the general's that made Rainsford uncomfortable. Whenever he looked up from his plate, he found the general studying him, appraising him narrowly.

PAUSE & REFLECT

PAUSE & REFLECT
Rainsford is uncomfortable when he notices that the general is studying him. What do you think the general is trying to do here?

Possible answer: The general is trying to understand Rainsford's character and is watching him closely to find out more about the man who has appeared at his home.

"Perhaps," said General Zaroff, "you were surprised that I recognized your name. You see, I read all books on hunting published in English, French, and Russian. I have but one passion in my life, Mr. Rainsford, and it is the hunt."

"You have some wonderful heads here," said Rainsford as he ate a particularly well cooked filet mignon. "That Cape buffalo is the largest I ever saw."

"Oh, that fellow. Yes, he was a monster."

"Did he charge you?"

"Hurled me against a tree," said the general. "Fractured my skull. But I got the brute."

11. **amenities** (uh MEN ih tees): things that make life easier or more pleasant.
12. **affable** (AF uh buhl): pleasant and easy to speak to.
13. **cosmopolite** (koz MOP uh lyt): a person who has traveled widely and feels at home everywhere in the world.

"I've always thought," said Rainsford, "that the Cape buffalo is the most dangerous of all big game."

For a moment the general did not reply; he was smiling his curious red-lipped smile. Then he said slowly: "No. You are wrong, sir. The Cape buffalo is not the most dangerous big game." He sipped his wine. "Here in my preserve on this island," he said, in the same slow tone, "I hunt more dangerous game." ❶

Rainsford expressed his surprise. "Is there big game on this island?"

The general nodded. "The biggest."

"Really?"

"Oh, it isn't here naturally, of course. I have to stock the island."

"What have you imported, General?" Rainsford asked. "Tigers?"

The general smiled. "No," he said. "Hunting tigers ceased to interest me some years ago. I exhausted their possibilities, you see. No thrill left in tigers, no real danger. I live for danger, Mr. Rainsford."

The general took from his pocket a gold cigarette case and offered his guest a long black cigarette with a silver tip; it was perfumed and gave off a smell like incense.

"We will have some capital hunting, you and I," said the general. "I shall be most glad to have your society."

"But what game—" began Rainsford.

"I'll tell you," said the general. "You will be amused, I know. I think I may say, in all modesty, that I have done a rare thing. I have invented a new sensation. May I pour you another glass of port, Mr. Rainsford?"

"Thank you, General."

The general filled both glasses and said: "God makes some men poets. Some he makes kings, some beggars. Me he made a hunter. My hand was made for the trigger, my father said. He was a very rich man with a quarter of a million acres in the Crimea, and he was an ardent[14] sportsman. When I was only five years old, he gave me a little gun, specially made in Moscow for me, to shoot

14. **ardent** (AR duhnt): dedicated and enthusiastic.

Monitor Your Comprehension

❶ CONFLICT

Circle what Rainsford thinks of as the most dangerous big game to hunt. What does Zaroff think about Rainsford's opinion?

Possible answer: Zaroff doesn't think that the Cape buffalo is the most dangerous big game and alludes to the more dangerous game that he hunts on his island preserve.

Monitor Your Comprehension

J LANGUAGE COACH

Informal language includes the use of contractions, short sentence fragments, slang, and other casual expressions. In most short stories, characters' **dialogue,** or speech, contains much informal language. Zaroff's dialogue, however, is more formal. **Formal language** includes challenging vocabulary and longer, more complicated sentences. With a partner, discuss what Zaroff's formal language tells you about his character.

Students should mention that Zaroff's formal language reinforces that his character is a rich and powerful man and a person in control.

K CONFLICT

Underline the sentence in this paragraph that states the conflict the general faced in his past.

sparrows with. When I shot some of his prize turkeys with it, he did not punish me; he complimented me on my marksmanship. I killed my first bear in the Caucasus[15] when I was ten. My whole life has been one prolonged hunt. I went into the army—it was expected of noblemen's sons—and for a time commanded a division of Cossack cavalry, but my real interest was always the hunt. I have hunted every kind of game in every land. It would be impossible for me to tell you how many animals I have killed." J

The general puffed at his cigarette.

"After the debacle in Russia I left the country, for it was imprudent for an officer of the Tsar[16] to stay there. Many noble Russians lost everything. I, luckily, had invested heavily in American securities, so I shall never have to open a tearoom in Monte Carlo or drive a taxi in Paris. Naturally, I continued to hunt—grizzlies in your Rockies, crocodiles in the Ganges,[17] rhinoceroses in East Africa. It was in Africa that the Cape buffalo hit me and laid me up for six months. As soon as I recovered, I started for the Amazon to hunt jaguars, for I had heard they were unusually cunning. They weren't." The Cossack sighed. "They were no match at all for a hunter with his wits about him, and a high-powered rifle. I was bitterly disappointed. I was lying in my tent with a splitting headache one night when a terrible thought pushed its way into my mind. Hunting was beginning to bore me! And hunting, remember, had been my life. I have heard that in America businessmen often go to pieces when they give up the business that has been their life." K

"Yes, that's so," said Rainsford.

The general smiled. "I had no wish to go to pieces," he said. "I must do something. Now, mine is an analytical mind, Mr. Rainsford. Doubtless that is why I enjoy the problems of the chase."

"No doubt, General Zaroff."

15. **Crimea** (kry MEE uh) **. . . Caucasus** (KAW kuh suhs): regions in the southern part of the former Russian Empire, near the Black Sea.
16. **debacle** (dih BAH kuhl) **in Russia . . . Tsar** (zar): A debacle is a disaster or complete failure. Zaroff is referring to the 1917 Russian Revolution, in which the emperor, Tsar Nicholas II, was overthrown.
17. **Ganges** (GAN jeez): a river in northern India.

"So," continued the general, "I asked myself why the hunt no longer fascinated me. You are much younger than I am, Mr. Rainsford, and have not hunted as much, but you perhaps can guess the answer."

"What was it?"

"Simply this: hunting had ceased to be what you call 'a sporting proposition.' It had become too easy. I always got my quarry. Always. There is no greater bore than perfection."

IN OTHER WORDS Over a fancy dinner, General Zaroff and Rainsford talk about hunting. The general tells about how he started hunting, the large animals he has hunted, and how he has become bored with the sport.

The general lit a fresh cigarette.

"No animal had a chance with me any more. That is no boast; it is a mathematical certainty. The animal had nothing but his legs and his instinct. Instinct is no match for reason. When I thought of this, it was a tragic moment for me, I can tell you."

Rainsford leaned across the table, absorbed in what his host was saying.

"It came to me as an inspiration what I must do," the general went on.

"And that was?"

The general smiled the quiet smile of one who has faced an obstacle and surmounted it with success. "I had to invent a new animal to hunt," he said. ●

"A new animal? You're joking."

"Not at all," said the general. "I never joke about hunting. I needed a new animal. I found one. So I bought this island, built this house, and here I do my hunting. The island is perfect for my purposes—there are jungles with a maze of trails in them, hills, swamps—"

"But the animal, General Zaroff?"

Monitor Your Comprehension

● **CONFLICT**

Foreshadowing is the use of clues to hint at what might happen next. Foreshadowing increases suspense as conflicts develop. Look for clues on this page that hint at what the "new animal" Zaroff hunts on the island is.

I think Zaroff hunts

an animal that has never been hunted before

because

he tells Rainsford that he had to invent a new type of animal to hunt.

"Oh," said the general, "it supplies me with the most exciting hunting in the world. No other hunting compares with it for an instant. Every day I hunt, and I never grow bored now, for I have a quarry with which I can match my wits."

Rainsford's bewilderment showed in his face.

"I wanted the ideal animal to hunt," explained the general. "So I said: 'What are the attributes of an ideal quarry?' And the answer was, of course: 'It must have courage, cunning, and, above all, it must be able to reason.' "

"But no animal can reason," objected Rainsford.

"My dear fellow," said the general, "there is one that can."

"But you can't mean—" gasped Rainsford.

"And why not?"

"I can't believe you are serious, General Zaroff. This is a grisly joke."

"Why should I not be serious? I am speaking of hunting."

"Hunting? Good God, General Zaroff, what you speak of is murder." **PAUSE & REFLECT**

PAUSE & REFLECT
Zaroff finally reveals his "new animal" to Rainsford. What is it?

The new animal is a human being.

The general laughed with entire good nature. He regarded Rainsford quizzically. "I refuse to believe that so modern and civilized a young man as you seem to be harbors romantic ideas about the value of human life. Surely your experiences in the war—"

"Did not make me **condone** cold-blooded murder," finished Rainsford, stiffly.

VOCABULARY
The word **condone** (kuhn DOHN) is a verb that means *to forgive or overlook.*

IN OTHER WORDS General Zaroff tells Rainsford about the most challenging animal he has found to hunt: human beings.

► How does Rainsford react to what Zaroff has revealed? What could this reaction mean for Rainsford? Share your thoughts with a classmate.

Possible answer: Rainsford is horrified by the idea that Zaroff hunts and kills people for sport. Rainsford could become an "animal" for Zaroff to hunt and kill.

Laughter shook the general. "How extraordinarily droll[18] you are!" he said. "One does not expect nowadays to find a young man of the educated class, even in America, with such a naïve, and, if I may say so, mid-Victorian point of view. It's like finding a snuffbox in a limousine. Ah, well, doubtless you had Puritan ancestors. So many Americans appear to have had. I'll wager you'll forget your notions when you go hunting with me. You've a genuine new thrill in store for you, Mr. Rainsford."

"Thank you, I'm a hunter, not a murderer."

"Dear me," said the general, quite unruffled, "again that unpleasant word. But I think I can show you that your scruples[19] are quite ill-founded."

"Yes?"

"Life is for the strong, to be lived by the strong, and, if needs be, taken by the strong. The weak of the world were put here to give the strong pleasure. I am strong. Why should I not use my gift? If I wish to hunt, why should I not? I hunt the scum of the earth—sailors from tramp ships—lascars,[20] blacks, Chinese, whites, mongrels—a thoroughbred horse or hound is worth more than a score of them."

"But they are men," said Rainsford, hotly.

"Precisely," said the general. "That is why I use them. It gives me pleasure. They can reason, after a fashion. So they are dangerous." **PAUSE & REFLECT**

"But where do you get them?"

The general's left eyelid fluttered down in a wink. "This island is called Ship Trap," he answered. "Sometimes an angry god of the high seas sends them to me. Sometimes, when Providence is not so kind, I help Providence a bit. Come to the window with me."

Rainsford went to the window and looked out toward the sea.

"Watch! Out there!" exclaimed the general, pointing into the night. Rainsford's eyes saw only blackness, and then, as the

---

18. **droll** (drohl): odd or funny.
19. **scruples** (SKROO puhlz): feelings of uneasiness that keep a person from doing something.
20. **lascars** (LAS kerz): sailors from India.

Monitor Your Comprehension

PAUSE & REFLECT

Reread lines 405–407. General Zaroff says that he enjoys hunting men because they can reason, or think logically. How does this make people more dangerous than animals such as tigers? Share your thoughts with a classmate.

Possible answer: While animals depend on instinct-based decisions, humans can strategize, solve problems, plan ahead, and make reason-based decisions.

Monitor Your Comprehension

general pressed a button, far out to sea Rainsford saw the flash of lights.

The general chuckled. "They indicate a channel," he said, "where there's none: giant rocks with razor edges crouch like a sea monster with wide-open jaws. They can crush a ship as easily as I crush this nut." He dropped a walnut on the hardwood floor and brought his heel grinding down on it. "Oh, yes," he said, casually, as if in answer to a question, "I have electricity. We try to be civilized here."

"Civilized? And you shoot down men?"

A trace of anger was in the general's black eyes, but it was there for but a second, and he said, in his most pleasant manner: "Dear me, what a righteous young man you are! I assure you I do not do the thing you suggest. That would be barbarous. I treat these visitors with every consideration. They get plenty of good food and exercise. They get into splendid physical condition. You shall see for yourself tomorrow."

"What do you mean?"

"We'll visit my training school," smiled the general. "It's in the cellar. I have about a dozen pupils down there now. They're from the Spanish bark Sanlúcar that had the bad luck to go on the rocks out there. A very inferior lot, I regret to say. Poor specimens and more accustomed to the deck than to the jungle."

He raised his hand, and Ivan, who served as waiter, brought thick Turkish coffee. Rainsford, with an effort, held his tongue in check.

"It's a game, you see," pursued the general, blandly. "I suggest to one of them that we go hunting. I give him a supply of food and an excellent hunting knife. I give him three hours' start. I am to follow, armed only with a pistol of the smallest caliber and range. If my quarry eludes me for three whole days, he wins the game. If I find him"—the general smiled—"he loses." (M)

"Suppose he refuses to be hunted?"

"Oh," said the general, "I give him his option, of course. He need not play that game if he doesn't wish to. If he does not wish to hunt, I turn him over to Ivan. Ivan once had the honor of

(M) CONFLICT

Reread lines 442–447. In your own words, describe the game that Zaroff plays with his "pupils."

Possible answer: The general tells the pupil that they will go hunting and supplies the pupil with food and a hunting knife and gives the person a head start. After three hours, Zaroff begins the hunt, using a small caliber gun. The hunt lasts three days. If the person eludes Zaroff for three days, the hunted person wins; however, if Zaroff catches up to the hunted person, he kills him.

serving as official knouter[21] to the Great White Tsar, and he has his own ideas of sport. Invariably, Mr. Rainsford, invariably they choose the hunt."

"And if they win?"

The smile on the general's face widened.

"To date I have not lost," he said.

IN OTHER WORDS **The general explains how he causes ships to crash, takes the survivors as prisoners, trains them, and hunts them. He sets it up like a game, with certain rules and supplies. Although it sounds as if the general gives his prisoners a fair chance, he always catches them in the end.**

Then he added, hastily: "I don't wish you to think me a braggart, Mr. Rainsford. Many of them afford only the most elementary sort of problem. Occasionally I strike a tartar.[22] One almost did win. I eventually had to use the dogs."

"The dogs?"

"This way, please. I'll show you."

The general steered Rainsford to a window. The lights from the windows sent a flickering illumination that made grotesque patterns on the courtyard below, and Rainsford could see moving about there a dozen or so huge black shapes; as they turned toward him, their eyes glittered greenly.

"A rather good lot, I think," observed the general. "They are let out at seven every night. If anyone should try to get into my house—or out of it—something extremely regrettable would occur to him." He hummed a snatch of song from the Folies Bergère.[23]

"And now," said the general, "I want to show you my new collection of heads. Will you come with me to the library?"

"I hope," said Rainsford, "that you will excuse me tonight, General Zaroff. I'm really not feeling at all well."

"Ah, indeed?" the general inquired, solicitously.[24] "Well, I suppose that's only natural, after your long swim. You need

---

21. **knouter** (NOW ter): a person who whipped criminals in Russia.
22. **strike a tartar** (TAHR ter): find a fierce opponent.
23. **Folies Bergère** (faw LEE ber ZHER): a music hall in Paris, famous for its variety shows.
24. **solicitously** (suh LIS ih tuhs lee): in a way that shows care or concern.

N LANGUAGE COACH

The word *resourceful* (line 485) contains the suffix *-ful*. This suffix turns nouns, such as *resource*, into adjectives. You can think of someone who is resourceful as being full of resources, such as intelligence and imagination. In other words, a resourceful person is able to handle difficult situations by using a lot of different skills.

a good, restful night's sleep. Tomorrow you'll feel like a new man, I'll wager. Then we'll hunt, eh? I've one rather promising prospect—"

Rainsford was hurrying from the room.

"Sorry you can't go with me tonight," called the general. "I expect rather fair sport—a big, strong black. He looks resourceful— Well, good night, Mr. Rainsford; I hope you have a good night's rest." N

The bed was good, and the pajamas of the softest silk, and he was tired in every fiber of his being, but nevertheless Rainsford could not quiet his brain with the opiate[25] of sleep. He lay, eyes wide open. Once he thought he heard stealthy steps in the corridor outside his room. He sought to throw open the door; it would not open. He went to the window and looked out. His room was high up in one of the towers. The lights of the château were out now, and it was dark and silent, but there was a fragment of sallow moon, and by its wan light he could see, dimly, the courtyard; there, weaving in and out in the pattern of shadow, were black, noiseless forms; the hounds heard him at the window and looked up, expectantly, with their green eyes. Rainsford went back to the bed and lay down. By many methods he tried to put himself to sleep. He had achieved a doze when, just as morning began to come, he heard, far off in the jungle, the faint report of a pistol. O

O VISUALIZE

When you visualize, you don't just imagine how things *look*. You also imagine how things *feel, sound, smell,* or even *taste*. Underline the words and phrases in this paragraph that help you visualize the scene. Be sure to focus on more than just your sense of sight.

IN OTHER WORDS The general shows off his fierce hunting dogs. He talks about hunting a man, and about his collection of human heads. That night, Rainsford cannot sleep. He realizes that he is a prisoner in this beautiful room. He hears someone leave in the evening. Then, in the morning, he hears a gunshot.

General Zaroff did not appear until luncheon. He was dressed faultlessly in the tweeds of a country squire. He was solicitous about the state of Rainsford's health.

25. **opiate** (OH pee it): anything that soothes or calms someone.

"As for me," sighed the general, "I do not feel so well. I am worried, Mr. Rainsford. Last night I detected traces of my old complaint."

To Rainsford's questioning glance the general said: "Ennui. Boredom."

Then, taking a second helping of crêpes suzettes, the general explained: "The hunting was not good last night. The fellow lost his head. He made a straight trail that offered no problems at all. That's the trouble with these sailors; they have dull brains to begin with, and they do not know how to get about in the woods. They do excessively stupid and obvious things. It's most annoying. Will you have another glass of Chablis,[26] Mr. Rainsford?" PAUSE & REFLECT

"General," said Rainsford, firmly, "I wish to leave this island at once."

The general raised his thickets of eyebrows; he seemed hurt. "But, my dear fellow," the general protested, "you've only just come. You've had no hunting—"

"I wish to go today," said Rainsford. He saw the dead black eyes of the general on him, studying him. General Zaroff's face suddenly brightened.

He filled Rainsford's glass with venerable Chablis from a dusty bottle.

"Tonight," said the general, "we will hunt—you and I."

Rainsford shook his head. "No, General," he said. "I will not hunt."

The general shrugged his shoulders and delicately ate a hothouse grape. "As you wish, my friend," he said. "The choice rests entirely with you. But may I not venture to suggest that you will find my idea of sport more diverting[27] than Ivan's?"

He nodded toward the corner to where the giant stood, scowling, his thick arms crossed on his hogshead of chest.

"You don't mean—" cried Rainsford.

26. **Chablis** (sha BLEE): a type of French white wine.
27. **diverting** (dih VUR ting): entertaining or amusing.

Monitor Your Comprehension

PAUSE & REFLECT

Reread lines 509–518. Why was the general bored by the hunt last night?

Possible answer: The person Zaroff hunted didn't provide enough of a challenge, making a straight trail that was easy to follow.

Monitor Your Comprehension

P CONFLICT

The main conflict in this story has become clear. Explain the conflict by filling in the blanks below.

The conflict is between

General Zaroff and Rainsford.

The conflict is that

General Zaroff wants to hunt and kill Rainsford

and Rainsford wants to escape from the island.

"My dear fellow," said the general, "have I not told you I always mean what I say about hunting? This is really an inspiration. I drink to a foeman worthy of my steel—at last." P

The general raised his glass, but Rainsford sat staring at him.

"You'll find this game worth playing," the general said, enthusiastically. "Your brain against mine. Your woodcraft against mine. Your strength and stamina against mine. Outdoor chess! And the stake is not without value, eh?"

"And if I win—" began Rainsford, huskily.

"I'll cheerfully acknowledge myself defeated if I do not find you by midnight of the third day," said General Zaroff. "My sloop will place you on the mainland near a town."

The general read what Rainsford was thinking.

"Oh, you can trust me," said the Cossack. "I will give you my word as a gentleman and a sportsman. Of course, you, in turn, must agree to say nothing of your visit here."

"I'll agree to nothing of the kind," said Rainsford.

"Oh," said the general, "in that case— But why discuss that now? Three days hence we can discuss it over a bottle of Veuve Clicquot,[28] unless—"

The general sipped his wine.

Then a businesslike air animated him. "Ivan," he said to Rainsford, "will supply you with hunting clothes, food, a knife. I suggest you wear **moccasins**; they leave a poorer trail. I suggest, too, that you avoid the big swamp in the southeast corner of the island. We call it Death Swamp. There's quicksand there. One foolish fellow tried it. The deplorable part of it was that Lazarus followed him. You can imagine my feelings, Mr. Rainsford. I loved Lazarus; he was the finest hound in my pack. Well, I must beg you to excuse me now. I always take a siesta after lunch. You'll hardly have time for a nap, I fear. You'll want to start, no doubt. I shall not follow till dusk. Hunting at night is so much more exciting than by day, don't you think? Au revoir,[29] Mr. Rainsford, au revoir."

VISUAL VOCABULARY

A **moccasin** (MOK uh sin) is a kind of soft leather shoe without a heel.

28. **Veuve Clicquot** (vuv klee KOH): a French champagne.
29. **au revoir** (oh ruh VWAHR): French for "goodbye."

Monitor Your Comprehension

General Zaroff, with a deep, courtly bow, strolled from the room.

IN OTHER WORDS At lunch, Rainsford asks to leave the island, but Zaroff insists that Rainsford go hunting with him. Zaroff explains the rules of the hunt, in which Rainsford will be Zaroff's prey. Zaroff also warns Rainsford of a dangerous swamp on the island.

► What must Rainsford do in order to be allowed to leave the island? Place brackets **[ ]** around the passage that tells you.

In order for Rainsford to leave the island, he must defeat Zaroff in the hunting game.

From another door came Ivan. Under one arm he carried khaki hunting clothes, a haversack of food, a leather sheath containing a long-bladed hunting knife; his right hand rested on a cocked revolver thrust in the crimson sash about his waist. . . .

Rainsford had fought his way through the bush for two hours. "I must keep my nerve. I must keep my nerve," he said, through tight teeth.

He had not been entirely clear-headed when the château gates snapped shut behind him. His whole idea at first was to put distance between himself and General Zaroff, and, to this end, he had plunged along, spurred on by the sharp rowels of something very like panic. Now he had got a grip on himself, had stopped, and was taking stock of himself and the situation.

He saw that straight flight was futile; inevitably it would bring him face to face with the sea. He was in a picture with a frame of water, and his operations, clearly, must take place within that frame.

"I'll give him a trail to follow," muttered Rainsford, and he struck off from the rude path he had been following into the trackless wilderness. He executed a series of intricate loops; he doubled on his trail again and again, recalling all the lore of the fox hunt, and all the dodges of the fox. Night found him leg-weary, with hands and face lashed by the branches, on a thickly wooded ridge. He knew it would be insane to blunder on through the dark, even if he had the strength. His need for

VOCABULARY

The word **imperative** (im PAIR uh tiv) is an adjective that means *absolutely necessary.*

rest was **imperative**, and he thought, "I have played the fox; now I must play the cat of the fable."[30] A big tree with a thick trunk and outspread branches was nearby, and, taking care to leave not the slightest mark, he climbed up into the crotch and, stretching out on one of the broad limbs, after a fashion, rested. Rest brought him new confidence and almost a feeling of security. Even so zealous[31] a hunter as General Zaroff could not trace him there, he told himself; only the devil himself could follow that complicated trail through the jungle after dark. But perhaps the general was a devil—

An apprehensive night crawled slowly by like a wounded snake, and sleep did not visit Rainsford, although the silence of a dead world was on the jungle. Toward morning, when a dingy gray was varnishing the sky, the cry of some startled bird focused Rainsford's attention in that direction. Something was coming through the bush, coming slowly, carefully, coming by the same winding way Rainsford had come. He flattened himself down on the limb, and through a screen of leaves almost as thick as tapestry, he watched. The thing that was approaching was a man.

It was General Zaroff. He made his way along with his eyes fixed in utmost concentration on the ground before him. He paused, almost beneath the tree, dropped to his knees, and studied the ground. Rainsford's impulse was to hurl himself down like a panther, but he saw that the general's right hand held something metallic—a small automatic pistol. **PAUSE & REFLECT**

PAUSE & REFLECT

Do you think Rainsford will behave like a panther and jump down from the tree? With a partner, discuss what you think will happen next and why.

Students may discuss that Rainsford will not jump on Zaroff because the general is holding a gun, and Rainsford knows what a good hunter Zaroff is.

The hunter shook his head several times, as if he were puzzled. Then he straightened up and took from his case one of his black cigarettes; its pungent, incenselike smoke floated up to Rainsford's nostrils.

Rainsford held his breath. The general's eyes had left the ground and were traveling inch by inch up the tree. Rainsford froze there, every muscle tensed for a spring. But the sharp eyes of the hunter stopped before they reached the limb where Rainsford

---

30. **I have played the fox . . . fable:** In Aesop's fable "The Cat and the Fox," the fox brags of knowing many ways to escape an enemy. The cat knows only one way to escape but is successful with it.
31. **zealous** (ZEL uhs): excited and eager.

lay; a smile spread over his brown face. Very deliberately he blew a smoke ring into the air; then he turned his back on the tree and walked carelessly away, back along the trail he had come. The swish of the underbrush against his hunting boots grew fainter and fainter. Ⓠ

The pent-up air burst hotly from Rainsford's lungs. His first thought made him feel sick and numb. The general could follow a trail through the woods at night; he could follow an extremely difficult trail; he must have **uncanny** powers; only by the merest chance had the Cossack failed to see his quarry.

Rainsford's second thought was even more terrible. It sent a shudder of cold horror through his whole being. Why had the general smiled? Why had he turned back?

Rainsford did not want to believe what his reason told him was true, but the truth was as evident as the sun that had by now pushed through the morning mists. The general was playing with him! The general was saving him for another day's sport! The Cossack was the cat; he was the mouse. Then it was that Rainsford knew the full meaning of terror. Ⓡ

IN OTHER WORDS Rainsford starts running, but then he stops to think. He creates a complicated trail that will be difficult to follow. At night, he climbs a tree. Just before dawn, General Zaroff reaches the tree. The general stops long enough to show that he has found Rainsford but leaves without harming him. Rainsford realizes that Zaroff could have killed him but chose not to so that he could keep playing the game.

"I will not lose my nerve. I will not."

He slid down from the tree and struck off again into the woods. His face was set, and he forced the machinery of his mind to function. Three hundred yards from his hiding place he stopped where a huge dead tree leaned precariously on a smaller, living one. Throwing off his sack of food, Rainsford took his knife from its sheath and began to work with all his energy.

Monitor Your Comprehension

Ⓠ VISUALIZE

Try to picture what happens in this important part of the plot. Underline phrases and sentences that help you imagine Zaroff's actions as he reaches Rainsford's hiding place.

VOCABULARY

The word **uncanny** (uhn KAN ee) is an adjective that means *far beyond what is normal.*

Ⓡ CONFLICT

Reread lines 643–651. The author adds to the suspense by having Rainsford ask himself questions. Underline the questions Rainsford asks. Rainsford's answers reveal that the conflict is building. Place brackets [ ] around his answers.

The job was finished at last, and he threw himself down behind a fallen log a hundred feet away. He did not have to wait long. The cat was coming again to play with the mouse.

Following the trail with the sureness of a bloodhound came General Zaroff. Nothing escaped those searching black eyes, no crushed blade of grass, no bent twig, no mark, no matter how faint, in the moss. So intent was the Cossack on his stalking that he was upon the thing Rainsford had made before he saw it. His foot touched the protruding bough[32] that was the trigger. Even as he touched it, the general sensed his danger and leaped back with the agility of an ape. But he was not quite quick enough; the dead tree, delicately adjusted to rest on the cut living one, crashed down and struck the general a glancing blow on the shoulder as it fell; but for his alertness, he must have been smashed beneath it. He staggered, but he did not fall; nor did he drop his revolver. He stood there, rubbing his injured shoulder, and Rainsford, with fear again gripping his heart, heard the general's mocking laugh ring through the jungle.

"Rainsford," called the general, "if you are within sound of my voice, as I suppose you are, let me congratulate you. Not many men know how to make a Malay man-catcher. Luckily for me I, too, have hunted in Malacca.[33] You are proving interesting, Mr. Rainsford. I am going now to have my wound dressed; it's only a slight one. But I shall be back. I shall be back."

IN OTHER WORDS Rainsford sets up a trap using a dead tree. General Zaroff walks into the trap but pulls back just in time. He escapes with only a small injury and promises to return.

When the general, nursing his bruised shoulder, had gone, Rainsford took up his flight again. It was flight now, a desperate, hopeless flight, that carried him on for some hours. Dusk came, then darkness, and still he pressed on. The ground grew softer under his moccasins; the vegetation grew ranker, denser; insects bit him savagely. Then, as he stepped forward, his foot sank

32. **protruding bough** (bow): a tree branch that extends or sticks out.
33. **Malay** (muh LAY) . . . **Malacca** (muh LAK uh): The Malays are a people of southeast Asia. Malacca is a region they live in, just south of Thailand.

into the ooze. He tried to wrench it back, but the muck sucked viciously at his foot as if it were a giant leech. With a violent effort he tore his foot loose. He knew where he was now. Death Swamp and its quicksand.

His hands were tight closed as if his nerve were something tangible that someone in the darkness was trying to tear from his grip. The softness of the earth had given him an idea. He stepped back from the quicksand a dozen feet or so, and like some huge prehistoric beaver, he began to dig.

Rainsford had dug himself in in France when a second's delay meant death. That had been a placid pastime compared to his digging now. The pit grew deeper; when it was above his shoulders, he climbed out and from some hard saplings cut stakes and sharpened them to a fine point. These stakes he planted in the bottom of the pit with the points sticking up. With flying fingers he wove a rough carpet of weeds and branches, and with it he covered the mouth of the pit. Then, wet with sweat and aching with tiredness, he crouched behind the stump of a lightning-charred tree.

He knew his pursuer was coming; he heard the padding sound of feet on the soft earth, and the night breeze brought him the perfume of the general's cigarette. It seemed to Rainsford that the general was coming with unusual swiftness; he was not feeling his way along, foot by foot. Rainsford, crouching there, could not see the general, nor could he see the pit. He lived a year in a minute. Then he felt an impulse to cry aloud with joy, for he heard the sharp crackle of the breaking branches as the cover of the pit gave way; he heard the sharp scream of pain as the pointed stakes found their mark. He leaped up from his place of concealment. Then he cowered back. Three feet from the pit a man was standing, with an electric torch in his hand.

"You've done well, Rainsford," the voice of the general called. "Your Burmese tiger pit[34] has claimed one of my best dogs. Again you score. I think, Mr. Rainsford, I'll see what you can do against

Monitor Your Comprehension

VISUALIZE

Reread this paragraph. Then in the first box of the chart below, list words and phrases that appeal to your senses. In the second box, describe what these details lead you to visualize.

Details from Story

"dusk came, then darkness"; "the ground grew softer"; "the vegetation grew ranker, denser"; "insects bit him savagely"; "his foot sank into the ooze"; "the muck sucked viciously at his foot as if it were a giant leech"

↓

What I Visualize

Possible answer: I visualize Rainsford running as quickly as possible through the dark jungle. As he crosses the soft earth, he is bitten by insects and can smell the rotting vegetation. His foot sinks into the Death Swamp quicksand, and he must struggle to free it.

---

34. **Burmese** (ber MEEZ) **tiger pit:** a trap used for catching tigers in Myanmar (myahn MAHR), a country in Southeast Asia formerly called Burma.

Monitor Your Comprehension

my whole pack. I'm going home for a rest now. Thank you for a most amusing evening."

IN OTHER WORDS Near the swamp, Rainsford makes a trap with a hidden pit. Something falls into it, but it is not the general. It is one of his dogs.

► With a partner, discuss what Zaroff says to Rainsford. What are Zaroff's plans now?

Zaroff tells Rainsford that he has done well but killed only his best hunting dog. The general plans to send a whole pack of hounds after Rainsford.

At daybreak Rainsford, lying near the swamp, was awakened by a sound that made him know that he had new things to learn about fear. It was a distant sound, faint and wavering, but he knew it. It was the baying of a pack of hounds. (T)

Rainsford knew he could do one of two things. He could stay where he was and wait. That was suicide. He could flee. That was postponing the inevitable. For a moment he stood there, thinking. An idea that held a wild chance came to him, and, tightening his belt, he headed away from the swamp.

The baying of the hounds grew nearer, then still nearer, nearer, ever nearer. On a ridge Rainsford climbed a tree. Down a watercourse, not a quarter of a mile away, he could see the bush moving. Straining his eyes, he saw the lean figure of General Zaroff; just ahead of him, Rainsford made out another figure whose wide shoulders surged through the tall jungle weeds; it was the giant Ivan, and he seemed pulled forward by some unseen force; Rainsford knew that Ivan must be holding the pack in leash.

They would be on him any minute now. His mind worked frantically. He thought of a native trick he had learned in Uganda.[35] He slid down the tree. He caught hold of a springy young sapling, and to it he fastened his hunting knife, with the blade pointing down the trail; with a bit of wild grapevine he tied back the sapling. Then he ran for his life. The hounds raised their voices as they hit the fresh scent. Rainsford knew now how an animal at bay feels.

(T) CONFLICT

Complications (kom plih KAY shuhnz) are plot events that make the conflict more difficult to resolve. What additional complication has now been added to the game?

Possible answer: Rainsford must defend himself against a pack of hounds.

35. **Uganda** (yoo GAN duh): a country in central Africa.

He had to stop to get his breath. The baying of the hounds stopped abruptly, and Rainsford's heart stopped, too. They must have reached the knife.

He shinned excitedly up a tree and looked back. His pursuers had stopped. But the hope that was in Rainsford's brain when he climbed died, for he saw in the shallow valley that General Zaroff was still on his feet. But Ivan was not. The knife, driven by the recoil of the springing tree, had not wholly failed.

Rainsford had hardly tumbled to the ground when the pack took up the cry again.

"Nerve, nerve, nerve!" he panted, as he dashed along. A blue gap showed between the trees dead ahead. Ever nearer drew the hounds. Rainsford forced himself on toward that gap. He reached it. It was the shore of the sea. Across a cove he could see the gloomy gray stone of the château. Twenty feet below him the sea rumbled and hissed. Rainsford hesitated. He heard the hounds. Then he leaped far out into the sea. . . .

When the general and his pack reached the place by the sea, the Cossack stopped. For some minutes he stood regarding the blue-green expanse of water. He shrugged his shoulders. Then he sat down, took a drink of brandy from a silver flask, lit a perfumed cigarette, and hummed a bit from *Madama Butterfly*.[36]

VISUALIZE
Reread lines 768–772. Underline details that appeal to your sense of sight. Circle details that appeal to your sense of smell. Place brackets [ ] around details that appeal to your sense of hearing.

IN OTHER WORDS As the general and his dogs get closer, Rainsford sets up one more trap with his knife. He misses the general but kills Ivan, who is holding the dogs. As Zaroff and the dogs continue the chase, Rainsford makes a final run and dives into the sea.

General Zaroff had an exceedingly good dinner in his great paneled dining hall that evening. With it he had a bottle of Pol Roger and half a bottle of Chambertin.[37] Two slight annoyances kept him from perfect enjoyment. One was the thought that it would be difficult to replace Ivan; the other was that his quarry had escaped him; of course the American hadn't played

36. ***Madama*** (muh DAM uh) ***Butterfly:*** a famous opera.
37. **Pol Roger** (PAWL raw ZHAY) **. . . Chambertin** (sham ber TAN): Pol Roger is a French champagne. Chambertin is a French red wine.

Monitor Your Comprehension

the game—so thought the general as he tasted his after-dinner liqueur. In his library he read, to soothe himself, from the works of Marcus Aurelius.[38] At ten he went up to his bedroom. He was deliciously tired, he said to himself, as he locked himself in. There was a little moonlight, so before turning on his light he went to the window and looked down at the courtyard. He could see the great hounds, and he called "Better luck another time" to them. Then he switched on the light.

A man, who had been hiding in the curtains of the bed, was standing there.

"Rainsford!" screamed the general. "How in God's name did you get here?"

"Swam," said Rainsford. "I found it quicker than walking through the jungle."

The general sucked in his breath and smiled. "I congratulate you," he said. "You have won the game."

Rainsford did not smile. "I am still a beast at bay," he said, in a low, hoarse voice. "Get ready, General Zaroff." Ⓥ

The general made one of his deepest bows.

"I see," he said. "Splendid! One of us is to furnish a repast[39] for the hounds. The other will sleep in this very excellent bed. On guard, Rainsford. . . ."

Ⓥ LANGUAGE COACH

Homophones (HOM uh fohnz) are words that are pronounced the same but have different meanings and sometimes different spellings, such as *hear* and *here*. The word *hoarse* (line 796), meaning "rough or harsh in sound," and the word *horse*, the animal, are homophones.

IN OTHER WORDS When General Zaroff goes to bed, Rainsford is waiting for him. The general says that Rainsford has won, but Rainsford is still "playing" the game. The two fight.

He had never slept in a better bed, Rainsford decided.

IN OTHER WORDS Rainsford thought he slept very well that night.

► Who won the game? Underline the details that tell you.

Rainsford won the game.

38. **Marcus Aurelius** (MAHR kuhs aw REE lee uhs): an ancient Roman emperor and philosopher.
39. **furnish a repast** (rih PAST): serve as a meal.

Text Analysis: Conflict

As an author develops a plot, he or she will often foreshadow, or hint at, future plot events before the main conflict is finally resolved. Find three examples of foreshadowing in "The Most Dangerous Game," and list them in the diagram below. Remember, each example should be a clue that suggests what might happen later in the story.

For this chart, answers will vary. See samples below.

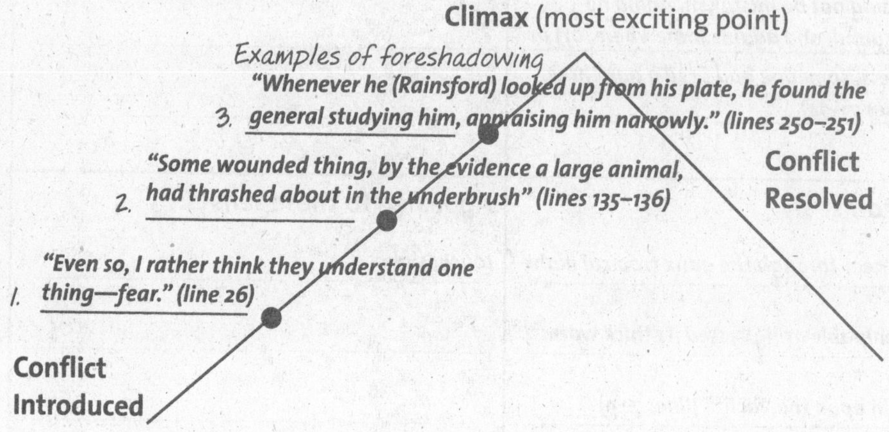

Climax (most exciting point)

Examples of foreshadowing

3. ***"Whenever he (Rainsford) looked up from his plate, he found the general studying him, appraising him narrowly." (lines 250–251)***

2. ***"Some wounded thing, by the evidence a large animal, had thrashed about in the underbrush" (lines 135–136)***

1. ***"Even so, I rather think they understand one thing—fear." (line 26)***

Conflict Introduced

Conflict Resolved

How did foreshadowing affect your understanding of the conflict in this story? How would the story have been different if the author had not used foreshadowing at all? Explain.

Possible answer: Foreshadowing helped me understand the following conflicts: Rainsford's realization that Zaroff hunts humans and that Zaroff was going to hunt Rainsford next, the conflict between hunter and prey, the conflict between right and wrong. The story's mysterious setting and the conflict between Zaroff and Rainsford would not have been as powerful without foreshadowing.

Reading Strategy: Visualize

Choose two descriptions from the story that created strong sensory images in your mind. List the words and phrases that helped create each image and note the senses to which each description appealed.

For this chart, answers will vary. See samples below.

Description 1:	Appealed to these senses:
"An abrupt sound startled him. Off to the right he heard it, and his ears, expert in such matters, could not be mistaken. Again he heard the sound, and again. Somewhere, off in the blackness, someone had fired a gun three times." (lines 71–74)	*hearing, sight*
Description 2:	**Appealed to these senses:**
"trying to peer through the dank tropical night that was palpable as it pressed its thick warm blackness in upon the yacht" (lines 7–9)	*touch, sight*

What does it take to be a SURVIVOR?

Look back at the "Traits of a Survivor" that you ranked on page 4. How does Rainsford demonstrate these traits in "The Most Dangerous Game"? For each of the traits that you ranked 1–3, give an example from the story.

Trait 1: *Rainsford demonstrates* __________ *when he* ________________.

Trait 2: *Rainsford demonstrates* __________ *when he* ________________.

Trait 3: *Rainsford demonstrates* __________ *when he* ________________.

Answers will vary but students should list examples from the story for each trait they've ranked 1–3.

Vocabulary Practice

Draw a line from the Vocabulary word in the first column to the word that is closest to its meaning in the second column.

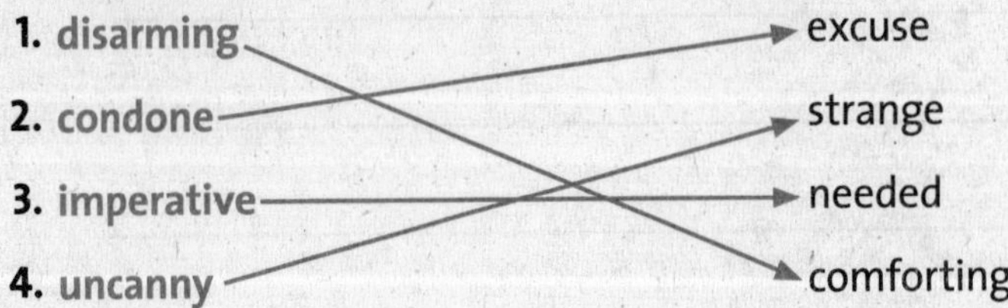

Academic Vocabulary in Writing

The word **sequence** (SEE kwuhns) is a noun that means *the order in which one thing follows another.*

When following a recipe to prepare food, it is important to perform the steps in the right **sequence.**

LIST IT What events in "The Most Dangerous Game" did you find most exciting? When in the story's **sequence** do these events happen? List three exciting events below, and then explain when each occurs. Be sure to use the word **sequence** in your response.

Encourage students to use the Academic Vocabulary word in their responses.

Assessment Practice

DIRECTIONS Use "The Most Dangerous Game" to answer questions 1–6.

1 Why does Zaroff "invent" a new kind of game?

- (A) He wants to impress Rainsford.
- (B) Hunting tigers has become too dangerous.
- (C) He is bored with the animals he has already hunted.
- (D) He wants to hunt animals without killing them.

2 Which sentence from the story foreshadows danger?

- (A) *"What island is it?" Rainsford asked.*
- (B) *"The old charts call it Ship-Trap Island," Whitney replied.*
- (C) *"The best sport in the world," agreed Rainsford.*
- (D) *"It will be light enough in Rio," promised Whitney.*

3 The main conflict Rainsford faces in this story is his effort to —

- (A) protect himself from wild animals
- (B) survive as Zaroff hunts him
- (C) swim to shore after falling off the boat
- (D) change Zaroff's mind about hunting

4 What causes Rainsford to know "the full meaning of terror" (line 651)?

- (A) Rainsford finds out that Zaroff is a better hunter than he is.
- (B) Zaroff has followed Rainsford all night.
- (C) Zaroff sees Rainsford in the tree.
- (D) Rainsford realizes Zaroff is playing with him.

5 Which of the following events happens first?

- (A) Rainsford kills Ivan.
- (B) Rainsford kills one of Zaroff's dogs.
- (C) Rainsford wounds Zaroff.
- (D) Rainsford falls in quicksand.

6 How is the story's main conflict resolved?

- (A) Rainsford kills Zaroff in Zaroff's bedroom.
- (B) Zaroff allows Rainsford to stay and rest at his home.
- (C) Rainsford jumps into the sea.
- (D) Zaroff reveals to Rainsford that he hunts humans.

The Gift of the Magi

Based on the short story by O. Henry

What are you willing to SACRIFICE?

Have you ever made a sacrifice in order to help others or make someone happy? In "The Gift of the Magi," a young couple show their love for each other by the sacrifices they are willing to make.

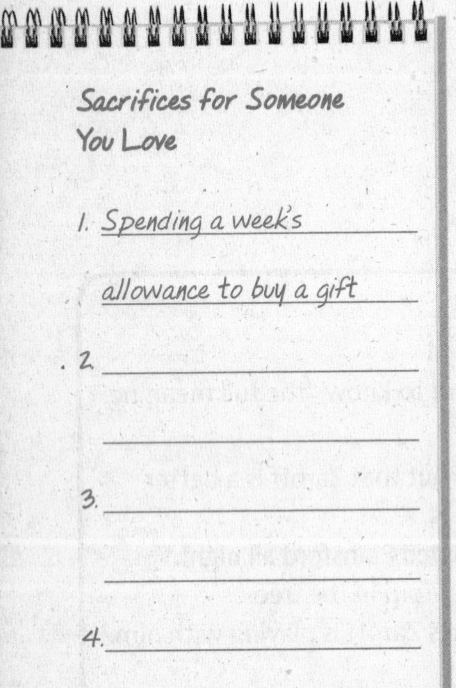

Sacrifices for Someone You Love
1. Spending a week's allowance to buy a gift
2.
3.
4.
5.

TURN AND TALK With a partner, talk about things that people sacrifice for those they love. Think about examples in real life as well as those in books, movies, and television shows. Write your examples in the chart to the left. Then, circle the sacrifice that you think would be hardest to make.

Answers will vary.

Text Analysis: Irony

Irony (EYE ruh nee) is the difference between what we expect to happen and what actually does happen. You will see three kinds of irony in literature. The chart below describes these types of irony.

Irony	Definition	Example
Situational Irony	when something happens that is the opposite of what you expected	You stay up all night studying for a test. However, the next day your teacher tells you there won't be a test.
Verbal Irony	when what is said is the opposite of what is meant	It's a rainy, dark day and you say, "What a beautiful day!"
Dramatic Irony	when what a character knows is different from what the audience knows	The audience is amazed when a champion boxer loses a big fight. The reader, however, knows the boxer has been paid to lose.

O. Henry is well known for using situational irony in his short stories. As you read "The Gift of the Magi," think about what you expect to happen next.

Reading Strategy: Predict

A good story will keep you wondering what happens next. Successful readers ask questions and predict possible answers. To make a prediction:

- Look for **clues** in the story to suggest what might happen next.
- Make a **prediction,** or a reasonable guess, about future events based on clues in the story and what you know from your own experience.
- Read on to confirm your prediction and see if it is correct.

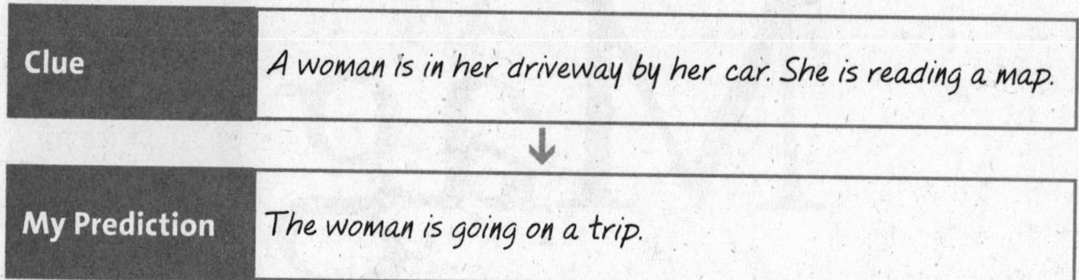

Clue	*A woman is in her driveway by her car. She is reading a map.*
My Prediction	*The woman is going on a trip.*

Vocabulary in Context

Note: Words are listed in the order in which they appear in the story.

Vestibule (VES tuh byool) is a noun that means *an entrance hall.*
The visitor waited in the **vestibule** while I came downstairs to meet him.

Ransack (RAN sak) is a verb that means *to search through every part of.*
Jane had to **ransack** her purse looking for change to pay the driver.

Covet (KUH vet) is a verb that means *to wish for or desire something owned by someone else.*
I **covet** Lisa's new computer, even though I have a computer of my own.

Vocabulary Practice

Review the words and sample sentences above. Then, predict with a partner what you think "Gift of the Magi" will be about based on these words. On the lines below, write down what you think will happen in the story.

Encourage students to use the Vocabulary words in their discussions.

SET A PURPOSE FOR READING
Read this story to find out what two people in love are willing to give up for each other's happiness.

The Gift of the Magi

Based on the short story by
O. HENRY

BACKGROUND In this story, the writer refers to the Magi (MAY jy). In the Christian Bible, the Magi were three wise men or kings. They traveled to Bethlehem, guided by a star. There they gave valuable gifts of gold, frankincense, and myrrh to the infant Jesus. This story was first published in 1906, when people were paid much less than today.

Della had saved one dollar and eighty-seven cents. That was all. And sixty cents of it was in pennies. She had saved the pennies one and two at a time by bargaining with the grocer, the vegetable seller, and the butcher to lower their prices. At times, her cheeks had burned with shame, for she was certain these sellers thought she was stingy. She counted her money three times. One dollar and eighty-seven cents. And the next day was Christmas.

Della decided there was nothing she could do except flop down on the shabby little couch and cry. So she did.

Della and her husband lived in a furnished apartment costing $8 per week. It didn't exactly look like the home of a beggar, but it had no extras, either.

Just inside the building's front door, in the **vestibule** below, there was a mailbox that a letter couldn't fit in and a doorbell that didn't ring. Near their doorbell was a card with the name *"Mr. James Dillingham Young"* on it.

For a short time, Mr. James Dillingham Young had done well for himself, making $30 per week. Now, his pay had shrunk to $20. With his pay cut, he'd lost his sense of place in the outside world. But whenever he came home, he was joyously greeted and hugged by his wife, Della. Which was all very good. Ⓐ

Della finished her crying and dried her cheeks. She stood by the window and looked out dully at a gray cat walking along the top of a gray fence in a gray backyard. Tomorrow would be Christmas Day, and after all her saving, she had only $1.87 to buy Jim a present. There were always more expenses than she thought. She had spent many happy hours planning a gift for him, something fine and rare and perfect, something worthy of her special Jim.

IN OTHER WORDS The main character is a woman named Della. Della and her husband don't have much money. She has tried to save money to buy a special Christmas gift for her husband, Jim, but she has saved very little.

Suddenly Della turned from the window and looked at herself in the tall, old mirror. Her eyes were shining brightly, but her face had become pale. Quickly she pulled down her hair and let it fall loosely around her.

Jim and Della were proud of two things—Jim's gold watch, which had been his father's and his grandfather's, and Della's hair. Della's beautiful, shiny hair now was so long that it hung below her knees. A few of her tears splashed on the worn carpet. Ⓑ

But she put on her coat and hat and, with a brilliant sparkle still in her eyes, hurried out. She stopped at a shop with a sign that read "Madame Sofronie. Hair Goods of All Kinds." Della

Monitor Your Comprehension

VOCABULARY

The word **vestibule** (VES tuh byool) is a noun that means *an entrance hall.*

Ⓐ IRONY

Irony is the difference between what you expect to happen and what actually happens. You might expect someone named Mr. James Dillingham Young to be rich. Is he? Underline two details that tell you he is not wealthy.

Ⓑ PREDICT

What are the two prized possessions described in lines 35–38? Write them in the "Clues" box below.

Clues
Jim's gold watch; Della's hair

What do you think Della might do with her prized possession? Write your prediction below.

My Prediction
Possible answer: Della will cut off her hair and sell it.

Monitor Your Comprehension

VOCABULARY
The word **ransack** (RAN sak) is a verb that means *to search or examine vigorously.*

VISUAL VOCABULARY
A **watch fob** is a short chain for a pocket watch.

C PREDICT
Did you predict that Della would buy the watch fob for Jim? What did you think she would buy with the money?

Possible answer: I knew that she would use it to buy him a Christmas present; however, I was not sure exactly what she would get him.

ran up the flight of stairs. After she calmed down, she said to Madame Sofronie, "Will you buy my hair?"

"Let's have a look at it," said Madame.

Della let down her beautiful hair.

Madame lifted the mass of hair. "Twenty dollars," she said.

"Give it to me quickly," said Della.

For the next two hours, Della **ransacked** the stores for Jim's present. At last she found a platinum **watch fob**, worthy of The Watch. It was like Jim— quiet and valuable.

She paid twenty-one dollars. With that chain, instead of the old leather strap he used now, Jim could proudly check the time in public. C

IN OTHER WORDS Della decides to sell her long, beautiful hair in order to buy her husband a Christmas gift. Della's hair and Jim's watch are the two things that are most precious to them.

At home, Della worked with her curling iron. After forty minutes, her head was covered with tiny curls. She studied herself in the mirror. "If Jim doesn't kill me right away," she said to herself, "he'll say I look cheap and flashy, like a chorus girl in a show. But what could I do with a dollar and eighty-seven cents!"

When she heard him on the stairs, her face turned white for a minute. She whispered, "Please, God, make him think I am still pretty."

The door opened and Jim entered. His eyes fixed on Della. He did not show anger, surprise, disapproval, or horror. He had a strange look on his face.

Della went to hug him.

"Jim, darling," she cried. "Don't look at me that way. I sold my hair because I couldn't have lived without giving you a Christmas present. It'll grow. You won't mind, will you?

"You've cut your hair?" asked Jim.

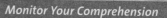

“Don’t you like me just as well, anyhow? I’m me without my hair.”

“You say your hair is gone?” he said. He seemed stunned.

“It’s sold. It’s Christmas Eve. Be good to me, because I sold it for you. I love you dearly.” **D**

Jim came out of his confusion.

“Don’t mind me, Dell,” he said. “You could cut or shave your hair any way you like and I wouldn’t love you less. But if you unwrap that package, you may see why I was so surprised.”

Della tore at the paper on the package. She screamed for joy and then began crying. Jim rose to comfort her. **E**

For he had given her The Combs— the set of combs, side and back, that Della had <u>**coveted**</u> for a long, long time. They would have been perfect in her hair. She had wanted them without ever believing she’d own them. And now, they were hers, but the beautiful hair to wear them in was gone.

IN OTHER WORDS Della’s husband is shocked when he comes home and sees that Della has cut her hair. He then gives Della her Christmas gift, a set of combs for her hair. She had wanted the combs very much for a long time, but now she has no need for them.

She smiled at Jim. “My hair grows fast!”

And then Della cried, “Oh, oh!”

Jim hadn’t seen his beautiful present yet. She held it out to him eagerly.

“Isn’t it a dandy, Jim? You’ll have to look at the time one hundred times a day now. Give me your watch. I want to see how the fob looks on it.”

Jim didn’t hand over the watch. “Dell,” he said, “let’s put away our Christmas presents. They’re too nice to use right now. I sold the watch to get the money to buy your combs.”

Monitor Your Comprehension

D LANGUAGE COACH

Contractions combine two words into one. The apostrophe (’) signals that something has been left out when two words are combined. For example, *didn’t* is *did not*; *isn’t* is *is not*; *let’s* is *let us*. Notice the contractions as you read the dialogue between Jim and Della in lines 67–75.

E PREDICT

What do you think Jim has bought for Della? In the first box below, write down a clue from lines 73–79. Then write down your prediction.

Clue

Jim is surprised to learn that

Della has cut her hair off.

My Prediction

I think that Jim has bought her a

gift that complements her hair.

VOCABULARY

The word **covet** (KUH vet) is a verb that means *to wish for or desire something owned by someone else.*

Monitor Your Comprehension

The Magi, as you know, were wise men. They brought gifts to the baby Jesus. They were the first people to give Christmas presents. They were wise, and probably so were their gifts. Here you have read the story of two foolish people in an apartment. They unwisely gave up the greatest treasures of their house for each other. But of all who give gifts, these two were the wisest. Everywhere they are the wisest. They are the Magi.

PAUSE & REFLECT

PAUSE & REFLECT

Reread lines 87–103. With a partner, discuss what is ironic about the end of the story.

Students should discuss that the end of the story is ironic because Jim sells his watch to buy the combs for Della, and she has sold her hair to buy a watch fob for him.

IN OTHER WORDS Della proudly gives Jim the watch chain she bought him. She asks Jim for the watch so she can see how it looks with the chain. But Jim explains that he sold the watch in order to buy the combs for Della's hair.

► Reread the last paragraph. Then, with a partner, discuss what the narrator thinks of Della's and Jim's actions.

Students should discuss that the narrator thinks that Jim and Della are foolish to give up their greatest treasures. However, the narrator also believes that they are wise for the gifts they chose to give each other and for their selfless acts to make each other happy.

After Reading

Text Analysis: Irony

"The Gift of the Magi" is famous for its **situational irony**—when something happens that is the opposite of what you expected. Fill in the Irony Map below to understand how the story's events create situational irony. The first row has been completed for you.

IRONY MAP

Della	Jim
What Della sells: *her hair*	What Jim sells: *his watch*
What Della buys: ***a watch fob for Jim's watch***	What Jim buys: ***a set of combs for Della's hair***
What Della receives: ***a set of combs that she had wanted for a long time***	What Jim receives: ***a watch fob for his gold watch***
Why the gift is useless: ***Della cut her hair off and cannot use the combs.***	Why the gift is useless: ***Jim sold his watch to buy a gift for Della.***

With a partner, review your notes for "The Gift of the Magi." Then, review your completed Irony Map, above. On the lines below, write a brief explanation of what O. Henry's use of irony tells us about Della and Jim's relationship.

O. Henry's use of irony in the story tells the reader that Jim and Della are willing to give up their most prized possessions in order to purchase gifts that will make the other one happy.

Reading Strategy: Predict

Look back at the **predictions** you made as you read. Place a checkmark [✓] next to the predictions that proved true and place an X next to those that did not. Then, choose one prediction. In the chart below, fill in the clue, your prediction, and the outcome—what actually happened in the story.

For this chart, answers will vary. See samples below.

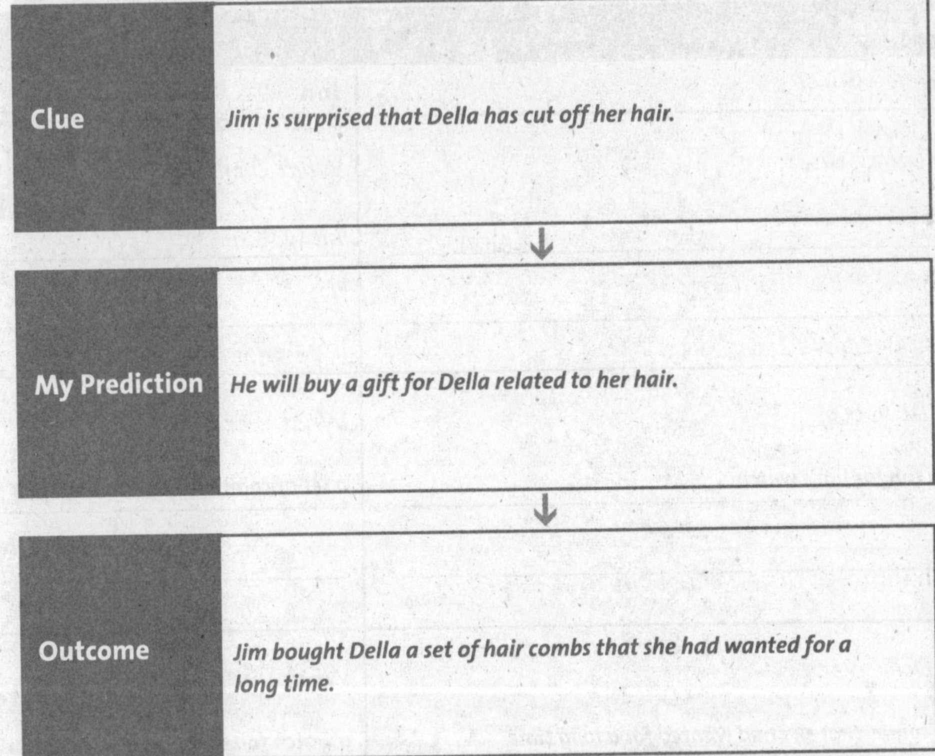

Clue	*Jim is surprised that Della has cut off her hair.*
My Prediction	*He will buy a gift for Della related to her hair.*
Outcome	*Jim bought Della a set of hair combs that she had wanted for a long time.*

What are you willing to SACRIFICE?

Of all the things you own, which could you live without?

Answers will vary.

Vocabulary Practice

Circle the word or phrase that is most different in meaning from the others.

1. (a) basement (b) vestibule (c) entryway
2. (a) throw away (b) ransack (c) look through
3. (a) desire (b) covet (c) dislike

Academic Vocabulary in Speaking

The word **element** (EL uh muhnt) is a noun that means *a needed or basic part of something.*

A short story has several **elements,** including plot and characters.

TURN AND TALK What **elements** in "The Gift of the Magi" help create the suspense, or excitement about what will happen? Think about what the narrator tells you and what the narrator leaves out. Be sure to use the word **element** in your conversation.

Encourage students to use the Academic Vocabulary word in their discussions.

Assessment Practice

DIRECTIONS Use "The Gift of the Magi" to answer questions 1–6.

1 Della buys a watch fob for Jim because —

(A) he lost his watch
(B) it does not cost much money
(C) he doesn't know how to tell time
(D) it's Christmas

2 When Jim sees Della's short hair, he realizes —

(A) she has been to a beauty parlor
(B) he likes her hair short
(C) his gift for her will be useless
(D) she couldn't always have long hair

3 Which statement best describes the situational irony in the story?

(A) The watch fob is as useless to Jim as the combs are to Della.
(B) Jim and Della bought each other expensive gifts.
(C) Della's combs were bought with the money she received for her hair.
(D) Jim and Della are as wise as the Magi.

4 O. Henry suggests that Della and Jim's "greatest treasure" is —

(A) a watch fob and a comb
(B) their foolishness
(C) their sacrifices
(D) their love for each other

5 To create a surprise ending, O. Henry —

(A) does not introduce Jim until the end of the story
(B) withholds information about Jim's plan
(C) explains right away what the characters know
(D) does not reveal Della's motivation for cutting her hair

6 What does the story reveal about Della and Jim?

(A) They are greedy and selfish.
(B) They put each other's happiness above their own.
(C) They don't know each other as well as they thought.
(D) They have fallen out of love.

Horse of the Century

Background

During the Great Depression, an American racehorse named Seabiscuit (SEE bis kit) became a hero even though he lost some early races. He even had a crooked leg. Seabiscuit was named Horse of the Year in 1938 after winning a race that almost 40 million people listened to on the radio. Read the following texts to understand why horseracing and Seabiscuit were so popular.

Standards Focus: Synthesize

Reading more than one source on a topic gives you more information. When you **synthesize** (SYN thuh syz) information, you put together the facts and ideas from each source. This gives you a more complete picture of the topic.

Use these steps to **synthesize** information from the following pieces about Seabiscuit.

1. Identify the key ideas in each piece as you read—ideas that are repeated or emphasized by the author.
2. When more than one piece discusses the same key idea, make notes about the information each source provides.
3. Sum up how all of the information about the key ideas fits together. This is your **synthesis statement.**

As you read, you will use a chart like the one below to keep track of your notes and questions.

Key Idea	Source	Information from the Source
Seabiscuit caused excitement in race fans.	*from "Four Good Legs Between Us"*	*"huge celebrity"; helped people forget troubles; record numbers of fans*
	Timeline: Seabiscuit	
	"Races on the Radio"	
How All of This Information Fits Together:		

SET A PURPOSE FOR READING

As you read these three selections, find at least one reason in each selection that helps explain why Seabiscuit was so popular.

from

Four Good Legs Between Us

Based on the magazine article by Laura Hillenbrand

Seabiscuit had lost the Santa Anita Handicap,[1] an important race, but he was becoming very famous. This was partly because his owner, Charles Howard, worked so hard to promote him, to get people to pay attention to him. Howard was a successful car salesman, with a lot of experience in advertising and promotion. Just as sports agents work for some athletes today, Howard worked for Seabiscuit.

1. A **handicap (HAN dee kap)**: is a type of horse race in which the horses carry different amounts of weight in their saddles. This helps even out the competition, since some horses are clearly faster and stronger than others.

No one had ever done this before. Howard shipped Seabiscuit thousands of miles all over North America. The horse ran races at eighteen tracks in the United States and Mexico.

The second reason for Seabiscuit's fame was timing. The nation was in the Great Depression and was about to enter World War II. During such hard times, people liked hearing a success story like Seabiscuit's. It was inspiring. It made them feel better about their own lives. (A)

Seabiscuit became very popular. In one year there were more newspaper stories about Seabiscuit than about Roosevelt, Hitler, or Mussolini, three of the most powerful and important people in the world at that time. A popular magazine, *Life,* even ran a story about his different facial expressions. Seabiscuit inspired record numbers of people to come to the racetrack. Because of him, more people than ever before were watching the races.

All this fame led to the success of California's new racing industry. Today horseracing in California is a business worth $4 billion a year. PAUSE & REFLECT

IN OTHER WORDS Seabiscuit became famous for two reasons. The first reason was that his owner worked very hard to promote him. The other reason was that Americans were going through hard times and Seabiscuit's story made them forget their troubles for a little while.

► Circle two things troubling Americans at the time.

(A) SYNTHESIZE

Reread lines 1–16; then, underline two reasons this passage gives for Seabiscuit's popularity.

PAUSE & REFLECT

With a partner, discuss whether a horse like Seabiscuit would be as popular today as during the 1930s. Give reasons to support your opinion.

Students' answers will vary.

Timeline: Seabiscuit

1937

- ***February 27:*** In his first try at the Santa Anita Handicap, Seabiscuit loses to a horse named Rosemont in a very close finish.
- ***March 6:*** Seabiscuit attracts a crowd of 45,000 excited fans and wins the San Juan Capistrano Handicap by finishing seven **lengths** ahead of the second-place horse. He breaks the track record.
- ***June 5:*** War Admiral captures the Triple Crown by winning three important races—the Belmont Stakes, the Kentucky Derby, and the Preakness Stakes—in the same year.
- ***June 26:*** Seabiscuit runs in a race called the Brooklyn Handicap, beating Rosemont.
- ***July:*** Seabiscuit wins the Butler Handicap and the Yonkers Handicap races easily, even though the rules make him carry much more weight than the other horses have to.
- ***September 11:*** At the Narragansett Special in Rhode Island, Seabiscuit finishes third.
- ***October 12:*** Seabiscuit wins the Continental Handicap in New York, making him the horse earning the most money in 1937, just ahead of War Admiral.
- ***October 30:*** Seabiscuit and War Admiral are supposed to race in the Washington Handicap. However, Seabiscuit's owner decides not to let him race because he might be injured if he falls on the muddy, slippery track. War Admiral wins the race easily.
- ***December 7:*** War Admiral is named horse of the year by the magazine *Turf and Sport Digest.*

VISUAL VOCABULARY
A **length** in horseracing is the distance of about one full body length of a horse from nose to tail—about eight feet.

1938

November 1: As 40 million people across the country listen to the race on their radios, Seabiscuit beats War Admiral, setting a new record for the Pimlico racetrack.

1939

February 14: Seabiscuit is injured while getting ready for the Santa Anita Handicap.

September 3: Britain and France declare war on Germany.

1940

March 2: Seabiscuit wins in his third try at the $100,000 Santa Anita Handicap. He runs the fastest mile and a quarter in the track's history, the second fastest time this distance has ever been run in the United States. The most people ever to attend an American horserace—75,000—watch as jockey Red Pollard leads Seabiscuit from way behind to win.

April 10: Seabiscuit retires from racing. B

IN OTHER WORDS Seabiscuit's career is detailed from 1937 to 1940, including victories, awards, and his retirement from racing.

B SYNTHESIZE

In the timeline, circle races Seabiscuit won and bracket [ ] races he did not win. Use the organizer below to synthesize this information into a statement about Seabiscuit's record.

Key Idea

Seabiscuit won more races than he lost. He also set many records in the races he won.

Races on the Radio

Santa Anita Handicap (1937)

Based on the commentary by Clem McCarthy and Buddy Twist

CLEM McCARTHY:

We don't have any starting barriers now, as you know. (No wall or fence is holding the horses in place.) Here they go. And they're on their way down the **stretch**. The start was good; every horse got a chance just as they left there.

As they come down here to the eighth pole, the leaders are Time Supply and Special Agent. Special Agent is trying to force his way to the front and he's going to do a good job of it as they pass the stands. Here on the outside comes Rosemont in a good position. And as they go by me it is Special Agent in the lead by one length. Special Agent has the lead and then comes Time Supply in second place right along beside him. Going to the first turn is Special Agent by a length. Time Supply is second and on the outside of him is Accolade. And Boxthorn is close up. Far back in the crowd, on the inside, in about twelfth place is Red Rain. Up there close is Rosemont in about sixth place.

They're going into the stretch (the straight part of the oval track); they've gone half a mile. They're turning into the backstretch with Special Agent on the lead. Special Agent has

VISUAL VOCABULARY

A **stretch** in horse racing is either of the two long sides of an oval racetrack a lead now of one length and a half. Right behind him comes Time Supply. And in there, slipping through on the inside is . . . Indian Broom is going up on the inside now in a good position. (C) Around that far turn, there's still no change in the positions. Rosemont is having a hard time working his way through, he's now in sixth position going around on the inside, he's got plenty of strength left. If he's a strong enough horse, he may get to the finish line first. And on the outside, here comes Indian Broom. And Goldeneye is moving up from the rear. Here comes Accolade in second position. And Seabiscuit is now moving up and is challenging as they turn for home. (D)

(C) LANGUAGE COACH
This transcript includes some **sentence fragments,** or incomplete sentences. For example, in line 21, Clem McCarthy interrupts himself and never completes the sentence "And in there, slipping through on the inside is. . . ." Story writers may use incomplete sentences in dialogue to make characters' conversations sound more realistic.

(D) SYNTHESIZE
This radio transcript includes the names of other horses who raced in the Santa Anita Handicap. Reread lines 5–31; then, underline the names of the other horses. Which horse is also mentioned in the timeline on pages 49–50?

Rosemont is also mentioned in the timeline.

IN OTHER WORDS The race begins. Through most of the race, other horses compete for first place.

► Discuss with a partner what happens in lines 24–31. What might happen next?

Students should discuss that the lead in the race is in question and that many horses, including Seabiscuit, are moving their position and challenging the leader. While the lead is uncertain, it is possible that Seabiscuit might win the race.

It's Special Agent and Seabiscuit challenging head-to-head as they swing into the stretch. And they've only got a quarter of a mile to come. They've stepped the first mile at a fast pace. Seabiscuit has got the lead half way down the stretch. And the battle is on. Indian Broom is coming fast and here comes Rosemont between horses. And Rosemont may take it all. It's gonna be a photograph finish. And it's anybody's race right to the end.

I think Rosemont was first. It was a very close finish. And Seabiscuit was the second horse. Seabiscuit was second and I think Indian Broom was third. It was very close. That was an eyelash finish. Rosemont was closing strong, but Seabiscuit hung on. The time of the race was 2:02 and four-fifths, which makes the track almost identically like the track of two years ago. . . .

BUDDY TWIST:

Oh boy, one of the most thrilling finishes I think that I've ever seen in a horse race in my life, Clem. The crowd down here has gone completely mad. The photographers are outside the charm circle, which is a white circle here, where the winner will come up in just a moment. Newsreel photographers are setting up on every hand. The horses are just coming back now. And everybody, depending on who was their favorite, was shouting "Rosemont," "Seabiscuit"—one would call Rosemont, one Seabiscuit. There were half-a-dozen here who were just as sure Rosemont won as Seabiscuit, they don't know what to think of it. One of the most beautiful driving finishes I think I've ever seen. PAUSE & REFLECT

CLEM McCARTHY:

Here's the photograph finish. Hold it now. Get ready for it. Just a few seconds and we'll know the winner of this race. I think Rosemont won it, but that's only my guess from where I stand. The photograph will tell us the actual winner. The naked eye is not as good as the photograph, we'll have it in a second. They're looking at it down there. Either horse won by a whisker and that's all. Just about a quarter of an inch, I can't see any more between them. I really shouldn't express an opinion on a finish that close. And they're still waiting. That shows you what a difficult . . . [There it is, Rosemont is the winner.] Rosemont by a nose. Seabiscuit is second. They haven't put up the numbers and they finished very close together. E

IN OTHER WORDS Four horses—Special Agent, Seabiscuit, Rosemont, and Indian Broom—race toward the finish line. The horses are so close together that the announcers have trouble identifying the winner.

► Which horse wins? Draw brackets [ ] around the sentence that tells you.

PAUSE & REFLECT

The scene that Buddy Twist describes helps build up suspense about which horse won the race. With a partner, discuss how determining the winner of the race would be different now than in 1937.

Students should discuss that races today can rely on instant replay to help determine the winner.

E SYNTHESIZE

All three selections mention the same key event: the Santa Anita Handicap. However, each source provides different details about it. What do you learn about the race from this transcript?

Key Event
Santa Anita Handicap

↓

Information from This Source
Possible answer: The race was so close that a photo finish was used to determine its winner.

Practicing Your Skills: Synthesize

Use the charts provided to develop two key ideas about Seabiscuit (one is provided for you) and to synthesize information about those ideas from the selections you have read. *For this chart, answers will vary. See samples below.*

Key Idea 1	Source	Information from the Source
Seabiscuit caused excitement in race fans.	from "Four Good Legs Between Us"	*In one year there were more newspaper stories about Seabiscuit than three of the most powerful people in the world. People attended races in record numbers.*
	Timeline: Seabiscuit	*45,000 people attend the March 1937 San Juan Capistrano Handicap to watch Seabiscuit. Forty million people listen to the November 1, 1940, race at Pimlico.*
	"Races on the Radio"	*The radio announcer calls the finish one of the most thrilling he has ever seen. At the end of the race, the crowd is wild with excitement.*
How All of This Information Fits Together: *Seabiscuit provided millions with exciting entertainment during a difficult time in U.S. history.*		

Key Idea 2	Source	Information from the Source
Seabiscuit did not win every race.	from "Four Good Legs Between Us"	*Seabiscuit lost the Santa Anita Handicap.*
	Timeline: Seabiscuit	*Seabiscuit lost to Rosemont at the Santa Anita Handicap in February 1937. Seabiscuit finished third in the September 1937 Narragansett Special.*
	"Races on the Radio"	*Rosemont defeated Seabiscuit in the 1937 Santa Anita Handicap.*
How All of This Information Fits Together: *Seabiscuit did not win every race in which he was entered.*		

Now use your "How All of This Information Fits Together" (synthesis) statements to help you complete the sentence starter below.

Even though Seabiscuit lost an important race, he was popular because *he was a strong competitor and inspired people at a tough time in the history of the United States.*

Academic Vocabulary in Speaking

The word **structure** (STRUK chuhr) means *something made of parts put together* or *the way something is put together.*

With its sturdy **structure,** the school was the only building on the block left standing after the hurricane.

TURN AND TALK With a partner, discuss how the selections organize information about Seabiscuit. Be sure to use the word **structure** in your conversation.

Encourage students to use the Academic Vocabulary word in their discussions.

Assessment Practice

DIRECTIONS Use the three selections in this section to answer questions 1–4.

1 What made Seabiscuit so popular?

- A He won every race in which he competed.
- B People felt sorry for him because of his injuries.
- C His owner promoted him with races across the country.
- D His variety of facial expressions charmed people.

2 Why is information about World War II in Europe included?

- A Seabiscuit's victories helped distract Americans from fears about the U.S. joining the war.
- B Seabiscuit's trainer or jockey might have had to fight in the war.
- C Seabiscuit would have gotten more attention if the war's leaders hadn't grabbed all of the newspaper headlines.
- D Seabiscuit's owner used publicity about his horse to express his opinion about the war.

3 What is a key way that the timeline and radio transcript are different?

- A Only the timeline is arranged in chronological (time) order.
- B The timeline states only facts, but the radio transcript includes opinions.
- C The radio transcript does not state who won the 1937 Santa Anita Handicap.
- D The radio transcript makes it less clear than the timeline how close the finish was.

4 A main idea common to all three selections is that —

- A Seabiscuit was everyone's favorite horse
- B Seabiscuit was popular only because his owner advertised him
- C People loved to watch Seabiscuit race
- D Rosemont should have gotten more recognition

The Raven

Poem by Edgar Allan Poe

Incident in a Rose Garden

Poem by Donald Justice

Why are we fascinated by the UNKNOWN?

Do you like television shows in which weird things happen? The writers of the poems you are about to read were also fascinated by the strange and unknown. These poems will introduce you to two strange–and perhaps imaginary–visitors.

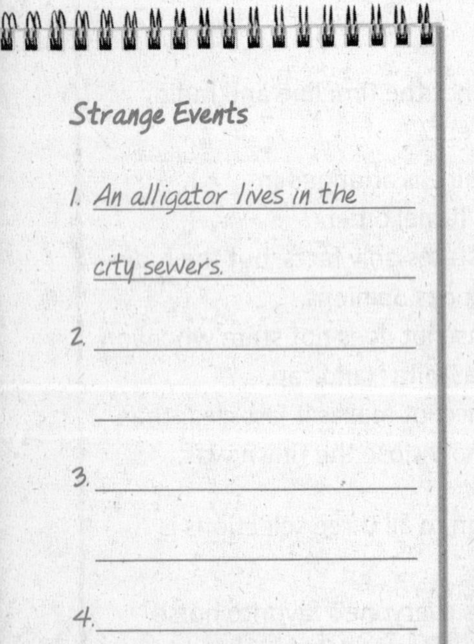

Strange Events
1. An alligator lives in the city sewers.
2.
3.
4.

TURN AND TALK With a partner, talk about three events from movies, television shows, or stories you have heard that you find weird or hard to believe. Write your answers in the notepad at the left.

Answers will vary.

Text Analysis: Narrative Poetry

Like fiction, **narrative poetry** contains the elements of plot, conflict, character, and setting. The **speaker** in the poems you are about to read is also the main character in the story. As you read, you will note the events each speaker describes and how these create an exciting story.

Narrative Element	"The Raven"	"Incident in a Rose Garden"
Characters	*a man who has lost his love Lenore* *a bird—the Raven*	
Setting	*dreary night in December - in the man's study*	*a rose garden*
Conflict	*he hears knocking on his door*	
Resolution (How does the poem end?)		

Reading Skill: Reading Poetry

To help you understand the events in a narrative poem, use the following strategies:

1. Read the poem silently to understand the basic story.
2. Read the poem aloud twice. Pay attention to sound devices such as **rhyme, rhythm, repetition,** and **alliteration.** (See the chart below for definitions of these terms.) As you read, circle or underline any instances you find of sound devices.
3. Look for clues that reveal something about the speaker. How does the speaker feel about the events in the poem?

As you read each poem, you will write down examples of sound devices.

Sound Device	Example from "The Raven"	Example from "Incident in a Rose Garden"
alliteration (uh lit uh RAY shuhn) noun: *repetition of consonant sounds*	"nodded, nearly napping"	
repetition (rep ih TISH uhn) noun: *repeating words, phrases, or lines*	"Quoth the Raven, 'Nevermore.'"	
rhyme (rym) noun: *similar sounds at the end of two or more words*		"breath" / "death"
rhythm (RITH uhm) noun: *pattern of stressed and unstressed syllables in a line of poetry*	"Once upon a midnight dreary"	

Monitor Your Comprehension

SET A PURPOSE FOR READING
"The Raven" is one of Poe's most famous works. Read this poem several times to enjoy its sound effects.

The Raven

Poem by
EDGAR ALLAN POE

BACKGROUND An obsession is an idea that we cannot get out of our minds. "The Raven" is about a man obsessed by the memory of Lenore, a woman he loved who is now dead. As he is thinking about her, a raven flies into his study. Ravens, like parrots, can imitate human speech. The raven in this story keeps repeating one word, causing the speaker to feel even worse.

Once upon a midnight dreary, while I pondered, weak and weary,
Over many a quaint and curious volume of forgotten lore—
While I nodded, nearly napping, suddenly there came a tapping,
As of someone gently rapping, rapping at my chamber door.
"'Tis some visitor," I muttered, "tapping at my chamber door—
Only this and nothing more." (A)

Ah, distinctly I remember it was in the bleak December;
And each separate dying ember wrought its ghost upon the floor.
Eagerly I wished the morrow;—vainly I had sought to borrow
From my books surcease of sorrow[1]—sorrow for the lost Lenore—

(A) READING POETRY
Circle the **rhyming words** in lines 1–6. With a partner, talk about what is happening at the beginning of the poem.

Students should discuss that as the poem begins the speaker is awake late at night reading and is about to fall asleep when there is a knock at his door.

1. **from my books surcease of sorrow:** from reading, an end to sorrow.

Monitor Your Comprehension

For the rare and radiant maiden whom the angels name Lenore—
Nameless *here* forevermore. Ⓑ

IN OTHER WORDS On a gloomy December night, the poem's speaker sits studying old books. He is trying to forget his sadness over the death of Lenore. Just as he is about to fall asleep, he hears a tapping. He tells himself it is just a visitor at the door.

And the silken, sad, uncertain rustling of each purple curtain
Thrilled me—filled me with fantastic terrors never felt before;
So that now, to still the beating of my heart, I stood repeating
"'Tis some visitor entreating entrance at my chamber door;—
Some late visitor entreating entrance at my chamber door;—
That it is and nothing more."

Presently my soul grew stronger; hesitating then no longer,
"Sir," said I, "or Madam, truly your forgiveness I implore;
But the fact is I was napping, and so gently you came rapping,
And so faintly you came tapping, tapping at my chamber door,
That I scarce was sure I heard you"—here I opened wide the door;—
Darkness there and nothing more.

IN OTHER WORDS The rustling of the curtains fills the speaker with terror. His heart races as he tells himself it is just a late visitor. Soon, he feels braver. He asks the visitor to forgive him for not answering the door. He says that he had been napping and that the tapping had been too quiet for him to hear. He opens the door, but no one is there.

Deep into that darkness peering, long I stood there wondering, fearing,
Doubting, dreaming dreams no mortal ever dared to dream before;
But the silence was unbroken, and the stillness gave no token,
And the only word there spoken was the whispered word, "Lenore!"

Ⓑ **NARRATIVE POETRY**
An **internal conflict** is a problem or struggle caused by a character's thoughts or emotions. With what internal conflict does the speaker struggle? Whom has he lost?

Possible answer: The speaker is struggling with his grief over the loss of his beloved Lenore, who has died.

Monitor Your Comprehension

C READING POETRY
Reread lines 25–30. Then underline one example of **alliteration**, the repetition of consonant sounds at the beginning of words.

This I whispered, and an echo murmured back the word
"Lenore!"
Merely this and nothing more. C

Back into the chamber turning, all my soul within me burning,
Soon again I heard a tapping somewhat louder than before.
"Surely," said I, "surely that is something at my window lattice;
Let me see, then, what thereat is, and this mystery explore—
Let my heart be still a moment and this mystery explore;—
'Tis the wind and nothing more!"

IN OTHER WORDS The speaker stares into the darkness. He whispers, "Lenore!"

► Reread lines 25–36. What does the speaker hear? With a partner, discuss the speaker's emotions at this point.

Students should discuss that the speaker hears a voice say "Lenore," which causes him to feel confused and fearful, and to wonder whether perhaps Lenore is alive. He tries to convince himself that the wind is the source of the noises he hears.

Open here I flung the shutter, when, with many a flirt and flutter,
In there stepped a stately Raven of the saintly days of yore.[2]
Not the least obeisance made he;[3] not a minute stopped or stayed he;
But, with mien of lord or lady,[4] perched above my chamber door—
Perched upon a **bust of Pallas** just above my chamber door—
Perched, and sat, and nothing more.

Then this ebony bird beguiling[5] my sad fancy into smiling,
By the grave and stern decorum of the countenance[6] it wore,
"Though thy crest be shorn and shaven, thou," I said, "art sure no
craven,[7]
Ghastly grim and ancient Raven wandering from the Nightly
shore—

VISUAL VOCABULARY
A **bust** is a sculpture of a person's head, shoulders, and chest. **Pallas** (PAL uhs) is another name for **Athena** (uh THEE nuh), the Greek goddess of war and wisdom.

2. **saintly days of yore:** sacred days of the past.
3. **not the least obeisance** (oh BAY suhns) **made he:** he did not bow or make any other gesture of respect.
4. **with mien of lord or lady:** with the appearance of a noble person.
5. **this ebony bird beguiling** (bih GYL ing): this black bird that is charming or delighting.
6. **grave and stern decorum . . . countenance** (KOUN tuh nuhns): serious and dignified expression on the face.
7. **art sure no craven:** are surely not cowardly.

Monitor Your Comprehension

Tell me what thy lordly name is on the Night's Plutonian[8] shore!"
Quoth the Raven, "Nevermore." D

IN OTHER WORDS The speaker opens the window covering. A raven steps in, then flies up and perches on a sculpture of the Greek goddess Athena. The speaker smiles at the bird's stern and serious look. He tells the bird that although its head feathers have been cut, it is not a coward. He asks its name. It answers, "Nevermore."

D READING POETRY

How does the speaker respond when he first sees the raven? Reread lines 43–48. What does his "smiling" reaction tell you about the speaker's state of mind?

Possible answer: When the speaker sees the raven, his spirits are lifted. He seems to welcome the raven as a source of relief from his sadness. The serious expression of the raven causes the speaker to smile. The speaker's reaction tells the reader that he is lonely and is grateful for the distraction that the raven provides.

Much I marveled this ungainly fowl to hear discourse so plainly,
Though its answer little meaning—little relevancy bore;
For we cannot help agreeing that no living human being
Ever yet was blessed with seeing bird above his chamber door—
Bird or beast upon the sculptured bust above his chamber door,
With such name as "Nevermore."

But the Raven, sitting lonely on the placid bust, spoke only
That one word, as if his soul in that one word he did outpour.
Nothing farther then he uttered—not a feather then he fluttered—
Till I scarcely more than muttered, "Other friends have flown before—
On the morrow he will leave me, as my hopes have flown before."
Then the bird said, ["Nevermore."]

IN OTHER WORDS The speaker does not understand the bird's answer. He decides that this has never happened before.

► What does the speaker say to the raven? Put brackets [ ] around the bird's answer.

The speaker tells the raven that it will leave him just as others have in the past.

Startled at the stillness broken by reply so aptly spoken,
"Doubtless," said I, "what it utters is its only stock and store
Caught from some unhappy master whom unmerciful Disaster
Followed fast and followed faster till his songs one burden bore—

8. **Plutonian:** having to do with Pluto, Roman god of the dead and ruler of the underworld.

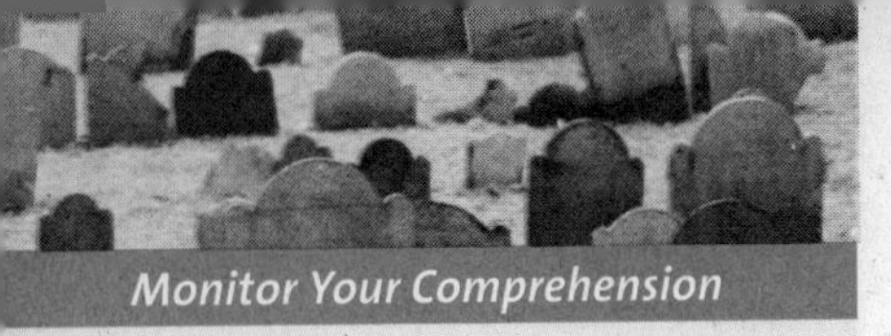

Monitor Your Comprehension

Till the dirges of his Hope[9] that melancholy burden bore
Of 'Never—nevermore.'"

But the Raven still beguiling all my fancy into smiling,
Straight I wheeled a cushioned seat in front of bird and bust and door;
Then, upon the velvet sinking, I betook myself to linking
Fancy unto fancy, thinking what this ominous bird of yore—
What this grim, ungainly, ghastly, gaunt, and ominous bird of yore
Meant in croaking, "Nevermore." E

E READING POETRY
Reread lines 67–72. Notice the internal **rhyme**—similar or identical sounds within a line—of the words *beguiling* and *smiling*. Circle those two words. Now underline another set of internal rhymes in this **stanza**, or grouping of lines.

IN OTHER WORDS The speaker is surprised that the bird's answer makes sense. He decides the bird has been trained to talk by an unhappy owner. Amused, he smiles, rolls a seat in front of the door, and looks up at the bird.

► What does the speaker think about? Reread lines 67–72. Then discuss your answer with a partner.

Students should discuss that the speaker is trying to figure out what the bird means by repeatedly saying "Nevermore."

This I sat engaged in guessing, but no syllable expressing
To the fowl whose fiery eyes now burned into my bosom's core;
This and more I sat divining,[10] with my head at ease reclining
On the cushion's velvet lining that the lamp-light gloated o'er,
But whose velvet violet lining with the lamp-light gloating o'er,
She shall press, ah, nevermore! F

F LANGUAGE COACH
Words have **connotations**, or feelings and ideas that we link to the words. These connotations may be positive, or they may be negative. Reread lines 74–75. With a partner, discuss whether you think *fiery* has a positive or a negative connotation.

Possible answer: Students may discuss that the word fiery has a negative connotation because it implies that the bird's eyes are burning into his chest.

Then, methought, the air grew denser, perfumed from an unseen censer
Swung by Seraphim[11] whose foot-falls tinkled on the tufted floor.
"Wretch," I cried, "thy God hath lent thee—by these angels he hath sent thee
Respite—respite and nepenthe[12] from thy memories of Lenore;
Quaff, oh quaff this kind nepenthe[13] and forget this lost Lenore!"

9. **dirges** (DUR jiz) **of his Hope:** funeral hymns mourning the loss of hope.
10. **divining** (dih VY ning): guessing or figuring out.
11. **censer swung by Seraphim** (SER uh fim): container of burning incense swung by angels of the highest rank.
12. **he hath sent thee respite** (RES pit) **... nepenthe** (nih PEN thee): God has sent you relief and forgetfulness of sorrow.
13. **quaff, oh quaff this kind nepenthe:** drink this beverage that eases pain.

Monitor Your Comprehension

Quoth the Raven, "Nevermore."

IN OTHER WORDS The speaker sits thinking. He feels as though the raven's eyes burn into his heart. He leans his head back against the velvet cushion. Then he realizes that Lenore will never rest her head against the same cushion again.

He imagines that the air smells of incense burned by an invisible angel. Suddenly, he yells that God and the angels have sent the raven to help him get over Lenore. He asks whether anything could help him forget her. The raven answers, "Nevermore."

"Prophet!" said I, "thing of evil!—prophet still, if bird or devil!—
Whether Tempter sent, or whether tempest tossed[14] thee here
ashore,
Desolate yet all undaunted,[15] on this desert land enchanted—
On this home by Horror haunted—tell me truly, I implore—
Is there—*is* there balm in Gilead?[16]—tell me—tell me, I
implore!"
Quoth the Raven, "Nevermore." G

"Prophet!" said I, "thing of evil!—prophet still, if bird or devil!
By that Heaven that bends above us—by that God we both
adore—
Tell this soul with sorrow laden if, within the distant Aidenn,[17]
It shall clasp a sainted maiden whom the angels name Lenore—
Clasp a rare and radiant maiden whom the angels name Lenore."
Quoth the Raven, "Nevermore."

"Be that word our sign of parting, bird or fiend!" I shrieked,
upstarting—
"Get thee back into the tempest and the Night's Plutonian shore!
Leave no black plume as a token of that lie thy soul hath spoken!
Leave my loneliness unbroken!—quit the bust above my door!

G **READING POETRY**
Underline the **repetition** in line 89. With a partner, talk about what this repetition tells you about the poem's speaker. Write down your answer below.

Possible answer: The repetition shows that the speaker is desperate for answers or consolation from the raven.

14. **whether Tempter sent . . . tempest tossed:** whether the devil sent or a violent storm carried.
15. **desolate yet all undaunted:** alone and yet unafraid.
16. **balm in Gilead** (GIL ee uhd): relief from suffering.
17. **Aidenn** (AYD en): heaven

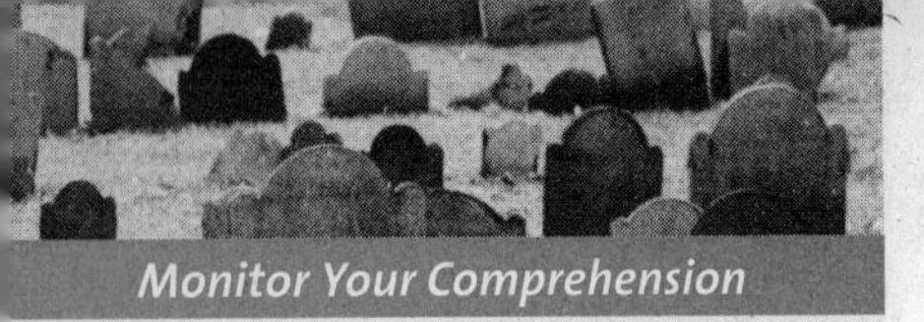

Monitor Your Comprehension

Take thy beak from out my heart, and take thy form from off my door!"
Quoth the Raven, "Nevermore."

IN OTHER WORDS **Angered by the bird's reply, the speaker says that he cannot tell whether the raven is a prophet of good or of evil. He asks if he will ever have relief from his sorrow. The raven says, "Nevermore." Then the speaker asks the bird whether he'll be able to hug Lenore in heaven one day. The raven answers, "Nevermore."**

► Reread lines 97–102. What does the speaker tell the raven to do? With a partner, talk about what the speaker tells the raven to do.

Students should discuss that the speaker tells the raven to leave his home and to leave him alone.

And the Raven, never flitting, still is sitting, *still* is sitting
On the pallid bust of Pallas just above my chamber door;
And his eyes have all the seeming of a demon's that is dreaming,
And the lamp-light o'er him streaming throws his shadow on the floor;
And my soul from out that shadow that lies floating on the floor
Shall be lifted—nevermore! PAUSE & REFLECT

IN OTHER WORDS **The speaker says that the demon raven has never flown away. It is still staring down at him from the statue. The speaker says his spirits will never be lifted.**

PAUSE & REFLECT

Think about whether the speaker's **conflict** is resolved at the end of the poem. What do you think will happen to him? Write your response on the lines below.

Possible answer: At the end of the poem, the speaker's conflict has not been resolved. He continues to be saddened by Lenore's death and says that his spirits will never be lifted. The raven's repetition of "Nevermore" has further agitated the speaker. His future will likely be bleak; he will continue to be unhappy.

Incident *in a* Rose Garden

Poem by
DONALD JUSTICE

BACKGROUND In this poem, the poet imagines Death as a man—or perhaps a skeleton—wearing black. Death carries a scythe (syth), a tool used to cut grain. Artists and writers have often used the scythe to symbolize, or stand for, death: just as it cuts the grain, it can cut down human life. The text in italics represents the voices of the different characters.

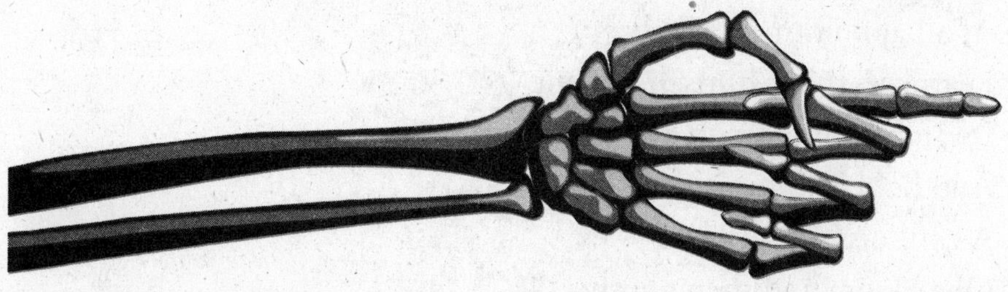

The gardener came running,
An old man, out of breath.
Fear had given him legs.
Sir, I encountered Death
Just now among the roses.
Thin as a scythe he stood there.
I knew him by his pictures.
He had his black coat on,
Black gloves, a broad black hat. H
I think he would have spoken,
Seeing his mouth stood open.
Big it was, with white teeth.
As soon as he beckoned, I ran.
I ran until I found you.

Monitor Your Comprehension

SET A PURPOSE FOR READING
Read this poem to find out what "incident" happens in the speaker's rose garden.

H READING POETRY
Reread lines 4–9. What word is repeated three times? Circle the word. Why do you think it is repeated?

Possible answer: To reinforce that Death was dressed in black from head to toe as he is often imagined to look.

Monitor Your Comprehension

Sir, I am quitting my job.
I want to see my sons
Once more before I die.
I want to see California. ❶
We shook hands; he was off.

IN OTHER WORDS The speaker says his gardener has run up to him, frightened. The gardener tells the speaker that he has just seen Death. He says he recognized Death from pictures he has seen. Death tries to get the gardener to come to him, but the gardener runs until he finds his master, the speaker. The gardener tells the speaker that he is leaving to see his sons and California before he dies.

And there stood Death in the garden,
Dressed like a Spanish waiter.
He had the air of someone
Who because he likes arriving
At all appointments early
Learns to think himself patient.
I watched him pinch one bloom off
And hold it to his nose—
A connoisseur[1] of roses—
One bloom and then another. ❶
They strewed the earth around him.
Sir, you must be that stranger
Who threatened my gardener.
This is my property, sir.
I welcome only friends here.

IN OTHER WORDS The speaker sees Death standing in the garden. He watches as Death picks blooms off the roses one by one and lets them fall to the ground.

► Reread lines 31–34. With a partner, discuss what the speaker tells Death.

Students should discuss that the speaker tells Death that he is not welcome in his garden.

❶ **NARRATIVE POETRY**
In lines 4–18, the gardener describes the character of Death. What do these lines suggest the **conflict** of the poem will be?

Possible answer: I think that the conflict will involve a character who does not want to die and the character Death.

❶ **READING POETRY**
Read aloud lines 26–29. As you read, listen to the **rhythm** of these shorter lines. Imagine Death slowly picking one rose at a time. How does this image fit the idea of what Death does?

Possible answer: The rhythm adds to the slow, deliberate actions of Death as he pinches off one bloom after another.

1. **connoisseur** (kon uh SUR): an expert.

Monitor Your Comprehension

Death grinned, and his eyes lit up
With the pale glow of those lanterns
That workmen carry sometimes
To light their way through the dusk.
Now with great care he slid
The glove from his right hand
And held that out in greeting,
A little cage of bone.
  Sir, I knew your father,
  And we were friends at the end.
  As for your gardener,
  I did not threaten him.
  Old men mistake my gestures.
  I only meant to ask him
  To show me to his master.
  I take it you are he? **PAUSE & REFLECT**

for Mark Strand

IN OTHER WORDS Death smiles, and his eyes begin to glow. When he takes off his glove to shake the speaker's hand, the speaker sees Death's hand is nothing but bones. Death says that he had become friends with the speaker's father near the end of his father's life. He tells the speaker that he didn't mean to scare the gardener. Old men, he says, misunderstand him.

Then Death tells the speaker he has been looking not for the gardener—but for the master.

PAUSE & REFLECT

What is the surprise ending in lines 48–50? With a partner, discuss what these last lines tell you about what Death has come to do. Then, write your answer on the lines below.

At the end of the poem, the surprise is that Death did not come for the gardener but for his master who is the speaker of the poem.

After Reading

Text Analysis: Narrative Poetry

Narrative poems like "The Raven" and "Incident in a Rose Garden" contain many of the same elements found in short stories. First, reread "The Raven" and review your notes. Next, fill in the middle column of the chart below. Then, review "Incident in a Rose Garden." Fill in the column on the right.

Narrative Element	"The Raven"	"Incident in a Rose Garden"
Characters	*the speaker who has lost his love Lenore, the Raven*	*the gardener, the speaker, Death*
Setting	*a cold, December night in the speaker's study*	*a rose garden*
Conflict	*The speaker wants to forget his lost love, Lenore.*	*Death has come to the garden to claim someone.*
Resolution (How does the poem end?)	*The speaker cannot rid himself of the Raven who has appeared outside his door.*	*Death has not come for the gardener but for the speaker.*

Reading Skill: Reading Poetry

Which of the sound devices used in these poems did you like most? Circle your favorite from the list below. In a complete sentence, explain what you liked about it. Then, write down an example from one of the poems, or make up your own. *Answers will vary. See samples below.*

alliteration (circled) **repetition** **rhyme** **rhythm**

Possible answer: I like alliteration the best because of how the words sounded next to each other. At times, the alliteration reinforces the meaning of each word, such as "grim, ungainly, ghastly, gaunt" in line 71 of "The Raven."

Why are we fascinated by the **UNKNOWN?**

What is it about unexplained events or occurrences that people find intriguing?

TURN AND TALK Review the list of strange events you made on page 56. Then, with a partner, review the strange events in the two poems. Use this information as you discuss why people find strange or bizarre events so interesting.

Have students consider what excites them or makes them fearful—or both—about the unknown.

Academic Vocabulary in Speaking

The word **analyze** (AN uh lyz) is a verb that means *to examine something by looking critically or closely at it.*

Betty will **analyze** the poem by reading it slowly and carefully.

The word **infer** (in FER) is a verb that means *to make a reasonable guess based on clues or facts.*

Based on the two examples he provided, I was able to **infer** the author's meaning.

TURN AND TALK With a partner, reread "The Raven" out loud. As you read, think about what the speaker's relationship with Lenore might have been like. What can you **infer** about that relationship? Be sure to use the words **analyze** and **infer** in your conversation.

Encourage students to use the Academic Vocabulary words in their discussions.

Assessment Practice

DIRECTIONS Use "The Raven" and "Incident in a Rose Garden" to answer questions 1–4.

1 In "The Raven" the speaker is trying to forget the loss of —

- (A) his life
- (B) his child
- (C) the raven
- (D) his love, Lenore

2 A poem's rhyme scheme can be written in letters; each letter stands for the same rhyming sound. The rhyme scheme of "The Raven" can be written as —

- (A) *a-b-a-b-b-b*
- (B) *a-b-c-b-b-b*
- (C) *a-b-b-c-b-a*
- (D) *a-b-a-b-b-c*

3 In "Incident in a Rose Garden," how does the gardener react to Death?

- (A) He runs from Death.
- (B) He greets Death calmly.
- (C) He demands that Death leave the garden.
- (D) He pretends not to notice Death.

4 The ending of "Incident in a Rose Garden" is ironic because —

- (A) the gardener is already dead
- (B) the speaker's father is already dead
- (C) Death has come for the speaker
- (D) Death knew the speaker's father

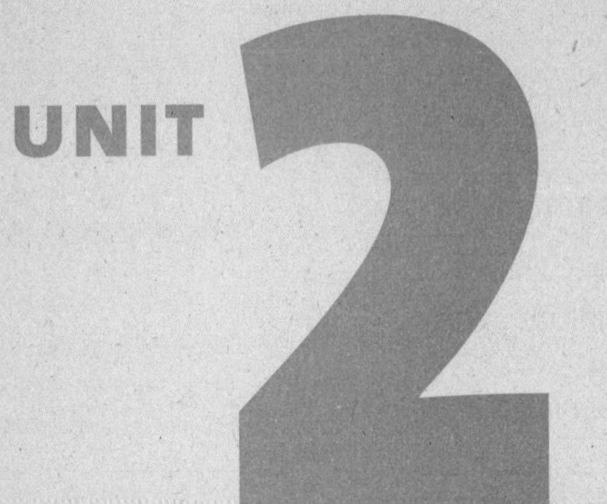

People Watching

CHARACTERIZATION AND POINT OF VIEW

Be sure to read the Text Analysis Workshop on pages 202–207 in *Holt McDougal Literature*.

Academic Vocabulary for Unit 2

You will see these Academic Vocabulary words as you work through this book. You will also be asked to use them as you write and talk about the selections in this unit.

Complex (kuhm PLEKS) is an adjective that means *made up of two or more parts.* It can also mean *not simple.*

The characters in the movie are **complex,** just like real people.

What is the most **complex** object in your classroom? Explain: ___________

Answers will vary.

Device (dih VYS) is a noun that means *a tool or method used to achieve a specific purpose.*

An interesting setting is one **device** of a good story.

What is a **device** you use to listen to music? ___________

Answers will vary.

Evaluate (ih VAL yoo ayt) is a verb that means *to judge the value or importance of something.*

Most schools use grades to **evaluate** student performance.

Describe how you **evaluate** something before you buy it: ___________

Answers will vary.

Interact (in tuhr AKT) is a verb that means *to act or work together with someone or something.*

Students must **interact** when they work on group projects.

Do you ever **interact** with students at another school? Explain. ___________

Answers will vary.

Perspective (per SPEK tiv) is a noun that means *point of view or a way of looking at things.*

The poem made Maria see birds from a different **perspective.**

What is your **perspective** on your elementary school years? ___________

Answers will vary.

The Necklace

Based on the short story by **Guy de Maupassant**

How important is **STATUS?**

What happens when people place too much importance on status, or the standing they have in a group? In "The Necklace," you'll meet Madame Loisel, a woman whose desire for status costs her more than she bargains for.

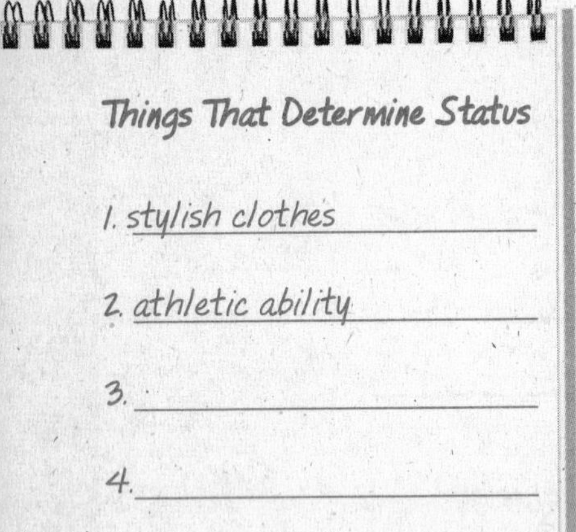

Things That Determine Status
1. stylish clothes
2. athletic ability
3.
4.
5.

TURN AND TALK With a partner, discuss how status is determined at your school. Then, add at least three of these things to the list at left. After you've finished your list, discuss with a partner whether you think the things on the list *should* determine status.

Answers will vary.

Text Analysis: Character Motivation

Motivation (MOH tuh VAY shuhn) is the reason behind someone's action. Motivation makes a person or character act in a certain way. In the chart below, a person's action is described in the left column. A possible motivation is in the right. In each of the last three rows, write down a possible reason for Ryan's action.

ACTION	MOTIVATION
Ignoring her pain, the runner sprints to the finish line.	*The runner wants to win the race.*
Serena secretly watches Justin in class all day.	*Serena has a crush on Justin.*
Ryan misses a friend's party to work on his science project.	
Ryan borrows money to buy new shoes.	
While at a coffee shop, Ryan shouts at one of his friends.	

As you read "The Necklace," you will consider what Madame Loisel's actions tell you about her motivation.

Reading Skill: Make Inferences

Sometimes writers tell you directly what a character is like. At other times, they will give clues. Using these clues, you can make an **inference** (IN fuhr uhns), or logical guess, about what the character is like. As you read, you will make inferences about the story by adding what you know from your own experience to these clues. Notice how a reader might make an inference in the chart below.

Clue from Story	My Experience	Inference
Mr. Loisel says, "We must replace the necklace." (line 70)	When I broke my friend's MP3 player, my mom made me work to replace it.	Mr. Loisel is honest and careful to do the right thing.

Vocabulary in Context

Note: Words are listed in the order in which they appear in the story.

Prospects (PROS pektz) is a noun meaning *chances of success.*
*Madame Loisel's **prospects** for obtaining wealth were limited.*

Pauper (PAW puhr) is a noun that means *a very poor person.*
*Mathilde thought her clothes made her look like a **pauper.***

Adulation (aj uh LAY shuhn) is a noun that means *too much praise.*
*The partygoers expressed **adulation** for Madame Loisel.*

Aghast (uh GAST) is an adjective that means *shocked or horrified.*
*Loisel was **aghast** when he heard that the necklace was lost.*

Askew (uh SKYOO) is an adjective meaning *crooked or leaning to one side.*
*Mathilde straightened the slightly **askew** necklace.*

Vocabulary Practice

Review the words and sample sentences above. Then, with a partner, discuss possible answers to each of the following questions. Use each boldface word at least once in your discussion.

1. How is a **prospect** different from a hope?
2. How is a **pauper** different from a beggar?
3. Why is respect better than **adulation?**
4. How is **aghast** different from surprised?
5. What is the difference between **askew** and messy?

Encourage students to use the Vocabulary words in their discussions.

SET A PURPOSE FOR READING

Read this story to find out how a borrowed necklace changes a woman's life.

The Necklace

Based on the short story by

GUY DE MAUPASSANT

BACKGROUND At the time of this story, France had three classes of society—upper, middle, and lower. A man could become rich enough to move into a higher class, but a woman had to marry to get into a higher class. To do that, her family had to pay a dowry (DOW ree)—money or property—to her new husband.

Mathilde was a pretty, charming, middle-class girl. She had no dowry—no money from her family to take to her marriage. She also had few **prospects** of meeting a rich man, so she married a clerk in the Ministry of Education.

She dressed plainly, and she was unhappy that she couldn't afford fine clothes. She daydreamed about being rich.

Her husband would say, "Ah! A good stew! There's nothing I like better." But she dreamed of fancy dinner parties.

She had no evening clothes or jewelry, yet she wanted them and felt she should have them. She needed to be charming. (A)

One evening her husband handed her an envelope. Excited, she opened it and found an invitation to a grand party at a **mansion**, the huge home of a government official.

She tossed it aside.

VOCABULARY

The word **prospects** (PROS pektz) is a noun meaning *chances of success*.

(A) MAKE INFERENCES

Underline words and phrases in lines 5–10 that describe how Mathilde Loisel looks. Then, circle words and phrases in the same lines that describe her emotions. Make an inference about what kind of person she is.

Possible answer: Mathilde is overly concerned with her appearance and her financial status.

VISUAL VOCABULARY

A **mansion** is a very large and fancy home.

Her husband said, "I thought you'd be thrilled since you never get to go out. Everybody wants to go, but few clerks can. The most important people will be there."

She gave him an irritated look and cried, "What do you think I would wear?"

He hadn't thought about that. "Why, the dress you wear to the theater. That looks quite nice."

He was surprised when she burst into tears. He gasped, "Why, what's the matter?"

Using all her control, she stopped crying. "Oh, nothing. I don't have an evening gown, so I can't go to that party." (B)

IN OTHER WORDS Mathilde is a pretty, young woman who wants things she can't afford. She marries a poor but happy clerk. One night, her husband brings home an invitation for an important party. Mathilde refuses to go because she doesn't have the proper clothes.

He was stunned. He said, "How much would the right outfit cost?"

She thought it over for several seconds. She thought of her allowance and about how much her husband might give her.

Finally, she answered, "I'm not sure exactly. Maybe I could manage with four hundred francs."[1]

He turned pale because he'd saved that much for a rifle and planned to go hunting with friends.

However, he said, "All right. I'll give you four hundred francs."

As the party neared, Madame[2] Loisel seemed sad. She was moody and upset although her outfit was ready. One evening her husband asked, "What's the matter?"

She answered, "I'm embarrassed not to have any jewelry. I'll look like a **pauper**, a poor person."

Her husband said, "Borrow some jewelry from your rich friend Madame Forestier."

1. **four hundred francs:** Francs are units of French currency. At the time of the story, four hundred francs would have been a large amount of money.
2. **Madame:** French title for married women, similar to *Mrs.* in English.

Monitor Your Comprehension

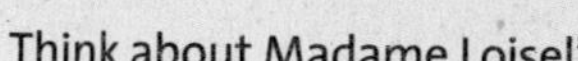

(B) MAKE INFERENCES

Think about Madame Loisel's response to the invitation. Have you ever wanted to go somewhere but didn't go because you might not fit in? Record your experience and an **inference** about Madame Loisel in the chart below.

Clue from Story
Mathilde refuses to go to the party because she doesn't have the right clothes.

↓

My Experience
Students' answers will vary.

↓

Inference
Possible answer: Madame Loisel is ashamed and embarrassed by her economic and social status.

VOCABULARY

The word **pauper** (PAW puhr) is a noun that means a *very poor person.*

Monitor Your Comprehension

C CHARACTER MOTIVATION

Of all the pieces of jewelry, why do you think Madame Loisel chooses the diamond necklace? Discuss your answer with a partner.

Students should discuss that Madame Loisel wants to borrow the diamond necklace because it is probably one of the more expensive pieces her friend owns. Madame Loisel wants to appear wealthy and be noticed by the others at the party.

VOCABULARY

The word **adulation** (aj uh LAY shuhn) is a noun that means *too much praise.*

She said, "Why didn't I think of that?"

The next day she went to her friend, who offered her a large jewelry box. "Pick out something, my dear."

Mathilde found a diamond necklace. Her heart beat faster as she picked it up. "Could I borrow this one?" she asked. C

"Why, of course."

She hugged her friend, kissed her warmly, and left.

Madame Loisel was a hit at the party. The prettiest one there, [she was stylish, warm, smiling, and wildly happy.] All the men turned to see her. They asked who she was and begged to meet her. The government's Cabinet members danced with her, and the head of the department noticed her.

She danced madly, wildly, [drunk with joy in her happiness of all the **adulation**, of all the admiring glances.] Around four o'clock the Loisels rode home in a shabby cab. For her, the excitement was over all too soon, but he had to get up the next morning to get to work by ten o'clock.

IN OTHER WORDS Mathilde buys the new dress she needs for the party, but she's upset that she doesn't have any jewelry. Her husband tells her to borrow a necklace from her wealthy friend, Madame Forestier.

► Circle the words that show you how people react to Mathilde at the party. Put brackets around [ ] the words that show you how this makes Mathilde feel.

At home, Mathilde looked at herself in the mirror one last time. The necklace was gone! She cried out.

Her husband, already half undressed, said, "What's wrong?"

Upset, she turned toward him. "I . . . I . . . I don't have my friend's necklace."

"That's impossible." They hunted everywhere in the apartment but found nothing. They looked at each other **aghast**. He retraced their steps, searching for hours. She slumped in a chair in the cold room.

VOCABULARY

The word **aghast** (uh GAST) is an adjective that means *shocked* or *horrified.*

Her husband came in around seven. He'd had no luck.

By the end of the week, they had given up all hope. Loisel looked five years older. He said, "We must replace the necklace."

They found a necklace exactly like the first. It cost forty thousand francs, but they could get it for thirty-six.

IN OTHER WORDS At home, Mathilde realizes that she has lost her friend's necklace. She and Loisel look for it everywhere. They can't find it, so they decide to buy a matching necklace. The new necklace will cost thirty-six thousand francs.

Loisel had eighteen thousand francs he had inherited from his father. He borrowed the rest. He got a thousand francs from one, four hundred from another—a hundred here, sixty there. He signed notes and made deals with loan sharks.[3] D

When Madame Loisel returned the necklace, her friend said coldly, "You should have returned it sooner."

Madame Forestier didn't open the case.

Madame Loisel bravely faced being poor. That debt had to be paid, and she would pay it. She let her maid go, and she and her husband moved to a cheap attic apartment. E

She cooked and did housework. She scrubbed the laundry, took out the garbage, carried up water, and dressed like a peasant. She watched every coin she spent. She bargained for food with the fruit dealer and the grocer, and they insulted her.

Her husband worked evenings as a bookkeeper and at night, he copied documents for very little pay.

This lasted for ten years.

Finally, all the debts and interest were paid.

Madame Loisel looked old now. Sometimes she'd remember when she had been so admired. Now her hair was messy, her skirts askew, her hands red, and her voice shrill.

What if she hadn't lost the necklace? Who knows? How little there is between joy and misery! PAUSE & REFLECT

3. **loan sharks:** People who lend money by requiring that borrowers pay a very large amount of money in addition to repaying the amount of the loan.

Monitor Your Comprehension

D CHARACTER MOTIVATION

What do you think motivates the Loisels to go into such great debt?

The Loisels need to replace the Madame Forestier's necklace, which Mathilde had borrowed and lost. By replacing the necklace, they hope to maintain their honor and dignity.

E LANGUAGE COACH

"She let her maid go" (line 81) is an **idiom**, an expression that is not meant to be taken literally. In this idiom, to "let someone go" means *to end a job.* The maid was not trapped and freed; the Loisels ended her job with them because they could not afford to pay her.

VOCABULARY

The word **askew** (uh SKYOO) is an adjective meaning *crooked* or *leaning to one side.*

PAUSE & REFLECT

With a partner, discuss what you think the Loisels' life would have been like if they hadn't lost the necklace.

If the Loisels had not lost the necklace, they would not have had to move or work so many jobs to earn extra money.

Monitor Your Comprehension

IN OTHER WORDS Using all of their wealth—along with a great deal of borrowed money—Loisel pays for the new necklace. Mathilde takes the new necklace to her friend, hoping she won't notice that it's not the one she borrowed. The Loisels live in poverty to repay the debt.

► With a partner, discuss how poverty changes Madame Loisel.

Students should discuss that poverty changes Madame Loisel physically (she looks much older). She also learns how to budget carefully, do her own cooking and housework, and bargain with vendors.

Then one Sunday, Mathilde went for a walk. She saw Madame Forestier. She still looked young and beautiful. Madame Loisel went toward her friend saying, "Hello, Jeanne."

The other woman stammered, "But . . . Madame . . . I don't recognize . . . You must be mistaken."

"No, I'm Mathilde Loisel."

Her friend cried, "Poor Mathilde! How you're changed!"

"Yes, I've had a hard time. And all because of you!" F

"Of me . . . what do you mean?" Madame Forestier asked.

"Do you remember the diamond necklace I borrowed?"

"Yes. What about it?"

"I lost it," Mathilde said.

"But you returned it."

"I bought another just like it, and we have been paying for it for ten years. Well, it's over now, and I am glad."

Madame Forestier was surprised. "You bought a diamond necklace to replace mine?"

"Yes. You never noticed, then? They were quite alike." Mathilde smiled with proud and simple joy. G

Madame Forestier, quite overcome, clasped her by the hands. "Oh, my poor Mathilde. Mine was fake. Why, at most it was worth only five hundred francs!"

IN OTHER WORDS Mathilde sees Madame Forestier, but her friend doesn't recognize her. Mathilde admits that she had lost the necklace and replaced it with another one. Madame Forestier is shocked.

► What do you learn about the necklace in lines 116–117? Underline the words that tell you.

Mrs. Forestier's necklace was not made of real diamonds.

F CHARACTER MOTIVATION

Why does Madame Loisel blame her problems on her friend?

Possible answer: Madame Loisel is unwilling admit that her unhappiness with her social status led her to borrow the necklace from Madame Forestier.

G MAKE INFERENCES

Look at the clue provided below. Then, based on this clue, make an inference about Mathilde.

Clue from Story

"Mathilde smiled with proud and simple joy." (line 114)

↓

My Experience

Answers will vary.

↓

Inference

Possible answer: Mathilde is pleased to learn that her replacement necklace fooled Mrs. Forestier and that she never knew that the original had been replaced.

Text Analysis: Character Motivation

Consider what you know about each character's feelings and goals. Review the actions listed in the left column of the chart below. In the right column, write down the motivation for each action. One motivation has been filled in for you.

Action	Motivation
Mathilde Loisel is upset because she does not have any jewelry to wear to the party. (lines 38–39)	*Mathilde wants to be well dressed so that others will admire and praise her.*
Mathilde looks at herself in the mirror one last time. (lines 59–60)	***Mathilde wants to remember how she looks wearing fine clothes and a beautiful necklace.***
Mathilde's husband searches everywhere for the lost necklace. (lines 64–68)	***Mathilde's husband desperately wants to find the necklace and is fearful of what will happen if he cannot locate it.***
The Loisels go into debt to pay for the new necklace. (lines 74–76)	***The Loisels are ashamed about the loss and do not want to tell Madame Forestier the truth.***
Madame Forestier is angry because Mathilde does not return the necklace immediately. (lines 77–79)	***Madame Forestier wants the things she loans to others to be returned promptly.***

How have Mathilde's motivations led her and her husband into difficulties? Write your answer on the lines below.

Possible answer: Mathilde's desire to appear wealthy for a short while causes her and her husband more trouble in the long run. Also, because she does not want to admit to losing the necklace, she has struggle to get enough money to buy a new necklace.

Reading Skill: Make Inferences

In the story, we learn a lot about the Loisels, but we don't know very much about Madame Forestier. Look back through the story to find three details about Madame Forestier and record them below. Then use the clues and your own knowledge to make an inference about her.
For this chart, answers will vary. See samples below.

Clues from the Story

1. *Madame Forestier lets Mathilde borrow any necklace she wants.*
2. *She says Mathilde should have returned the necklace sooner.*

↓

My Experience

1. *It is nice to share your things with others.*
2. *When I borrow clothing from my friends, I always return it.*

↓

Inference

Madame Forestier is a generous friend who loans her possessions to her friends as long as they are returned in a timely manner.

How important is STATUS?

Do you think popularity, or status, is an important thing to have or pursue? Why or why not?

Possible answer: No, I do not think it is important to pursue it because there will always be someone who has more of something than you and, as a result, your quest to achieve will never end.

Vocabulary Practice

With a partner, discuss why each statement below is true or false. Use each Vocabulary word once in your discussion.
Encourage students to use the Vocabulary words in their discussions.

1. If you have **prospects** of wealth, you believe you will be a **pauper.**
2. If someone heaps **adulation** on you, you must have done something well.
3. If you are **aghast** about something, you are not surprised at all.
4. If a picture is **askew,** it is perfectly straight.

Academic Vocabulary in Speaking

The word **complex** (kuhm PLEKS) means *made up of two or more parts.*

Richard could not find all the pieces for the **complex** tool.

Complex can also mean *not simple.*

That story is very **complex** and confusing.

The word **evaluate** (ih VAL yoo ayt) means *to judge the value or importance of something.*

The store owner wants to **evaluate** my collection of baseball cards to see how much they are worth.

TURN AND TALK In "The Necklace," you learned about characters with **complex** motivations. With a partner, **evaluate** your own motivations for achieving a goal. Be sure to use **complex** and **evaluate** in your discussion.

Encourage students to use the Academic Vocabulary words in their discussions.

Assessment Practice

DIRECTIONS Use "The Necklace" to answer questions 1–4.

1 Madame Loisel is unhappy at the beginning of the story because —

- (A) she wishes she were pretty and charming
- (B) she does not like her husband
- (C) she wishes she had wealth and luxuries
- (D) she does not like housework

2 What is Madame Loisel's motivation for borrowing the necklace from her friend?

- (A) She wants to appear elegant and well dressed at the party.
- (B) She wants to add glamour to the old dress she has to wear.
- (C) She likes her friend's jewelry better than her own.
- (D) She does not want to appear too dressed up at the party.

3 What inference can you make about why the Loisels are so willing to replace the necklace?

- (A) They are embarrassed by the situation.
- (B) They want everyone to think highly of them.
- (C) They are trying to trick Madame Forestier.
- (D) They want to keep the necklace for themselves.

4 What unexpected plot twist occurs at the end of the story?

- (A) Madame Forestier learns that the Loisels have been paying off a debt.
- (B) Monsieur Loisel goes into debt to pay off the necklace.
- (C) Madame Loisel learns that the necklace she borrowed was fake.
- (D) Madame Forestier immediately recognizes Madame Loisel.

I Know Why the Caged Bird Sings

Autobiography by Maya Angelou

What is a TEACHER?

Other than your teachers at school, who else teaches you important things? In this selection, you'll meet Mrs. Flowers, a woman who acted as a mentor—a trusted teacher—to a young Maya Angelou.

LIST IT Think of people who have taught you, helped you see things in a new way, or encouraged you. What traits, or qualities, did these people have? Write these traits on the lines at left.

Answers will vary.

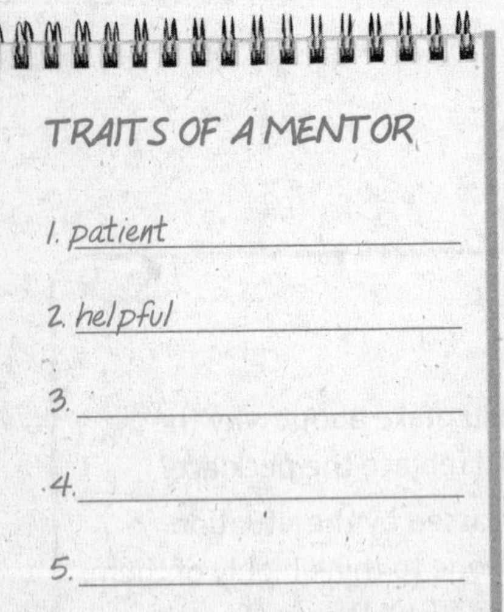

Text Analysis: Characterization in Autobiography

In an **autobiography** (aw tuh by OG ruh fee) the author writes about his or her own life. Writers of autobiographies use **characterization** (kayr uhk tuhr ih ZAY shuhn) to reveal what a character is like. Two types of characterization are direct and indirect. **Direct characterization** tells you exactly what a character is like. **Indirect characterization** reveals a character through

- the character's appearance
- the character's words
- the character's actions
- the character's thoughts and feelings
- other characters' reactions to the character

As you read this selection, notice how Angelou uses both direct and indirect characterization to show you what Mrs. Flowers is like.

Reading Skill: Analyze Perspectives

Autobiographies often include two different **perspectives** (puhr SPEK tihvz), or viewpoints:

- that of a writer as he or she experiences events
- that of the writer looking back on those events years later

As you read, you will use a chart like the one below to record Angelou's thoughts from both her childhood and adult perspectives.

Child's Viewpoint	Adult's Viewpoint
"My name was beautiful when she said it." (lines 79–80)	*I have tried often to search behind the sophistication of years for the enchantment I so easily found in those gifts. (lines 224–225)*

Vocabulary in Context

Note: Words are listed in the order in which they appear in the selection.

Clarity (KLAYR ih tee) is a noun meaning *clearness.*
Mrs. Flowers always spoke with such **clarity.**

Infuse (in FYOOZ) is a verb that means *to fill.*
Marguerite wanted to **infuse** her words with meaning.

Illiteracy (ih LIT uhr uh see) is a noun that means *the condition of being unable to read and write.*
According to Mrs. Flowers, **illiteracy** is not the same as stupidity.

Homely (HOHM lee) is an adjective that means *simple, plain, and everyday.*
Sometimes **homely** sayings contain great wisdom.

Cascade (kas KAYD) is a verb that means *to flow like a waterfall.*
Mrs. Flowers's words **cascade** like music.

Review the words and sample sentences above. Then, based on these words, predict with a partner what you think this selection will be about. Write your predictions on the lines below.

Encourage students to use the Vocabulary words in their discussions.

SET A PURPOSE FOR READING

Read this excerpt from *I Know Why the Caged Bird Sings* to discover how a neighbor helps a young girl in need.

I KNOW WHY THE *Caged Bird* SINGS

Autobiography by

MAYA ANGELOU

BACKGROUND The following story about Marguerite Johnson—who later changed her name to Maya Angelou—is true. After being abused by a family friend, Angelou spoke to no one but her brother Bailey for five years. During this time she first visited Mrs. Flowers, who was a respected woman in her community.

For nearly a year, I sopped around the house, the Store, the school and the church, like an old biscuit, dirty and inedible. Then I met, or rather got to know, the lady who threw me my first life line.

Mrs. Bertha Flowers was the aristocrat of Black Stamps. She had the grace of control to appear warm in the coldest weather, and on the Arkansas summer days it seemed she had a private breeze which swirled around, cooling her. She was thin without the taut[1] look of wiry people, and her printed voile dresses and flowered hats were as right for her as denim overalls for a farmer. She was our side's answer to the richest white woman in town. Ⓐ

Her skin was a rich black that would have peeled like a plum if snagged, but then no one would have thought of getting close enough to Mrs. Flowers to ruffle her dress, let alone snag her skin. She didn't encourage familiarity. She wore gloves too.

Ⓐ CHARACTERIZATION IN AUTOBIOGRAPHY

In lines 1–12, what do you learn about Mrs. Flowers?

Possible answer: Mrs. Flowers is an elegant African American woman who lives in Black Stamps. She is always dressed properly whatever the weather.

Circle the answer below that tells you how you know this:

The writer tells you directly.

The writer tells you indirectly.

1. **taut** (tawt): pulled or drawn tight.

I don't think I ever saw Mrs. Flowers laugh, but she smiled often. A slow widening of her thin black lips to show even, small white teeth, then the slow, effortless closing. When she chose to smile on me, I always wanted to thank her. The action was so graceful and inclusively benign.

She was one of the few gentlewomen I have ever known, and has remained throughout my life the measure of what a human being can be.

Momma had a strange relationship with her. Most often when she passed on the road in front of the Store, she spoke to Momma in that soft yet carrying voice, "Good day, Mrs. Henderson." Momma responded with "How you, Sister Flowers?"

Mrs. Flowers didn't belong to our church, nor was she Momma's familiar.[2] Why on earth did she insist on calling her Sister Flowers? Shame made me want to hide my face. Mrs. Flowers deserved better than to be called Sister. Then, Momma left out the verb. Why not ask, "How *are* you, Mrs. Flowers?" With the unbalanced passion of the young, I hated her for showing her ignorance to Mrs. Flowers. It didn't occur to me for many years that they were as alike as sisters, separated only by formal education. (B)

Although I was upset, neither of the women was in the least shaken by what I thought an unceremonious greeting. Mrs. Flowers would continue her easy gait up the hill to her little bungalow, and Momma kept on shelling peas or doing whatever had brought her to the front porch.

Occasionally, though, Mrs. Flowers would drift off the road and down to the Store and Momma would say to me, "Sister, you go on and play." As I left I would hear the beginning of an intimate conversation, Momma persistently using the wrong verb, or none at all.

IN OTHER WORDS Marguerite is very unhappy and feels sad and unwanted. Then one day she gets to know the lady who changes her life: Mrs. Flowers is an elegant black woman whom Marguerite respects.

► In lines 43–47, how does Momma treat Mrs. Flowers? Discuss your answer with a partner.

Students should discuss that Momma treats Mrs. Flowers as someone that she can confide in, talking to her about private, personal matters.

2. **familiar:** a close friend or associate.

Monitor Your Comprehension

(B) ANALYZE PERSPECTIVES

Reread lines 29–37. What does the adult Angelou see looking back on this situation that the younger Angelou does not? Fill in the chart below.

Child's Viewpoint
Possible answer: The embarrassment over Mrs. Flowers being called "Sister" and Momma's grammatical errors reflects the child's viewpoint.

↓

Adult's Viewpoint
Possible answer: The realization that only a formal education separated Momma and Mrs. Flowers and that the two women really were like sisters with many shared qualities and experiences reflects the adult's viewpoint.

Monitor Your Comprehension

C ANALYZE PERSPECTIVES

Why is Angelou upset with Momma in lines 48–49? Underline the words that tell you this.

Angelou is upset with Momma because of the grammatical errors she uses when speaking.

VISUAL VOCABULARY

Humpty Dumpty is an egg-shaped character in a nursery rhyme who fell off a wall and cracked and could not be put back together again.

"Brother and Sister Wilcox is sho'ly the meanest—" "Is," Momma? "Is"? Oh, please, not "is," Momma, for two or more. But they talked, and from the side of the building where I waited for the ground to open up and swallow me, I heard the soft-voiced Mrs. Flowers and the textured voice of my grandmother merging and melting. They were interrupted from time to time by giggles that must have come from Mrs. Flowers (Momma never giggled in her life). Then she was gone. C

She appealed to me because she was like people I had never met personally. Like women in English novels who walked the moors[3] (whatever they were) with their loyal dogs racing at a respectful distance. Like the women who sat in front of roaring fireplaces, drinking tea incessantly from silver trays full of scones and crumpets.[4] Women who walked over the "heath"[5] and read morocco-bound[6] books and had two last names divided by a hyphen. It would be safe to say that she made me proud to be Negro, just by being herself.

She acted just as refined as whitefolks in the movies and books and she was more beautiful, for none of them could have come near that warm color without looking gray by comparison.

It was fortunate that I never saw her in the company of powhitefolks. For since they tend to think of their whiteness as an evenizer, I'm certain that I would have had to hear her spoken to commonly as Bertha, and my image of her would have been shattered like the unmendable **Humpty-Dumpty**.

One summer afternoon, sweet-milk fresh in my memory, she stopped at the Store to buy provisions. Another Negro woman of her health and age would have been expected to carry the paper sacks home in one hand, but Momma said, "Sister Flowers, I'll send Bailey up to your house with these things."

She smiled that slow dragging smile, "Thank you, Mrs. Henderson. I'd prefer Marguerite, though." My name was

3. **moors**: broad open areas of countryside with marshes and patches of low shrubs.
4. **scones** (skonz) **and crumpets** (KRUM pits): Scones are small, biscuitlike pastries; crumpets are rolls similar to English muffins.
5. **heath** (heeth): another word for a moor.
6. **morocco-bound:** Morocco is a soft leather sometimes used for expensive book covers.

beautiful when she said it. "I've been meaning to talk to her, anyway." They gave each other age-group looks.

Momma said, "Well, that's all right then. Sister, go and change your dress. You going to Sister Flowers's."

IN OTHER WORDS Marguerite is embarrassed about the way her grandmother (whom she calls Momma) talks to Mrs. Flowers. One day, Mrs. Flowers asks if Marguerite can carry her groceries home for her because she wants to talk to Marguerite.

The chifforobe[7] was a maze. What on earth did one put on to go to Mrs. Flowers's house? I knew I shouldn't put on a Sunday dress. It might be sacrilegious.[8] Certainly not a house dress, since I was already wearing a fresh one. I chose a school dress, naturally. It was formal without suggesting that going to Mrs. Flowers's house was equivalent to attending church.

I trusted myself back into the Store.

"Now, don't you look nice." I had chosen the right thing, for once.

"Mrs. Henderson, you make most of the children's clothes, don't you?"

"Yes, ma'am. Sure do. Store-bought clothes ain't hardly worth the thread it take to stitch them."

"I'll say you do a lovely job, though, so neat. That dress looks professional."

Momma was enjoying the seldom-received compliments. Since everyone we knew (except Mrs. Flowers, of course) could sew competently, praise was rarely handed out for the commonly practiced craft.

"I try, with the help of the Lord, Sister Flowers, to finish the inside just like I does the outside. Come here, Sister."

I had buttoned up the collar and tied the belt, apronlike, in back. Momma told me to turn around. With one hand she pulled the strings and the belt fell free at both sides of my waist. Then

7. **chifforobe** (SHIF uh rohb): a chest of drawers combined with a small closet for hanging clothes.
8. **sacrilegious** (sak ruh LIJ uhs): disrespectful toward a sacred person, place, or thing.

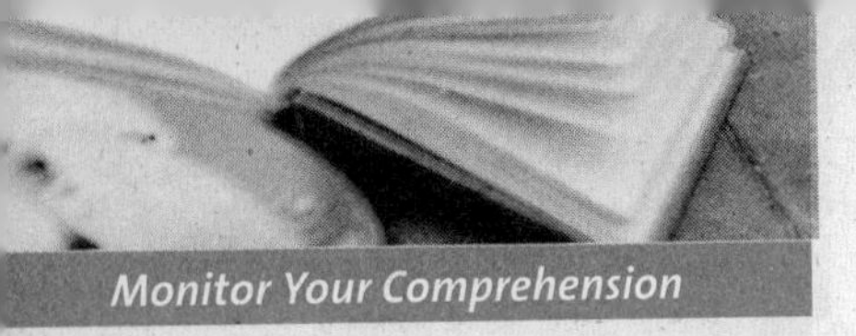

her large hands were at my neck, opening the button loops. I was terrified. What was happening?

"Take it off, Sister." She had her hands on the hem of the dress.

"I don't need to see the inside, Mrs. Henderson, I can tell . . ." But the dress was over my head and my arms were stuck in the sleeves. Momma said, "That'll do. See here, Sister Flowers, I French-seams[9] around the armholes." Through the cloth film, I saw the shadow approach. "That makes it last longer. Children these days would bust out of sheet-metal clothes. They so rough."

"That is a very good job, Mrs. Henderson. You should be proud. You can put your dress back on, Marguerite."

"No ma'am. Pride is a sin. And 'cording to the Good Book, it goeth before a fall."

"That's right. So the Bible says. It's a good thing to keep in mind."

I wouldn't look at either of them. Momma hadn't thought that taking off my dress in front of Mrs. Flowers would kill me stone dead. If I had refused, she would have thought I was trying to be "womanish" and might have remembered St. Louis. Mrs. Flowers had known that I would be embarrassed and that was even worse. I picked up the groceries and went out to wait in the hot sunshine. It would be fitting if I got a sunstroke and died before they came outside. Just dropped dead on the slanting porch. **D**

There was a little path beside the rocky road, and Mrs. Flowers walked in front swinging her arms and picking her way over the stones.

D CHARACTERIZATION IN AUTOBIOGRAPHY
Reread lines 123–130. What do these lines tell you about Marguerite? List two things you learn about her.

Possible answer: Marguerite is proud—she does not like to be embarrassed—yet obedient, allowing her grandmother to take off her dress in front of Mrs. Flowers.

IN OTHER WORDS Marguerite puts on a school dress to go to Mrs. Flowers's house. Then, Momma makes her take the dress partway off to show Mrs. Flowers the stitching. Marguerite is embarrassed.

She said, without turning her head, to me, "I hear you're doing very good school work, Marguerite, but that it's all written. The teachers report that they have trouble getting you to talk in class." We passed the triangular farm on our left and the path widened

9. **French-seams:** sew seams that are turned in and stitched on the wrong side so that the unfinished edges of the cloth are not visible.

to allow us to walk together. I hung back in the separate unasked and unanswerable questions.

"Come and walk along with me, Marguerite." I couldn't have refused even if I wanted to. She pronounced my name so nicely. Or more correctly, she spoke each word with such **clarity** that I was certain a foreigner who didn't understand English could have understood her.

"Now no one is going to make you talk—possibly no one can. But bear in mind, language is man's way of communicating with his fellow man and it is language alone which separates him from the lower animals." That was a totally new idea to me, and I would need time to think about it.

"Your grandmother says you read a lot. Every chance you get. That's good, but not good enough. Words mean more than what is set down on paper. It takes the human voice to **infuse** them with the shades of deeper meaning."

I memorized the part about the human voice infusing words. It seemed so valid and poetic.

IN OTHER WORDS As they are walking, Mrs. Flowers talks to Marguerite about her schoolwork and the fact that Marguerite does not talk in school.

► Why does Mrs. Flowers say speaking aloud is important? Circle the words that tell you this.

Mrs. Flowers tells Marguerite that speaking aloud is what shapes the meanings of words.

She said she was going to give me some books and that I not only must read them, I must read them aloud. She suggested that I try to make a sentence sound in as many different ways as possible. E

"I'll accept no excuse if you return a book to me that has been badly handled." My imagination boggled at the punishment I would deserve if in fact I did abuse a book of Mrs. Flowers'. Death would be too kind and brief.

The odors in the house surprised me. Somehow I had never connected Mrs. Flowers with food or eating or any other common experience of common people. There must have been an **outhouse**, too, but my mind never recorded it.

Monitor Your Comprehension

VOCABULARY

The word **clarity** (KLAYR ih tee) is a noun meaning *clearness*.

VOCABULARY

The word **infuse** (in FYOOZ) is a verb that means *to fill*.

E CHARACTERIZATION IN AUTOBIOGRAPHY

In lines 140–158, Angelou uses **indirect characterization** to show you that Mrs. Flowers wants to help Marguerite. Underline one example of indirect characterization in these lines showing how Marguerite reacts to Mrs. Flowers.

VISUAL VOCABULARY

An **outhouse** is an outdoor toilet without plumbing in its own small building.

Monitor Your Comprehension

The sweet scent of vanilla had met us as she opened the door.

"I made tea cookies this morning. You see, I had planned to invite you for cookies and lemonade so we could have this little chat. The lemonade is in the icebox."

It followed that Mrs. Flowers would have ice on an ordinary day, when most families in our town bought ice late on Saturdays only a few times during the summer to be used in the wooden ice-cream freezers.

She took the bags from me and disappeared through the kitchen door. I looked around the room that I had never in my wildest fantasies imagined I would see. Browned photographs leered[10] or threatened from the walls and the white, freshly done curtains pushed against themselves and against the wind. I wanted to gobble up the room entire and take it to Bailey, who would help me analyze and enjoy it.

"Have a seat, Marguerite. Over there by the table." She carried a platter covered with a tea towel. Although she warned that she hadn't tried her hand at baking sweets for some time, I was certain that like everything else about her the cookies would be perfect.

IN OTHER WORDS **Mrs. Flowers says she will give Marguerite some books to read. Marguerite looks at Mrs. Flowers's house and wishes her brother, Bailey, could see it, too. Mrs. Flowers offers Marguerite cookies and lemonade.**

They were flat round wafers, slightly browned on the edges and butter-yellow in the center. With the cold lemonade they were sufficient for childhood's lifelong diet. Remembering my manners, I took nice little lady like bites off the edges. She said she had made them expressly for me and that she had a few in the kitchen that I could take home to my brother. So I jammed one whole cake in my mouth and the rough crumbs scratched the insides of my jaws, and if I hadn't had to swallow, it would have been a dream come true. F

As I ate she began the first of what we later called "my lessons in living." She said that I must always be intolerant of ignorance

F CHARACTERIZATION IN AUTOBIOGRAPHY

Reread lines 186–194. Based on Mrs. Flowers's actions, what do you learn about her?

Possible answer: Mrs. Flowers is generous and kind, wanting to make Marguerite a special treat just for her.

10. **leered** (lihrd): gave sly, evil glances.

but understanding of **illiteracy**. That some people, unable to go to school, were more educated and even more intelligent than college professors. She encouraged me to listen carefully to what country people called mother wit. That in those **homely** sayings was couched the collective wisdom of generations.

When I finished the cookies she brushed off the table and brought a thick, small book from the bookcase. I had read *A Tale of Two Cities*[11] and found it up to my standards as a romantic novel. She opened the first page and I heard poetry for the first time in my life.

IN OTHER WORDS Marguerite feels special because Mrs. Flowers made the cookies just for her. Mrs. Flowers talks to her about important things in life.

► In lines 195–201, put brackets [ ] around the two lessons Mrs. Flowers tells Marguerite. Then, with a partner, discuss what both lessons mean.

Students should discuss that Mrs. Flowers wants Marguerite to understand that a formal education does not always lead to knowledge and that people can learn much from the wisdom found in "mother wit".

"It was the best of times and the worst of times . . ."[12] Her voice slid in and curved down through and over the words. She was nearly singing. I wanted to look at the pages. Were they the same that I had read? Or were there notes, music, lined on the pages, as in a hymn book? Her sounds began **cascading** gently. I knew from listening to a thousand preachers that she was nearing the end of her reading, and I hadn't really heard, heard to understand, a single word.

"How do you like that?"

It occurred to me that she expected a response. The sweet vanilla flavor was still on my tongue and her reading was a wonder in my ears. I had to speak.

I said, "Yes, ma'am." It was the least I could do, but it was the most also.

"There's one more thing. Take this book of poems and memorize one for me. Next time you pay me a visit, I want you to recite."

---

11. ***A Tale of Two Cities:*** a novel by Charles Dickens, set in Paris and London during the French Revolution (1789–1799).

12. **"It was . . . the worst of times . . .":** the famous opening sentence of *A Tale of Two Cities.*

Monitor Your Comprehension

VOCABULARY

The word **illiteracy** (ih LIT uhr uh see) is a noun that means *the condition of being unable to read and write.*

VOCABULARY

The word **homely** (HOHM lee) is an adjective that means *simple, plain, and everyday.*

VOCABULARY

The word **cascade** (kas KAYD) is a verb that means *to flow like a waterfall.*

How does Mrs. Flowers's voice sound? Underline the words that tell you this.

Possible answer: Mrs. Flowers voice sounds fluid like water.

Monitor Your Comprehension

IN OTHER WORDS Mrs. Flowers reads aloud from a familiar book, and Marguerite is amazed. She thinks it sounds like singing rather than reading. Mrs. Flowers asks Marguerite what she thinks of her reading. Marguerite feels that she must answer her, so she speaks aloud.

I have tried often to search behind the sophistication of years for the enchantment I so easily found in those gifts. The essence escapes but its aura remains.[13] To be allowed, no, invited, into the private lives of strangers, and to share their joys and fears, was a chance to exchange the Southern bitter wormwood for a cup of mead with Beowulf or a hot cup of tea and milk with Oliver Twist.[14] When I said aloud, "It is a far, far better thing that I do, than I have ever done . . ."[15] tears of love filled my eyes at my selflessness.

On that first day, I ran down the hill and into the road (few cars ever came along it) and had the good sense to stop running before I reached the Store.

I was liked, and what a difference it made. I was respected not as Mrs. Henderson's grandchild or Bailey's sister but for just being Marguerite Johnson. PAUSE & REFLECT

Childhood's logic never asks to be proved (all conclusions are absolute). I didn't question why Mrs. Flowers had singled me out for attention, nor did it occur to me that Momma might have asked her to give me a little talking to. All I cared about was that she had made tea cookies for me and read to me from her favorite book. It was enough to prove that she liked me. G

IN OTHER WORDS Mrs. Flowers tells Marguerite to take a book of poems. Next time Marguerite visits her, Mrs. Flowers wants her to recite a poem from the book.

PAUSE & REFLECT

Why do you think it's important to Marguerite that Mrs. Flowers likes her? Discuss your answer with a partner.

Students should discuss that it is important for Marguerite to be liked just for herself—not for her relationship to anyone else in her family. As a result, her self-confidence is boosted.

G ANALYZE PERSPECTIVES

Underline the words in lines 224–243 in which Angelou is telling about her experience from a child's view. Circle the lines in which she shares her insights as an adult.

13. **The essence . . . remains:** The basic quality of a thing or event escapes, but the feelings or atmosphere that it creates remains.
14. **a chance to exchange . . . with Oliver Twist:** Angelou compares her life as a black child in the South to wormwood, a bitter herb. Mead and tea with milk were common drinks in the respective eras of Beowulf and Oliver Twist, two characters from English literature. Angelou suggests that reading about such characters provided an escape from her racist surroundings.
15. **"It is a far . . . than I have ever done . . .":** the final line of *A Tale of Two Cities*, spoken by a man who sacrifices his own life to save that of another.

Text Analysis: Characterization in Autobiography

Look back at the selection and find examples of indirect characterization used in Angelou's autobiography. Include one example for each type of indirect characterization below.

For this chart, answers will vary. See samples below.

Methods of Characterization	Examples
1. How a character looks	*She was thin without the taut look of wiry people, and her printed voile dresses and flowered hats were as right for her as denim overalls for a farmer. (Lines 8–11)*
2. What a character says	*"Mrs. Henderson, you make most of the children's clothes, don't you?" "Yes, ma'am. Sure do. Store-bought clothes ain't hardly worth the thread it take to stitch them." "I'll say you do a lovely job, though, so neat. That dress looks professional." (Lines 93–98)*
3. How a character acts	*"I wouldn't look at either of them....I picked up the groceries and went out to wait in the hot sunshine.' (Lines 123, 128)*

What is a TEACHER?

Think about teachers in your life—not only school teachers but other people in your life who help to guide you. Why are these people important to you?

Possible answer: These people have helped me learn a variety of things, including values and life lessons, in addition to learning things that are a part of my formal education in school.

Reading Skill: Analyze Perspectives

In her autobiography, Angelou tells the events of her childhood. She also tells you how, as an adult, she thinks about those events. Find one example of each perspective, or viewpoint, and enter it into the chart below.

For this chart, answers will vary. See samples below.

Child's Viewpoint	Adult's Viewpoint
I knew from listening to a thousand preachers that she was nearing the end of her reading, and I hadn't really heard, heard to understand, a single word. "How do you like that?" It occurred to me that she expected a response. The sweet vanilla flavor was still on my tongue and her reading was a wonder in my ears. I had to speak. (Lines 211–218)	*I have tried often to search behind the sophistication of years for the enchantment I so easily found in those gifts. The essence escapes but its aura remains. To be allowed, no, invited, into the private lives of strangers, and to share their joys and fears, was a chance to exchange the Southern bitter wormwood for a cup of mead with Beowulf or a hot cup of tea and milk with Oliver Twist. (Lines 224–229)*

How does Angelou's adult perspective help you understand how Mrs. Flowers helped her as a child?

Possible answer: Angelou's adult viewpoint tells the reader that Mrs. Flowers, by allowing Marguerite to spend time with her, showed her what it was like to be treated as someone's equal and also exposed Marguerite to different worlds.

Vocabulary Practice

Circle the sentence that most accurately shows the meaning of each Vocabulary word.

1. **clarity** 1) Tyson gave his speech in a careful manner that was easy for the audience to understand. 2) Tyson gave his speech in a loud and confident manner.
2. **infuse** 1) The scent of baking bread seeped out of the kitchen. 2) The scent of baking bread filled the whole house with a lovely smell.
3. **illiteracy** 1) Sometimes adults who cannot read or write take classes at night to learn more. 2) Sometimes adults who are not very intelligent take beginning college classes.
4. **homely** 1) Laramie remembers a simple saying her grandmother told her about how to predict the weather. 2) Laramie remembers a difficult recipe her grandmother gave her years ago.
5. **cascade** 1) The little girl's hair gleamed in the sunlight. 2) The little girl's hair fell over her shoulders in waves.

Academic Vocabulary in Speaking

The word **interact** (in tuhr AKT) is a verb that means *to act or work together with someone or something.*

Small-group discussions require you to **interact** with other people in your class.

TURN AND TALK For people to **interact** well together (such as in a small group), it is important to follow certain rules. With a partner, discuss two or three rules that might be important as you **interact.** Be sure to use the word **interact** in your discussion.

Encourage students to use the Academic Vocabulary word in their discussions.

Assessment Practice

DIRECTIONS Use "I Know Why the Caged Bird Sings" to answer questions 1–6.

1 Why does Mrs. Flowers ask Marguerite to come to her house?

- (A) She is too weak to carry her own groceries.
- (B) Momma asks Mrs. Flowers to watch Marguerite for the afternoon.
- (C) She wants to help Marguerite start talking again.
- (D) She wants Marguerite to take some cookies to her brother.

2 Which of the following is an example of Angelou's adult perspective?

- (A) *For nearly a year, I sopped around the house, the Store, the school and the church, like an old biscuit, dirty and inedible.*
- (B) *She smiled that slow dragging smile. . . .*
- (C) *My name was beautiful when she said it.*
- (D) *I didn't question why Mrs. Flowers had singled me out for attention, nor did it occur to me that Momma might have asked her to give me a little talking to.*

3 Mrs. Flowers asks Marguerite to —

- (A) memorize a poem
- (B) talk in class the next day
- (C) give her opinion of the cookies
- (D) read from *A Tale of Two Cities*

4 What is the most important gift that Mrs. Flowers gives Marguerite?

- (A) a book of her own
- (B) cookies
- (C) her attention
- (D) a hug

5 Which of the following characterizes Mrs. Flowers through her actions?

- (A) "Come and walk along with me, Marguerite."
- (B) She was one of the few gentlewomen I have ever known. . . .
- (C) She opened the first page and I heard poetry for the first time in my life.
- (D) I was certain that like everything else about her the cookies would be perfect. . . .

6 Mrs. Flowers can *best* be described as —

- (A) quiet but angry
- (B) kind and helpful
- (C) proud and foolish
- (D) polite but nervous

Before Reading

from Rosa Parks

Biography by **Douglas Brinkley**

Rosa

Poem by **Rita Dove**

What is DIGNITY?

Rosa Parks had true dignity—a quiet strength and a strong sense of self-respect. This biography and poem portray her dignity and courage when Parks, an African American, refused to give up her seat on a bus in protest of unfair rules.

LIST IT With a partner, list three people, living or dead, real or fictional, whom you consider to have dignity. What is it about their personalities or actions that makes each of them dignified? Note your responses on the list at left.

Answers will vary.

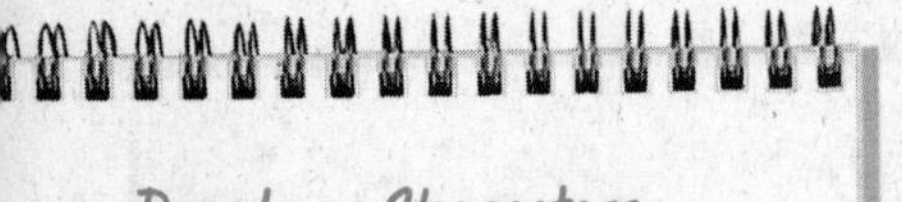

People or Characters with Dignity

1. Dr. Martin Luther King, Jr.

What makes him/her dignified?

2.

What makes him/her dignified?

3.

What makes him/her dignified?

Text Analysis: Characterization Across Genres

Douglas Brinkley and Rita Dove both praise Rosa Parks, but they **characterize,** or describe, her using two different **genres,** or types of literature.

Brinkley writes a biographical piece about Parks. He includes several factual details such as descriptions of Parks's physical appearance and daily life, as well as quotations from her that reveal her personality and point of view. Dove writes a poem. She includes a small number of carefully chosen words and images to characterize Parks in a few powerful lines. As you read, consider how each genre shapes the writer's characterization of Parks.

Rosa Parks	In Biography	In Poem
Physical Appearance	tired, body in pain (lines 38–41)	wears a sensible coat (line 6)
Daily Life (job, friends, etc.)		
Personality		

Reading Strategy: Set a Purpose for Reading

When you **set a purpose for reading,** you find specific reasons for reading a work. Your purpose for reading the two selections that follow is to compare and contrast the ways each work presents Rosa Parks. What do they have in common? What does each work do differently? Comparing and contrasting two works can help you understand each work better. As you read, also look for other purposes to keep you involved in your reading.

Vocabulary in Context

Note: Words are listed in the order in which they appear in the selections.

Frenetically (fruh NET ik lee) is an adverb meaning *in a wildly hurrying or frantic way.*

There was too much work to do, so she had to work **frenetically** to finish it all on time.

Exhortation (eg zawr TAY shuhn) is a noun meaning *a statement strongly urging that something be done.*

She remembered John's Brown's **exhortation** to act, not just talk, to try to change the situation.

Serene (suh REEN) is an adjective meaning *calm and peaceful.*

The bus driver was angry with her, but Parks remained **serene.**

Retrieve (rih TREEV) is a verb meaning *to find and bring back.*

The police officer bent down to **retrieve** the purse she had dropped.

Vocabulary Practice

Review the words and sentences above. Answer each item that follows using the boldface Vocabulary word.

1. What is something you might do **frenetically**?

Possible answer: He frenetically cleaned his room while waiting for the school bus to arrive.

2. What **exhortation** would you give your favorite sports team?

Possible answer: I would give my school's team, the Badgers, an exhortation to win the state tennis championship.

3. Describe a place that makes you feel **serene**.

Possible answer: Sitting on the beach with a book to read makes me feel serene.

4. When might it be best not to **retrieve** something you left behind?

Possible answer: I would not try to retrieve my coat from the library when the building is closed.

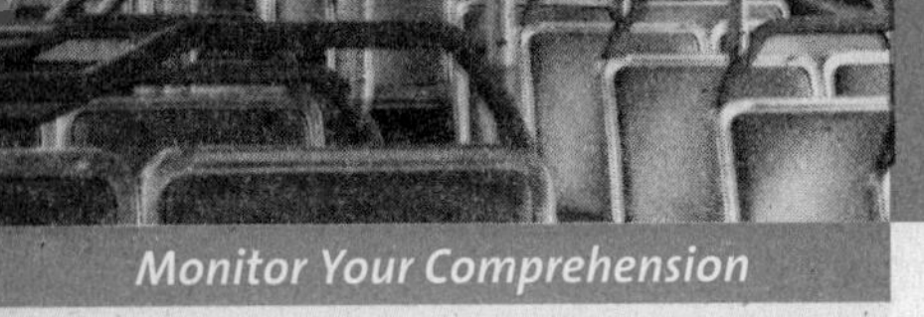

Monitor Your Comprehension

SET A PURPOSE FOR READING
Read this biography to discover how Rosa Parks made history.

Rosa Parks

Biography by
DOUGLAS BRINKLEY

BACKGROUND In parts of the United States in the past, state and local laws sometimes forced people of different races to live and work apart from each other. These laws were known as Jim Crow laws. One law forced African American people to sit separately from white people on buses. They also had to give up their seats to white people on demand.

Rosa Parks headed to work on December 1, 1955, on the Cleveland Avenue bus to Court Square. It was a typical prewinter morning in the Alabama capital, chilly and raw, topcoat weather. Outside the Montgomery Fair Department Store a Salvation Army Santa rang his bell for coins in front of window displays of toy trains and mannequins modeling reindeer sweaters. Every afternoon when school let out, hordes of children would invade the store to gawk at the giant Christmas tree draped with blinking lights, a mid-1950s electrical marvel. But Rosa Parks saw little of the holiday glitter down in the small tailor shop in the basement next to the huge steam presses, where the only hint of Yuletide cheer came from a sagging, water-stained banner reading "Merry Christmas and a Happy New Year."

Not that many of Montgomery Fair's lower-level employees had the time to let the faded decoration make them sad. The department store rang up nearly half of its sales between Thanksgiving and New Year's Day, which turned the tailor shop into a beehive of activity every December. But even on days spent **frenetically** hemming, ironing, and steam-pressing, Parks's mind was more with the NAACP[1] than her workday duties. She was in the midst of organizing a workshop to be held at Alabama State University on December 3–4 and spent the morning during her coffee break telephoning H. Council Trenholm, president of the university, applying enough quiet persuasion to be granted the use of a classroom over the weekend. "I was also getting the notices in the mail for the election of officers of the senior branch of the NAACP, which would be [the] next week," Parks recalled. That afternoon, she lunched with Fred Gray, the lawyer who defended Claudette Colvin and was serving as Clifford Durr's protégé[2] at his law office above the Sears Auto Tire Store. (A)

IN OTHER WORDS Rosa Parks, an African American woman, has a job sewing and ironing clothes in a department store. It is the holiday season, so the store is busy, but Parks isn't thinking about work. Instead, she is thinking about the civil rights workshop she is helping to plan.

"When 1:00 P.M. came and the lunch hour ended, Mrs. Parks went back to her work as a seamstress," Gray would write in his civil rights memoir, *Bus Ride to Justice.* "I continued my work and left the office in the early afternoon for an out-of-town engagement."

Shortly after 5:00 P.M., Rosa Parks clocked out of work and walked the block to Court Square to wait for her bus home. It

1. **NAACP:** a civil rights organization, the National Association for the Advancement of Colored People.
2. **Claudette Colvin . . . Clifford Durr's protégé** (PRO tuh zhay): Earlier that year, Claudette Colvin had refused to give up her seat on a Montgomery city bus. Clifford Durr was a white lawyer who worked for civil rights. As Durr's protégé, Gray was guided by Durr regarding his law career.

Monitor Your Comprehension

VOCABULARY

The word **frenetically** (fruh NET ik lee) is an adverb meaning *in a wildly hurrying, or frantic way.*

(A) CHARACTERIZATION

With a partner, discuss how Parks's work for the NAACP is different from her job in the department store. What does this contrast tell you about the kind of person Parks is?

Students should discuss that at the department store Parks sews and irons clothing whereas for the NAACP she organizes a civil rights workshop to be held at Alabama State University. While Parks is a talented seamstress, her true interests lie in community organization. She is capable of doing two very different types of work.

Monitor Your Comprehension

(B) CHARACTERIZATION

Brinkley spends a full paragraph describing what Parks does after she leaves work. Reread the paragraph, and then add to the chart below.

Rosa Parks	In Biography
Physical Appearance	tired, body in pain (lines 38–41)
Daily Life	*long and busy, filled with work (lines 41–43)*
Personality	*patient and practical (lines 45–49)*

had been a hard day, and her body ached, from her feet swollen from the constant standing to her shoulders throbbing from the strain and her chronic bursitis.[3] But the bus stand was packed, so Parks, disinclined to jockey for a rush-hour seat, crossed Dexter Avenue to do a little shopping at Lee's Cut-Rate Drug. She had decided to treat herself to a heating pad but found them too pricey. Instead, she bought some Christmas gifts, along with aspirin, toothpaste, and a few other sundries, and headed back to the bus stop wondering how her husband's day had been at the Maxwell Air Force Base Barber Shop and thinking about what her mother would cook for dinner. (B)

It was in this late-day reverie that Rosa Parks dropped her dime in the box and boarded the yellow-olive city bus. She took an aisle seat in the racially neutral middle section,[4] behind the movable sign which read "colored." She was not expecting any problems, as there were several empty spaces at the whites-only front of the bus. A black man was sitting next to her on her right and staring out the window; across the aisle sat two black women deep in conversation. At the next two stops enough white passengers got on to nearly fill up the front section. At the third stop, in front of the Empire Theater, a famous shrine to country-music fans as the stage where the legendary Hank Williams got his start, the last front seats were taken, with one man left standing. (C)

(C) CHARACTERIZATION

When she gets on the bus, what does Parks think her ride home will be like? Underline the statement that tells you.

IN OTHER WORDS On the way home from work, Parks sits down in the middle section of the bus. By law, only white people could sit in the front of the bus. Black people had to sit in the back. If enough white passengers got on the bus, black passengers in the middle section had to give up their seats. Parks's bus fills up, and one white man is left standing.

The bus driver twisted around and locked his eyes on Rosa Parks. Her heart almost stopped when she saw it was James F. Blake, the bully who had put her off his bus twelve years earlier.

3. **bursitis** (ber SY tis): a painful swelling, usually near the shoulder or hip.
4. **racially neutral middle section:** a section of the bus where African Americans could sit, as long as no whites wanted or needed seats there.

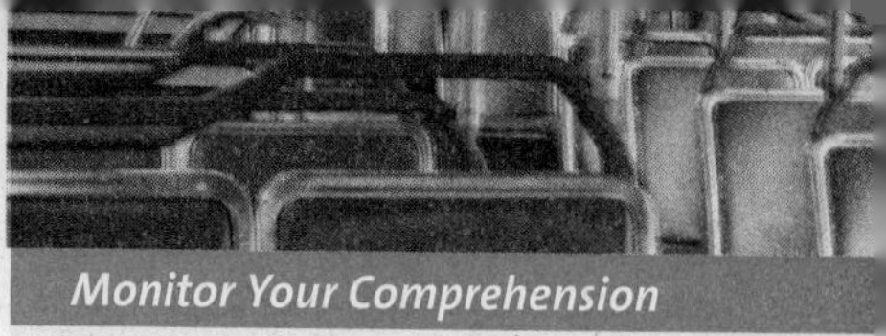

She didn't know his name, but since that incident in 1943, she had never boarded a bus that Blake was driving. This day, however, she had absentmindedly stepped in. "Move y'all, I want those two seats," the driver barked on behalf of Jim Crow, which dictated that all four blacks in that row of the middle section would have to surrender their seats to accommodate a single white man, as no "colored" could be allowed to sit parallel[5] with him. A stony silence fell over the bus as nobody moved. "Y'all better make it light on yourselves and let me have those seats," Blake sputtered, more impatiently than before. Quietly and in unison[6], the two black women sitting across from Parks rose and moved to the back. Her seatmate quickly followed suit, and she swung her legs to the side to let him out. **D** Then Parks slid over to the window and gazed out at the Empire Theater marquee promoting *A Man Alone,* a new Western starring Ray Milland. **E**

IN OTHER WORDS The bus driver, James F. Blake, had forced Rosa Parks off a bus twelve years earlier. Today, she got on his bus without noticing who was driving. Blake expects four black passengers to give up their seats so a white man will not have to sit next to a black passenger. He becomes angry, telling them to move. Three get up and move, but Parks does not.

► Underline the words that tell you that Parks ignores the bus driver.

The next ten seconds seemed like an eternity to Rosa Parks. As Blake made his way toward her, all she could think about were her forebears, who, Maya Angelou would put it, took the lash, the branding iron, and untold humiliations while only praying that their children would someday "flesh out" the dream of equality. But unlike the poet, it was not Africa in the days of the slave trade that Parks was thinking about; it was racist Alabama in the here and now. She shuddered with the memory of her grandfather back in Pine Level keeping watch for

5. **parallel** (PAIR uh lel): next to, or side by side.
6. **in unison:** together

Monitor Your Comprehension

D LANGUAGE COACH

Adverbs Adverbs are often formed by adding an *-ly* to the end of an adjective. In line 68, the word *absentmindedly,* meaning "without thinking," is formed by adding *-ly* to the adjective *absentminded* to describe why Parks fails to notice Blake when she gets on the bus. There are three other adverbs ending in *-ly* in this paragraph. Circle them.

E CHARACTERIZATION

With a partner, discuss how you would describe Parks's attitude when she refuses to move out of her seat.

Students should discuss that Parks is quietly defiant—she does not make a big deal about the fact that she will not give up her seat.

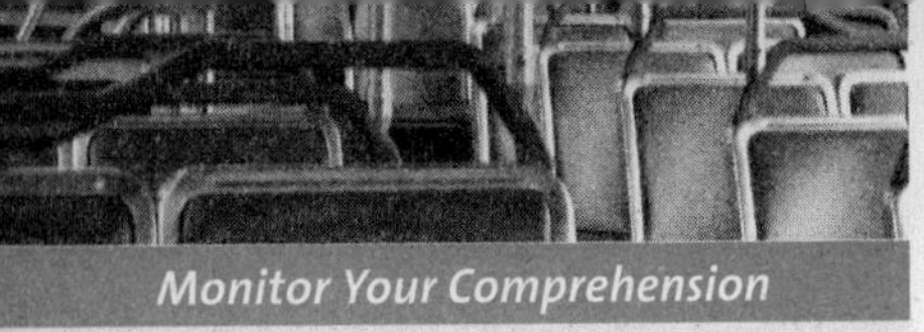

Monitor Your Comprehension

VOCABULARY

The word **exhortation** (eg zawr TAY shuhn) is a noun meaning *a statement strongly urging that something be done.*

VOCABULARY

The word **serene** (suh REEN) is an adjective meaning *calm and peaceful.*

PAUSE & REFLECT

Reread this paragraph. With a partner, discuss what causes Parks to stop fearing the bus driver. Why does she pity him instead?

Students should discuss that Parks realizes that by calmly taking action, she will put events into motion that will do more to change racism in Alabama than talking about it would ever do. She was taking a stand for what she believed was right.

VISUAL VOCABULARY

The **gallows** is a structure used for executing prisoners by hanging.

F SET A PURPOSE FOR READING

As you read this biography, what kept you interested in what would happen?

Possible answer: The first paragraph described the event but did not tell what led up to it.

the KKK[7] every night with a loaded shotgun in his lap, echoing abolitionist John Brown's[8] **exhortation**: "Talk! Talk! Talk! That didn't free the slaves. . . . What is needed is action! Action!" So when Parks looked up at Blake, his hard, thoughtless scowl filled her with pity. She felt fearless, bold, and **serene**. "Are you going to stand up?" the driver demanded. Rosa Parks looked straight at him and said: "No." Flustered and not quite sure what to do, Blake retorted, "Well, I'm going to have you arrested." And Parks, still sitting next to the window, replied softly, "You may do that." **PAUSE & REFLECT**

Her majestic use of "may" rather than "can" put Parks on the high ground, establishing her as a protester, not a victim. "When I made that decision," Parks stated later, "I knew I had the strength of my ancestors with me," and obviously their dignity as well. And her formal dignified "No," uttered on a suppertime bus in the cradle of the Confederacy as darkness fell, ignited the collective "no" of black history in America,[9] a defiance[10] as liberating as John Brown's on the **gallows** in Harpers Ferry. **F**

IN OTHER WORDS Parks remembers how her ancestors suffered under slavery and racism. Thinking of them, she decides not to give in to the bus driver. By saying "no" to the driver, Parks begins an important movement in black history.

7. **KKK:** The Ku Klux Klan (KKK) was a group that often violently terrorized black people in the South.
8. **abolitionist John Brown's:** John Brown, a white man, tried to force slavery to come to an end; he led a failed attempt to steal guns from the U.S. arsenal at Harpers Ferry, Virginia. Later, he was hanged for the crime.
9. **"ignited the collective 'no' of black history in America":** Parks's action caused many others to object to the oppression of African Americans throughout American history.
10. **defiance** (dih FY uhns): resistance against those in power.

Rosa

Poem by
RITA DOVE

BACKGROUND In this poem, Rita Dove presents her own impression of Rosa Parks's arrest.

How she sat there,
the time right inside a place
so wrong it was ready.

That trim name with
its dream of a bench
to rest on. Her sensible coat.

IN OTHER WORDS Rosa Parks sat where the law said it was wrong for her to sit. But that law was so wrong that it was time for change. Parks sat, wanting nothing more than a place to sit down and rest.

[Doing nothing was the doing:
the clean flame of her gaze]
carved by a camera flash.

Monitor Your Comprehension

SET A PURPOSE FOR READING
Read this poem to compare and contrast the characterization of Rosa Parks in the biography and the poem.

Monitor Your Comprehension

VOCABULARY

The word **retrieve** (rih TREEV) is a verb meaning *to find and bring back.*

G CHARACTERIZATION

What words or phrases does Dove use to show that Parks is dignified? Put brackets [ ] around them.

[How she stood up
when they bent down to **retrieve**
her purse.] That courtesy. G

IN OTHER WORDS By doing nothing—by refusing to move—Parks had done something. A photograph of Parks shows her steady strength and determination. As she was being arrested, she dropped her purse. The police picked it up for her. She politely stood up.

Text Analysis: Characterization Across Genres

You have just read works by two different authors describing Rosa Parks. Now use your completed version of the chart like the one below to help you analyze how Brinkley and Dove characterize Parks using two different genres.

For this chart, answers will vary. See samples below.

Rosa Parks	In Biography	In Poem
Physical Appearance	*tired, body in pain (lines 38–41)*	*wears a sensible coat (line 6)*
Daily Life (job, friends, etc.)	*busy, long, filled with work and errands (lines 37–49)*	*long and exhausting (lines 5–6)*
Personality	*patient and practical (lines 37–49)*	*polite, calm and quiet (lines 10–12)*

What overall impression of Parks do you get from the biography?

Possible answer: Parks is a hard worker who is polite and soft spoken.

What impression of her do you get from the poem?

Possible answer: Parks is tired. She is calm and quiet in her actions.

Explain which characterization of Rosa Parks you find stronger or more appealing, and explain why.

Possible answer: I prefer the biography because it explains what Parks is like in greater detail.

What is **DIGNITY?**

Look back at the notes you made on page 96 about what makes someone dignified. Which of the personality traits or actions you listed fit Rosa Parks? Explain.

Answers will vary.

After Reading

Reading Strategy: Set a Purpose for Reading

Now that you have compared and contrasted the two works about Rosa Parks, what are the strongest similarities you notice between them? What are the biggest differences? On the lines below, record specific examples from each work for two similarities and two differences. Then compare and contrast your list with a partner's.

For this chart, answers will vary. See samples below.

Similarities	Differences
Both describe the same event, both describe Parks as heroic	*Length of selections (biography excerpt is long; poem is brief); Writing style (biography is concrete; poem is abstract)*

Vocabulary Practice

Use the Vocabulary words to fill in the blanks.

WORD LIST
frenetically
exhortation
retrieve
serene

1. She recalled the *exhortation* to act for change, rather than simply think about it.
2. Her belief that what she did was right made her calm and *serene*.
3. She knew that if she lost her self-respect now, she might never *retrieve* it.
4. The only way to finish on time was to work *frenetically*.

Academic Vocabulary in Speaking

The word **perspective** (per SPEK tiv) is a noun that means *a point of view or a way of looking at things.*

My negative **perspective** about her changed after she apologized to me.

The word **device** (dih VYS) is a noun that means *a tool or method used to achieve a specific purpose.*

He told jokes at the party as a **device** to overcome his shyness.

TURN AND TALK What is a situation you would like to change? With a partner, explain your **perspective** on the situation and a **device** or approach you might use to help change the situation. Be sure to use the words **perspective** and **device** in your conversation.

Encourage students to use the Academic Vocabulary words in their discussions.

Assessment Practice

DIRECTIONS Use "Rosa Parks" and "Rosa" to answer questions 1–4.

1 The bus driver ordered Parks to change seats because —

- (A) she was taking up too much space
- (B) he wanted an empty row for one white passenger
- (C) he remembered that she was a troublemaker
- (D) he was trying to irritate her

2 What did Parks decide to do on the bus?

- (A) She decided not to give up her seat even if it meant getting arrested.
- (B) She decided to move to the back of the bus.
- (C) She decided to yell at the bus driver.
- (D) She decided to quit her job.

3 Which of the following word pairs best describes how both selections characterize Parks?

- (A) loud, angry
- (B) sweet, kind
- (C) dignified, noble
- (D) uncaring, selfish

4 Which of the following phrases from Dove's poem best expresses Parks's dignity?

- (A) *the time right inside a place*
- (B) *That trim name with its dream of a bench*
- (C) *Her sensible coat*
- (D) *How she stood up when they bent down to retrieve her purse*

UNIT 3

A Sense of Place

SETTING, MOOD, AND IMAGERY

Be sure to read the Text Analysis Workshop on pp. 330–335 in *Holt McDougal Literature*.

Academic Vocabulary for Unit 3

You will see these Academic Vocabulary words as you work through this book. You will also be asked to use them as you write and talk about the selections in this unit.

Aspect (AS pekt) is a noun that means *a part or a side of something.*
One memorable **aspect** of the concert was Zoe's cello solo.

What **aspect** of your day do you enjoy the most? ______

Answers will vary.

Circumstance (SER kuhm stans) is a noun that means *a situation or detail connected with an event.*
An unusual **circumstance** of my childhood was our family's constant traveling.

Write a sentence about a **circumstance** of your social life: ______

Answers will vary.

Contribute (kuhn TRIB yoot) is a verb that means *to provide a thing or idea that helps create a result.*
All the team members will **contribute** equally to the project.

Explain briefly how you **contribute** to your household: ______

Answers will vary.

Distinct (dih STINGKT) is an adjective that means *separate* or *different.* It can also mean *sharp and clear.*
Ali had a **distinct** dislike of the lunch served yesterday.

Name two **distinct** areas of your classroom: ______

Answers will vary.

Perceive (puhr SEEV) is a verb that means *to notice or become aware of.*
Scientists think that people **perceive** colors differently.

Describe something that you did not **perceive** before this year: ______

Answers will vary.

A Christmas Memory

Short story by Truman Capote

What do you look for in a **FRIEND?**

What is it that makes two people friends? Does a friend have to be someone your own age? Do you and your friends always have the same interests and attitudes? "A Christmas Memory" shows how important friendship can be to two very different people.

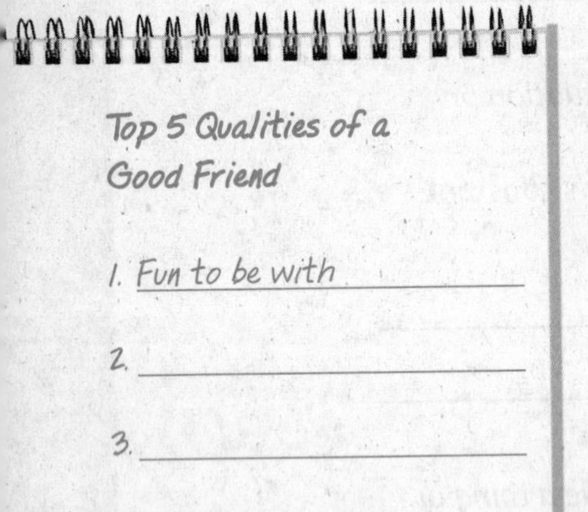

Top 5 Qualities of a Good Friend
1. Fun to be with
2.
3.
4.
5.

QUICKWRITE Make a "top five" list of the key qualities you look for in a friend. Then compare your list with your classmates' lists. Has everyone listed similar qualities?

Answers will vary.

Text Analysis: Details of Setting

The **setting** of a story is more than just the time and place in which the story happens. Through **details of setting,** writers can give information about the characters' lives and what is important to them. Details of setting also reveal information about the time period—the buildings, people, and customs that exist at the time the story takes place. In some stories, the setting may even create conflict for the characters and influence the choices they make.

Role of Setting	Example of Setting
Setting can influence characters by • determining how people live and the jobs they can have • shaping their personalities, their dreams, and their values	***A poor farm town during the Great Depression*** Even after Joe has spent months of back-breaking work, his crops are dying. Realizing that life may never get better, Joe becomes depressed and angry.
Setting can create conflict by • exposing the characters to dangerous weather • making characters live through a difficult time period	The town has gone seven years without enough rain, and most of the farms are failing. People have begun to sell their prized possessions in order to get money.

Reading Skill: Analyze Imagery

Memorable writing is often filled with **imagery**—words and phrases that appeal to the senses (sight, smell, hearing, taste, and touch). Truman Capote uses imagery to give readers a vivid description of a holiday memory. For example, note how this language appeals to your sense of sight:

Dollar bills, tightly rolled and green as May buds.

As you read, you will be asked to note words and phrases from the story that appeal to your senses.

Vocabulary in Context

Note: Words are listed in the order in which they appear in the story.

Exhilarate (ig ZIL uh rayt) is a verb meaning *to excite or make lively.*
Holiday celebrations **exhilarate** me; the decorations, music, and food make me as happy as a child.

Squander (SKWON duhr) is a verb that means *to spend or use wastefully.*
Don't **squander** your money on candy and other useless items.

Potent (POH tuhnt) is an adjective that means *powerful.*
The man added milk to make the strong coffee less **potent.**

Vocabulary Practice

Review the vocabulary words and sample sentences above. Then complete each sentence with the most appropriate vocabulary word.

1. The ___*potent*___ smell of spilled gasoline warned of danger.

2. A quick peek at the room full of presents and balloons was enough to ___*exhilarate*___ the child.

3. A gifted singer shouldn't ___*squander*___ her talent by performing only for her pets!

SET A PURPOSE FOR READING

Read this story to discover why a young boy and his elderly cousin are best friends.

A Christmas Memory

Short story by

TRUMAN CAPOTE

BACKGROUND This story is based on Truman Capote's childhood during the Great Depression of the 1930s. The Great Depression was a time when many people lost their jobs and had little money. Set in an old house in the Alabama countryside, the narrator remembers the last Christmas season he shared with his "best friend," an elderly female cousin.

Imagine a morning in late November. A coming of winter morning more than twenty years ago. Consider the kitchen of a spreading old house in a country town. A great black stove is its main feature; but there is also a big round table and a fireplace with two rocking chairs placed in front of it. Just today the fireplace commenced its seasonal roar. Ⓐ

Ⓐ **DETAILS OF SETTING**

Reread lines 1–6. Circle three details of setting that are included in this paragraph.

A woman with shorn white hair is standing at the kitchen window. She is wearing tennis shoes and a shapeless gray sweater over a summery calico dress. She is small and sprightly,[1] like a bantam hen; but, due to a long youthful illness, her shoulders are pitifully hunched. Her face is remarkable—not unlike Lincoln's, craggy like that, and tinted by sun and wind; but it is delicate too, finely boned, and her eyes are sherry-colored

1. **sprightly** (SPRYT lee): lively.

and timid. "Oh my," she exclaims, her breath smoking the windowpane, "it's fruitcake weather!"

The person to whom she is speaking is myself. I am seven; she is sixty-something. We are cousins, very distant ones, and we have lived together—well, as long as I can remember. Other people inhabit the house, relatives; and though they have power over us, and frequently make us cry, we are not, on the whole, too much aware of them. We are each other's best friend. She calls me Buddy, in memory of a boy who was formerly her best friend. The other Buddy died in the 1880's, when she was still a child. She is still a child. **PAUSE & REFLECT**

"I knew it before I got out of bed," she says, turning away from the window with a purposeful excitement in her eyes. "The courthouse bell sounded so cold and clear. And there were no birds singing; they've gone to warmer country, yes indeed. Oh, Buddy, stop stuffing biscuit and fetch our buggy. Help me find my hat. We've thirty cakes to bake."

It's always the same: a morning arrives in November, and my friend, as though officially inaugurating[2] the Christmas time of year that **exhilarates** her imagination and fuels the blaze of her heart, announces: "It's fruitcake weather! Fetch our buggy. Help me find my hat."

IN OTHER WORDS The story begins on a fall morning in an old country house. A small woman stands at the window. The seven-year-old narrator, Buddy, says the woman is a much older cousin who still seems like a child. The woman is excited by the beginning of the Christmas season and the idea of making fruitcakes.

► What makes the woman think that it is the right time to make fruitcakes?

Possible answer: The woman always makes fruitcakes at the start of the Christmas season, which begins once the weather turns cooler.

The hat is found, a straw cartwheel corsaged with velvet roses out-of-doors has faded: it once belonged to a more fashionable relative. Together, we guide our buggy, a dilapidated[3] baby carriage, out to the garden and into a grove of pecan trees. The

2. **inaugurating** (in AW gyuh rayt ing): marking a formal beginning of.
3. **dilapidated** (duh LAP uh day tihd): falling to pieces.

PAUSE & REFLECT

Where do Buddy and his friend live? Who do they live with?

Possible answer: Buddy and his friend live together in a large old house in a country town. They live with some of their relatives.

VOCABULARY

The word **exhilarate** (ig ZIL uh rayt) is a verb meaning *to excite or make lively.*

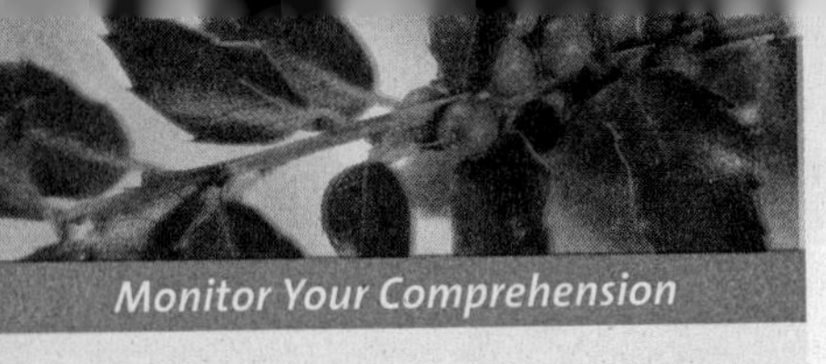

Monitor Your Comprehension

B DETAILS OF SETTING

This story is set during the Great Depression, a time when most Americans had little, if any, money to spare. What do the details about the buggy in lines 38–42 tell you about the lives of those who push it?

Possible answer: The rundown condition of the buggy indicates that the people who own it do not have the money to repair or replace it.

C ANALYZE IMAGERY

Reread lines 56–64. The description of the kitchen includes several vivid images. Fill in each box below with an appropriate example of imagery. An example has been done for you.

1. Hearing:

"Caarackle! A cheery crunch"

↓

2. Hearing:

Possible answer: "scraps of miniature thunder sound"

↓

3. Taste:

Possible answer: "the golden mound of sweet oily ivory meat"

↓

4. Sight:

Possible answer: "Dusk turns the window into a mirror: our reflections mingle with the rising moon as we work by the fireside in the firelight."

buggy is mine; that is, it was bought for me when I was born. It is made of wicker, rather unraveled, and the wheels wobble like a drunkard's legs. But it is a faithful object; springtimes, we take it to the woods and fill it with flowers, herbs, wild fern for our porch pots; in the summer, we pile it with picnic paraphernalia[4] and sugar-cane fishing poles and roll it down to the edge of a creek; it has its winter uses, too: as a truck for hauling firewood from the yard to the kitchen, as a warm bed for Queenie, our tough little orange and white rat terrier who has survived distemper and two rattlesnake bites. Queenie is trotting beside it now. **B**

Three hours later we are back in the kitchen hulling a heaping buggyload of windfall pecans. Our backs hurt from gathering them: how hard they were to find (the main crop having been shaken off the trees and sold by the orchard's owners, who are not us) among the concealing leaves, the frosted, deceiving grass. Caarackle! A cheery crunch, scraps of miniature thunder sound as the shells collapse and the golden mound of sweet oily ivory meat mounts in the milk-glass bowl. Queenie begs to taste, and now and again my friend sneaks her a mite, though insisting we deprive ourselves. "We mustn't, Buddy. If we start, we won't stop. And there's scarcely enough as there is. For thirty cakes." The kitchen is growing dark. Dusk turns the window into a mirror: our reflections mingle with the rising moon as we work by the fireside in the firelight. At last, when the moon is quite high, we toss the final hull into the fire and, with joined sighs, watch it catch flame. The buggy is empty, the bowl is brimful. **C**

We eat our supper (cold biscuits, bacon, blackberry jam) and discuss tomorrow. Tomorrow the kind of work I like best begins: buying. Cherries and citron, ginger and vanilla and canned Hawaiian pineapple, rinds and raisins and walnuts and whiskey and oh, so much flour, butter, so many eggs, spices, flavorings: why, we'll need a pony to pull the buggy home.

But before these purchases can be made, there is the question of money. Neither of us has any. Except for skinflint sums

4. **paraphernalia** (par uh fur NAYL yuh): the articles needed for a particular event or activity.

persons in the house occasionally provide (a dime is considered very big money); or what we earn ourselves from various activities: holding rummage sales, selling buckets of hand-picked blackberries, jars of homemade jam and apple jelly and peach preserves, rounding up flowers for funerals and weddings. Once we won seventy-ninth prize, five dollars, in a national football contest. Not that we know a fool thing about football. It's just that we enter any contest we hear about: at the moment our hopes are centered on the fifty-thousand-dollar Grand Prize being offered to name a new brand of coffee (we suggested "A.M."; and, after some hesitation, for my friend thought it perhaps sacrilegious,[5] the slogan "A.M.! Amen!"). To tell the truth, our only *really* profitable enterprise was the Fun and Freak Museum we conducted in a back-yard woodshed two summers ago. The Fun was a stereopticon[6] with slide views of Washington and New York lent us by a relative who had been to those places (she was furious when she discovered why we'd borrowed it); the Freak was a three-legged biddy chicken hatched by one of our own hens. Everybody hereabouts wanted to see that biddy: we charged grownups a nickel, kids two cents. And took in a good twenty dollars before the museum shut down due to the decease of the main attraction. **D**

But one way and another we do each year accumulate Christmas savings, a Fruitcake Fund. These moneys we keep hidden in an ancient bead purse under a loose board under the floor under a chamber pot under my friend's bed. The purse is seldom removed from this safe location except to make a deposit or, as happens every Saturday, a withdrawal; for on Saturdays I am allowed ten cents to go to the picture show. My friend has never been to a picture show, nor does she intend to: "I'd rather hear you tell the story, Buddy. That way I can imagine it more. Besides, a person my age shouldn't **squander** their eyes. When the Lord comes, let me see him clear." In addition to never having seen a movie, she has never: eaten in a restaurant, traveled more than five miles from home, received or sent a telegram, read anything except funny papers and the

5. **sacrilegious** (sak ruh LIJ uhs): insulting to sacred persons or objects.
6. **stereopticon** (stehr ee OP tuh kuhn): an early slide projector that could merge two images of the same scene on a screen, resulting in a 3-D effect.

Monitor Your Comprehension

D DETAILS OF SETTING

Reread lines 74–97. What do these details about the money-raising activities of Buddy and his friend tell you about the story's time and place?

Possible answer: The story is set in the past—the amounts of money, e.g., a dime being considered "big money" and a nickel for admission, are much lower than amounts would be today. It is set in a rural area where people grow and pick a variety of fruits and have large yards.

VOCABULARY

The word **squander** (SKWON duhr) is a verb that means *to spend or use wastefully.*

Monitor Your Comprehension

Bible, worn cosmetics, cursed, wished someone harm, told a lie on purpose, let a hungry dog go hungry. Here are a few things she has done, does do: killed with a hoe the biggest rattlesnake ever seen in this county (sixteen rattles), dip snuff[7] (secretly), tame hummingbirds (just try it) till they balance on her finger, tell ghost stories (we both believe in ghosts) so tingling they chill you in July, talk to herself, take walks in the rain, grow the prettiest japonicas in town, know the recipe for every sort of old-time Indian cure, including a magical wart remover. PAUSE & REFLECT

Now, with supper finished, we retire to the room in a faraway part of the house where my friend sleeps in a scrap-quilt-covered iron bed painted rose pink, her favorite color. Silently, wallowing in the pleasures of conspiracy, we take the bead purse from its secret place and spill its contents on the scrap quilt. Dollar bills, tightly rolled and green as May buds. Somber fifty-cent pieces, heavy enough to weight a dead man's eyes.[8] Lovely dimes, the liveliest coin, the one that really jingles. Nickels and quarters, worn smooth as creek pebbles. But mostly a hateful heap of bitter-odored pennies. E Last summer others in the house contracted to pay us a penny for every twenty-five flies we killed. Oh, the carnage of August: the flies that flew to heaven! Yet it was not work in which we took pride. And, as we sit counting pennies, it is as though we were back tabulating dead flies. Neither of us has a head for figures; we count slowly, lose track, start again. According to her calculations, we have $12.73. According to mine, exactly $13. "I do hope you're wrong, Buddy. We can't mess around with thirteen. The cakes will fall. Or put somebody in the cemetery. Why, I wouldn't dream of getting out of bed on the thirteenth." This is true: she always spends thirteenths in bed. So, to be on the safe side, we subtract a penny and toss it out the window.

7. **dip snuff:** to place a small amount of finely ground tobacco (snuff) in one's mouth.
8. **heavy enough to weight a dead man's eyes:** from the custom of putting coins on the closed eyes of corpses to keep the eyelids from opening.

PAUSE & REFLECT

With a partner, discuss what Buddy tells about his friend in lines 108–121. What kind of a person is she? How would you describe her?

Possible answer: She has religious faith and has led a sheltered life. She is gentle and kind yet tough.

E ANALYZE IMAGERY

Reread lines 124–131. Write down three examples of imagery in these lines, and tell what sense each one appeals to. An example has been done for you.

"Dollar bills, tightly rolled and green as May buds."—sight

1. *Possible answer: "iron bed painted rose pink"—sight*
2. *Possible answer: "the liveliest coin, the one that really jingles"—hearing*
3. *Possible answer: "worn smooth as creek pebbles"—touch*

IN OTHER WORDS The cousins collect and then shell pecans for their fruitcakes. They need many more ingredients, which they will have to buy. Buddy tells about some of the money-raising activities of past years, including selling things and charging people to see their three-legged chick. The cousins count their money and find that they have $13.00. They throw out a penny so they won't have such an unlucky number.

Of the ingredients that go into our fruitcakes, whiskey is the most expensive, as well as the hardest to obtain: State laws forbid its sale. But everybody knows you can buy a bottle from Mr. Haha Jones. And the next day, having completed our more prosaic[9] shopping, we set out for Mr. Haha's business address, a "sinful" (to quote public opinion) fish-fry and dancing café down by the river. We've been there before, and on the same errand; but in previous years our dealings have been with Haha's wife, an iodine-dark Indian woman with brassy peroxided hair and a dead-tired disposition. Actually, we've never laid eyes on her husband, though we've heard that he's an Indian too. A giant with razor scars across his cheeks. They call him Haha because he's so gloomy, a man who never laughs. As we approach his café (a large log cabin festooned inside and out with chains of garish-gay naked light bulbs and standing by the river's muddy edge under the shade of river trees where moss drifts through the branches like gray mist) our steps slow down. Even Queenie stops prancing and sticks close by. People have been murdered in Haha's café. Cut to pieces. Hit on the head. There's a case coming up in court next month. F

Naturally these goings-on happen at night when the colored lights cast crazy patterns and the Victrola[10] wails. In the daytime Haha's is shabby and deserted. I knock at the door, Queenie barks, my friend calls: "Mrs. Haha, ma'am? Anyone to home?"

Footsteps. The door opens. Our hearts overturn. It's Mr. Haha Jones himself! And he *is* a giant; he *does* have scars; he *doesn't* smile. No, he glowers at us through Satan-tilted eyes and demands to know: "What you want with Haha?"

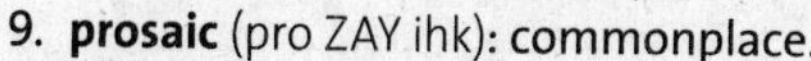

9. **prosaic** (pro ZAY ihk): commonplace.
10. **Victrola:** a trademark for a brand of old record player.

Monitor Your Comprehension

F DETAILS OF SETTING

From 1919–1933 prohibition was in force in the United States. This law made it illegal to make, sell, or transport alcohol. What do you think Buddy means when he calls Mr. Haha's cafe a "sinful" place?

Possible answer: Buddy means that since Mr. Haha's café is a place where you can buy liquor, as a result you are breaking the law and committing a sin.

Circle the details in lines 145–163 that tell you the café is a dangerous and "sinful" place.

For a moment we are too paralyzed to tell. Presently my friend half-finds her voice, a whispery voice at best: "If you please, Mr. Haha, we'd like a quart of your finest whiskey."

His eyes tilt more. Would you believe it? Haha is smiling! Laughing, too. "Which one of you is a drinkin' man?"

"It's for making fruitcakes, Mr. Haha. Cooking."

This sobers him. He frowns. "That's no way to waste good whiskey." Nevertheless, he retreats into the shadowed café and seconds later appears carrying a bottle of daisy-yellow unlabeled liquor. He demonstrates its sparkle in the sunlight and says: "Two dollars."

We pay him with nickels and dimes and pennies. Suddenly, as he jangles the coins in his hand like a fistful of dice, his face softens. "Tell you what," he proposes, pouring the money back into our bead purse, "just send me one of them fruitcakes instead."

"Well," my friend remarks on our way home, "there's a lovely man. We'll put an extra cup of raisins in *his* cake."

IN OTHER WORDS **Buddy and his cousin go to the cafe of Mr. Haha Jones to buy whiskey illegally. Mr. Haha tells them it will cost two dollars, but when they tell him it's for fruitcakes he returns the money and tells them to give him a fruitcake instead.**

► Why are Buddy and his cousin so surprised when Mr. Haha returns their money?

Possible answer: Buddy and his cousin are surprised by Mr. Haha's generosity, which does not match his gruff, unsmiling appearance.

The black stove, stoked with coal and firewood, glows like a lighted pumpkin. Eggbeaters whirl, spoons spin round in bowls of butter and sugar, vanilla sweetens the air, ginger spices it; melting, nose-tingling odors saturate the kitchen, suffuse[11] the house, drift out to the world on puffs of chimney smoke. In four days our work is done. Thirty-one cakes, dampened with whiskey, bask on windowsills and shelves.

Who are they for?

Friends. Not necessarily neighbor friends: indeed, the larger share is intended for persons we've met maybe once, perhaps not

11. **suffuse** (suh FYOOZ): to gradually spread through or over.

Monitor Your Comprehension

at all. People who've struck our fancy. Like President Roosevelt. Like the Reverend and Mrs. J. C. Lucey, Baptist missionaries to Borneo[12] who lectured here last winter. Or the little knife grinder who comes through town twice a year. Or Abner Packer, the driver of the six o'clock bus from Mobile, who exchanges waves with us every day as he passes in a dust-cloud whoosh. Or the young Wistons, a California couple whose car one afternoon broke down outside the house and who spent a pleasant hour chatting with us on the porch (young Mr. Wiston snapped our picture, the only one we've ever had taken). Is it because my friend is shy with everyone *except* strangers that these strangers, and merest acquaintances, seem to us our truest friends? I think yes. Also, the scrapbooks we keep of thank-you's on White House stationery, time-to-time communications from California and Borneo, the knife grinder's penny post cards, make us feel connected to eventful worlds beyond the kitchen with its view of a sky that stops. **PAUSE & REFLECT**

PAUSE & REFLECT

Reread lines 197–212. With a partner, discuss why Buddy and his friend give their fruitcakes to strangers and people they don't know well.

Buddy and his friend live an isolated life. As a result, they have few friends of their own with whom they can share the fruitcakes.

Now a nude December fig branch grates against the window. The kitchen is empty, the cakes are gone; yesterday we carted the last of them to the post office, where the cost of stamps turned our purse inside out. We're broke. That rather depresses me, but my friend insists on celebrating—with two inches of whiskey left in Haha's bottle. Queenie has a spoonful in a bowl of coffee (she likes her coffee chicory-flavored and strong). The rest we divide between a pair of jelly glasses. We're both quite awed at the prospect of drinking straight whiskey; the taste of it brings screwed-up expressions and sour shudders. But by and by we begin to sing, the two of us singing different songs simultaneously. I don't know the words to mine, just: *Come on along, come on along, to the dark-town strutters' ball.* But I can dance: that's what I mean to be, a tap dancer in the movies. My dancing shadow rollicks on the walls; our voices rock the chinaware; we giggle: as if unseen hands were tickling us. Queenie rolls on her back, her paws plow the air, something like a grin stretches her black lips. Inside myself, I feel warm **G**

G ANALYZE IMAGERY

Reread lines 231–234 and Underline the imagery in these lines. What senses does Capote appeal to?

Capote appeals to the sense of hearing and touch.

12. **Borneo** (BOR nee oh): a large island in the South China Sea.

Monitor Your Comprehension

and sparky as those crumbling logs, carefree as the wind in the chimney. My friend waltzes round the stove, the hem of her poor calico skirt pinched between her fingers as though it were a party dress: *Show me the way to go home,* she sings, her tennis shoes squeaking on the floor. *Show me the way to go home.*

Enter: two relatives. Very angry. **Potent** with eyes that scold, tongues that scald. Listen to what they have to say, the words tumbling together into a wrathful tune: "A child of seven! whiskey on his breath! are you out of your mind? feeding a child of seven! must be loony! road to ruination! remember Cousin Kate? Uncle Charlie? Uncle Charlie's brother-in-law? shame! scandal! humiliation! kneel, pray, beg the Lord!"

Queenie sneaks under the stove. My friend gazes at her shoes, her chin quivers, she lifts her skirt and blows her nose and runs to her room. PAUSE & REFLECT

VOCABULARY

The word **potent** (POH tuhnt) is an adjective that means *powerful.*

PAUSE & REFLECT

Reread lines 241–250. What impression do you get of the relatives? Circle words and phrases in these lines that give you this impression.

The relatives are angry and judgmental. They appear to notice only mistakes and problems.

IN OTHER WORDS Buddy and his friend spend four days making fruitcakes. They use the rest of their money mailing them to "friends." Most of their "friends" are people they've only met once or never at all. To celebrate, the two share the last bit of whiskey. They hate the taste, but they begin to sing and dance. Two relatives get angry because Buddy has had whiskey.

Long after the town has gone to sleep and the house is silent except for the chimings of clocks and the sputter of fading fires, she is weeping into a pillow already as wet as a widow's handkerchief.

"Don't cry," I say, sitting at the bottom of her bed and shivering despite my flannel nightgown that smells of last winter's cough syrup, "don't cry," I beg, teasing her toes, tickling her feet, "you're too old for that."

"It's because," she hiccups, "I *am* too old. Old and funny."

"Not funny. Fun. More fun than anybody. Listen. If you don't stop crying you'll be so tired tomorrow we can't go cut a tree."

She straightens up. Queenie jumps on the bed (where Queenie is not allowed) to lick her cheeks. "I know where we'll find real pretty trees, Buddy. And holly, too. With berries big as your eyes. It's way off in the woods. Farther than we've ever been. Papa used to bring us Christmas trees from there: carry them on his shoulder. That's fifty years ago. Well, now: I can't wait for morning."

Morning. Frozen rime[13] lusters the grass; the sun, round as an orange and orange as hot-weather moons, balances on the horizon, burnishes the silvered winter woods. A wild turkey calls. A renegade hog grunts in the undergrowth. Soon, by the edge of knee-deep, rapid-running water, we have to abandon the buggy. Queenie wades the stream first, paddles across barking complaints at the swiftness of the current, the pneumonia-making coldness of it. We follow, holding our shoes and equipment (a hatchet, a burlap sack) above our heads. A mile more: of chastising thorns, burrs and briers that catch at our clothes; of rusty pine needles brilliant with gaudy fungus and molted feathers. Here, there, a flash, a flutter, an ecstasy of shrillings remind us that not all the birds have flown south. Always, the path unwinds through lemony sun pools and pitch-black vine tunnels. Another creek to cross: a disturbed armada of speckled trout froths the water round us, and frogs the size of plates practice belly flops; beaver workmen are building a dam. On the farther shore, Queenie shakes herself and trembles. My friend shivers, too: not with cold but enthusiasm. One of her hat's ragged roses sheds a petal as she lifts her head and inhales the pine-heavy air. "We're almost there; can you smell it, Buddy?" she says, as though we were approaching an ocean. (H)

And, indeed, it is a kind of ocean. Scented acres of holiday trees, prickly-leafed holly. Red berries shiny as Chinese bells: black crows swoop upon them screaming. Having stuffed our burlap sacks with enough greenery and crimson to garland a dozen windows, we set about choosing a tree. "It should be," muses my friend, "twice as tall as a boy. So a boy can't steal the star." The one we pick is twice as tall as me. A brave handsome brute that survives thirty hatchet strokes before it keels with a creaking rending cry. Lugging it like a kill, we commence the long trek out.

13. **rime** (rym): a white frost.

Monitor Your Comprehension

(H) ANALYZE IMAGERY

Reread lines 276–285. Find two examples of imagery in these lines and write them below. Tell what sense each example appeals to.

1. *Possible answer: "chastising thorns, burrs and briers that catch at our clothes"—touch*

2. *Possible answer: "lemony sun pools and pitchblack vine tunnels"—sight*

Monitor Your Comprehension

Every few yards we abandon the struggle, sit down and pant. But we have the strength of triumphant huntsmen; that and the tree's virile, icy perfume revive us, goad[14] us on. Many compliments accompany our sunset return along the red clay road to town; but my friend is sly and noncommittal when passers-by praise the treasure perched in our buggy: what a fine tree, and where did it come from? "Yonderways," she murmurs vaguely. Once a car stops, and the rich mill owner's lazy wife leans out and whines: "Giveya two-bits[15] cash for that ol tree." Ordinarily my friend is afraid of saying no; but on this occasion she promptly shakes her head: "We wouldn't take a dollar." The mill owner's wife persists. "A dollar, my foot! Fifty cents. That's my last offer. Goodness, woman, you can get another one." In answer, my friend gently reflects: "I doubt it. There's never two of anything." **PAUSE & REFLECT**

PAUSE & REFLECT

What do you learn about the narrator's friend based on her words and actions in lines 305–312?

She is proud; she thinks little of people whom she sees as lazy; she appreciates the value of hard work.

Home: Queenie slumps by the fire and sleeps till tomorrow, snoring loud as a húman.

A trunk in the attic contains: a shoebox of **ermine** tails (off the opera cape of a curious lady who once rented a room in the house), coils of frazzled tinsel gone gold with age, one silver star, a brief rope of dilapidated, undoubtedly dangerous candylike light bulbs. Excellent decorations, as far as they go, which isn't far enough: my friend wants our tree to blaze "like a Baptist window," droop with weighty snows of ornament. But we can't afford the made-in-Japan splendors at the five-and-dime. So we do what we've always done: sit for days at the kitchen table with scissors and crayons and stacks of colored paper. I make sketches and my friend cuts them out: lots of cats, fish too (because they're easy to draw), some apples, some watermelons, a few winged angels devised from saved-up sheets of Hershey-bar tin foil. We use safety pins to attach these creations to the tree; as a final touch, we sprinkle the branches with shredded cotton (picked in August for this purpose). My friend, surveying the effect, clasps her hands together. "Now honest, Buddy. Doesn't it look good enough to eat?" Queenie tries to eat an angel.

VISUAL VOCABULARY

An **ermine** (UR muhn) is a type of weasel. In winter the ermine's coat is all white except for its tail, which has a black tip.

---

14. **goad** (gohd): to drive or urge.
15. **two-bits:** 25 cents.

Monitor Your Comprehension

IN OTHER WORDS Buddy and his friend walk far into the woods to find a Christmas tree. The tree they bring back draws many compliments. At home, they drag old decorations out of the attic and make new ones from colored paper and crayons.

► What do Buddy and his friend use for Christmas tree decorations?

Buddy and his friend use a trunk full of old decorations as well as making new ones from construction paper and crayons.

After weaving and ribboning holly wreaths for all the front windows, our next project is the fashioning of family gifts. Tie-dye scarves for the ladies, for the men a home-brewed lemon and licorice and aspirin syrup to be taken "at the first Symptoms of a Cold and after Hunting." But when it comes time for making each other's gift, my friend and I separate to work secretly. I would like to buy her a pearl-handled knife, a radio, a whole pound of chocolate-covered cherries (we tasted some once, and she always swears: "I could live on them, Buddy, Lord yes I could—and that's not taking his name in vain"). Instead, I am building her a kite. She would like to give me a bicycle (she's said so on several million occasions: "If only I could, Buddy. It's bad enough in life to do without something *you* want; but confound it, what gets my goat is not being able to give somebody something you want *them* to have. Only one of these days I will, Buddy. Locate you a bike. Don't ask how. Steal it, maybe"). Instead, I'm fairly certain that she is building me a kite—the same as last year and the year before: the year before that we exchanged slingshots. All of which is fine by me. For we are champion kite fliers who study the wind like sailors; my friend, more accomplished than I, can get a kite aloft when there isn't enough breeze to carry clouds.

Christmas Eve afternoon we scrape together a nickel and go to the butcher's to buy Queenie's traditional gift, a good gnawable beef bone. The bone, wrapped in funny paper, is placed high in the tree near the silver star. Queenie knows it's there. She squats at the foot of the tree staring up in a trance of greed: when bedtime arrives she refuses to budge. Her excitement is equaled by my own. I kick the covers and turn my pillow as though it were a scorching summer's night. Somewhere a rooster crows: falsely, for the sun is still on the other side of the world.

"Buddy, are you awake?" It is my friend, calling from her room, which is next to mine; and an instant later she is sitting

DETAILS OF SETTING

Buddy and his friend are making ornaments, wreaths, tie-dyed scarves, cold medicine and kites. How do these details relate to the time and place of the story? How might this scene be different if the story took place today?

Possible answer: The details tell the reader that the story takes place in the past. If the story were to take place today, the decorations and gifts might be purchased at a shop instead of being homemade.

LANGUAGE COACH

Many words in English begin with *kn-* or *gn-*, in which the first letter is silent. How would you pronounce the word *gnawable* in line 355? ***naw-able***

on my bed holding a candle. "Well, I can't sleep a hoot," she declares. "My mind's jumping like a jack rabbit. Buddy, do you think Mrs. Roosevelt will serve our cake at dinner?" We huddle in the bed, and she squeezes my hand I-love-you. "Seems like your hand used to be so much smaller. I guess I hate to see you grow up. When you're grown up, will we still be friends?" I say always. "But I feel so bad, Buddy. I wanted so bad to give you a bike. I tried to sell my cameo Papa gave me. Buddy"—she hesitates, as though embarrassed—"I made you another kite." Then I confess that I made her one, too; and we laugh. The candle burns too short to hold. Out it goes, exposing the starlight, the stars spinning at the window like a visible caroling that slowly, slowly daybreak silences. Possibly we doze; but the beginnings of dawn splash us like cold water: we're up, wide-eyed and wandering while we wait for others to waken. Quite deliberately my friend drops a kettle on the kitchen floor. I tap dance in front of closed doors. One by one the household emerges, looking as though they'd like to kill us both; but it's Christmas, so they can't. First, a gorgeous breakfast: just everything you can imagine—from flapjacks and fried squirrel to hominy grits and honey-in-the-comb. Which puts everyone in a good humor except my friend and me. Frankly, we're so impatient to get at the presents we can't eat a mouthful.

Well, I'm disappointed. Who wouldn't be? With socks, a Sunday school shirt, some handkerchiefs, a hand-me-down sweater, and a year's subscription to a religious magazine for children. *The Little Shepherd*. It makes me boil. It really does.

PAUSE & REFLECT

My friend has a better haul. A sack of satsumas,[16] that's her best present. She is proudest, however, of a white wool shawl knitted by her married sister. But she *says* her favorite gift is the kite I built her. And it is very beautiful; though not as beautiful as the one she made me, which is blue and scattered with gold and green Good Conduct stars;[17] moreover, my name is painted on it, "Buddy."

16. **satsumas** (sat SOO muh): fruit similar to tangerines.
17. **Good Conduct stars:** small, shiny, glued paper stars often awarded to children for good behavior.

LANGUAGE COACH

A *hand-me-down* (line 388) is a piece of clothing that has been passed down, or handed down, from one person to another. Hand-me-downs are often clothes passed from an older family member to a younger one.

PAUSE & REFLECT

Why is Buddy disappointed with most of his Christmas presents?

Possible answer: Buddy is disappointed with his gifts because they are all practical (e.g., clothing and religious magazines) and do not include anything fun, such as toys, for him.

"Buddy, the wind is blowing."

The wind is blowing, and nothing will do till we've run to a pasture below the house where Queenie has scooted to bury her bone (and where, a winter hence, Queenie will be buried, too). There, plunging through the healthy waist-high grass, we unreel our kites, feel them twitching at the string like sky fish as they swim into the wind. Satisfied, sun-warmed, we sprawl in the grass and peel satsumas and watch our kites cavort.[18] Soon I forget the socks and hand-me-down sweater. I'm as happy as if we'd already won the fifty-thousand-dollar Grand Prize in that coffee-naming contest.

"My, how foolish I am!" my friend cries, suddenly alert, like a woman remembering too late she has biscuits in the oven. "You know what I've always thought?" she asks in a tone of discovery and not smiling at me but a point beyond. "I've always thought a body would have to be sick and dying before they saw the Lord. And I imagined that when he came it would be like looking at the Baptist window: pretty as colored glass with the sun pouring through, such a shine you don't know it's getting dark. And it's been a comfort: to think of that shine taking away all the spooky feeling. But I'll wager it never happens. I'll wager at the very end a body realizes the Lord has already shown himself. That things as they are"—her hand circles in a gesture that gathers clouds and kites and grass and Queenie pawing earth over her bone—"just what they've always seen, was seeing him. As for me, I could leave the world with today in my eyes."

IN OTHER WORDS Buddy and his friend make Christmas presents for their family members and for each other. On Christmas morning, they eat a holiday breakfast and exchange their gifts of homemade kites. Later they run to a pasture to fly the kites. They lie in the warm grass eating oranges. Buddy and his friend are happy.

► Why does Buddy's friend say "I could leave the world with today in my eyes"? Discuss your ideas with a partner.

Possible answer: Buddy's friend means that she could die happy after the day's events.

This is our last Christmas together.

18. **cavort** (kuh VORT): to leap or romp about.

Monitor Your Comprehension

Ⓛ DETAILS OF SETTING

Reread lines 424–428, the setting of the story changes. How has Buddy's life changed since the last Christmas with his friend?

Possible answer: Buddy has been sent to a military school as well as summer camps and no longer lives at home with his friend.

Life separates us. Those who Know Best decide that I belong in a military school. And so follows a miserable succession of bugle-blowing prisons, grim reveille-ridden[19] summer camps. I have a new home too. But it doesn't count. Home is where my friend is, and there I never go. Ⓛ

And there she remains, puttering around the kitchen. Alone with Queenie. Then alone. ("Buddy dear," she writes in her wild hard-to-read script, "yesterday Jim Macy's horse kicked Queenie bad. Be thankful she didn't feel much. I wrapped her in a Fine Linen sheet and rode her in the buggy down to Simpson's pasture where she can be with all her Bones . . ."). For a few Novembers she continues to bake her fruitcakes single-handed; not as many, but some: and, of course, she always sends me "the best of the batch." Also, in every letter she encloses a dime wadded in toilet paper: "See a picture show and write me the story." But gradually in her letters she tends to confuse me with her other friend, the Buddy who died in the 1880's; more and more, thirteenths are not the only days she stays in bed: a morning arrives in November, a leafless birdless coming of winter morning, when she cannot rouse herself to exclaim: "Oh my, it's fruitcake weather!"

And when that happens, I know it. A message saying so merely confirms a piece of news some secret vein had already received, severing[20] from me an irreplaceable part of myself, letting it loose like a kite on a broken string. That is why, walking across a school campus on this particular December morning, I keep searching the sky. As if I expected to see, rather like hearts, a lost pair of kites hurrying toward heaven. **PAUSE & REFLECT**

PAUSE & REFLECT

What happens to Buddy's friend after he leaves?

Possible answer: After Buddy leaves his friend, she stays at home. At first, she continues to bake the fruitcakes without him. Later on, she begins to confuse him with another Buddy who died in the 1880s. Finally, she passes away.

IN OTHER WORDS Buddy and his friend never spend Christmas together again. He is sent to a military school, and she is left alone with her dog. For a few more years, Buddy's friend sends him fruitcakes for Christmas, but one year they stop coming. When that happens, Buddy knows she has died. He says it makes him feel as if a part of himself has been lost.

19. **reveille-ridden** (REV uh lee RID uhn): dominated by an early-morning signal, as on a bugle, to wake soldiers or campers.
20. **severing** (SEV er ing): cutting off.

Text Analysis: Details of Setting

Find one example of how the setting of "A Christmas Memory" influences the characters. Then find an example of how the setting creates a conflict for the characters. Record this information in the right-hand column of the chart.

For this chart, answers will vary. See samples below.

Role of Setting	Example of Setting
Setting can influence characters by • determining how people live and the jobs they can have • shaping their personalities, their dreams, and their values	*"Of the ingredients that go into our fruitcakes, whiskey is the most expensive, as well as the hardest to obtain: State laws forbid its sale." (Lines 144–146)*
Setting can create conflict by • exposing the characters to dangerous weather, such as a storm • making characters live through a difficult time period, such as the Great Depression	*"But before these purchases can be made, there is the question of money. Neither of us has any. Except for skinflint sums persons in the house occasionally provide (a dime is considered very big money); or what we earn ourselves from various activities..." (Lines 74–78)*

How would the story change if it were set in a city instead of the country, or in modern times instead of the past? Choose one detail from the story and explain how the story would be different if the setting were changed.

Possible answer: If the story were set in a city, a number of the events in the story would not take place. For example, Buddy and his friend would not gather windfall pecans from neighboring farms to make fruitcakes, nor, would they be able to cut down a Christmas tree for free.

After Reading

Reading Skill: Imagery

Review the description of the walk to pick out a Christmas tree in lines 268–289. The author uses vivid imagery to help you imagine the setting. In the chart below, record five examples of imagery from the passage and identify which sense each example appeals to. The first has been done for you.

For this chart, answers will vary. See samples below.

Sensory Images	
1. *"the sun, round as an orange" (line 268)*	*Sight*
2. ***"burnishes the silvered winter woods" (line 270)***	***Sight***
3. ***"the pneumonia-making coldness" (lines 274–275)***	***Touch***
4. ***"rusty pine needles brilliant with gaudy fungus and molted feathers" (lines 278–279)***	***Sight***
5. ***"the pine-heavy air" (line 288)***	***Smell***

What do you look for in a FRIEND?

Look back at the list you made on page 110 of the Top 5 Qualities of a Good Friend. Do you know someone who has all or most of those qualities? What have you learned from being friends with that person?

Answers will vary and should be based on students' lists on page 110.

Vocabulary Practice

For each set of words, circle the word whose meaning is different from the other three.

1. **(a)** depress **(b)** excite **(c)** energize **(d)** exhilarate
2. **(a)** squander **(b)** waste **(c)** save **(d)** misuse
3. **(a)** potent **(b)** mighty **(c)** possible **(d)** strong

Academic Vocabulary in Speaking

The word **distinct** (dis TINGKT) is an adjective that means *separate or different*.

I heard three **distinct** voices coming from the kitchen; two strangers were speaking with my mother.

TURN AND TALK With a partner, discuss Buddy and his friend and their **distinct** relationship. Talk about how their friendship is different and separate from the way they relate to others in the house. Be sure to use the word **distinct** in your conversation.

Encourage students to use the Academic Vocabulary word in their discussions.

Assessment Practice

DIRECTIONS Use "A Christmas Memory" to answer questions 1–6.

1 Buddy and his friend make fruitcakes each year because —

- (A) they enjoy eating them
- (B) they sell them to raise money
- (C) they send them as gifts to people they admire
- (D) they give them as gifts to their family members

2 How is Buddy's friend different from most people her age?

- (A) She still enjoys the Christmas holiday.
- (B) She is childlike in her attitudes and actions.
- (C) She has fewer friends than most.
- (D) She takes care of a young child.

3 Mr. Haha surprises Buddy most when he —

- (A) asks for a fruitcake
- (B) answers the door himself
- (C) shows him his giant razor scars
- (D) smiles and laughs

4 What happens to the two friends after the Christmas in the story?

- (A) They separate and never see each other again.
- (B) They separate but visit each other often.
- (C) They continue their yearly holiday traditions.
- (D) They both move away from home.

5 The setting affects this story because at the time —

- (A) there were few ways to entertain oneself
- (B) there wasn't enough rain to water the crops
- (C) the Great Depression meant that there was little money
- (D) America was at war

6 The following excerpt from "A Christmas Memory" is from the description of baking fruitcakes. Read the excerpt and identify the senses to which it appeals.

Eggbeaters whirl, spoons spin round in bowls of butter and sugar, vanilla sweetens the air, ginger spices it; melting, nose-tingling odors saturate the kitchen, suffuse the house, drift out to the world on puffs of chimney smoke.

- (A) touch and smell
- (B) sight and smell
- (C) hearing and sight
- (D) taste and touch

Through the Tunnel

Based on the short story by **Doris Lessing**

When is a **RISK** worth taking?

Sometimes people take risks to prove something to themselves or others. These risks can be physical, emotional, or social. But when is an action too risky?

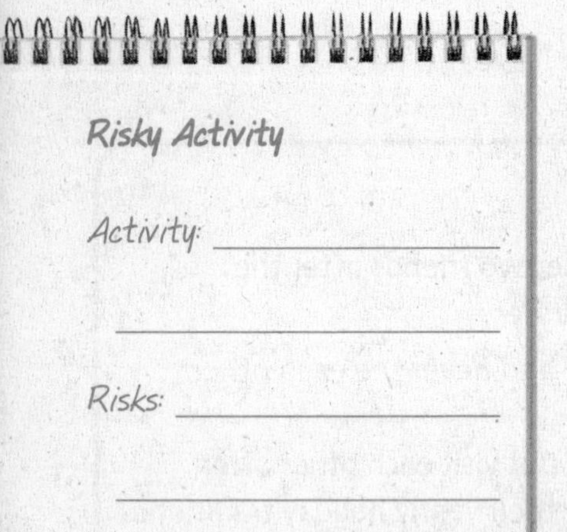

TURN AND TALK Think about a time when you or someone you know took a risk to prove something. In the notepad on the left, list the risky activity. Then, list the risks involved and the possible benefits of the activity. Finally, discuss the following question with a partner: Was the activity worth the risk?

Answers will vary.

Text Analysis: Setting as Symbol

A **symbol** is a person, place, object, or activity that stands for something else. For example, you know that a car is something that a person can drive to get somewhere. In a story, a car might also symbolize, or stand for, freedom. The **setting** of a story—the time and place in which the story takes place—can serve as a symbol, as shown in the example below.

Setting can serve as a symbol by	Example
• representing an important idea in the story • representing some element of a character or of a character's experience	A shy girl grows up on a small island but dreams of moving to the mainland. The island symbolizes the girl's loneliness and feeling of being separated from the rest of the world.

As you read "Through the Tunnel," think about what its different settings might symbolize and what they tell you about its main character, Jerry.

Reading Skill: Analyze Details

In order to understand the importance and symbolism of each setting in "Through the Tunnel," you must analyze **descriptive details** and think about the larger meanings they suggest. For example, the big beach is a familiar place where Jerry's mother goes. It might symbolize safety to Jerry. As you read, keep track of words and phrases from the text that describe each setting. Then, you can try to draw conclusions about what each setting symbolizes.

Big Beach	Bay	Tunnel
crowded *familiar*	*wild and rocky*	

Vocabulary in Context

Note: Words are listed in the order in which they appear in the story.

Inquisitive (in KWIZ ih tiv) is an adjective that means *questioning* or *curious.*

Although Jerry's mother wonders what he does at the bay, she tries not to act too **inquisitive.**

Persistence (per SIS tuhns) is a noun that means *the act of continuing to do something.*

Jerry's **persistence** in practicing helps him learn to hold his breath underwater.

Incredulous (in KREJ uh luhs) is an adjective that means *disbelieving* or *full of doubt.*

Jerry's progress seems unbelievable, so he is **incredulous** at first about how well he is doing.

Vocabulary Practice

Review the Vocabulary words and sample sentences above. Then, based on these words and sentences, answer the following question: What can you guess about Jerry's character, the kind of person he is?

Encourage students to use the Vocabulary words in their answers.

SET A PURPOSE FOR READING
Read this story to find out what one risk symbolizes to a young boy named Jerry.

THROUGH THE Tunnel

Based on the short story by
DORIS LESSING

BACKGROUND Many groups of people hold events for children who are about to become adults. In the Jewish community, thirteen-year-olds take part in a ceremony that shows they are considered adults. The Apache (uh PACH ee) people often hold a dance for teenage girls. In this story, the main character, an English boy, decides on his own to complete a difficult task and prove that he is no longer a child.

On the first morning of vacation, the young English boy looked down at a [rocky] bay and then over to the (crowded) beach. He knew the beach well. They had spent their vacation in this country in other years. His mother walked in front of him. He looked at the water and back to his mother. "Why, darling," she smiled. "Would you rather not come with me?" Jerry's contrition, or feeling of having done something wrong, sent him running after her. And yet he looked back at the [wild] bay. As he played on the (safe) beach all morning, he was thinking of it. Ⓐ

Next morning, when it was time for swimming and sunbathing, his mother said, "Are you tired of the usual beach, Jerry? Would you like to go somewhere else?"

"Oh, no!" he said quickly. Yet, walking down the path with her, he said, "I'd like to go and have a look at those rocks down there."

Ⓐ ANALYZE DETAILS
Reread lines 1–9. Circle the words or phrases that describe the big beach, and place brackets [ ] around those that describe the bay. Then place your circled words in the first box below and your bracketed words in the second box.

Big Beach
crowded safe

Bay
rocky, wild

IN OTHER WORDS Jerry and his mother are on vacation at the same beach they have visited for many years. Jerry's mother can tell that he wants to explore on his own this year. He spends the first day with her. On the second day, he admits that he would like to go to a different part of the beach.

She thought about it. It was a wild-looking place, and there was no one there, but she said, "Of course, Jerry." She walked away. He almost ran after her, but he did not.

She was thinking, Of course he's old enough to be safe without me. Have I been keeping him too close?

He was an only child, eleven years old. She was a widow; her husband had died. She wanted to take care of Jerry without being too protective. She worried as she went off to her beach. B

Once Jerry saw that his mother had reached her beach, he began the steep climb down to the bay. He slid down the last few yards. He saw the shining movement of water over white sand and sharp rocks. Beyond the bay, the sea was a solid, heavy blue.

He ran into the water. He was a good swimmer. He went out fast over the sand. Then he crossed a middle area where rocks lay like monsters under the surface. Finally he was in the real sea—a warm sea with cold currents from the deep water.

IN OTHER WORDS Jerry's mother tells him he can go play on the rocks. Even though she is still worried, she wants to trust that Jerry will be safe without her. She is afraid that she has been babying him. Jerry goes to the bay and swims out to sea.

Jerry swam out past the **promontory** of land that jutted out into the open sea. He could see his mother, like a speck of yellow under an umbrella. He swam back to shore. He felt relieved that she was there, but all at once very lonely.

Monitor Your Comprehension

B SETTING AS SYMBOL

Reread lines 19–23. What does Jerry's mother worry about? What do her fears lead you to think the bay might symbolize?

Possible answer: Jerry's mother worries about her son's safety and about her ability to care for him without being overly protective. The bay symbolizes the excitement and dangers of adulthood from which she cannot protect Jerry.

VISUAL VOCABULARY

A **promontory** (PROM uhn tawr ee) is a high ridge of land or rock sticking out into a body of water.

Looking up, he saw some boys run down to the rocks. They spoke a language he did not understand. He wanted badly to be one of them. One of them smiled and waved. In a minute, Jerry swam to the rocks beside them. He smiled with a nervous supplication,[1] letting them know without words that he was asking to join them. They shouted cheerful greetings at him. When he didn't understand, they realized that he was a foreigner—that he had come from another country. But he was happy to be included in the group. **C**

C LANGUAGE COACH
A **pronoun** is a word that stands for one or more nouns or other pronouns. A pronoun's **antecedent** is the word or words for which the pronoun stands. Circle each instance of *they* and *them* in this paragraph. *They* and *them* are pronouns, and *some boys* (line 37) is their antecedent.

The boys began diving from a high point into the blue sea. They were big boys—men, to Jerry. They watched him dive. He felt accepted, as if he were part of the group.

Soon the biggest boy dove into the water, and did not come up. The others watched. Jerry waited, scared. After a long time, the boy came up on the other side of a big dark rock. The rest of them dived in. Through the heavy blue water, dark shapes moved.

IN OTHER WORDS Jerry sees some older boys playing on the rocks. He wants to be friends, but he doesn't understand their language. Jerry admires the boys and is happy when they pay attention to him. One of the boys dives in but doesn't come up right away. Jerry worries about the boy.

► Where and when does the boy finally surface? Underline the sentence that tells you.

Jerry dived. He passed the underwater swimmers. He saw a black wall of rock ahead, touched it, and rose to the surface. Under him, in the water, the swimmers had disappeared. Then one by one, the boys came up on the far side of the rock. He understood that they had swum through some hole in it. He plunged down again but could see only the blank rock. When he came up, the boys were preparing to dive again. In a panic of failure, he yelled up, in English, "Look at me!" He began splashing and kicking in the water like a foolish dog. **D**

D ANALYZE DETAILS
Underline details in lines 54–62 that explain what the bigger boys are doing. What does Jerry do in response?

Jerry plunges down into the water to find the hole; however, he finds only blank rock. To distract the boys, he yells and splashes and kicks in the water to get their attention.

1. **supplication** (suhp lih KAY shuhn): a humble request or prayer.

They looked down, frowning. He knew the frown. At moments of failure, when he clowned to get his mother's attention, she looked at him the same way.

The boys dove into the water again. Jerry started counting: one, two, three. . . . When he reached fifty, he was terrified. They must all be drowning! At a hundred, he wondered if he should yell for help. He counted faster, as if to hurry them up. And then, at a hundred and sixty, the water beyond the rock was full of boys. They swam back to the shore without looking at him.

IN OTHER WORDS Jerry dives into the water to find out how the older boy reached the other side of the rocks. The other boys swim through a gap in the rock to the other side. Jerry tries to get their attention by being silly, but they look at him and frown. Frightened, Jerry counts how long it takes the boys to swim through the tunnel.

Jerry climbed back to the diving rock and sat down, embarrassed. The boys were gathering their clothing and running away. There was no one to see him, and he cried. **E**

After a long time had passed, he swam out to where he could see his mother. He swam back and dived down again into the blue pool until he touched the wall of rock. But the salt hurt his eyes and he could not see.

He swam to shore, and then returned to the house to wait for his mother. "I want some swimming goggles," he said when she arrived.

She gave him a patient, **inquisitive** look and said, "Well, of course, darling." But he wanted them now—this very minute! He bothered his mother until she took him to a shop. She bought the goggles, and he grabbed them and ran off to the bay.

IN OTHER WORDS The older boys leave and Jerry cries. He looks for his mother and then dives down to look at the tunnel through the rock. The salt water hurts his eyes, so he asks his mother for swimming goggles. He gets the goggles and runs back to the bay.

Monitor Your Comprehension

E SETTING AS SYMBOL

How has the setting changed in lines 70–75? What makes Jerry upset?

The boys have swum back to shore, leaving Jerry on the swimming rock. Jerry gets upset because he feels like the boys are deliberately abandoning him.

VOCABULARY

The word **inquisitive** (in KWIZ ih tiv) is an adjective that means *questioning* or *curious.*

Why does Jerry's mother give him an *inquisitive* look? Why does she find his request a bit strange?

Possible answer: She is unsure what Jerry will do with the goggles and cannot figure out why he needs them to play on the rocks.

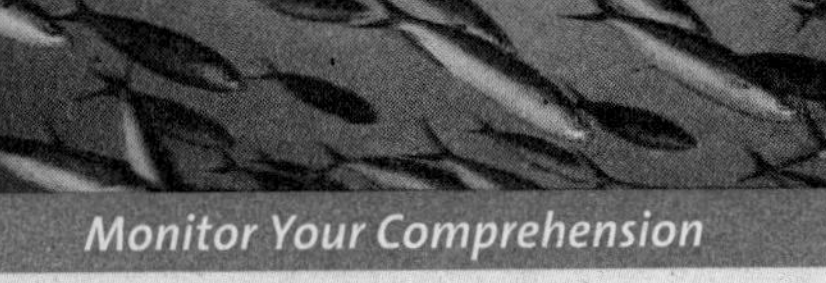

Monitor Your Comprehension

PAUSE & REFLECT

How do you think Jerry feels at this moment?

Possible answer: I think that Jerry feels happy that he has succeeded in finding the tunnel through the rock.

Jerry swam out to the big rock. He put the goggles on tightly, filled his lungs, and floated, face down. Now he could see the white sand six or seven feet down, and fish swimming beneath him. There was the great rock the big boys had swum into. He could see no hole in it. He swam down to its bottom.

Again and again he rose, filled his lungs with air, and went down. Again and again he touched the surface of the rock until he found the opening. **PAUSE & REFLECT**

Holding a rock to weigh him down, he sank to the sandy bottom. He could see the hole, but not inside it. He tried to go in.

He got his head in, found his shoulders slightly stuck, moved them in sidewise, and was inside up to his waist. Something soft and clammy touched his mouth, making him think of octopuses. Frightened, he pushed himself out backward and saw a harmless bit of seaweed. But it was enough. He swam to shore. He knew he must find his way through that cave and out the other side. F

F LANGUAGE COACH

In English, the letter combination *gh* is pronounced several different ways. Very often, *gh* is silent, as in *taught* (tawt), or pronounced like the letter *f*, as in *cough* (kawf). The *gh* combination appears in five words in lines 95–104. Find the words. Then, underline the ones in which *gh* is silent and circle the one in which *gh* is pronounced like the letter *f*.

IN OTHER WORDS Wearing his goggles, Jerry finds the tunnel through the rock. He swims into the tunnel up to his waist, but he is scared and backs out. Then he makes a decision.

► What has Jerry decided he will do? With a partner, discuss why this is so important to him.

Jerry decides that he will figure out how to get through the cave and out the other side of the rock. It is important to him to figure it out because he wants to feel grown up enough to do the same things as the other boys.

First he must learn to control his breathing. Jerry let himself down into the water and counted. Fifty-one, fifty-two. . . . His chest hurt. He went up into the air. The late afternoon sun was low, and he rushed to the villa, the nice house in which they were staying. His mother said, "Did you enjoy yourself?" He answered, "Yes."

All night the boy dreamed of the water-filled cave in the rock. As soon as breakfast was over, he went to the bay.

That night, his nose bled badly. For hours he had been underwater, learning to hold his breath. Now he felt weak and dizzy.

That day and the next, Jerry exercised his lungs as if his whole life depended upon it. Again his nose bled at night. The next day, his mother made him come with her to that other beach. To Jerry, it now seemed like a place for small children. It was not his beach. G

IN OTHER WORDS Jerry practices holding his breath. Each time he practices, he is able to hold it a little longer, but practicing makes him feel sick. It also makes his nose bleed. Jerry's mother makes him stay with her and rest for a day.

The next day he did not ask for permission to go to his beach. A day's rest, he discovered, had improved his count by ten. The big boys had made the passage while he counted a hundred and sixty. Probably now, if he tried, he could get through that tunnel, but he was not going to try yet. **Persistence** made him wait. In the meantime, he lay underwater on the white sand and studied the entrance to the tunnel until he knew every corner of it.

He could now hold his breath without effort for two minutes. He was **incredulous** and then proud. He felt very close to having his adventure.

One morning his mother told him that they would go home in four days. Two days before they were to leave—a day of triumph when he increased his count by fifteen—his nose bled so badly that he felt dizzy and had to lie down. He was frightened. [What if he got dizzy in the tunnel? What if he died there, trapped?] He thought maybe he would return to the house and lie down. Next summer, perhaps, he would go through the hole. PAUSE & REFLECT

Monitor Your Comprehension

G SETTING AS SYMBOL
Underline the sentences that tell what Jerry now thinks of the big beach. What might this beach symbolize to Jerry now? Share your thoughts with a classmate.

To Jerry, the beach symbolizes the rejected world of childhood.

VOCABULARY
The word **persistence** (per SIS tuhns) is a noun that means *the act of continuing to do something.*

VOCABULARY
The word **incredulous** (in KREJ uh luhs) is an adjective that means *disbelieving* or *full of doubt.*

PAUSE & REFLECT
Reread lines 132–139. Place brackets [ ] around Jerry's doubts and fears. Do you think his fears are reasonable? Why or why not?

Possible answer: The journey through the tunnel is dangerous, so, I think that Jerry's fears are reasonable. Also, since no one knows what he is doing, no one would know where to look for him if he were to get stuck.

IN OTHER WORDS Once again Jerry practices holding his breath. He thinks he might be able to get through the tunnel but decides to keep practicing instead. Then his mother tells him that they'll be leaving soon. He is determined to swim through the rock before they leave, but then he suffers another bloody nose and more dizziness. He begins to doubt that he will swim through the hole this year.

► With a partner, discuss what you think Jerry will do.

Students may discuss that Jerry will try one last time to swim through the tunnel before he and his mother leave for the summer.

But even after he made the decision, he knew that now, when his nose had only just stopped bleeding, when his head was still sore—this was the moment to try. If he did not do it now, he never would.

He put on his goggles. His hands were shaking. He filled his lungs twice, and then sank to the bottom and began to count. He wiggled his shoulders into the hole and kicked himself along.

Soon he was inside a small hole. It was filled with water that pushed him up against the sharp roof. He pulled himself along with his hands—fast, fast—and used his legs as levers. His head knocked against something. A sharp pain dizzied him. Fifty, fifty-one, fifty-two. . . . It was dark, and the water pressed upon him. Seventy-one, seventy-two. . . . There was no strain on his lungs, but his head ached.

IN OTHER WORDS Jerry decides to swim through the tunnel. He puts on his goggles, takes a deep breath, and swims in. He grabs on to the rocks to pull himself along, counting to keep track of how long he has been underwater.

► How is Jerry feeling so far? Underline the details that tell you.

Jerry feels nervous but determined to try one more time to swim through the tunnel.

He kept being pressed against the sharp, slimy roof. He kicked forward, ducked his head, and swam. His feet and hands moved freely. The hole must have widened out. (H)

A hundred, a hundred and one. . . . The water became lighter. Victory filled him. His lungs were beginning to hurt.

(H) ANALYZE DETAILS

In the box below, list details from lines 147–156 that describe how the tunnel looks and feels to Jerry now that he is inside it.

Tunnel
small hole, filled with water, *sharp, slimy roof, dark, water pressing on him, hole widened at end of tunnel*

A few more strokes and he would be out. He was counting wildly. The water was a clear jewel-green all around him. Then he saw, above his head, a crack running up through the rock. Sunlight was falling through it, showing only darkness ahead. He wished the crack were filled with air, not water.

IN OTHER WORDS As Jerry swims, he is pushed into the top of the tunnel. He begins to tire. Suddenly, he sees light and thinks he is almost out. Then he realizes the light is not coming from the end of the tunnel after all.

► Where is the light coming from? Circle the source of the light.

The light is coming through a crack in the rock.

He was at the end of what he could do, but he must go on into the blackness, or he would drown. He clutched at rocks in the dark, hanging on to one and then the next to pull himself forward. He struggled on in the darkness, feeling that he was dying. Pain filled his head, and then the darkness cracked with an explosion of green light. He pushed himself out into the open sea.

The boy drifted to the surface, his face turned up to the air. He was gasping like a fish. Then he was pulling himself onto the diving rock. He lay down and pulled off his goggles, full of blood from the bleeding of his nose.

After a time, his heart slowed down, his eyes cleared, and he sat up. He could see the local boys diving and playing half a mile away. [He did not want them.] He only wanted to get home and lie down. ❶

IN OTHER WORDS Just when Jerry thinks he can't go on, he reaches the end of the tunnel. He comes up gasping for air with his goggles full of blood. Jerry sees the local boys, but he isn't interested in them anymore. He just wants to go home.

---

❶ ANALYZE DETAILS

How have Jerry's feelings toward the local boys changed? Place brackets [ ] around the sentence that tells you.

At the house, Jerry threw himself on his bed and slept. He woke at the sound of his mother returning. He rushed to the bathroom. She must not see his face with blood or tears on it. He met her as she walked inside, smiling. **PAUSE & REFLECT**

"Have a nice morning?" she asked.

"Oh, yes, thank you," he said.

"You look a bit pale." And then, sharp and anxious, "How did you bang your head?"

"Oh, just banged it," he told her.

She looked at him closely. He was strained; his eyes were glazed-looking. She was worried. And then she said to herself, Oh, don't fuss!

They sat down to lunch.

"Mummy," he said, "I can stay underwater for two minutes—three minutes, at least."

"Can you, darling?" she said. "Well, I wouldn't overdo it. I don't think you ought to swim anymore today."

She was ready for an argument, but he gave in at once. It was no longer of the least importance to go to the bay. (J)

IN OTHER WORDS Jerry falls asleep, and his mother wakes him up. Jerry doesn't want to scare her, so he quickly washes the blood and tears away. His mother is worried about him. Jerry tells her he can hold his breath for two to three minutes. Jerry's mother tells him that he had better not swim anymore that day. He does not disagree.

► Why is Jerry no longer eager to swim in the bay? Share your thoughts with a classmate.

Students should discuss that Jerry is no longer eager to swim in the bay because he has already achieved what he wanted to do there—swim through the tunnel.

Monitor Your Comprehension

PAUSE & REFLECT

With a partner, discuss why Jerry doesn't want his mother to see his blood or tears. Do you think he would feel differently if he had given up instead of swimming through the tunnel?

Students should discuss that Jerry does not want his mother to worry about his safety or to restrict his activities to the beach for the remainder of their visit.

(J) SETTING AS SYMBOL

Does the bay still symbolize the same things for Jerry as it did at the beginning of the story? Explain.

Possible answer: For Jerry, the bay no longer has the same appeal as it did at the story's beginning because he has accomplished what the other boys have done.

After Reading

Text Analysis: Setting as Symbol

Consider each of the following aspects, or features, of the tunnel and write down your thoughts about it. Then decide what you think Jerry's swim through the tunnel symbolizes.

For this chart, answers will vary. See samples below.

Aspect of the Tunnel	My Thoughts
1. The danger it represents for Jerry	*Its danger represents the physical and psychological limitations that Jerry must overcome to pass through the tunnel.*
2. Its connection to the older boys	*Its connection to the older boys represents is association with the excitement and challenges of adulthood.*
3. How it looks and feels	*Its look and feel represents the uncertainties and unknown aspects of growing older.*
4. How Jerry feels about it	*Jerry's interest in the tunnel represents his interest in growing up and moving away from his mother.*
5. What Jerry's swim though the tunnel symbolizes	*Jerry's swim represents his ability to overcome his fears of the unknown and the start of his transition into adulthood.*

Review the thoughts you noted in the chart above. Does Jerry accomplish his goal? What is Jerry like before his swim? What is he like after it? How has he changed?

Jerry does accomplish his goal of swimming through the tunnel. Before the swim, he scares easily and worries a lot. After the swim, he seems more confident and sure of himself.

Reading Skill: Analyze Details

Look back at the details you recorded about each setting as you read "Through the Tunnel." For the big beach and the bay, find a passage in the text that best sums up each place and write it in the chart below. Then, write a sentence explaining the major differences between the two settings.

For this chart, answers will vary. See samples below.

Big Beach	Bay
"The next day, his mother made him come with her to that other beach. To Jerry, it now seemed like a place for small children. It was not his beach." (lines 117–120)	*"he began the steep climb down to the bay. He slid down the last few yards. He saw the shining movement of water over white sand and sharp rocks. Beyond the bay, the sea was a solid, heavy blue." (lines 24–28)*
Differences: *At the big beach, families can easily supervise children playing nearby, but the bay is full of steep cliffs, sharp rocks, and fast-moving water.*	

When is a **RISK** worth taking?

How would you decide if the possible rewards of a risk are worth taking that risk?

Possible answer: I would calculate that the ratio of the upside (reward) versus the downside (danger) must be high.

Vocabulary Practice

Circle T or F below to tell whether each statement is true or false. If necessary, review the definitions of the Vocabulary words on page 131.

T (F) 1. An **inquisitive** child will rarely ask why.

(T) F 2. A person shows **persistence** by repeating a job until she gets it right.

(T) F 3. If you are **incredulous** about a friend's advice, you will probably ignore it.

Academic Vocabulary in Speaking

The word **contribute** (kuhn TRIB yoot) is a verb that means *to provide a thing or idea that helps create a result.*

Mark's feelings of loneliness **contribute** to his longing for new friends.

TURN AND TALK With a partner, talk about how the older boys and their actions **contribute** to Jerry's desire to swim through the tunnel. Be sure to use the word **contribute** in your conversation.

Encourage students to use the Academic Vocabulary word in their discussions.

Assessment Practice

DIRECTIONS Use "Through the Tunnel" to answer questions 1–6.

1 Which word best describes Jerry's journey through the tunnel?

- (A) Interesting
- (B) Relaxing
- (C) Boring
- (D) Frightening

2 What happens between Jerry and the older boys?

- (A) They show him how to swim through the tunnel.
- (B) They ask if he will join them.
- (C) They are friendly at first but then ignore him.
- (D) They make fun of him.

3 Which detail from the story shows that Jerry's mother wants him to grow up, even if it is difficult for her?

- (A) She lets him go to the bay by himself.
- (B) She refuses to buy him goggles.
- (C) She makes him stay home and rest one day.
- (D) She worries about him.

4 Which word best describes Jerry's character?

- (A) Scared
- (B) Shy
- (C) Mature
- (D) Determined

5 The sharp rocks in the tunnel may symbolize —

- (A) the bravery of the older boys
- (B) painful, pointy rocks
- (C) Jerry's mother's worries about him
- (D) the unexpected difficulties of growing up

6 Which sentence best expresses the symbolic meaning of the story?

- (A) Children have to rebel against their parents to grow up.
- (B) Mothers and sons will never understand each other.
- (C) The journey to adulthood can be dangerous and frightening.
- (D) It is difficult to be friends with people from other cultures.

The Cask of Amontillado

Based on the short story by **Edgar Allan Poe**

Is **REVENGE** ever justified?

The narrator of "The Cask of Amontillado" wants revenge against another man he believes has harmed him. When you take revenge against someone, you harm that person to get even with him or her for harming you.

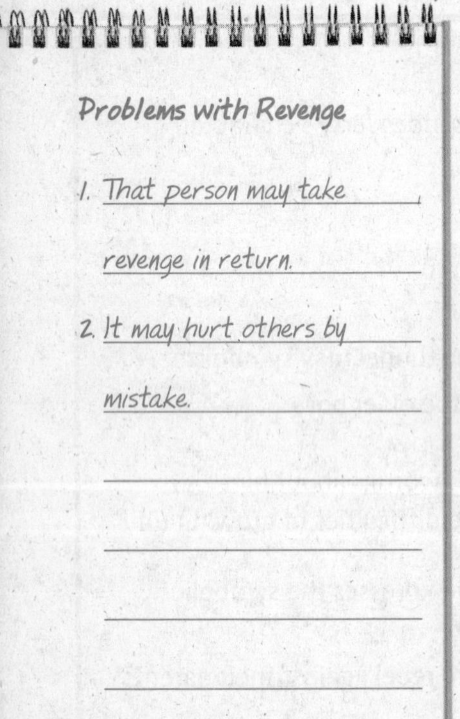

Problems with Revenge
1. That person may take revenge in return.
2. It may hurt others by mistake.

TURN AND TALK Taking revenge may sound like a satisfying way to get even with someone, but it can have negative consequences. What are some of the problems that may result from taking revenge on another person? Write your examples in the notepad to the left. Then, discuss your list with a partner.

Answers will vary.

Text Analysis: Mood

Mood is the feeling or atmosphere the writer creates for the reader. "The Cask of Amontillado" is a terrifying story about a man who plots a shocking act of revenge. Poe does not reveal what this act of revenge is until the story is almost over. Instead, he keeps us in **suspense,** a continual state of excitement about will happen next. But from the beginning, the mood Poe creates makes us feel that something horrifying is about to happen.

Poe creates this mood of suspense and horror by using **imagery** to describe the story's **setting,** where the story takes place. To create this imagery, he uses sensory details—details that appeal to sight, hearing, taste, touch, or smell. As you read, you will fill out a chart like the one below. This step will help you identify how Poe uses imagery to create a suspenseful mood.

MOOD: Suspenseful, horrifying	
Example of imagery	**Which senses does imagery use?**
"Drops of moisture trickle among the bones." (lines 73–74)	touch, sight

Reading Skill: Paraphrase

To make sure you understand the events in this story, try **paraphrasing**—restating in your own words the information you've read. A paraphrase contains all the details of the original text. In this example, the narrator, who tells the story, meets a man against whom he secretly plans revenge.

Text		My paraphrase
"I smiled at him as usual whenever I met him. He didn't guess that I smiled at the thought of destroying him." (lines 5–6)	→	*The narrator pretends he is happy to see the other man, but he is lying. What he really wants to do is crush him.*

As you read this story, you will fill out a chart like the one above to help you understand difficult passages in the story.

Vocabulary in Context

Note: Words are listed in the order in which they appear in the story.

Impunity (im PYOO nuh tee) is a noun that means *freedom from punishment.*

He is not afraid of being punished for what he does because he has **impunity.**

Repose (rih POHZ) is a verb that means *to lie dead or at rest.*

Many buried bodies **repose** in the tombs underground.

Aperture (AP uhr chuhr) is a noun that means *an opening, such as a doorway.*

He entered the dark room through an **aperture** in the wall.

Subside (sub SYD) is a verb that means *to slow or decrease.*

When he realizes that no one hears him, his screams **subside.**

Vocabulary Practice

Review the words and sample sentences above. Then, based on these words, discuss with a partner what you think might happen in "The Cask of Amontillado." Be sure to use the words in your discussion.

Encourage students to use the Vocabulary words in their discussions.

SET A PURPOSE FOR READING
Read this story to find out how a mysterious narrator plans revenge against his worst enemy.

The Cask of Amontillado

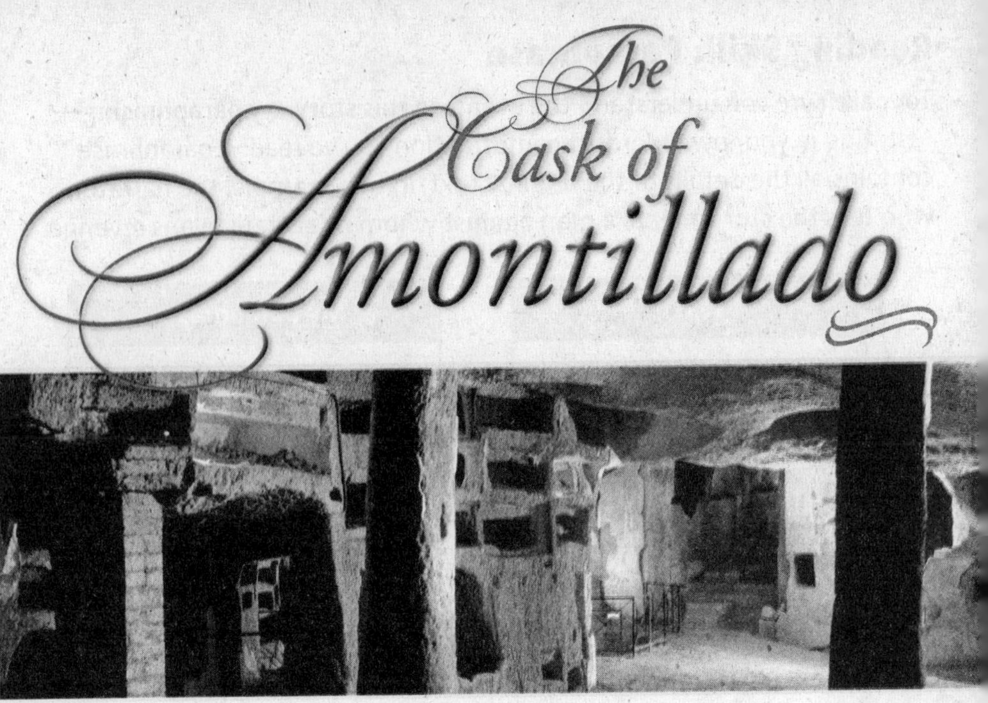

Based on the short story by
EDGAR ALLAN POE

BACKGROUND Long ago in Italy, Christians buried their dead in small rooms inside long underground tunnels called catacombs (KAT uh kohmz). Later, rich families built catacombs underneath their homes, storing containers of wine in the tunnels' cool, dark rooms. Much of this story takes place in catacombs under the home of the story's main character. The title refers to a container of a rare and expensive type of wine.

I put up with Fortunato[1] for years. When he insulted me, however, I decided to fight back. I wouldn't threaten him. Instead, I would punish him with **impunity**—I wanted to make him suffer, but I did not want to get caught.

VOCABULARY
The word **impunity** (im PYOO nuh tee) is a noun that means *freedom from punishment.*

I smiled at him as usual whenever I met him. He didn't guess that I smiled at the thought of destroying him.

Fortunato was a man to respect and fear. But he had a weakness: He was too proud of his knowledge of wines. He thought he knew everything about them. I plotted to use his pride against him.

1. **Fortunato** (for too NAH toh).

One evening during carnival[2] I ran into Fortunato. He wore a clown costume, and bells jingled on his cone-shaped cap. He was drunk.

I said, "It's lucky we met. I just bought some wine. It's supposed to be Amontillado.[3] I have my doubts."

"Amontillado? To buy such a fine wine during carnival—impossible!"

"Silly me, I paid the full price. I should have talked to you first. But I couldn't find you and I was afraid of losing a bargain."

"Amontillado!"

"I have my doubts," I said.

"Amontillado!"

"I want to know the truth."

"Amontillado!"

IN OTHER WORDS Montresor, the character telling the story, says that Fortunato has somehow insulted him. Montresor plans revenge on Fortunato to get even for this insult. Montresor tells Fortunato that he is worried that the expensive wine he recently bought may be fake.

"Since you're busy, I'll go to Luchesi.[4] If anyone knows wine, he does. He'll tell me—"

"Luchesi!" Fortunato snorted, laughing loudly to show his low opinion of the man. "He just pretends to know about wine. He doesn't know what he's talking about."

"Some think he knows as much as you do about wine."

"Let's go to your cellars so I can taste the Amontillado."

"No. The cellars are damp; I can see that you already have a bad cold. Besides, you have other plans. Luchesi—"

"I don't have plans. Come," he insisted.

"You obviously have a bad cold. The cellars are very damp." Your cold will get much worse."

"Let's go anyway. This cold is nothing."

I pulled on a cloak to keep warm and let him lead me to my palace. Ⓐ

---

2. **carnival** (KAR nuh vuhl): a festival that includes colorful costumes, masks, and feasts.
3. **Amontillado** (uh mahn tee YAH doh): a type of pale, dry wine.
4. **Luchesi** (loo KEH see).

Monitor Your Comprehension

Answer to discussion question at the bottom of the page: Students should discuss that the reader already knows that Montresor wants revenge on Fortunato and wants to lure Fortunato to his home. As a result, Montresor may not be telling the truth about the wine, using it to get Fortunato to come to his home.

Ⓐ PARAPHRASE

Paraphrase lines 33–35 below:

My Paraphrase

Possible answer: Fortunato says he doesn't have plans, but the narrator tells him not to come because it will be bad for his health.

Then, with a partner, discuss whether Montresor is honest with Fortunato.

IN OTHER WORDS Montresor says he will ask Luchesi, another wine lover, to judge the wine. Fortunato wants to prove that he knows more about wine than Luchesi. He insists that they go to Montresor's wine cellar to taste and judge the wine.

► With a partner, discuss how Montresor persuades Fortunato to visit his palace.

Students should discuss that Montresor persuades Fortunato to visit his palace by tempting him with a bottle of what he believes to be Amontillado and by appealing to Fortunato's vanity in suggesting that he could get advice from Luchesi as well.

As I expected, the servants had all gone to the carnival, so no one was home. Carrying torches, we went down many stairs to the catacombs, a series of cold, damp cellars under my palace. They held the bones of my ancestors, the Montresors. I also used them to store wine.

My drunken friend walked unsteadily, as if he might fall down; his bells jingled.

"The Amontillado?" he said.

"It's farther on." I said. "Look; do you see the white lines like cobwebs on the walls? It is niter, salt deposits left because of the dampness. . . . How long have you had that cough?" B

B MOOD

Reread lines 39–49. Underline the words or phrases that establish a mood of suspense and horror in this description of the story's **setting.**

"Ugh! ugh! ugh!— ugh! ugh! ugh!"

My friend coughed so hard he could not answer me for several minutes.

"It's nothing," he said at last.

"Come," I said. "We'll go back. Your health is important. You are rich, respected. You are happy—as I was once. Besides, I can ask Luchesi—"

"I won't die of a cough," he said.

"True," I replied. "But you should be careful. Here, this wine will keep you warm."

I offered him wine from a bottle that lay in our path.

"I drink to the dead that **repose** here," Fortunato said.

"And I drink to your long life," I replied. PAUSE & REFLECT

VOCABULARY

The word **repose** (rih POHZ) is a verb that means *to lie dead or at rest.*

PAUSE & REFLECT

Reread lines 47–62. Montresor plans to take revenge on Fortunato. But he pretends to be worried about Fortunato's health, gives him more wine, and drinks to his long life. With a partner, discuss why Montresor does this.

Students should discuss that Montresor expresses concern about Fortunato's health because he does not want Fortunato to suspect that he plans to harm him.

IN OTHER WORDS Montresor leads Fortunato into the catacombs where his ancestors are buried and his wine is stored. Fortunato is sick and Montresor pretends to try to persuade him to leave the cold and damp catacombs. Fortunato insists that they keep going.

"These tombs go on and on," he said as we continued.

"The Montresors were a great family," I answered.

"I forget what your family's coat of arms is."

"Two symbols represent the Montresors: a human foot crushing a snake. The snake is biting deeply into the heel."

"And the motto?" he asked.

"'Nobody attacks me without being punished.'" I replied.

"Good!" he said.

We went farther into the catacombs. I paused.

"The niter!" I said. "See how much more there is. We're below the river. The air is *terribly* damp. Drops of moisture trickle among the bones. Let's return before it's too late. Your cough—!"

"No," he said. "Let's go on. But first, more wine." C

C MOOD

In lines 71–74, Poe creates **suspense** by having Montresor describe the **setting** as he and Fortunato go deeper into the catacombs. Underline the **imagery** Poe uses to describe the setting. With a partner, discuss how this imagery creates a scary **mood.**

Students should discuss that the imagery creates a scary mood because the reader senses just how far underground the two men have gone, how damp and dark it is in the catacombs, and how close they are to the bones resting within the catacombs.

IN OTHER WORDS Montresor's family motto means "Nobody attacks me without being punished for it." Fortunato does not realize this motto reveals Montresor's desire to punish him. Montresor suggests that they turn back. Fortunato refuses again. He is already drunk, but he asks for more wine.

► What image appears on the coat of arms of Montresor's family? Circle the statement that tells you.

The coat of arms is a human foot crushing a snake; the snake is biting into the heel of the foot.

I broke open another bottle. He drank it all and then, with his hand, made a strange gesture I did not understand. I looked at him in surprise.

"Aha," he said. "I see you are not a Mason."[5]

---

5. **Mason** (MAY suhn): a Freemason, a member of a secret club with its own rituals and signs. Members use secret signs to recognize each other.

VISUAL VOCABULARY

A **trowel** (TROW uhl) is a tool used for building walls. The trowel is used to smooth mortar (MAWR ter), material that holds bricks or stones together.

"Oh, yes," I said, "Yes, I am."

"You? Impossible! Show me the secret sign," he said.

"It is this," I answered, pulling a **trowel** from my cape.

"You're joking," he said, drawing back. "But let's go on."

IN OTHER WORDS Fortunato is a member of a secret group, the Freemasons. He insults Montresor by saying that Montresor could never be a Mason, a member of this group. Fortunato asks Montresor to show him the secret sign that proves he is a Mason. Montresor reveals that he secretly has been carrying a trowel, a tool used by builders called masons. Fortunato thinks Montresor is making a joke based on the word *mason*.

As we continued, our torches barely glowed in the bad air. Finally, we entered a small chamber. Bones lined three of its walls. The bones from the fourth wall were on the ground. This bare wall opened into another small room that ended in a wall of solid rock.

"The Amontillado is inside," I said. "As for Luchesi—"

"He's a fool," said Fortunato. He swayed into the dark **aperture** with me behind him as we entered the room. Even with his torch, he could barely see where it ended. Bumping into the rock wall, he stopped, confused. Quickly I chained him to the wall. He was too surprised to stop me. I stepped back.

VOCABULARY

The word **aperture** (AP uhr chuhr) is a noun that means *an opening, such as a doorway.*

"Move your hand along the wall," I said. "You'll feel the niter. It is *very* damp. Once more let me *beg* you to return. No? Then I must leave you."

"The Amontillado!" he cried.

"True," I replied, "the Amontillado." Among the pile of bones I found building stones and cement. Using my trowel, I began to build a wall in front of the room's opening.

IN OTHER WORDS Montresor leads Fortunato deep into the damp catacombs. All around them are the bones of the dead. They reach a small room. Before Fortunato knows what is happening, Montresor chains him to one of the room's walls. Montresor begins to build a wall in front of the room's entrance.

► Discuss with a partner what may happen next.

Students may discuss that they think that Montresor is going to bury Fortunato alive by building a wall to close off the room's entrance.

The wine's effect on Fortunato was wearing off. His moaning wasn't the cry of a drunken man. Then there was a long silence. I added several more rows to the wall. Then I heard the furious rattling of the chain. It went on for several minutes. I stopped working briefly, listening to it with satisfaction.

When the rattling **subsided**, I continued building the wall. It was now as high as my chest. I shone my torch into the room to see how my work was going. Then the chained man screamed—so loudly that I became worried. But feeling the thick walls of the catacomb, I became calm again. I simply screamed back, longer and louder until Fortunato's screams stopped. D

IN OTHER WORDS Fortunato rattles his chains and screams. But Montresor is sure that the walls of the catacombs are so thick that no one can hear Fortunato scream.

Around midnight, I was almost finished. I was putting the last stone in place in the wall. Then I heard a low laugh that made my hair stand up. It was followed by a sad voice. "Ha! ha! ha!— a very good joke. We'll laugh about it later. Over our wine—he! he! he!" E

"The Amontillado!" I said.

"He! he! he—yes, the Amontillado. But isn't it late? Lady Fortunato will be waiting for me. Let's go."

"Yes," I said, "Let's go."

"For the love of God, Montresor!"

Monitor Your Comprehension

VOCABULARY

The word **subside** (sub SYD) is a verb that means *to slow down or wear off.*

D MOOD

Reread lines 107–112. Bracket [ ] the sensory **imagery** in these lines. Identify which of the five senses Poe uses to create a feeling of horror in these lines. Add them to the box below.

Which senses does Poe use?
sight, hearing, touch

E PARAPHRASE

Reread lines 113–117. In your own words, write what happens below.

My Paraphrase
Montresor is placing the last stone into the wall when Fortunato begins to laugh, remarking that Montresor is playing a joke on him that they will look back on and laugh about while drinking wine.

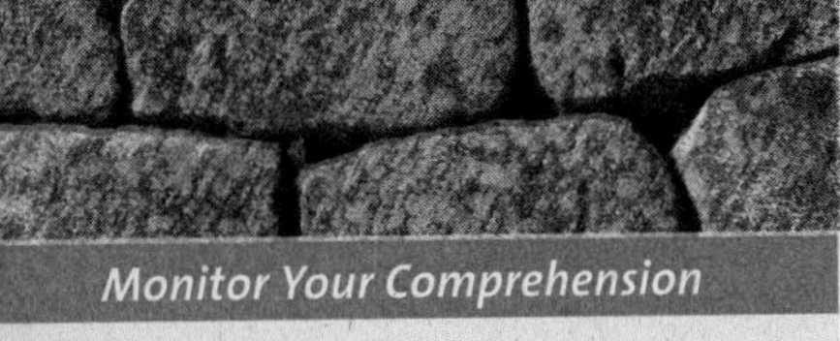

"Yes," I said, "for the love of God!" He didn't answer. I called out, "Fortunato!"

No answer. I heard only the jingling of bells. My heart grew sick—because of the dampness. I hurried to complete my work. I finished sealing up the wall. I piled the bones up against it. For half a century no one has moved them. May he rest in peace.

PAUSE & REFLECT

PAUSE & REFLECT

Reread lines 125–128. With a partner, discuss what happens in the last lines of the story. Does Montresor succeed in taking revenge against Fortunato? Does Fortunato deserve what Montresor does to him? Why or why not?

Students should discuss that Montresor succeeds in taking revenge against Fortunato by chaining him to the wall of a room and sealing the room off from view. They may discuss that the revenge Montresor took on Fortunato was too extreme and by burying Fortunato alive Montresor had committed an even greater crime.

IN OTHER WORDS Fortunato begs Montresor to release him. Montresor puts the last stone in place and seals up Fortunato forever. He piles the bones against the wall to hide his work. Since then, no one has found Fortunato.

After Reading

Text Analysis: Mood

The unique setting of "The Cask of Amontillado" helps create a frightening **mood,** or feeling of horror and suspense, in the story. Poe uses sensory **imagery** that appeals to one or more of the five senses to describe the catacombs, which are dark, damp, and filled with the bones of the dead.

Fill out the chart below with the examples of imagery from the story that gave you the strongest feeling of suspense.

For this chart, answers will vary. See samples below.

MOOD: Suspenseful, horrifying	
Example of imagery	**Which senses does imagery use?**
"Drops of moisture trickle among the bones." (lines 73–74)	touch, sight
"His moaning wasn't the cry of a drunken man: Then there was a long silence.... Then I heard the furious rattling of the chain." (lines 102–105)	*hearing*
"Carrying torches, we went down many stairs to the catacombs, a series of cold, damp cellars under my palace. They held the bones of my ancestors..." (lines 40–42)	*sight, touch*
"the chained man screamed—so loudly that I became worried. But feeling the thick walls of the catacomb, I became calm again. I simply screamed back, longer and louder until Fortunato's screams stopped." (lines 109–112)	*hearing, touch*

Why do you think these examples of imagery had such a powerful effect?

Possible answer: I think these images had a powerful effect because they communicated the sense of panic and abandonment felt by Fortunato as he realized what was happening to him in the dark, creepy catacombs.

Is REVENGE ever justified?

What do you think is the right thing to do when you believe someone has wronged or harmed you? Explain.

Suggest that students support their opinions with specific, reasoned examples as though arguing their point of view in a debate.

After Reading

Reading Skill: Paraphrase

Reread the following passage from "The Cask of Amontillado," and then paraphrase it in the space below. Include the names of characters in your paraphrase.

Text
The wine's effect on Fortunato was wearing off. His moaning wasn't the cry of a drunken man. Then there was a long silence. I added several more rows to the wall. Then I heard the furious rattling of the chain. It went on for several minutes. I stopped working briefly, listening to it with satisfaction. (lines 102–106)

My paraphrase
Possible answer: Fortunato is no longer drunk and cries out for help as he realizes what is happening to him. Montresor continues building the wall until Fortunato begins to rattle the chains, which Montresor has used to imprison him. Montresor stops his work and listens to Fortunato, taking pleasure in his prisoner's panic.

Vocabulary Practice

Circle the part of each sentence that answers the question.

1. If you act with **impunity**, will you be punished for something you did or get away with it?
2. If you have a headache and the pain begins to **subside**, do you feel better or worse?
3. If you are in a state of **repose**, are you standing up or lying down?
4. If someone tells you to wait at the nearest **aperture**, will they meet you at a doorway or a wall?

Academic Vocabulary in Speaking

The word **perceive** (puhr SEEV) is a verb that means *to notice or become aware of.*

When he **perceives** that one of his friends is in need, he offers to help.

TURN AND TALK Why is Montresor able to trick Fortunato so successfully? How well does Fortunato **perceive** what Montresor is thinking? Discuss your ideas with a partner. Be sure to use the word **perceive** in your discussion.
Encourage students to use the Academic Vocabulary word in their discussions.

Assessment Practice

DIRECTIONS Use "The Cask of Amontillado" to answer questions 1–6.

1 Montresor, the narrator, wants revenge because —

- A Fortunato stole his Amontillado
- B Fortunato insulted him
- C Fortunato prefers Luchesi
- D Luchesi dislikes Fortunato

2 Which of the following does Montresor do to ensure the success of his plan?

- A He tells Fortunato why he is angry.
- B He goes to Fortunato's house.
- C He buys a poor-quality wine.
- D He gives Fortunato wine to drink.

3 Which of these lines from the story is an example of imagery?

- A *My friend coughed so hard he could not answer me for several minutes.*
- B *I broke open another bottle.*
- C *As we continued, our torches barely glowed in the bad air.*
- D *He was too surprised to stop me.*

4 Which of the following is the *best* paraphrase of the following quotation?

"You are rich, respected. You are happy—as I was once."

- A I am as happy as you are.
- B People have a more positive opinion of me than they do of you.
- C You are unhappy and want to seek revenge against me.
- D I used to be as happy as you are now.

5 Which of the following is not a result of the carnival setting?

- A Fortunato does not respect Luchesi.
- B Fortunato has been drinking.
- C Montresor's servants are not at home.
- D Montresor and Fortunato wear costumes.

6 Which of the following words best describes the story's mood?

- A Amusing
- B Cheerful
- C Frightening
- D Sad

A Walk in the Woods

Travel narrative by **Bill Bryson**

Where do you find ADVENTURE?

Where do you find adventure? In this selection, you'll read about the adventures of Bill Bryson, a well-known travel writer whose hike along the Appalachian Trail takes him into some unexpected situations.

TURN AND TALK If you could explore any place on Earth, what would it be? The ocean, a jungle, a city, or somewhere else? Write a list of places that sound adventurous to visit. With a partner, discuss what excites you about visiting each of these places.

Answers will vary.

Places I Want to Explore

1. *A jungle in Africa*
2. ____________
3. ____________
4. ____________
5. ____________
6. ____________
7. ____________

Text Analysis: Setting and Mood

Setting, where and when a story takes place, plays an important role in creating **mood**—the feeling the text creates for the reader. Often a writer's description of setting helps set the mood of the selection. In this selection, Bill Bryson describes the setting of the Appalachian Trail by using **sensory language**—language that appeals to one or more of the five senses (sight, smell, sound, touch, or taste). As you read, pay attention to the language Bryson uses to describe the setting and create a particular mood.

Description of Setting		Mood
"But then the wind rose, then rose again, until it was blowing with an end-of-the-world fury that seemed to have even the trees in a panic. . . ." (lines 40–42)	→	*Dangerous, threatening*
	→	
	→	

Reading Skill: Identify Author's Perspective

People often look at a subject from different perspectives, or points of view. Bill Bryson's perspective on hiking the Appalachian Trail changes when he is trapped there by a sudden snowstorm. To identify an author's perspective, pay attention to the following clues:

- Statements of the writer's opinion
- Details the writer includes

Statements and Details	What They Reveal About Author's Perspective
"Distance changes utterly when you take the world on foot." (line 1)	*Bryson believes that hiking changes the way you experience the world around you.*

As you read, you will use a chart like this one to help you identify Bill Bryson's perspective on hiking the Appalachian Trail.

Vocabulary in Context

Note: Words are listed in the order in which they appear in the selection.

Unnerving (uhn NURV ing) is an adjective that means *frightening.*
Climbing down the steep hill was **unnerving.**

Abysmal (uh BIZ muhl) is an adjective that means *very bad.*
The weather was so **abysmal** that we decided it was not safe to continue our hike.

Daunted (DAWNT ed) is an adjective that means *discouraged.*
The trail was so steep that we were **daunted** by the idea of climbing it.

Vocabulary Practice

Write a description of a dangerous landscape. Use all of the Vocabulary words in your description.

Encourage students to use the Vocabulary words in their descriptions.

SET A PURPOSE FOR READING
Read this narrative to find out how a walk in the woods can also be an exciting adventure.

A Walk in the Woods

Travel Narrative by
BILL BRYSON

BACKGROUND In this selection the narrator is hiking, or walking, the Appalachian (ap uh LAY chun) Trail with his friend Katz. The Appalachian National Scenic Trail is part of America's national park system. The trail stretches over 2,000 miles across 14 states. Hikers call it the AT. Hiking the entire AT usually takes five to seven months.

Distance changes utterly when you take the world on foot. A mile becomes a long way, two miles literally considerable, ten miles whopping, fifty miles at the very limits of conception. The world, you realize, is enormous in a way that only you and a small community of fellow hikers know. Planetary scale is your little secret.

Life takes on a neat simplicity, too. Time ceases to have any meaning. When it is dark, you go to bed, and when it is light again you get up, and everything in between is just in between. It's quite wonderful, really. Ⓐ

You have no engagements, commitments, obligations, or duties; no special ambitions and only the smallest, least complicated of wants; you exist in a tranquil tedium,[1] serenely beyond the reach of exasperation,[2] "far removed from the seats of strife," as the early explorer and botanist William Bartram put it. All that is required of you is a willingness to trudge.

Ⓐ **AUTHOR'S PERSPECTIVE**
Review lines 1–10. According to Bryson, what makes hiking "wonderful"?

Possible answer: The simplicity that life takes on as well as the way in which it changes your perspective of the world around you are two of the reasons why Bryson thinks hiking is wonderful.

1. **tranquil tedium** (TRANG kwhul TEE dee uhm): calm and peaceful boredom.
2. **exasperation** (ehg zas puh RAY shuhn): annoyance, frustration.

There is no point in hurrying because you are not actually going anywhere. However far or long you plod, you are always in the same place: in the woods. It's where you were yesterday, where you will be tomorrow. The woods is one boundless singularity. Every bend in the path presents a prospect indistinguishable from every other, every glimpse into the trees the same tangled mass. For all you know, your route could describe a very large, pointless circle. In a way, it would hardly matter. Ⓑ

At times, you become almost certain that you slabbed this hillside three days ago, crossed this stream yesterday, clambered[3] over this fallen tree at least twice today already. But most of the time you don't think. No point. Instead, you exist in a kind of mobile Zen mode,[4] your brain like a balloon tethered with string, accompanying but not actually part of the body below. Walking for hours and miles becomes as automatic, as unremarkable, as breathing. At the end of the day you don't think, "Hey, I did sixteen miles today," any more than you think, "Hey, I took eight-thousand breaths today." It's just what you do.

And so we walked, hour upon hour, over rollercoaster hills, along knife-edge ridges and over grassy balds, through depthless ranks of oak, ash, chinkapin, and pine.[5] The skies grew sullen and the air chillier, but it wasn't until the third day that the snow came. It began in the morning as thinly scattered flecks, hardly noticeable. But then the wind rose, then rose again, until it was blowing with an end-of-the-world fury that seemed to have even the trees in a panic, and with it came snow, great flying masses of it. By midday we found ourselves plodding into a stinging, cold, hard-blowing storm. Soon after, we came to a narrow **ledge** of path along a wall of rock.

IN OTHER WORDS Bill Bryson writes about his experience hiking the Appalachian Trail. He describes how huge the world seems to hikers, how simple trail life is, and how each day of hiking is much like other days. One day, however, a snowstorm blows in.

3. **slabbed . . . clambered** (KLAM buhrd): both terms mean "to climb with effort."
4. **mobile Zen mode:** feeling at one with your surroundings as you walk through them.
5. **balds . . . oak, ash, chinkapin, and pine:** areas of a mountain that are bare due to lack of trees; four types of trees common to mountain forests.

Monitor Your Comprehension

Ⓑ SETTING AND MOOD

Reread lines 17–24. Write the words and phrases that Bryson uses to describe the trail. What **mood** do they convey?

Description of Setting
"However far or long you plod, you are always in the same place: in the woods"; "The woods is one boundless singularity."; "Every bend in the path presents a prospect indistinguishable from every other"; "every glimpse into the trees the same tangled mass"; "your route could describe a very large, pointless circle"

↓

Mood
Bryson's description creates a mood of pleasant monotony—the feeling that you are experiencing the same things over and over.

VISUAL VOCABULARY

A **ledge** is a narrow shelf or ridge attached to the side of a mountain or building. Walking on a ledge can be very dangerous.

Even in ideal circumstances this path would have required delicacy and care. It was like a window ledge on a skyscraper, no more than fourteen or sixteen inches wide, and crumbling in places, with a sharp drop on one side of perhaps eighty feet, and long, looming stretches of vertical granite on the other. Once or twice I nudged foot-sized rocks over the side and watched with faint horror as they crashed and tumbled to improbably remote resting places. The trail was cobbled with rocks and threaded with wandering tree roots against which we constantly stubbed and stumbled, and veneered[6] everywhere with polished ice under a thin layer of powdery snow. At exasperatingly frequent intervals, the path was broken by steep, thickly bouldered streams, frozen solid and ribbed with blue ice, which could only be negotiated in a crablike crouch. And all the time, as we crept along on this absurdly narrow, dangerous perch, we were half-blinded by flying snow and jostled by gusts of wind, which roared through the dancing trees and shook us by our packs. This wasn't a blizzard; it was a tempest. We proceeded with painstaking deliberativeness, placing each foot solidly before lifting the one behind. Even so, twice Katz made horrified, heartfelt, comic-book noises ("AIEEEEE!" and "EEEARGH!") as his footing went, and I turned to find him hugging a tree, feet skating, his expression bug-eyed and fearful. C

It was deeply **unnerving**. It took us over two hours to cover six-tenths of a mile of trail. By the time we reached solid ground at a place called Bearpen Gap, the snow was four or five inches deep and accumulating fast. The whole world was white, filled with dime-sized snowflakes that fell at a slant before being caught by the wind and hurled in a variety of directions. We couldn't see more than fifteen or twenty feet ahead, often not even that.

The trail crossed a logging road, then led straight up Albert Mountain, a bouldered summit 5,250 feet above sea level, where the winds were so wild and angry that they hit the mountain with an actual wallop sound and forced us to shout to hear each other. We started up and hastily retreated. Hiking packs leave you with

C SETTING AND MOOD
Underline the sensory language in lines 47–68 that shows how dangerous the trail has become.

VOCABULARY
The word **unnerving** (uhn NURV ing) is an adjective that means *frightening*.

6. **veneered** (vuh NIHRD): covered with a thin layer of material.

no recognizable center of gravity at the best of times; here we were literally being blown over. Confounded, we stood at the bottom of the summit and looked at each other. This was really quite grave. We were caught between a mountain we couldn't climb and a ledge we had no intention of trying to renegotiate. Our only apparent option was to pitch our tents—if we could in this wind—crawl in, and hope for the best. I don't wish to reach for melodrama, but people have died in less trying circumstances. **D**

IN OTHER WORDS It is extremely difficult to walk the trail. It has a steep drop-off on one side. It takes them two hours to walk along the ledge to a safer place. They try to follow the trail up a mountain, but they have to turn around because of the strong winds. They don't know what to do next.

► With a partner, discuss what you think will happen next.

Students may discuss that the hikers decide to set up camp and wait for the storm to pass before continuing their journey.

I dumped my pack and searched through it for my trail map. Appalachian Trail maps are so monumentally useless that I had long since given up using them. They vary somewhat, but most are on an **abysmal** scale of 1:100,000, which ludicrously compresses every kilometer of real world into a mere centimeter of map.[7] Imagine a square kilometer of physical landscape and all that it might contain—logging roads, streams, a mountaintop or two, perhaps a fire tower, a knob or grassy bald, the wandering AT,[8] and maybe a pair of important side trails—and imagine trying to convey all that information on an area the size of the nail on your little finger. That's an AT map.

Actually, it's far, far worse than that because AT maps—for reasons that bewilder me beyond speculation—provide less detail than even their meager scale allows. For any ten miles of trail, the maps will name and identify perhaps only three of the dozen or more peaks you cross. Valleys, lakes, gaps, creeks, and other important, possibly vital, topographical[9] features are routinely

---

7. **"kilometer . . . centimeter":** a kilometer, which is equal to 5/8 of a mile, is represented on the map by a centimeter, or only about .4 inches.
8. **AT:** Appalachian Trail.
9. **topographical** (top uh GRAF uh kuhl): the science of making an accurate description or drawing of a place, such as making a map.

Monitor Your Comprehension

D AUTHOR'S PERSPECTIVE

What does Bryson's statement that "people have died in less trying circumstances" (line 88) tell you about his perspective on the situation?

Possible answer: Bryson is communicating to the reader just how serious the hikers' situation is and what a grave danger they are facing.

VOCABULARY

The word **abysmal** (uh BIHZ mal) is an adjective that means *very bad.*

E AUTHOR'S PERSPECTIVE

Why does Bryson find the map "useless" (line 90)? Write your answer on the lines below.

Bryson thinks the map is useless because its scale compresses too much "real" area into too small of a space on the map. Also, the map does not list a sufficient number of details to describe the area. Additionally, it does not include coordinates, directions, or references to towns located just outside of its area.

left unnamed. Forest Service roads are often not included, and, if included, they're inconsistently identified. Even side trails are frequently left off. There are no coordinates, no way of directing rescuers to a particular place, no pointers to towns just off the map's edge. These are, in short, seriously inadequate maps. E

In normal circumstances, this is merely irksome. Now, in a blizzard, it seemed closer to negligence.[10] I dragged the map from the pack and fought the wind to look at it. It showed the trail as a red line. Nearby was a heavy, wandering black line, which I presumed to be the Forest Service road we stood beside, though there was no actual telling. According to the map, the road (if a road is what it was) started in the middle of nowhere and finished half a dozen miles later equally in the middle of nowhere, which clearly made no sense—indeed, wasn't even possible. (You can't start a road in the middle of forest; earth-moving equipment can't spontaneously appear among the trees. Anyway, even if you could build a road that didn't go anywhere, why would you?) There was, obviously, something deeply and infuriatingly wrong with this map.

"Cost me eleven bucks," I said to Katz a little wildly, shaking the map at him and then crumpling it into an approximately flat shape and jabbing it into my pocket.

"So what're we going to do?" he said.

I sighed, unsure, then yanked the map out and examined it again. I looked from it to the logging road and back. "Well, it looks as if this logging road curves around the mountain and comes back near the trail on the other side. If it does and we can find it, then there's a shelter we can get to. If we can't get through, I don't know, I guess we take the road back downhill to lower ground and see if we can find a place out of the wind to camp." I shrugged a little helplessly. "I don't know. What do you think?"

He issued a single bitter guffaw[11] and returned to the hysterical snow. I hoisted my pack and followed.

We plodded up the road, bent steeply, buffeted by winds. Where it settled, the snow was wet and heavy and getting deep

10. **negligence** (NEHG luh juhnz): carelessness, disregard.
11. **bitter guffaw** (BHIT er guh FAW): harsh, loud laugh.

enough that soon it would be impassable and we would have to take shelter whether we wanted to or not. There was no place to pitch a tent here, I noted uneasily—only steep, wooded slope going up on one side and down on the other. For quite a distance—far longer than it seemed it ought to—the road stayed straight. Even if, farther on, it did curve back near the trail, there was no certainty (or even perhaps much likelihood) that we would spot it. In these trees and this snow you could be ten feet from the trail and not see it. It would be madness to leave the logging road and try to find it. Then again, it was probably madness to be following a logging road to higher ground in a blizzard. F

IN OTHER WORDS Bryson gets out his map, but it is not very useful. It doesn't include the details that hikers need. After studying the map, the hikers decide to seek shelter around the side of the mountain by following a loggers' road.

► Reread lines 139–151. With a partner, discuss what challenges Bryson and Katz face at this point.

Students should discuss that Katz and Bryson are lost in a snowstorm, deciding whether they should continue to follow a logger's road, try to find their original trail, or set up their tents on a steep, wooded slope not well suited for use as a camp site.

Gradually, and then more decidedly, the trail began to hook around behind the mountain. After about an hour of dragging sluggishly through ever-deepening snow, we came to a high, windy, level spot where the trail—or at least a trail—emerged down the back of Albert Mountain and continued on into level woods. I regarded my map with bewildered exasperation. It didn't give any indication of this whatever, but Katz spotted a white blaze[12] twenty yards into the woods, and we whooped with joy. We had refound the AT. A shelter was only a few hundred yards farther on. It looked as if we would live to hike another day.

The snow was nearly knee deep now, and we were tired, but we all but pranced through it, and Katz whooped again when we reached an arrowed sign on a low limb that pointed down a side trail and said "BIG SPRING SHELTER." The shelter, a simple wooden affair, open on one side, stood in a snowy glade—a little winter wonderland—150 yards or so off the main

12. **blaze** (blayz): a marker or sign to show the way.

Monitor Your Comprehension

F AUTHOR'S PERSPECTIVE

On the basis of the statements and details Bryson includes in lines 142–151, what is his perspective about his situation at this point? Write your answer in the boxes below.

Statements and Details
"I noted uneasily"; "there was no certainty (or even perhaps much likelihood)"; "it would be madness"; "then again, it was probably madness"

↓

What They Reveal About the Author's Perspective
Possible answer: Bryson is worried that they may not find their way to safety and that none of their current options are really appealing to him.

Monitor Your Comprehension

G SETTING AND MOOD
Bryson and Katz seem relieved to be nearing the shelter. Underline the descriptive words and phrases in lines 162–171 that convey this mood of relief.

VOCABULARY
The word **daunted** (DAWNT ed) is an adjective that means *discouraged.*

H AUTHOR'S PERSPECTIVE
Reread lines 174–179. How does Bryson's perspective on the snowstorm differ from Jim and Heath's? Write the differences between their perspectives on the lines below.

Possible answer: Bryson is exhausted and disoriented (noting he does not know what day it is) by the storm; however, Jim and Heath are cheerful, friendly and seemingly not at all bothered by the weather.

trail. Even from a distance we could see that the open side faced into the wind and that the drifting snow was nearly up to the lip of the sleeping platform. Still, if nothing else, it offered at least a sense of refuge. G

We crossed the clearing, heaved our packs onto the platform, and in the same instant discovered that there were two people there already—a man and a boy of about fourteen. They were Jim and Heath, father and son, from Chattanooga, and they were cheerful, friendly, and not remotely **daunted** by the weather. They had come hiking for the weekend, they told us (I hadn't even realized it was a weekend), and knew the weather was likely to be bad, though not perhaps quite this bad, and so were well prepared. Jim had brought a big clear plastic sheet, of the sort decorators use to cover floors, and was trying to rig it across the open front of the shelter. Katz, uncharacteristically, leapt to his assistance. The plastic sheet didn't quite reach, but we found that with one of our groundcloths lashed alongside it we could cover the entire front. The wind walloped ferociously against the plastic and from time to time tore part of it loose, where it fluttered and snapped, with a retort like gunshot, until one of us leaped up and fought it back into place. The whole shelter was, in any case, incredibly leaky of air—the plank walls and floors were full of cracks through which icy wind and occasional blasts of snow shot—but we were infinitely snugger than we would have been outside. H

IN OTHER WORDS Bryson and Katz follow the logging road and find a shelter that has been built for all hikers to use. Two other people, a father and his son, are already inside. The strong wind blows through the shelter, but the group uses a plastic sheet and a blanket to block out most of the cold wind.

So we made a little home of it for ourselves, spread out our sleeping pads and bags, put on all the extra clothes we could find, and fixed dinner from a reclining position. Darkness fell quickly and heavily, which made the wildness outside seem even more severe. Jim and Heath had some chocolate cake, which they shared with us (a treat beyond heaven), and then the four of us settled down to a long, cold night on hard wood, listening to a banshee[13] wind and the tossing of angry branches.

When I awoke, all was stillness—the sort of stillness that makes you sit up and take your bearings. The plastic sheet before me was peeled back a foot or so and weak light filled the space beyond. Snow was over the top of the platform and lying an inch deep over the foot of my sleeping bag. I shooed it off with a toss of my legs. Jim and Heath were already stirring to life. Katz slumbered heavily on, an arm flung over his forehead, his mouth a great open hole. It was not quite six. ❶

I decided to go out to reconnoiter and see how stranded we might be. I hesitated at the platform's edge, then jumped out into the drift—it came up over my waist and made my eyes fly open where it slipped under my clothes and found bare skin—and pushed through it into the clearing, where it was slightly (but only slightly) shallower. Even in sheltered areas, under an umbrella of conifers,[14] the snow was nearly knee deep and tedious to churn through. But everywhere it was stunning. Every tree wore a thick cloak of white, every stump and boulder a jaunty snowy cap, and

❶ **LANGUAGE COACH**

Context Clues *Lying* is a word that can have different meanings depending on the context in which it is used. *Lying* may refer to the act of not telling the truth. It can also refer to something resting in a flat position. The context, or situation, in which this word occurs can provide you with clues to its correct meaning. Which is the correct meaning of the word *lying* in line 203? Underline the context clues that help you identify the meaning.

The snow was resting in a flat position.

13. **banshee** (BAN shee): in Gaelic folklore, a female spirit who screams as a sign that death is coming.
14. **conifers** (KOH nuh fuhrs): family of trees including pine and fir trees.

there was that perfect, immense stillness that you get nowhere else but in a big woods after a heavy snowfall. Here and there clumps of snow fell from the branches, but otherwise there was no sound or movement. I followed the side trail up and under heavily bowed limbs to where it rejoined the AT. The AT was a plumped blanket of snow, round and bluish, in a long, dim tunnel of overbent rhododendrons. It looked deep and hard going. I walked a few yards as a test. It was deep and hard going. J

When I returned to the shelter, Katz was up, moving slowly and going through his morning groans, and Jim was studying his maps, which were vastly better than mine. I crouched beside him and he made room to let me look with him. It was 6.1 miles to Wallace Gap and a paved road, old U.S. 64. A mile down the road from there was Rainbow Springs Campground, a private campsite with showers and a store. I didn't know how hard it would be to walk seven miles through deep snow and had no confidence that the campground would be open this early in the year. Still, it was obvious this snow wasn't going to melt for days and we would have to make a move sometime; it might as well be now, when at least it was pretty and calm. Who knew when another storm might blow in and really strand us?

Jim had decided that he and Heath would accompany us for the first couple of hours, then turn off on a side trail called Long Branch, which descended steeply through a ravine for 2.3 miles and emerged near a parking lot where they had left their car. He had hiked the Long Branch trail many times and knew what to expect. Even so, I didn't like the sound of it and asked him hesitantly if he thought it was a good idea to go off on a little-used side trail, into goodness knows what conditions, where no one would come across him and his son if they got in trouble. Katz, to my relief, agreed with me. "At least there's always other people on the AT," he said. "You don't know what might happen to you on a side trail." Jim considered the matter and said they would turn back if it looked bad. K

J SETTING AND MOOD
Although Bryson knows he and the other hikers are in danger of being stranded, he is also appreciative of the beautiful setting. Underline the details in lines 215–224 that convey a mood of appreciation.

K AUTHOR'S PERSPECTIVE
Reread lines 238–250. Circle the statements and details that convey Bryson's attitude toward Jim's plan. How would you describe Bryson's opinion of the situation?

Bryson does not agree with Jim's plan to use a lesser-known trail to reach his car. He asks Jim to reconsider his plans.

Katz and I treated ourselves to two cups of coffee, for warmth, and Jim and Heath shared with us some of their oatmeal, which made Katz intensely happy. Then we all set off together. It was cold and hard going. The tunnels of boughed rhododendrons, which often ran on for great distances, were exceedingly pretty, but when our packs brushed against them they dumped volumes of snow onto our heads and down the backs of our necks. The three adults took it in turns to walk in front because the lead person always received the heaviest dumping, as well as having all the hard work of dibbing[15] holes in the snow.

IN OTHER WORDS The next morning, Bryson goes outside and discovers that the snow is deep, making it hard to walk. Jim's map shows the way to a campground. Jim decides that he and Heath will take a side path. Bryson and Katz are not sure this will work and prefer to stay on the trail. They all travel together for the first few miles.

The Long Branch trail, when we reached it, descended steeply through bowed pines—too steeply, it seemed to me, to come back up if the trail proved impassable, and it looked as if it might. Katz and I urged Jim and Heath to reconsider, but Jim said it was all downhill and well-marked, and he was sure it would be all right. "Hey, you know what day it is?" said Jim suddenly and, seeing our blank faces, supplied the answer. "March twenty-first."

Our faces stayed blank.

"First day of spring," he said.

We smiled at the pathetic[16] irony of it, shook hands all around, wished each other luck, and parted. **PAUSE & REFLECT**

Katz and I walked for three hours more, silently and slowly through the cold, white forest, taking it in turns to break snow. At about one o'clock we came at last to old 64, a lonesome, superannuated two-lane road through the mountains. It hadn't been cleared, and there were no tire tracks through it. It was

---

15. **dibbing** (DIH bing): making holes in soil, as if to plant seeds; here, the first hiker steps into deep snow, leaving holes into which followers may step.
16. **pathetic** (puh THEHT ihk): pitiful, sad.

Monitor Your Comprehension

PAUSE & REFLECT

Irony occurs when a situation turns out to be the opposite of what someone expects. With a partner, discuss why Bryson thinks it is ironic that it is the first day of spring.

Students should discuss that Bryson thinks it is ironic because spring typically brings warmer weather; however, they are in a wintry, snow-covered world.

starting to snow again, steadily, prettily. We set off down the road for the campground and had walked about a quarter of a mile when from behind there was the crunching sound of a motorized vehicle proceeding cautiously through snow. We turned to see a big jeep-type car rolling up beside us. The driver's window hummed down. It was Jim and Heath. They had come to let us know they had made it, and to make sure we had likewise. "Thought you might like a lift to the campground," Jim said. L

IN OTHER WORDS Jim and Heath turn off on another trail to find their parked car, while Bryson and Katz continue on the trail. As the author hikes toward the campground, he hears a car pull up beside him. In it are Jim and Heath. They offer them a ride to the campground.

L SETTING AND MOOD

Reread lines 273–285. Describe the setting where Bryson and Katz are walking. How does the arrival of Jim and Heath in this setting change the mood of the story to a humorous one?

Description of Setting
Katz and Bryson walk through a quiet, cold, snow-covered forest whose roads remain untouched since the last snowfall.

↓

What Makes the Mood Change
The mood of the story becomes humorous when Jim and Heath appear in their car to offer Bryson and Katz a ride to the campground.

After Reading

Text Analysis: Setting and Mood

Where do you find **ADVENTURE?**

Bill Bryson uses sensory language to describe the unexpected changes in landscape and weather he encounters in the **setting** of this selection. These descriptions help set a distinct **mood,** the feeling the writer creates for the reader. To communicate different moods, Bryson describes the Appalachian Trail in different ways at different points in the story. Three different moods are listed below. Look back at the selection, and then list sensory language Bryson uses to create each mood—sights, sounds, smells, and sensations.

For this chart, answers will vary. See samples below.

Mood	Description of Setting
Peaceful	***"Every tree wore a thick cloak of white, every stump and boulder a jaunty snowy cap, and there was that perfect, immense stillness that you get nowhere else but in a big woods after a heavy snowfall. Here and there clumps of snow fell from the branches, but otherwise there was no sound or movement." (lines 215–220)***
Frightening	***"It was like a window ledge on a skyscraper, no more than fourteen or sixteen inches wide, and crumbling in places, with a sharp drop on one side of perhaps eighty feet, and long, looming stretches of vertical granite on the other" (lines 47–50)***
Humorous	***"your brain like a balloon tethered with string, accompanying but not actually part of the body below" (lines 29–30)***

Reading Skill: Identify Author's Perspective

Look back at the selection for statements and details that reveal Bryson's perspective about hiking the Appalachian Trail—both before the snowstorm and during it. In the chart below, sum up his perspective about hiking the trail at each of these times. Then answer the question that follows the chart.

For this chart, answers may vary. See samples below.

Bryson's Perspective About Hiking the Appalachian Trail	
Before the Snowstorm	**During the Snowstorm**
Possible answer: Before the storm, Bryson finds the trail peaceful, relaxing, and beautiful and enjoys the repetition of hiking.	*Possible answer: During the storm, Bryson finds the trail dangerous, terrifying, and life-threatening.*

How does Bryson's perspective about hiking the Appalachian Trail change by the end of his narrative? Use the statements and details from the selection as evidence to show how Bryson's perspective changes.

Possible answer: By the end of the narrative, Bryson learns that the hiking can be a dangerous experience and one in which hikers need to be prepared for emergencies, such as storms.

Vocabulary Practice

For each group of words below, circle the word that means the same as the Vocabulary word.

1. **daunted:** confident, careless, afraid
2. **unnerving:** startling, soothing, entertaining
3. **abysmal:** joyful, crazy, terrible

Academic Vocabulary in Speaking

The word **circumstance** (SER kuhm stans) is a noun that means *a situation or detail connected with an event.*

He realized that this new **circumstance** meant he had to change his plans.

TURN AND TALK With a partner, discuss the benefits and risks of exploring a new place. Consider the kinds of situations you might find yourself in and what you might gain from the experience. Be sure to use the word **circumstance** in your discussion.

Encourage students to use the Academic Vocabulary word in their discussions.

Assessment Practice

DIRECTIONS Use "A Walk in the Woods" to answer questions 1–6.

1 Bill Bryson and his friend have set out to —
- (A) see how long they can survive in the wilderness
- (B) vacation at Rainbow Springs Campground
- (C) rescue Jim and Heath from the storm
- (D) hike the Appalachian Trail

2 Bryson dislikes AT maps because —
- (A) they are difficult to fold
- (B) they don't offer detailed information
- (C) they never hold up in the rain or snow
- (D) they show only one route

3 Other than the storm, which of the following contributes to the suspense of the narrative?
- (A) Bryson's poor preparations
- (B) Meeting Jim and Heath
- (C) Difficulty finding the campground
- (D) Katz's negative attitude

4 The hikers survive the storm by —
- (A) calling for help
- (B) huddling together
- (C) following a logging route to shelter
- (D) sharing food and warm clothes

5 Which word best describes the mood when Bryson and Katz cross the narrow ledge in lines 46–70?
- (A) Sorrowful
- (B) Lighthearted
- (C) Peaceful
- (D) Frightening

6 When Bryson and Katz reach the shelter, the mood shifts from —
- (A) worried to relieved
- (B) hopeful to gloomy
- (C) joyful to nervous
- (D) confused to humorous

Wilderness Letter

By Wallace Stegner

Background

The writer Wallace Stegner fought to protect the environment. In this letter, he argues that we should save wilderness areas, places where people do not live and have not changed the natural landscape. He says the wilderness is an important part of American history. In modern times, Stegner argues, wilderness helps people find rest and spiritual renewal. Stegner's letter—sent to an official group studying public lands—helped persuade Congress to pass the Wilderness Act in 1964.

Standards Focus: Read Primary Sources

A **primary source** is a document about events written by someone who actually experienced those events. Letters, speeches, and journals are examples of primary sources. To get the most from reading a primary source, you should consider the **form** and **purpose** of the text, when and where it was written, the intended **audience,** and the **author's credibility** (kred uh BIL ih tee), how believable he or she is. You will use a chart like the one below to help you find this information as you read Wallace Stegner's letter.

Things to Consider	Ask Yourself . . .	My Answers
form of the text	Is this a letter, a speech, a journal entry or some other type of primary source document?	
purpose of the text	Why did the author write this document?	
where and when it was written	Are any dates or locations mentioned in the document? What do other sources say about where and when it was written?	
the intended **audience**	To whom was the author writing?	
the author's **credibility**	Is the author reliable? Can you trust what he or she says?	

As part of reading a primary source, you will summarize the writer's ideas. When you **summarize** a text, you simplify it and put it in your own words, focusing on the main idea. The **main idea** is the writer's most important point or message.

Wilderness Letter

By Wallace Stegner

Los Altos, Calif.
Dec. 3, 1960

David E. Pesonen
Wildland Research Center
Agricultural Experiment Station
243 Mulford Hall
University of California
Berkeley 4, Calif. (A)

Dear Mr. Pesonen:

I believe that you are working on the wilderness portion of the Outdoor Recreation Resources Review Commission's report. If I may, I should like to urge some arguments for wilderness preservation that involve recreation, as it

SET A PURPOSE FOR READING

Read this letter to find out why Wallace Stegner believes in protecting wilderness.

(A) READ PRIMARY SOURCES

Read lines 1–8. Then use this information to fill in the chart below.

form of the text	*The text is a letter.*
the intended **audience**	*Mr. David E. Pesonen at the University of California's Wildland Research Center*

is ordinarily conceived, hardly at all. Hunting, fishing, hiking, mountain-climbing, camping, photography, and the enjoyment of natural scenery will all, surely, figure in your report. So will the wilderness as a genetic reserve, a scientific yardstick by which we may measure the world in its natural balance against the world in its man-made imbalance. What I want to speak for is not so much the wilderness uses, valuable as those are, but [the wilderness idea, which is a resource in itself.] Being an intangible and spiritual resource, it will seem mystical to the practical-minded—but then anything that cannot be moved by a bulldozer is likely to seem mystical to them.

I want [to speak for the wilderness idea as something that has helped form our character and that has certainly shaped our history as a people. . . .] B

IN OTHER WORDS Stegner says that Mr. Pesonen's report is likely to say that wilderness areas are important for sporting activities. But Stegner points out that the wilderness is also important simply because it exists.

Something will have gone out of us as a people if we ever let the remaining wilderness be destroyed; if we permit the last virgin forests to be turned into comic books and plastic cigarette cases; if we drive the few remaining members of the wild species into zoos or to extinction; if we pollute the last clear air and dirty the last clean streams and push our paved roads through the last of the silence, so that never again will Americans be free in their own country from the noise, the exhausts, the stinks of human and automotive waste. And so that never again can we have the chance to see ourselves single, separate, vertical and individual in the world, part of the environment of trees and rocks and soil, brother to the other animals, part of the natural world and competent

B READ PRIMARY SOURCES

Read lines 19–28 again. What is Stegner's **purpose** for writing this document? Put brackets [ ] around the sentences that tell you why he wrote. Include this information in your chart.

purpose of the text	*Stegner's purpose is to speak for the idea of the wilderness as a resource, as a former of our character, and as a shaper of our history.*

to belong in it. Without any remaining wilderness we are committed wholly, without chance for even momentary reflection and rest, to a headlong drive into our technological termite-life, the Brave New World[1] of a completely man-controlled environment. We need wilderness preserved—as much of it as is still left, and as many kinds—because it was the challenge against which our character as a people was formed. **C** The reminder and the reassurance that it is still there is good for our spiritual health even if we never once in ten years set foot in it. It is good for us when we are young, because of the incomparable sanity it can bring briefly, as vacation and rest, into our insane lives. It is important to us when we are old simply because it is there—important, that is, simply as idea.

IN OTHER WORDS Stegner asks Mr. Pesonen to consider what America would be like if there were no forests, no wild animals, no clean air.

► In lines 51–55, in what ways does Stegner say the wilderness is good for people of all ages? Underline the answer.

C READ PRIMARY SOURCES

Reread lines 29–49. Put a checkmark ✔ beside the **summary** below that is most likely the writer's most important point—his **main idea**:

✔**1.** If the wilderness is destroyed, we will have lost something of importance.
2. Killing animals and cutting down trees will destroy the wilderness.
3. The wilderness keeps us connected to nature.
4. Wilderness lands need to be protected.

We are a wild species. . . . Nobody ever tamed or domesticated or scientifically bred us. But for at least three millennia we have been engaged in a cumulative and ambitious race to modify and gain control of our environment, and in the process we have come close to domesticating ourselves. Not many people are likely, any more, to look upon what we call "progress" as an unmixed blessing. Just as surely as it has brought us increased comfort and more material goods, it has brought us spiritual losses, and it threatens now to become the Frankenstein that will

1. **Brave New World:** a reference to Aldous Huxley's 1932 science fiction novel *Brave New World,* about a society in which technology controls every aspect of life, including happiness.

destroy us. One means of sanity is to retain a hold on the natural world, to remain, insofar as we can, good animals. Americans still have that chance, more than many peoples; for while we were demonstrating ourselves the most efficient and ruthless environment-busters in history, and slashing and burning and cutting our way through a wilderness continent, the wilderness was working on us. It remains in us as surely as Indian names remain on the land. If the abstract dream of human liberty and human dignity became, in America, something more than an abstract dream, mark it down at least partially to the fact that we were in subtle ways subdued by what we conquered. . . .

The American experience has been the confrontation by old peoples and cultures of a world as new as if it had just risen from the sea. That gave us our hope and our excitement, and the hope and excitement can be passed on to newer Americans, Americans who never saw any phase of the frontier. But only so long as we keep the remainder of our wild as a reserve and a promise—a sort of wilderness bank. . . .

IN OTHER WORDS Stegner says that humans are free and not easily tamed. Still, he says, our attempts to change and control nature have almost tamed us. Progress, Stegner claims, gives us good things but can also destroy us. He says that connecting with nature keeps us mentally healthy.

Stegner then claims that early Americans tried to defeat the wilderness but were changed by it. The struggle of people against the wild, he says, is important enough to pass down to the next generation. But there must be a wilderness for this to happen.

We need to demonstrate our acceptance of the natural world, including ourselves; we need the spiritual refreshment that being natural can produce. And one of the best places for us to get that is in the wilderness where the fun houses, the bulldozers, and the pavements of our civilization are shut out. D

D READ PRIMARY SOURCES

Reread lines 85–89. Using your own words, **summarize** one reason Stegner says we need the wilderness.

Possible answer: People need the respite that the wilderness provides from the noise and distraction of our daily existence.

Sherwood Anderson, in a letter to Waldo Frank in the 1920's, said it better than I can. "Is it not likely that when the country was new and men were often alone in the fields and the forest they got a sense of bigness outside themselves that has now in some way been lost . . . Mystery whispered in the grass, played in the branches of trees overhead, was caught up and blown across the American line in clouds of dust at evening on the **prairies** . . . I am old enough to remember tales that strengthen my belief in a deep semi-religious influence that was formerly at work among our people. The flavor of it hangs over the best work of Mark Twain . . . I can remember old fellows in my home town speaking feelingly of an evening spent on the big empty plains. It had taken the shrillness out of them. They had learned the trick of quiet . . ."

We could learn it too, even yet; even our children and grand-children could learn it. But only if we save, for just such absolutely non-recreational, impractical, and mystical uses as this, all the wild that still remains to us. . . .

For myself, I grew up on the empty plains of Saskatchewan and Montana and in the mountains of Utah, and I put a very high valuation on what those places gave me. And if I had not been able periodically to renew myself in the mountains and deserts of western America I would be very near bughouse.[2] Even when I can't get to the back country, the thought of the colored deserts of southern Utah, or the reassurance that there are still stretches of prairie where the world can be instantaneously perceived as disk and bowl, and where the little but intensely important human being is exposed to the five directions and the thirty-six winds, is a positive consolation. The idea alone can sustain me. (E) But as the wilderness areas are progressively exploited or "improved," as the jeeps and bulldozers of uranium prospectors scar up the deserts and the roads are cut into the alpine timberlands,

2. **bughouse:** slang for crazy.

VISUAL VOCABULARY

A **prairie** is a grassy, flat land with very few trees.

(E) READ PRIMARY SOURCES

In lines 108–119, Stegner gives an example from his own life. Does his example lead you to believe that he knows what he's talking about? Why or why not? Discuss your answer with a partner.

Students may discuss that the example Stegner gives leads them to believe that he knows what he is talking about because he grew up in the wilderness of Saskatchewan, Montana, and Utah, noting that his memories of these untouched places provide him with great consolation.

and as the remnants of the unspoiled and natural world are progressively eroded, every such loss is a little death in me. In us. . . .

IN OTHER WORDS Stegner says that nature has a healing power. He quotes writer Sherwood Anderson, who says that nature filled frontier people with wonder. Stegner believes that everyone can and should learn to feel the wonder of those frontier people. He notes nature's importance to him personally and says that the destruction of wilderness is painful to him.

Let me say something on the subject of the kinds of wilderness worth preserving. Most of those areas contemplated are in the national forests and in high mountain country. For all the usual recreational purposes, the alpine and forest wildernesses are obviously the most important, both as genetic banks and as beauty spots. F But for the spiritual renewal, the recognition of identity, the birth of awe, other kinds will serve every bit as well. Perhaps, because they are less friendly to life, more abstractly nonhuman, they will serve even better. On our Saskatchewan prairie, the nearest neighbor was four miles away, and at night we saw only two lights on all the dark rounding earth. The earth was full of animals—field mice, ground squirrels, weasels, ferrets, badgers, coyotes, burrowing owls, snakes. I knew them as my little brothers, as fellow creatures, and I have never been able to look upon animals in any other way since. The sky in that country came clear down to the ground on every side, and it was full of great weathers, and clouds, and winds, and hawks. I hope I learned something from knowing intimately the creatures of the earth; I hope I learned something from looking a long way, from looking up,

F LANGUAGE COACH
Banks in line 131 is a **multiple-meaning word**. Multiple meaning words are words that have more than one definition. Here are some definitions of *bank* that you may already know: "the edge of a river," "a pile or mound of something, as in a *bank of clouds*," and "a business that keeps people's money safe." In this sentence, *banks* means "places where something is kept safe for future use."

from being much alone. A prairie like that, one big enough to carry the eye clear to the sinking, rounding horizon, can be as lonely and grand and simple in its forms as the sea. It is as good a place as any for the wilderness experience to happen; the vanishing prairie is as worth preserving for the wilderness idea as the alpine forests.

So are great reaches of our western deserts, scarred somewhat by **prospectors** but otherwise open, beautiful, waiting. . . . PAUSE & REFLECT

These are some of the things wilderness can do for us. That is the reason we need to put into effect, for its preservation, some other principle than the principles of exploitation or "usefulness" or even recreation. We simply need that wild country available to us, even if we never do more than drive to its edge and look in. For it can be a means of reassuring ourselves of our sanity as creatures, a part of the geography of hope.

Very sincerely yours,

Wallace Stegner

IN OTHER WORDS Most of the planned wilderness areas are mountain forests. Stegner says that plains and deserts will work well, too. Because he grew up on the plains, Stegner appreciates the wide-open spaces and animals there.

► With a partner, discuss the reasons Stegner gives in lines 156–163 for why the wilderness is needed.

*Students should discuss that Stegner says that wilderness needs to be available to people because of its ability to reassure them of their own sanity and of the possibility **of hope**.*

VISUAL VOCABULARY

A **prospector** (PRAHS pek ter) is a person who explores places for gold, silver, and other resources.

PAUSE & REFLECT

In lines 127–155, Stegner talks about mountain forests, prairies, and deserts as valuable wilderness areas. What other kinds of places might make good wilderness areas? Discuss your answer with a partner.

Students should discuss other examples of good wilderness areas, such as rivers, streams, oceans, and beaches.

Practicing Your Skills: Read Primary Sources

Now that you have finished reading the letter, complete the chart below.

For this chart, answers will vary. See samples below.

Things to Consider	Ask Yourself . . .	My Answers
form of the text	Is this a letter, a speech, a journal entry or some other type of primary source document?	*The text is a letter.*
purpose of the text	Why did the author write this document?	*To explain why he believes the wilderness should be protected*
where and when it was written	Are any dates or locations mentioned in the document? What do other sources say about where and when it was written?	*It was written in 1960 from Los Angeles, California.*
the intended **audience**	To whom was the author writing?	*A person who makes decisions about wilderness land use.*
the author's **credibility** (kred uh BIL ih tee)	Is the author reliable? Can you trust what he or she says?	*I believe that the author is reliable and trustworthy.*

Look back at the notes you made while reading. What do you think is the main idea of this document?

Possible answer: The main idea of Stegner's letter is to explain why he believes that the wilderness must be protected and its benefits to people who live in the United States.

Academic Vocabulary in Speaking

The word **aspect** (AS pekt) is a noun that means *a part or a side of something.*

Sometimes a person can only look at one **aspect** of a problem rather than seeing all different sides of it.

TURN AND TALK How important is it to you to spend time in nature? What parts of the natural world do you most appreciate? Discuss your answer with a partner. Be sure to use the word **aspect** in your discussion.

Encourage students to use the Academic Vocabulary word in their discussions.

Assessment Practice

DIRECTIONS Use "Wilderness Letter" to answer questions 1–4.

1 Stegner's purpose for writing "Wilderness Letter" is —

- (A) to protect animals that have nearly been wiped out due to humans
- (B) to ask that homes be torn down to create parks
- (C) to protect what's left of the wilderness
- (D) to ask that humans never enter protected areas

2 The intended audience for Stegner's letter is —

- (A) construction company owners
- (B) people who make decisions about public lands
- (C) people who use wilderness areas
- (D) people who conduct scientific research

3 Which of the following aspects of Stegner's letter *most* helps establish his credibility on the subject?

- (A) Personal accounts of his experiences with the wilderness
- (B) Pointing out the benefits that progress has brought to people
- (C) Quotations from Mark Twain and Sherwood Anderson on the same subject
- (D) References to literary works such as *Frankenstein* and *Brave New World*

4 Stegner believes that wilderness areas help us —

- (A) even if we only hear about them
- (B) only if we visit them often
- (C) only when we are upset and stressed
- (D) even if very few of them are left

UNIT 4

Getting the Message

THEME AND SYMBOL

Be sure to read the Text Analysis Workshop on pages 434–439 in *Holt McDougal Literature.*

Academic Vocabulary for Unit 4

You will see these Academic Vocabulary words as you work through this book. You will also be asked to use them as you write and talk about the selections in this unit.

Context (KON tekst) is a noun that means *the conditions in which an event or idea happens or exists.*
In the **context** of talking about good manners, Sara's comment about turning off cell phones made sense.

Describe a **context** in which it is important to be quiet.

Answers will vary.

Interpret (in TER prit) is a verb that means *to explain or make clear the meaning of something.*
Jolie can **interpret** the computer code without looking at a book.

Why do some people **interpret** rules differently?

Answers will vary.

Reveal (rih VEEL) is a verb that means *to show or make known.*
The dictionary helped **reveal** the meaning of the word.

How do you **reveal** your thoughts?

Answers will vary.

Significant (sig NIF ih kuhnt) is an adjective that means *important* or *having meaning.*
A **significant** part of the speech focused on sports.

Describe the most **significant** person in your life.

Answers will vary.

Tradition (truh DISH uhn) is a noun that means *a custom, belief, or practice passed down from one generation to the next.*
The school's **tradition** of giving each graduate a book was started nearly fifty years ago.

What **tradition** do you enjoy at home?

Answers will vary.

The Scarlet Ibis

Adapted from the short story by **James Hurst**

Why do we **HURT** the ones we **LOVE?**

Sometimes it's easy to be mean when you feel angry or disappointed, even if you're not a mean person. What do we do when we are angry with people we love? How much harm can come from one angry word or action?

Why do we sometimes get angrier at loved ones than we do at others?

Sometimes I get mad at ______________________

because ______________________

____

____

I think we demand more of people we love because

____

____

____

____

____

____

TURN AND TALK Why do we sometimes demand more of loved ones than we do of others? With a partner, talk about times you get angry with someone you love and care about. Then, fill in the blanks at the left.
Answers will vary.

Text Analysis: Symbol

A **symbol** is a person, animal, place, object, or activity that stands for something beyond itself. For example, sometimes an eagle stands for freedom and a four-leaf clover stands for good luck.

To find symbols in "The Scarlet Ibis," use these strategies:

- Look for ideas that the writer emphasizes.
- Note vivid images and character descriptions.

Once you've identified a symbol, note how you respond to it. Then think about what the symbol may stand for. As you read, you will use a chart like this one to help you identify symbols and their meanings.

Clue from the Story	→	My Response
bleeding tree		*symbol for injury or death?*

Understanding what a symbol may stand for can help you identify the story's **theme**—its underlying message about life or human nature.

Reading Skill: Make Inferences About Characters

Rather than directly tell you what characters are like, writers often *show* you instead: they show what characters say and do, how they look, and how others respond to them. You can add these clues to what you know from your own experience to make **inferences,** or educated guesses, about characters. As you read, you will make inferences about characters using a chart like this one.

Detail from Text	My Experience	My Inference
Doodle "was a disappointment."	I get disappointed when I expect something great and it doesn't happen.	The narrator expects a lot from Doodle.

Vocabulary in Context

Note: Words are listed in the order in which they appear in the story.

Infallibility (in fal uh BIL uh tee) is a noun that means *an inability to make mistakes.*
The accident proved his idea of **infallibility** wrong.

Precariously (prih KAIR ee uhs lee) is an adverb that means *insecurely* or *in a dangerous or unstable way.*
Precariously balanced on a tree limb, the bird almost fell.

Exotic (ig ZOT ik) is an adjective that means *excitingly strange.*
We'd never seen such **exotic** and colorful feathers before.

Heresy (HEHR ih see) is a noun that means *an action or opinion that goes against what is generally thought of as right.*
People strongly disagreed with her idea, calling it a **heresy.**

Vocabulary Practice

With a partner, discuss answers to the following questions.
Encourage students to use the Vocabulary words in their discussions.

1. What might lead you to believe in your own **infallibility**?
2. What would you do if you saw something breakable balanced **precariously**?
3. Name something **exotic**. What makes it exotic?
4. What is the difference between a **heresy** and an unusual idea?

SET A PURPOSE FOR READING
Read this story to find out what happens when a boy tries to change his younger brother.

The *Scarlet* Ibis

Adapted from the short story by
JAMES HURST

BACKGROUND The narrator of this story recalls his childhood relationship with his brother, Doodle. The boys live in North Carolina in 1918. It is the last year of World War I. The story's title refers to a bright red bird, a scarlet ibis (EYE bis). The bird lands in the family's backyard, and Doodle is drawn to the bird. As the story opens, the narrator remembers Doodle's birth.

It was between the end of summer and the beginning of autumn that the ibis landed in the bleeding tree.[1] Another bird's deserted nest rocked back and forth in the elm like an empty cradle. The last flowers in the graveyard were blooming. Their smell drifted through every room of our house, reminding us of the names of our war dead. A

It's strange that all this is still so clear to me, now that so much time has passed. The bleeding tree is gone now. But sometimes time seems to disappear—and I remember Doodle.

Doodle was born when I was six. He was a disappointment from the beginning, not what I had hoped for. He seemed to be all head, with a tiny, red, wrinkled body. No one but Aunt Nicey expected him to live long. Daddy had a carpenter build a little coffin for him. But he didn't die, so Mama and Daddy

A SYMBOL
Symbols can be a clue to a story's theme. Reread lines 1–6 and circle words associated with death or dying.

1. **bleeding tree:** a tree that has been cut so it leaks sap, or liquid, from inside.

decided to name him. They called him William Armstrong, which was like tying a big tail on a small kite. A name like that only sounds good on a tombstone.

I thought I was good at things like holding my breath, running, jumping, or climbing vines. More than anything else, I wanted someone to do these things with me. I wanted a brother. But Mama, crying, told me that even if William Armstrong lived, he would never do these things. He might not, she sobbed, even be "all there." He might, as long as he lived, lie on the rubber sheet in the center of the bed in the front bedroom.

It was bad enough having an invalid[2] brother. Having one who might not be "all there" was unbearable. So I began to make plans to kill him by covering his face with a pillow so he couldn't breathe. However, one afternoon as I watched him, he looked straight at me and grinned. I skipped through the rooms, down the halls, shouting, "Mama, he smiled. He's all there! He's all there!" And he was. B

IN OTHER WORDS The narrator remembers his younger brother, William. When William is born, no one thinks he will survive. Even if he lives, he might have serious mental and physical disabilities. One day the baby smiles at him. The narrator realizes that his brother is "all there," or mentally okay.

When he was two, if you laid him on his stomach, he began to move himself, straining terribly because it was so hard for him. The doctor said that with his weak heart this strain would probably kill him, but it didn't. I can still see Mama watching him, her eyes wide with fear. But he learned to crawl. We brought him out of the front bedroom and put him on the rug in front of the fireplace. For the first time he became one of us.

As long as he stayed in bed all the time, we called him William Armstrong. But now he was crawling and beginning to talk. Something had to be done about his name. When he crawled, he crawled backward, moving in reverse. Crawling backward made him look like a doodlebug,[3] so I began to call

2. **invalid** (IN vuh lid): a person who is sick and must remain in bed.
3. **doodlebug:** a type of insect that can only walk backward.

Monitor Your Comprehension

B MAKE INFERENCES

Reread lines 18–31. Underline **details** about the narrator. Based on these details, what inferences can you make about the narrator's feelings about his brother?

Details About the Narrator

Possible answer: The narrator is good at holding his breath, running, jumping, and climbing vines. However, he wants someone, such as a little brother, to do those things with him. At first, he plans to kill his invalid brother. Later, his brother smiles at him, and the narrator changes his mind, reacting with great joy and excitement.

My Experience

Answers will vary.

My Inferences About the Narrator's Feelings

Answers will vary.

him Doodle. Giving my brother a new name was perhaps the kindest thing I ever did for him, because nobody expects much from someone called Doodle.

IN OTHER WORDS The baby does not die. With great effort, he learns to crawl. Because he crawls backward like a doodlebug, the narrator calls him "Doodle."

Although Doodle learned to crawl, he showed no signs of walking. But he talked all the time. I had to pull him around in a go-cart, an open box on wheels that Daddy built. At first I just pulled him up and down the porch, but then he started crying to go into the yard. Finally, I had to take him wherever I went. If I got ready to go anywhere, he'd start crying to go with me, and Mama would make me take him.

He was a burden in many ways, complicating my life. The doctor said he had to be treated very gently. I ignored the doctor once we got out of the house. To keep Doodle from wanting to come with me, I'd pull him roughly in the go-cart around corners. Sometimes I accidentally turned him over, but he never told Mama. Finally, I gave up. Doodle was my brother, and he was going to hang on to me forever, no matter what I did. So I decided to share with him the only beauty I knew, Old Woman **Swamp**. When we got there I put him in the soft grass. His eyes were round with wonder as he looked around. His little hands began to stroke the grass. Then he began to cry.

"What's the matter?" I asked, annoyed.

"It's so pretty," he said. "So pretty, pretty, pretty." C

After that day Doodle and I often went to the swamp. We made flower necklaces and crowns and wore them. We were beyond the touch of the everyday world.

IN OTHER WORDS Doodle does not walk, but he wants to spend time outside the house. The narrator pulls him around in an open box on wheels. He takes Doodle to his favorite place, a beautiful swamp. Doodle loves it. The brothers often go back to the swamp.

VISUAL VOCABULARY

A **swamp** is a low, wet area of land, often filled with trees and shrubs.

C MAKE INFERENCES

Underline details in lines 54–66 that show you what Doodle is like. How would you describe Doodle's personality?

Though Doodle was frail, he wanted to spend time with his brother, eagerly following him everywhere.

There is cruelty within me. At times I was mean to Doodle. One day I took him to the loft high up in the barn. I showed him his coffin, telling him how we all had believed he would die.

Doodle said, "It's not mine." **D**

"It is," I said. "And before I'll help you down from here, you have to touch it."

"I won't touch it," he said.

"Then I'll leave you here by yourself," I threatened. I started climbing down.

Doodle was afraid of being left alone. "Don't go leave me, Brother," he cried. He leaned toward the coffin. His hand shook as he reached toward it. He touched the coffin and screamed. Then Doodle couldn't move. I put him on my shoulder and carried him down the ladder. Even when we were outside, he held on to me, crying, "Don't leave me. Don't leave me."

PAUSE & REFLECT

IN OTHER WORDS The narrator takes Doodle to the barn. He shows Doodle the coffin that was made when he was a baby. He threatens to leave unless Doodle touches the coffin. Doodle touches the coffin, but he is too scared to move. His brother carries him out. Doodle continues to beg his brother not to leave him.

When Doodle was five years old, I was embarrassed because I had a brother who couldn't walk. We were down in Old Woman Swamp. "I'm going to teach you to walk, Doodle," I said.

"Why?" he asked.

I hadn't expected such an answer. "So I won't have to drag you around with me all the time."

"I can't walk, Brother," he said.

"Who says so?" I demanded.

"Mama, the doctor—everybody."

"Oh, you can walk," I said. I took him by the arms and stood him up. He collapsed and fell onto the grass as if he had no bones in his little legs.

Monitor Your Comprehension

D SYMBOL

In lines 71–72, the narrator shows Doodle a coffin stored in a barn. What response do you have to the narrator's action?

Possible answer: I think that the narrator is being mean, cruel, and nasty to Doodle by showing him a coffin and telling him that, at one time, everyone thought he would die.

What might the coffin symbolize, or stand for?

Possible answer: The coffin represents impending death or isolation.

PAUSE & REFLECT

Reread lines 71–84. With a partner, discuss what Doodle fears most. What do Doodle's fears tell you about him?

Students should discuss that Doodle most fears being left alone. Possible answer: Doodle knows that he is small and frail and would be helpless without his brother.

"Don't hurt me, Brother," he warned.

"I'm not going to hurt you. I'm going to teach you to walk." I pulled him up on his feet again, and again he collapsed.

"I just can't do it."

"Oh yes you can, Doodle," I said. "All you got to do is try." It seemed so hopeless that it's a miracle I didn't give up. But all of us must have something or someone to be proud of, and Doodle had become mine. I did not know then that pride is a seed that bears two vines, life and death. Every day we went to the swamp. I put him on his feet again and again. Sometimes I became discouraged because I didn't think he was trying. I would say, "Doodle, don't you *want* to learn to walk?" E

He'd nod his head, and I'd say, "Well, if you don't keep trying, you'll never learn." Then I told him to imagine us as old men and me still pulling him around in the go-cart. This never failed to make him try again.

After many weeks of practice, he finally stood alone for a few seconds. When he fell, I grabbed him and hugged him. Now we knew it could be done.

We decided not to tell anyone until he could actually walk. Each day we practiced until Doodle was ready to show what he could do. He still wasn't able to walk far, but we could wait no longer. We chose to show all on Doodle's sixth birthday. For weeks before, we promised everybody a big surprise.

On Doodle's birthday, Mama, Daddy, and Aunt Nicey were in the dining room. I brought Doodle to the door and had them turn their backs. I helped Doodle up, and when he was standing alone, I let them look. There wasn't a sound as Doodle walked slowly across the room and sat down at the table. Then Mama began to cry and hugged him and kissed him. Daddy hugged him, too. Aunt Nicey prayed her thanks in the doorway.

Doodle told them I taught him to walk, so everyone wanted to hug me, and I began to cry.

"What are you crying for?" asked Daddy, but I couldn't answer. They did not know that I did it for myself, out of pride. Doodle walked only because [I was ashamed of having a crippled brother.] F

E MAKE INFERENCES
Why does the narrator try so hard to teach Doodle to walk?

Possible answer: The narrator becomes determined to teach Doodle how to walk. His pride will not let him give up on the seemingly impossible task.

Underline the statements in lines 101–108 that support your answer.

F MAKE INFERENCES
Reread lines 121–133. Why does Mama cry?

Possible answer: Doodle walks—something she never expected him to be able to do.

Why does the narrator cry?

Possible answer: He knows that Doodle's walking is the result of his selfish pride.

Underline the words that explain why the narrator cries.

IN OTHER WORDS The narrator decides to teach Doodle to walk. On Doodle's sixth birthday, the boys surprise the family by showing them that Doodle can walk. They are happy, but the narrator knows that he taught Doodle to walk for selfish reasons.

► Why does the narrator really want his brother to learn to walk? Mark brackets [ ] around the statement that tells you.

Within a few months Doodle had learned to walk. Now, when we wandered, we never went back home until we reached where we had planned to go. To help pass the time, we took up lying. Doodle was a terrible liar, and he got me in the habit of telling lies, too.

My lies were scary, complicated, and usually pointless, but Doodle's were twice as crazy. People in his stories all had wings and flew wherever they wanted to go. His favorite lie was about a boy named Peter who had a pet peacock with a ten-foot tail. When Peter was ready to go to sleep, the peacock spread his huge, magnificent tail, folding the boy gently in its colorful feathers like a closing go-to-sleep flower. Doodle and I spent lots of time thinking about our future. We decided that when we were grown we'd live at the swamp. G

IN OTHER WORDS Doodle and the narrator spend a lot of time together at the swamp. They make up stories. Doodle's stories are beautiful and colorful, such as the story he tells about a boy and his pet peacock. The brothers plan to live together at the swamp when they grow up.

Once I had taught Doodle to walk, I began to believe in my own <u>infallibility</u>. I prepared a terrific list of skills for him to learn, unknown to Mama and Daddy. I would teach him to run, to swim, to climb trees, and to fight. <u>He, too, believed that I could never be wrong</u>, so we decided that he'd learn how to do everything in less than a year, when Doodle could start school.

G SYMBOL

Reread lines 139–147. Think about the kinds of "lies" Doodle tells. What might Doodle's "lies" symbolize, or stand for?

Possible answer: Doodle's impending death

VOCABULARY

The word **infallibility** (in fal uh BIL uh tee) is a noun that means *an inability to make mistakes.*

Underline the words that show that Doodle believes in the narrator's *infallibility.*

That winter we didn't get far because I was in school and Doodle was sick with colds a lot. But when spring came, we tried again. I gave Doodle swimming lessons or showed him how to row a boat. Sometimes we climbed vines or boxed beneath the tree where he had learned to walk. Promise hung about us like the leaves.

That summer of 1918 was a disaster. There was no rain and the crops dried up, then died. In July a hurricane's winds tore trees out of the ground. And during that summer, we heard the names of World War I battlefields in France. In her blessing at the supper table, Mama once said, "And bless the Pearsons, whose boy Joe was lost at Belleau Wood."[4]

IN OTHER WORDS After Doodle learns to walk, the narrator feels confident that he can teach Doodle to do much more. He wants to teach Doodle to swim and row. The summer of 1918 is very bad. Storms destroy crops and many men die in France as the war goes on.

We were between summer and fall. School was only a few weeks away, and Doodle was far behind schedule. He could barely get up off the ground when he climbed the vines, and he still couldn't swim well. [We decided to work twice as hard.] [I made him swim and row until he was exhausted, with no energy left at all.] Wherever we went, [I walked fast on purpose.] Although he kept up, he was very tired. Once, he could go no further. He collapsed on the ground and began to cry.

"Aw, come on, Doodle," I urged. "You can do it. Do you want to be different from everybody else when you start school?"

"Does it make any difference?"

"It certainly does," I said. "Now, come on," and I helped him up. **H**

H MAKE INFERENCES
Reread lines 166–178. Draw brackets [ ] around each thing the narrator does because Doodle is "far behind schedule."

Why is the narrator so worried about Doodle starting school?

Possible answer: He wants Doodle to be able to do the same things as everyone else.

Doodle began to look hot and feverish, and Mama asked him if he felt ill. At night he didn't sleep well. Sometimes he had

4. **Belleau Wood** (beh LOH wud): a place in France where famous battles were fought near the end of World War I (1914–1918).

nightmares, crying out until I touched him and said, "Wake up, Doodle. Wake up."

IN OTHER WORDS School starts soon, so the brothers decide to work even harder to reach their goal. Doodle tires easily, but his brother wants him to keep working. He asks Doodle if he wants to be different from other kids at school. But things aren't easy for Doodle, and he struggles. He looks sick and has bad dreams.

It was a few days before school started. Doodle still couldn't do all the things I had been teaching him. I should already have given up and admitted defeat, but my pride wouldn't let me. Our training no longer excited us, but we still kept on. ❶

Daddy, Mama, Doodle, and I were seated at the dining-room table having lunch. "It's so calm, I wouldn't be surprised if we had a storm this afternoon," Daddy remarked.

"I haven't heard a rain frog," said Mama, who believed in signs.[5]

"I did," declared Doodle. "Down in the swamp."

"He didn't," I said, disagreeing.

"You did, eh?" said Daddy to Doodle, ignoring my denial.

"I certainly did," Doodle repeated.

Suddenly, from out in the yard, came a strange croaking noise. "What's that?" Doodle whispered.

Doodle slipped out into the yard. He was looking up into the bleeding tree. "It's a great big red bird!" he called.

The bird croaked loudly again, and Mama and Daddy came out into the yard. On the highest branch a bird the size of a chicken, with scarlet feathers and long legs, was perched **precariously** as if it might fall. As we watched, one of its feathers dropped away and floated down.

"It looks tired," Daddy added. "Or maybe sick."

I had never seen Doodle stand still for so long. "What is it?" he asked.

Daddy shook his head. "I don't know, maybe it's—."

5. **signs:** warnings of events to come.

Monitor Your Comprehension

❶ MAKE INFERENCES

Neither Doodle nor the narrator enjoys Doodle's training. Still, they continue to work toward their goal together.

Why does the narrator continue training Doodle?

His pride will not let him give up.

Why does Doodle continue training with the narrator?

Possible answer: Doodle enjoys spending time with his brother.

Based on your answers above, how would you describe the relationship between the narrator and Doodle?

Possible answer: They love each other, but Doodle is more innocent and needy, while the narrator is full of pride and self interest.

VOCABULARY

The word **precariously** (prih KAIR ee uhs lee) is an adverb that means *insecurely* or *in a dangerous or unstable way.*

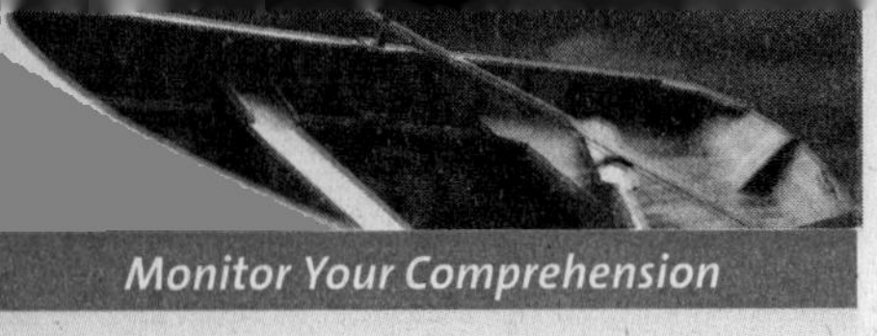

Monitor Your Comprehension

At that moment the bird began to beat its wings, but it lost its balance. It tumbled down, bumping through the limbs of the tree. It landed at our feet with a thud. Its long, graceful neck jerked twice. Then the bird was still. Its legs were crossed and its feet were curved at rest. It was graceful even in death. It lay on the earth like a broken vase of red flowers, and we stood around it, awed by its **exotic** beauty. ❶

"It's dead," Mama said.

"What is it?" Doodle repeated.

"Go bring me the bird book," said Daddy.

Daddy looked through the book. "It's a scarlet ibis," he said, pointing to a picture. "It lives from South America to Florida. A storm must have brought it here."

Sadly, we all looked back at the bird. A scarlet ibis! How many miles it had traveled to die like this, in *our* yard, beneath the bleeding tree.

IN OTHER WORDS A strange noise interrupts lunch. A beautiful and unusual red bird lands on a tree outside. As the narrator and his family watch, the bird falls to the ground and dies. They find out that the bird is a scarlet ibis. It has wandered far from its home.

"Let's finish lunch," Mama said.

"I'm not hungry," said Doodle, and he knelt down beside the ibis. "I'm going to bury him."

"Don't you dare touch him," Mama warned. "There's no telling what disease he might have had."

"All right," said Doodle. "I won't."

Daddy, Mama, and I watched Doodle through the open door. He took out a piece of string from his pocket and, without touching the ibis, looped one end around its neck. Slowly, while singing a hymn, he carried the bird to the front yard. He dug a hole in the flower garden. He looked awkward and clumsy as he dug the hole with a shovel whose handle was twice as long as

VOCABULARY

The word **exotic** (ig ZOT ik) is an adjective that means *excitingly strange.*

❶ SYMBOL

Reread lines 200–216. The description of the bird seems to give it a special, symbolic meaning.

What character in the story does the bird remind you of?

Possible answer: Doodle

Why does the bird remind you of that character?

Possible answer: Both the bird and Doodle seem out of place. The bird is fragile and clumsy like Doodle.

he was. It made us laugh, and we covered our mouths with our hands so he wouldn't hear. **PAUSE & REFLECT**

"Did you get the scarlet ibis buried?" asked Daddy when Doodle returned.

Doodle nodded his head.

"Go wash your hands, and then you can have some dessert," said Mama.

"I'm not hungry," he said.

"Dead birds is bad luck," said Aunt Nicey, poking her head out the kitchen door. "Specially *red* dead birds!"

IN OTHER WORDS The death of the ibis upsets Doodle. He refuses to finish lunch. Instead, he buries the bird. No one offers to help him. The others laugh as he struggles to bury it. The boys' aunt says that dead birds are bad luck.

As soon as I had finished eating, Doodle and I hurried off to practice. Time was short. (K) Doodle had a long way to go if he was going to keep up with the other boys at school. Doodle said he was too tired to swim, so we got into a boat and floated down the creek. I put the oars in place and made Doodle row back against the outgoing tide to where we had started. It was hard work. Black clouds began to gather, and he kept watching them, trying to row a little faster. By the time we reached the shore, lightning was flashing across half the sky and thunder roared. The clouds hid the sun, making it dark as night.

Doodle was both tired and frightened. When he stepped from the boat he collapsed onto the mud. I helped him up and he smiled at me, ashamed. He had failed and we both knew it. We started back home, racing the storm. We never spoke, but I knew he was watching me for a sign of mercy, a little kindness. The lightning was near now. He was afraid and walked so close behind me he kept stepping on my heels. The faster I walked, the faster he walked, so I began to run. The rain was coming. Then a gum tree ahead of us was blasted apart by a bolt of

Monitor Your Comprehension

PAUSE & REFLECT
With a partner, discuss how Doodle's reaction to the death of the ibis differs from the reaction of the rest of the family.

Students should discuss that Doodle identifies with the ibis right away. The rest of the family only sees the ibis as a dead bird.

(K) LANGUAGE COACH
An **idiom** is an expression whose meaning differs from the meaning of the expression's individual words. For example, in line 248, the narrator tells you that "time was short." The word *short* usually refers to height. However, the idiom means that little time is left.

lightning. I heard Doodle, who couldn't run as fast and had fallen behind, cry out, "Brother, Brother, don't leave me! Don't leave me!"

IN OTHER WORDS The narrator makes Doodle row a boat. A thunderstorm approaches. When they reach land, Doodle falls to the ground. The narrator is angry. When he and Doodle run home to escape the storm, he leaves Doodle behind. Doodle cries out.

▶ Reread lines 257–268. Discuss with a partner why the narrator leaves Doodle behind.

Students should discuss that the narrator is frustrated or irritated with Doodle because he is behind schedule in his swimming and rowing.

Knowing that our plans had come to nothing woke up that streak of cruelty within me. I ran as fast as I could, leaving him far behind. Soon I couldn't hear his voice. I hadn't run too far before I became tired. I stopped and waited for Doodle. As I waited, I peered through the heavy rain, hoping I'd see him, but he did not come. Finally I went back. I found him huddled beneath a red nightshade bush[6] beside the road. He was sitting on the ground, his face buried in his arms, which were resting on his drawn-up knees. "Let's go, Doodle," I said.

He didn't answer, so I placed my hand on his forehead and lifted his head. Limply, he fell backward. He had been bleeding from the mouth, and his neck and the front of his shirt were stained a brilliant red.

"Doodle! Doodle!" I cried, shaking him, but there was no answer. He lay with his head thrown far back, making his red neck appear unusually long and slim. His little legs, bent sharply at the knees, had never before seemed so fragile, so thin. Ⓛ

I began to weep. "Doodle!" I screamed and threw my body over his. It seemed that I lay there forever crying, sheltering my fallen scarlet ibis from the heresy of rain.

Ⓛ SYMBOL

The color red appears three times in this section of the story. It also appears in several other sections of the story.

What do you think the color red might symbolize? Why?

Possible answer: The scarlet ibis; because the narrator realizes that Doodle is fragile like the bird

VOCABULARY

The word **heresy** (HEHR ih see) is a noun that means *an action or opinion that goes against what is generally thought of as right.*

IN OTHER WORDS The narrator stops to wait for Doodle. When Doodle does not appear, he goes back to look for him. He finds the little boy curled under a bush. Doodle is unmoving and covered in blood. The narrator cries and holds his dead brother. He calls him his scarlet ibis.

---

6. **red nightshade bush:** a poisonous flowering plant.

After Reading

Text Analysis: Symbol

In "The Scarlet Ibis," some of the people, places, things, and events are also symbols; they stand both for themselves and for something beyond themselves. Fill out the chart below to identify the meanings of some of the story's symbols.

For this chart, answers will vary. See samples below.

Symbol	My Response	Meaning
Peacock (lines 143–145)	*In the passage, the peacock is comforting and beautiful.*	*love and protection; a kinder, happier world*
Coffin (lines 71–73)	*The narrator showed Doodle a coffin and told him that the family believed he would die.*	*cruelty*
Scarlet ibis (lines 222–224)	*The bird flew many miles only to die beneath the bleeding tree.*	*sadness*

What do the symbols in the story reveal about its theme—its underlying message about life or human nature? State the story's theme in a complete sentence.

Possible answer: Delicate creatures need to be cared for and protected.

Why do we HURT the ones we LOVE?

What harm can come from being cruel to loved ones?

Possible answer: The loved one can end up feeling more hurt than was intended. The loved one may even change his or her feelings toward the person who was cruel.

Reading Skill: Make Inferences About Characters

When you make inferences about characters, you make educated guesses about them based on their appearance, speech, actions, and thoughts and on the reactions of other characters.

Find three details from the text that describe Doodle. Choose one detail that describes his appearance, another that describes his speech, and a third detail that describes his actions. Then make an inference for each one.

For this chart, answers will vary. See samples below.

Detail from Text	My Experience	My Inference
Appearance: *When he was born, Doodle was all head. He had a tiny body which was red and shriveled.*	*When a baby is born and weighs very little, the baby may have problems developing.*	*Doodle may have physical disabilities.*
Speech: *When Doodle sat in the grass he cried and said "So pretty, pretty, pretty."*	*When someone experiences something for the first time, they may cry tears of joy.*	*Doodle has never seen anything as beautiful as the swamp.*
Actions: *When Doodle touched the coffin he screamed.*	*People often scream when they are afraid.*	*Doodle is afraid of the coffin.*

Vocabulary Practice

Circle the word that is closest in meaning to the boldface Vocabulary word.

1. **infallibility** **(a)** clumsiness **(b)** perfection **(c)** risk-taking
2. **precariously** **(a)** dangerously **(b)** cleverly **(c)** foolishly
3. **exotic** **(a)** ordinary **(b)** unusual **(c)** comfortable
4. **heresy** **(a)** disobedience **(b)** agreement **(c)** repetition

Academic Vocabulary in Speaking

The word **reveal** (rih VEEL) is a verb that means *to show or make known.*

The writer chose to **reveal** the personality of one of her story's characters by showing how that character acts.

The word **significant** (sig NIF ih kuhnt) is an adjective that means *important or having meaning.*

He explained why the symbols in his painting were **significant.**

TURN AND TALK The author of "The Scarlet Ibis" uses **significant** symbols to help **reveal** the story's theme. With a partner, discuss how the story's many symbols help show you the theme. Be sure to use the words **significant** and **reveal** in your conversation.

Encourage students to use the Academic Vocabulary words in their discussions.

Assessment Practice

DIRECTIONS Use "The Scarlet Ibis" to answer questions 1–6.

1 Why does the narrator teach Doodle to walk?

- A He likes teaching Doodle new things.
- B His parents asked him to teach Doodle.
- C He wants to prove that Doodle can walk.
- D He feels embarrassed because Doodle can't walk.

2 Why does the narrator take Doodle to Old Woman Swamp?

- A The narrator has to take him because their parents are waiting for them there.
- B The narrator wants to frighten Doodle out of wanting to be with him.
- C The narrator accepts Doodle and decides to share a beautiful place with him.
- D The narrator thinks it is the best place to teach someone to run, swim, and climb trees.

3 The scarlet ibis serves as a symbol for Doodle because both the child and the bird are —

- A able to move very quickly
- B lost and lonely
- C rare and delicate
- D likely to be found outside

4 Which of the following themes does the symbolism of the ibis best support?

- A Anger sometimes leads people to be cruel.
- B Delicate creatures need to be protected and cared for.
- C Brothers often compete for their parents' attention.
- D Life in the swamps can be full of surprises.

5 Which of the following does *not* describe the narrator's feelings toward Doodle?

- A Generous
- B Disappointed
- C Ashamed
- D Jealous

6 From his efforts to bury the ibis, what inference can you make about Doodle?

- A He killed the bird.
- B He likes to bury things.
- C He feels sorry for the bird.
- D He does what his mother tells him to do.

Poem on Returning to Dwell in the Country

Poem by T'ao Ch'ien

My Heart Leaps Up

Poem by William Wordsworth

The Sun

Poem by Mary Oliver

Where do you go to GET AWAY from it all?

What does nature do for you? Whether it's watching fish in an aquarium or hiking in the mountains, many people look to nature for beauty, serenity, and relaxation. The poems that follow reflect on things in nature.

WRITE IT On the lines at left, list types of nature activities you enjoy and the reasons why you enjoy them.

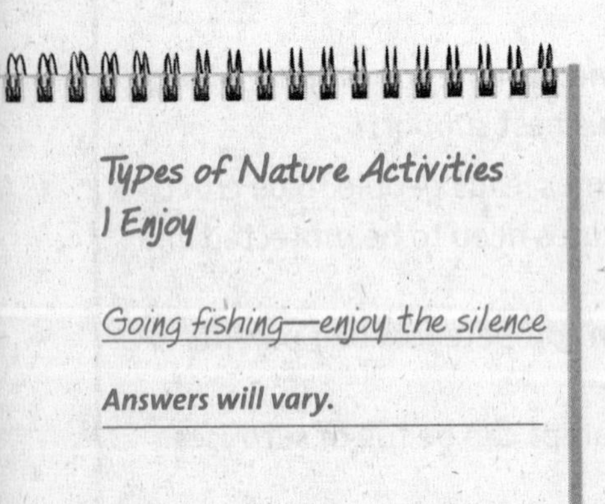

Types of Nature Activities I Enjoy
Going fishing—enjoy the silence
Answers will vary.

Text Analysis: Universal Theme

Some themes, or messages, in poetry are universal. A **universal theme** is an idea that people from many cultures and times have found to be true. The poems you are about to read all describe a love of nature. Although the poems come from different cultures and times, all three poems talk about the same universal theme. As you read each poem, use these questions to think about this universal theme:

- What idea about nature does each poem mention?
- What theme does each poem contain on its own?
- How are the poems similar or different?

Reading Strategy: Reading Poetry for Theme

The **theme** of a work is the message about life or human nature that it reveals. The words in a poem are carefully chosen and arranged to show the poem's message. To understand theme in poetry, you need to look at details differently than you would when reading a story. Use the questions in the chart below to help you identify the theme in each poem.

Clue	Ask Yourself	Details from the Poem
Title	What is the title of the poem? Often the title of a work offers clues to its theme.	
Speaker	Who is the speaker, the person talking in the poem? What is the speaker's attitude toward the subject of the poem?	
Key Words and Phrases	Are there any words or phrases that may hint at the writer's message? Watch for words that are repeated or presented at the beginning or end of a line.	
Images	Are there any key images or ideas that are emphasized in the poem? Why are they important?	

Monitor Your Comprehension

SET A PURPOSE FOR READING

Read this poem to find out why the speaker returns to the mountains and hills that he loved as a child.

Poem on Returning to Dwell in the Country

Poem by
T'AO CH'IEN
Translated by William Acker

BACKGROUND Chinese poet T'ao Ch'ien lived from 365–427. He grew up in the country, but he left his farm to work in the city. When he got tired of the city, he decided to move back to his family farm. His poetry reflects the idea of living simply and close to nature.

In youth I had nothing
  that matched the vulgar tone,
For my nature always
  loved the hills and mountains.
Inadvertently I fell
  into the Dusty Net,
Once having gone
  it was more than thirteen years.
The tame bird
  longs for his old forest—
The fish in the house-pond
  thinks of his ancient pool. Ⓐ

IN OTHER WORDS The speaker remembers his life as a youth when he loved nature. Then one day he left for the city. He felt trapped there, as if caught in a net.

► How long does the speaker say he was trapped? Circle the answer.

Ⓐ **READING POETRY FOR THEME**

Think about the images in lines 9–12. The words *tame* and *house-pond* might make you think of captivity. Why would a tame bird want to go back to his old forest?

Possible answer: He misses the surroundings where he once flew free.

Why does the fish in the house-pond think of his ancient pool?

Possible answer: He wants to return to his home in nature.

I too will break the soil
    at the edge of the southern moor,
I will guard simplicity
    and return to my fields and garden.
My land and house—
    a little more than ten acres,
In the thatched cottage—
    only eight or nine rooms.
Elms and willows
    shade the back verandah,
Peach and plum trees
    in rows before the hall.

IN OTHER WORDS The speaker decides to return home and farm the land. He describes the fields, house, and trees around his home.

Hazy and dimly seen
    a village in the distance,
Close in the foreground
    the smoke of neighbors' houses.
A dog barks
    amidst the deep lanes,
A cock is crowing
    atop a mulberry tree.
No dust and confusion
    within my doors and courtyard;
In the empty rooms
    more than sufficient leisure. **PAUSE & REFLECT**

PAUSE & REFLECT

Reread lines 33–36. What is the speaker saying about the difference between life in the country and life elsewhere?

Possible answer: Life is simpler in the country where there is no dust or confusion and there are places to relax.

Too long I was held
　　within the barred cage.
Now I am able
　　to return again to Nature. (B)

IN OTHER WORDS Next, the speaker talks about the sights and sounds of home—the town in the distance, dogs barking, a rooster crowing. The speaker says his home is clean and orderly.

► With a partner, discuss how the speaker feels about the country.

Students should discuss what the speaker doesn't like about where he used to live and what the speaker likes about the country.

(B) UNIVERSAL THEME

Reread lines 37–40. What do you think the poet means by the "barred cage"?

Possible answer: The "barred cage" is the way of life the speaker is giving up.

My Heart Leaps Up

SET A PURPOSE FOR READING
Read this poem to find out what makes the speaker's heart leap.

Poem by
WILLIAM WORDSWORTH

BACKGROUND As a child, British poet William Wordsworth loved being outdoors. His appreciation of nature never left him. Many of his poems show how much he loved and admired the natural world.

My heart leaps up when I behold
  A rainbow in the sky:
So was it when my life began;
So is it now I am a man;
So be it when I shall grow old,
  Or let me die! C
The Child is father of the Man;
And I could wish my days to be
Bound each to each by natural piety.[1]

IN OTHER WORDS The speaker talks about how happy he was when he saw a rainbow as a child. As a grown man, he feels the same joy. He believes that when he's old, he will still love nature, and he hopes that his childlike view will stay with him throughout his life.

C UNIVERSAL THEME
What does the speaker say in lines 1–6 about his feelings toward nature?
Possible answer: He feels joy whenever he sees a rainbow. He had the same feeling as a child and wishes to still have the same feeling when he is old.

1. **piety** (PY ih tee): religious devotion.

Monitor Your Comprehension

SET A PURPOSE FOR READING

Read this poem to understand the speaker's appreciation of the sun.

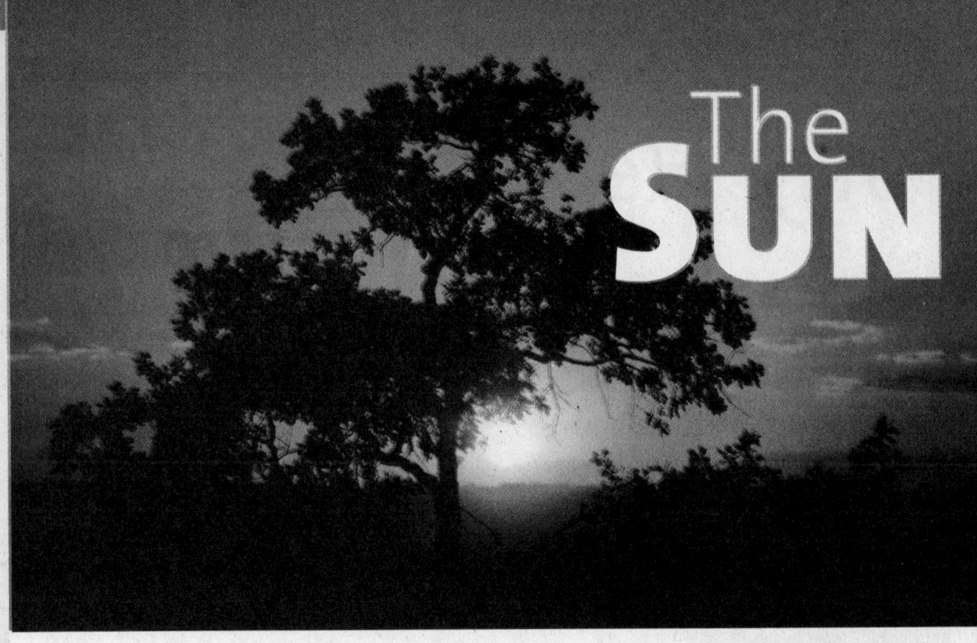

The SUN

Poem by

MARY OLIVER

BACKGROUND Nature poets often focus on one part of the world. In this poem, Mary Oliver explores emotions people have when they see and think about the sun.

Have you ever seen
anything
in your life
more wonderful

than the way the sun,
every evening,
relaxed and easy,
floats toward the horizon

and into the clouds or the hills,
or the rumpled sea,
and is gone— **PAUSE & REFLECT**
and how it slides again

PAUSE & REFLECT

How would you answer the question the speaker asks in lines 1–11? Explain your response.

Answers will vary.

out of the blackness,
every morning,
on the other side of the world,
like a red flower **D**

streaming upward on its heavenly oils,
say, on a morning in early summer,
at its perfect imperial distance— **E**
and have you ever felt for anything

such wild love—
do you think there is anywhere, in any language,
a word billowing enough
for the pleasure

that fills you,
as the sun
reaches out,
as it warms you

as you stand there,
empty-handed—
or have you too
turned from this world—

or have you too
gone crazy
for power,
for things? **F**

IN OTHER WORDS The speaker of this poem asks: Have you ever seen anything as wonderful as the sun setting and rising? Have you ever felt happy to be warmed by the sun?

► Reread lines 31–36. With a partner, discuss the meaning of the speaker's questions in these lines.

Students should discuss how power and material things might interfere with people's appreciation of nature.

Monitor Your Comprehension

D READING POETRY FOR THEME

Circle the visual images you find in lines 5–16.

E READING POETRY FOR THEME

Look back at the speaker's description of the sun in lines 1–19. What can you infer, or guess, about how the speaker feels toward nature based on this description?

Possible answer: The speaker looks at nature with a mix of wonder and joy.

F UNIVERSAL THEME

Reread lines 31–36. What question does the speaker ask?

Possible answer: Have we rejected nature for power and possessions?

Why does the speaker talk about power and things as separate from nature?

Possible answer: The speaker probably feels that power and material things often distract us from the wonders of nature.

Text Analysis: Universal Theme

Think about the three poems about nature you just read. In the chart below, identify the theme, or message, expressed in each poem. Then write down a single universal theme that all of the pieces share.

For this chart, answers will vary. See samples below.

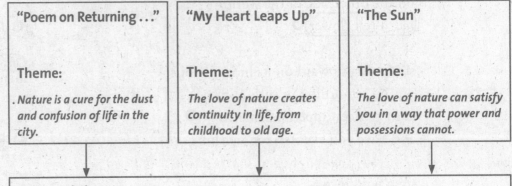

"Poem on Returning . . ."	"My Heart Leaps Up"	"The Sun"
Theme: *Nature is a cure for the dust and confusion of life in the city.*	Theme: *The love of nature creates continuity in life, from childhood to old age.*	Theme: *The love of nature can satisfy you in a way that power and possessions cannot.*

Universal Theme:
Connecting to the natural world provides a simple but powerful joy.

Reading Strategy: Reading Poetry for Theme

In the previous chart you named the themes of the three poems you just read. What clues led you to those themes? Identify those clues in the chart below.

For this chart, answers will vary. See samples below.

Poem	Theme	Clues: Title, Speaker, Key Words/Phrases, Images
Poem on Returning to Dwell in the Country	*Nature is a cure for the dust and confusion of life in the city.*	*title; "dust and confusion" (line 33), "barred cage" (line 38)*
My Heart Leaps Up	*The love of nature creates continuity in life, from childhood to old age.*	*title; "behold a rainbow in the sky" (lines 1–2)*
The Sun	*The love of nature can satisfy you in a way that power and possessions cannot.*	*title; first two stanzas*

Where do you go to **GET AWAY** from it all?

Is there a place in nature that's all your own—a backyard, a park, or a truly wild area? Describe that place and why it is special to you below.

Answers will vary.

Academic Vocabulary in Speaking

The word**interpret** (in TER prit) is a verb that means *to explain or make clear the meaning of something.*

Joshua was able to **interpret** the real meaning of the story.

TURN AND TALK Choose one of these poems and decide how you would **interpret** it. With a classmate, discuss what you think the poem means. Be sure to use the word**interpret** in your discussion.

Encourage students to use the Academic Vocabulary word in their discussions.

Assessment Practice

DIRECTIONS Use the poems to answer questions 1–4.

1 In "Poem on Returning to Dwell in the Country," what change does the speaker make in his life?

- A He moves from the country to the city.
- B The speaker moves to the country.
- C He decides he no longer enjoys the country.
- D He does not make any changes.

2 In "My Heart Leaps Up," the speaker wishes to —

- A never grow old
- B see a rainbow every day
- C always love nature
- D fall in love

3 In "The Sun," what does the speaker think is the most wonderful thing in life?

- A Sunrises and sunsets
- B The beauty of red flowers
- C The sky and sea
- D Summertime

4 Which of the following best expresses the universal theme found in all three poems?

- A People cannot live without nature.
- B Nature can be powerful and dangerous.
- C Connecting to nature provides a simple but powerful joy.
- D Some types of nature are more beautiful than others.

Two Kinds

Short story by **Amy Tan**

Rice and Rose Bowl Blues

Poem by **Diane Mei Lin Mark**

How do **EXPECTATIONS** affect what we do?

Has someone ever set really high goals for you? Maybe your parents expected you to make top grades or a coach expected you to win a race. How did you respond to those expectations? Did you work harder to meet their goals? Or did you rebel?

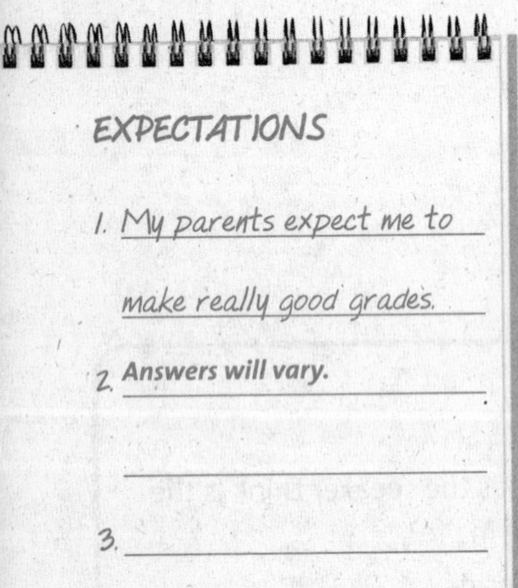

EXPECTATIONS
1. My parents expect me to
make really good grades.
2. Answers will vary.
3.

TURN AND TALK At left, list two or three expectations others have had for you. Then, choose one of those expectations to discuss with a partner. Talk about how you responded to the expectations.

Text Analysis: Theme Across Genres

You will read a short story and a poem about young people trying to discover their identity as they face the expectations of their parents. Both works have a similar **theme,** or insight about life, even though they are different types of literature. The short story writer and the poet use different techniques to express the theme of their work. The chart below lists questions that will help you uncover the theme.

Points of Comparison	In the Story	In the Poem
What is the main conflict, or struggle?		
What lesson does the narrator or speaker learn?		
What do you learn from the title?		
What is the theme, or message, of the work?		

As you read, try to identify the theme of each work.

Reading Strategy: Set a Purpose for Reading

When you **set a purpose** for reading, you have a specific reason for reading a work. Your main purpose for reading "Two Kinds" and "Rice and Rose Bowl Blues" is to identify the theme of each work. As you read, you may find that other purposes keep you involved in the selections. For example, if you have been in a similar situation, you may read with the purpose of comparing what you did with what the narrator does when faced with pressure to excel.

Vocabulary in Context

Note: Words are listed in the order in which they appear in the story.

Prodigy (PROD uh jee) is a noun that means *a person who is very talented or intelligent.*
The young **prodigy** played the piano with great confidence.

Reproach (rih PROHCH) is a noun that means *blame or criticism.*
Jing-mei often felt her parents' **reproach.**

Discordant (dis KOR duhnt) is an adjective that means *having clashing sounds.*
The sounds coming from the piano were very **discordant.**

Lament (luh MENT) is a verb that means *to express sorrow or regret.*
Jing-mei might one day **lament** her failure to practice the piano.

Vocabulary Practice

Review the words and sample sentences above. Then, answer these questions.

1. What is one area in which you would like to be a **prodigy**? Why?

Answers will vary.

2. If you received a **reproach** for something, how would you feel?

Answers will vary.

3. What is something that sounds **discordant**? Why?

Answers will vary.

4. What is one thing you **lament** either doing or not doing? Why?

Answers will vary.

SET A PURPOSE FOR READING
Read this short story to discover how one girl rebels against her mother's high expectations.

Two Kinds

Short story by
AMY TAN

BACKGROUND In Chinese culture, children are expected to respect and obey their parents. The storyteller in "Two Kinds" is Jing-mei (JENG may), a young Chinese American girl. The narrator's mother expects Jing-mei to obey her and honor her every wish. However, Jing-mei soon begins to rebel against her mother.

My mother believed you could be anything you wanted to be in America. You could open a restaurant. You could work for the government and get good retirement. You could buy a house with almost no money down. You could become rich. You could become instantly famous.

"Of course you can be **prodigy**, too," my mother told me when I was nine. "You can be best anything. What does Auntie Lindo know? Her daughter, she is only best tricky."

VOCABULARY
The word **prodigy** (PROD uh jee) is a noun that means *a person who is very talented or intelligent.*

America was where all my mother's hopes lay. She had come here in 1949 after losing everything in China: her mother and father, her family home, her first husband, and two daughters, twin baby girls. But she never looked back with regret. There were so many ways for things to get better.

We didn't immediately pick the right kind of prodigy. At first my mother thought I could be a Chinese Shirley Temple.[1] We'd watch Shirley's old movies on TV as though they were training films. My mother would poke my arm and say, "*Ni kan*"—You

1. **Shirley Temple:** a popular child movie star from 1930–50.

watch. And I would see Shirley tapping her feet, or singing a sailor song, or pursing her lips into a very round O while saying, "Oh my goodness."

IN OTHER WORDS The narrator, Jing-mei, begins by telling about her mother's views of America as a land of opportunity. Jing-mei's mother came to America to live in 1949 after facing much loss in China. She hopes her daughter will be a prodigy (PROD uh jee), maybe as a child movie star.

"*Ni kan,*" said my mother as Shirley's eyes flooded with tears. "You already know how. Don't need talent for crying!"

Soon after my mother got this idea about Shirley Temple, she took me to a beauty training school in the Mission district and put me in the hands of a student who could barely hold the scissors without shaking. Instead of getting big fat curls, I emerged with an uneven mass of crinkly black fuzz. My mother dragged me off to the bathroom and tried to wet down my hair.

"You look like Negro Chinese," she lamented, as if I had done this on purpose.

The instructor of the beauty training school had to lop off these soggy clumps to make my hair even again. "Peter Pan is very popular these days," the instructor assured my mother. I now had hair the length of a boy's, with straight-across bangs that hung at a slant two inches above my eyebrows. I liked the haircut, and it made me actually look forward to my future fame.

In fact, in the beginning, I was just as excited as my mother, maybe even more so. I pictured this prodigy part of me as many different images, trying each one on for size. I was a dainty **ballerina** girl standing by the curtains, waiting to hear the right music that would send me floating on my tiptoes. I was like the Christ child lifted out of the straw manger, crying with holy indignity. I was Cinderella stepping from her pumpkin carriage with sparkly cartoon music filling the air.

VISUAL VOCABULARY
A **ballerina** (bal uh REE nuh) is a female ballet dancer.

Monitor Your Comprehension

In all of my imaginings, I was filled with a sense that I would soon become *perfect*. My mother and father would adore me. I would be beyond **reproach**. I would never feel the need to sulk for anything.

VOCABULARY

The word **reproach** (rih PROHCH) is a noun that means *blame* or *criticism*.

IN OTHER WORDS Jing-mei's mother takes Jing-mei to get a haircut, but she ends up looking more like the boy character Peter Pan than Shirley Temple. Jing-mei doesn't see this as a problem. She soon is excited about the idea of becoming a prodigy. She tries to be perfect and wants her parents' approval.

► Underline the three people that Jing-mei thinks she is like.

But sometimes the prodigy in me became impatient. "If you don't hurry up and get me out of here, I'm disappearing for good," it warned. "And then you'll always be nothing." Ⓐ

Every night after dinner, my mother and I would sit at the Formica kitchen table. She would present new tests, taking her examples from stories of amazing children she had read in *Ripley's Believe It or Not*, or *Good Housekeeping*, *Reader's Digest*, and a dozen other magazines she kept in a pile in our bathroom. My mother got these magazines from people whose houses she cleaned. And since she cleaned many houses each week, we had a great assortment. She would look through them all, searching for stories about remarkable children.

The first night she brought out a story about a three-year-old boy who knew the capitals of all the states and even most of the European countries. A teacher was quoted as saying the little boy could also pronounce the names of the foreign cities correctly.

"What's the capital of Finland?" my mother asked me, looking at the magazine story.

All I knew was the capital of California, because Sacramento was the name of the street we lived on in Chinatown. "Nairobi!"[2] I guessed, saying the most foreign word I could think of. She checked to see if that was possibly one way to pronounce "Helsinki" before showing me the answer.

Ⓐ **THEME**

Reread lines 38–49. In these lines, how does Jing-mei feel about becoming a prodigy?

She is excited about it.

Now reread lines 50–52. In these lines, how does she feel about becoming a prodigy?

Possible answer: She is impatient and insecure about the likelihood of succeeding if it doesn't happen very soon.

2. **Nairobi** (ny ROH bee): the capital of the African nation of Kenya.

Monitor Your Comprehension

IN OTHER WORDS As time passes, Jing-mei begins to worry that she may not become a prodigy. Jing-mei's mother refuses to give up. She reads many magazine articles about remarkable children. She keeps testing Jing-mei to see if she might have similar traits or abilities.

The tests got harder—multiplying numbers in my head, finding the queen of hearts in a deck of cards, trying to stand on my head without using my hands, predicting the daily temperatures in Los Angeles, New York, and London.

One night I had to look at a page from the Bible for three minutes and then report everything I could remember. "Now Jehoshaphat had riches and honor in abundance and . . . that's all I remember, Ma," I said. B

And after seeing my mother's disappointed face once again, something inside of me began to die. I hated the tests, the raised hopes and failed expectations. Before going to bed that night, I looked in the mirror above the bathroom sink and when I saw only my face staring back—and that it would always be this ordinary face—I began to cry. Such a sad, ugly girl! I made high-pitched noises like a crazed animal, trying to scratch out the face in the mirror.

And then I saw what seemed to be the prodigy side of me—because I had never seen that face before. I looked at my reflection, blinking so I could see more clearly. The girl staring back at me was angry, powerful. This girl and I were the same. I had new thoughts, willful thoughts, or rather thoughts filled with lots of won'ts. I won't let her change me, I promised myself. I won't be what I'm not. C

So now on nights when my mother presented her tests, I performed listlessly, my head propped on one arm. I pretended to be bored. And I was. I got so bored I started counting the bellows of the foghorns out on the bay while my mother drilled me in other areas. The sound was comforting and reminded me of the cow jumping over the moon. And the next day, I played a game with myself, seeing if my mother would give up on me

B THEME

Reread lines 62–80. Why do you think Jing-mei's mother asks her to do such impossible things?

Possible answer: She hopes Jing-mei is a prodigy.

C SET A PURPOSE FOR READING

Reread lines 89–95. How is Jing-mei's attitude changing about the tests her mother gives her? With a partner, discuss what you hope to find out about this change in Jing-mei as you read.

Students should discuss what they will find out about Jing-mei's attitude and how she will react to her mother in the future.

before eight bellows. After a while I usually counted only one, maybe two bellows at most. At last she was beginning to give up hope.

Two or three months had gone by without any mention of my being a prodigy again. And then one day my mother was watching *The Ed Sullivan Show* on TV. The TV was old and the sound kept shorting out. Every time my mother got halfway up from the sofa to adjust the set, the sound would go back on and Ed would be talking. As soon as she sat down, Ed would go silent again. She got up, the TV broke into loud piano music. She sat down. Silence. Up and down, back and forth, quiet and loud. **D** It was like a stiff, embraceless dance between her and the TV set. Finally she stood by the set with her hand on the sound dial.

D LANGUAGE COACH
Sometimes writers use **sentence fragments,** or incomplete sentences, to help express events that happen quickly or abruptly. In lines 113–114, the writer uses two fragments: The one-word fragment "Silence" and the next fragment starting with "Up and down, . . ." are used to help you understand what is happening with the mother and the TV.

She seemed entranced by the music, a little frenzied piano piece with this mesmerizing[3] quality, sort of quick passages and then teasing lilting ones before it returned to the quick playful parts.

"*Ni kan,*" my mother said, calling me over with hurried hand gestures, "Look here."

I could see why my mother was fascinated by the music. It was being pounded out by a little Chinese girl, about nine years old, with a Peter Pan haircut. The girl had the sauciness of a Shirley Temple. She was proudly modest like a proper Chinese child. And she also did this fancy sweep of a curtsy, so that the fluffy skirt of her white dress cascaded slowly to the floor like the petals of a large carnation.

In spite of these warning signs, I wasn't worried. Our family had no piano and we couldn't afford to buy one, let alone reams of sheet music and piano lessons. So I could be generous in my comments when my mother bad-mouthed the little girl on TV.

IN OTHER WORDS A few months later, Jing-mei's mother sees a young Chinese girl playing the piano on TV. She is fascinated by the sound and calls Jing-mei to watch.

► Circle the reason why Jing-mei is not worried about becoming a famous piano player.

3. **mesmerizing** (MEZ mur eyez ing): holding someone's complete attention.

"Play note right, but doesn't sound good! No singing sound," complained my mother.

"What are you picking on her for?" I said carelessly. "She's pretty good. Maybe she's not the best, but she's trying hard." I knew almost immediately I would be sorry I said that.

"Just like you," she said. "Not the best. Because you not trying." She gave a little huff as she let go of the sound dial and sat down on the sofa.

The little Chinese girl sat down also to play an encore[4] of "Anitra's Dance" by Grieg. I remember the song, because later on I had to learn how to play it.

Three days after watching *The Ed Sullivan Show,* my mother told me what my schedule would be for piano lessons and piano practice. She had talked to Mr. Chong, who lived on the first floor of our apartment building. Mr. Chong was a retired piano teacher and my mother had traded housecleaning services for weekly lessons and a piano for me to practice on every day, two hours a day, from four until six.

When my mother told me this, I felt as though I had been sent to hell. I whined and then kicked my foot a little when I couldn't stand it anymore.

"Why don't you like me the way I am? I'm *not* a genius! I can't play the piano. And even if I could, I wouldn't go on TV if you paid me a million dollars!" I cried.

My mother slapped me. "Who ask you be genius?" she shouted. "Only ask you be your best. For you sake. You think I want you be genius? Hnnh! What for! Who ask you!"

IN OTHER WORDS Jing-mei's mother arranges piano lessons and practice time from a retired piano teacher. In exchange, she cleans his apartment. Jing-mei protests this plan and her mother slaps her angrily.

"So ungrateful," I heard her mutter in Chinese. "If she had as much talent as she has temper, she would be famous now."

Mr. Chong, whom I secretly nicknamed Old Chong, was very strange, always tapping his fingers to the silent music of an

4. **encore** (AHN kor): a repeated or additional performance.

Monitor Your Comprehension

invisible orchestra. He looked ancient in my eyes. He had lost most of the hair on top of his head and he wore thick glasses and had eyes that always looked tired and sleepy. But he must have been younger than I thought, since he lived with his mother and was not yet married.

I met Old Lady Chong once and that was enough. She had this peculiar smell like a baby that had done something in its pants. And her fingers felt like a dead person's, like an old peach I once found in the back of the refrigerator; the skin just slid off the meat when I picked it up.

I soon found out why Old Chong had retired from teaching piano. He was deaf. "Like Beethoven!" he shouted to me. "We're both listening only in our head!"[5] And he would start to conduct his frantic silent sonatas.

Our lessons went like this. He would open the book and point to different things, explaining their purpose: "Key! Treble! Bass! No sharps or flats! So this is C major! Listen now and play after me!"

And then he would play the C scale a few times, a simple chord, and then, as if inspired by an old, unreachable itch, he gradually added more notes and running trills and a pounding bass until the music was really something quite grand.

IN OTHER WORDS Jing-mei begins piano lessons with Mr. Chong. She quickly realizes that he retired from teaching because he is partly deaf. Jing-mei finds Mr. Chong a bit odd. He is balding and still lives with his mother, but he is very good at playing the piano.

I would play after him, the simple scale, the simple chord, and then I just played some nonsense that sounded like a cat running up and down on top of garbage cans. Old Chong smiled and applauded and then said, "Very good! But now you must learn to keep time!"

5. **Beethoven . . . in our head!** (BAY toh ven): Ludwig van Beethoven (1770–1827) continued to compose great music even after becoming totally deaf during the last years of his life.

So that's how I discovered that Old Chong's eyes were too slow to keep up with the wrong notes I was playing. He went through the motions in half-time. To help me keep rhythm, he stood behind me, pushing down on my right shoulder for every beat. He balanced pennies on top of my wrists so I would keep them still as I slowly played scales and arpeggios. He had me curve my hand around an apple and keep that shape when playing chords. He marched stiffly to show me how to make each finger dance up and down, staccato[6] like an obedient little soldier.

He taught me all these things, and that was how I also learned I could be lazy and get away with mistakes, lots of mistakes. If I hit the wrong notes because I hadn't practiced enough, I never corrected myself. I just kept playing in rhythm. And Old Chong kept conducting his own private reverie. **E**

So maybe I never really gave myself a fair chance. I did pick up the basics pretty quickly, and I might have become a good pianist at that young age. But I was so determined not to try, not to be anybody different, that I learned to play only the most ear-splitting preludes, the most **discordant** hymns.

IN OTHER WORDS Jing-mei quickly discovers that Mr. Chong, who has trouble hearing and seeing, cannot tell if she is playing correctly. She learns the basics of piano quickly.

► With a partner, discuss why Jing-mei doesn't play the piano well.

Over the next year, I practiced like this, dutifully in my own way. And then one day I heard my mother and her friend Lindo Jong both talking in a loud, bragging tone of voice so others could hear. It was after church, and I was leaning against the brick wall wearing a dress with stiff white petticoats. Auntie Lindo's daughter, Waverly, who was about my age, was standing

6. **staccato** (stuh KAHT oh): producing distinct, sudden breaks between one tone and the next.

E THEME

Review lines 202–206. How does Jing-mei, approach her piano lessons? Put brackets [ ] around the words that show you her attitude.

VOCABULARY

The word **discordant** (dis KOR duhnt) is an adjective that means *having clashing sounds.*

farther down the wall about five feet away. We had grown up together and shared all the closeness of two sisters squabbling over crayons and dolls. In other words, for the most part, we hated each other. I thought she was snotty. Waverly Jong had gained a certain amount of fame as "Chinatown's Littlest Chinese Chess Champion."

VOCABULARY
The word **lament** (luh MENT) is a verb that means *to express sorrow or regret.* What is Auntie Lindo expressing regret about? Circle your answer.

"She bring home too many trophy," **lamented** Auntie Lindo that Sunday. "All day she play chess. All day I have no time do nothing but dust off her winnings." She threw a scolding look at Waverly, who pretended not to see her.

"You lucky you don't have this problem," said Auntie Lindo with a sigh to my mother.

And my mother squared her shoulders and bragged: "Our problem worser than yours. If we ask Jing-mei wash dish, she hear nothing but music. It's like you can't stop this natural talent."

And right then, I was determined to put a stop to her foolish pride. PAUSE & REFLECT

PAUSE & REFLECT
Why do you think Jing-mei is so determined to put a stop to her mother's "foolish" bragging? Discuss your answer with a partner.

Students should discuss that Jing-mei's mother's foolish pride and ambition for Jing-mei may be why Jing-mei wants to stop her mother's bragging.

A few weeks later, Old Chong and my mother conspired to have me play in a talent show which would be held in the church hall. By then, my parents had saved up enough to buy me a secondhand piano, a black Wurlitzer spinet with a scarred bench. It was the showpiece of our living room.

IN OTHER WORDS Jing-mei continues practicing half-heartedly for a year. One day at church she hears her mother brag that she is an amazing piano player. Jing-mei decides to make her mother stop bragging about her.

For the talent show, I was to play a piece called "Pleading Child" from Schumann's *Scenes from Childhood.* It was a simple, moody piece that sounded more difficult than it was. I was supposed to memorize the whole thing, playing the repeat parts twice to make the piece sound longer. But I dawdled over it,

Monitor Your Comprehension

playing a few bars and then cheating, looking up to see what notes followed. I never really listened to what I was playing. I daydreamed about being somewhere else, about being someone else.

The part I liked to practice best was the fancy curtsy: right foot out, touch the rose on the carpet with a pointed foot, sweep to the side, left leg bends, look up and smile.

My parents invited all the couples from the Joy Luck Club[7] to witness my debut.[8] Auntie Lindo and Uncle Tin were there. Waverly and her two older brothers had also come. The first two rows were filled with children both younger and older than I was. The littlest ones got to go first. They recited simple nursery rhymes, squawked out tunes on miniature violins, twirled **Hula-Hoops**, pranced in pink ballet tutus, and when they bowed or curtsied, the audience would sigh in unison, "Awww," and then clap enthusiastically.

VISUAL VOCABULARY
Hula Hoops are plastic hoops that whirl around the body when the hips are moved.

IN OTHER WORDS Jing-mei's mother enters her in a talent show, but Jing-mei continues to put little effort into her practicing. Her parents invite all of their friends to the performance.

When my turn came, I was very confident. I remember my childish excitement. It was as if I knew, without a doubt, that the prodigy side of me really did exist. I had no fear whatsoever, no nervousness. I remember thinking to myself, This is it! This is it! I looked out over the audience, at my mother's blank face, my father's yawn, Auntie Lindo's stiff-lipped smile, Waverly's sulky expression. I had on a white dress layered with sheets of lace, and a pink bow in my Peter Pan haircut. As I sat down I envisioned people jumping to their feet and Ed Sullivan rushing up to introduce me to everyone on TV. (F)

And I started to play. It was so beautiful. I was so caught up in how lovely I looked that at first I didn't worry how I would sound. So it was a surprise to me when I hit the first wrong note

(F) THEME
Reread lines 262–271. What expectation does Jing-mei have about her performance at the talent show? Underline two sentences that tell you this.

Possible answer: Jing-mei thinks that she will perform well and that everyone will praise her. She is looking forward to her audience's reaction.

7. **Joy Luck Club:** the social club to which the family in this story belongs.
8. **debut** (day BYOO): a person's first performance.

and I realized something didn't sound quite right. And then I hit another and another followed that. A chill started at the top of my head and began to trickle down. Yet I couldn't stop playing, as though my hands were bewitched. I kept thinking my fingers would adjust themselves back, like a train switching to the right track. I played this strange jumble through two repeats, the sour notes staying with me all the way to the end.

When I stood up, I discovered my legs were shaking. Maybe I had just been nervous and the audience, like Old Chong, had seen me go through the right motions and had not heard anything wrong at all. I swept my right foot out, went down on my knee, looked up and smiled. [The room was quiet, except for Old Chong, who was beaming and shouting, "Bravo! Bravo! Well done!"] But then I saw my mother's face, her stricken face. [The audience clapped weakly,] and as I walked back to my chair, with my whole face quivering as I tried not to cry, [I heard a little boy whisper loudly to his mother, "That was awful," and the mother whispered back, "Well, she certainly tried."]

IN OTHER WORDS Before performing, Jing-mei feels confident. She plays well at first but soon begins messing up. She hopes no one will notice her mistakes.

► How does the audience respond to Jing-mei's performance? Put brackets [ ] around the sentences that tell you.

And now I realized how many people were in the audience, the whole world it seemed. I was aware of eyes burning into my back. I felt the shame of my mother and father as they sat stiffly throughout the rest of the show.

We could have escaped during intermission. Pride and some strange sense of honor must have anchored my parents to their chairs. And so we watched it all: the eighteen-year-old boy with a fake mustache who did a magic show and juggled flaming hoops while riding a unicycle. The breasted girl with white makeup who sang from *Madama Butterfly* and got honorable

Monitor Your Comprehension

mention. And the eleven-year-old boy who won first prize playing a tricky violin song that sounded like a busy bee.

After the show, the Hsus, the Jongs, and the St. Clairs from the Joy Luck Club came up to my mother and father.

"Lots of talented kids," Auntie Lindo said vaguely, smiling broadly.

"That was somethin' else," said my father, and I wondered if he was referring to me in a humorous way, or whether he even remembered what I had done.

Waverly looked at me and shrugged her shoulders. "You aren't a genius like me," she said matter-of-factly. And if I hadn't felt so bad, I would have pulled her braids and punched her stomach.

IN OTHER WORDS Even though they are embarrassed, Jing-mei and her family stay for the rest of the show. Their conversation with their friends afterward is awkward. Most of the friends are polite, except for Waverly. She insults Jing-mei.

But my mother's expression was what devastated me: a quiet, blank look that said she had lost everything. I felt the same way, and it seemed as if everybody were now coming up, like gawkers at the scene of an accident, to see what parts were actually missing. When we got on the bus to go home, my father was humming the busy-bee tune and my mother was silent. I kept thinking she wanted to wait until we got home before shouting at me. But when my father unlocked the door to our apartment, my mother walked in and then went to the back, into the bedroom. No accusations. No blame. And in a way, I felt disappointed. I had been waiting for her to start shouting, so I could shout back and cry and blame her for all my misery. G

I assumed my talent-show fiasco[9] meant I never had to play the piano again. But two days later, after school, my mother came out of the kitchen and saw me watching TV.

"Four clock," she reminded me as if it were any other day. I was stunned, as though she were asking me to go through the

G THEME

Reread lines 315–326. Underline the words that tell you how Jing-mei's mother feels after the talent show. Put checkmarks beside the sentences that tell you how Jing-mei feels.

---

9. **fiasco** (fee AS koh): a complete failure.

talent-show torture again. I wedged myself more tightly in front of the TV.

"Turn off TV," she called from the kitchen five minutes later.

I didn't budge. And then I decided. I didn't have to do what my mother said anymore. I wasn't her slave. This wasn't China. I had listened to her before and look what happened. She was the stupid one.

She came out from the kitchen and stood in the arched entryway of the living room. "Four clock," she said once again, louder.

"I'm not going to play anymore," I said nonchalantly. "Why should I? I'm not a genius."

She walked over and stood in front of the TV. I saw her chest was heaving up and down in an angry way.

IN OTHER WORDS After the talent show, Jing-mei expects to give up the piano. Her mother insists that she continue. Jing-mei argues that she should stop because she is not a piano "genius."

"No!" I said, and I now felt stronger, as if my true self had finally emerged. So this was what had been inside me all along.

"No! I won't!" I screamed.

She yanked me by the arm, pulled me off the floor, snapped off the TV. She was frighteningly strong, half pulling, half carrying me toward the piano as I kicked the throw rugs under my feet. She lifted me up and onto the hard bench. I was sobbing by now, looking at her bitterly. Her chest was heaving even more and her mouth was open, smiling crazily as if she were pleased I was crying.

"You want me to be someone that I'm not!" I sobbed. "I'll never be the kind of daughter you want me to be!"

"Only two kinds of daughters," she shouted in Chinese. "Those who are obedient and those who follow their own mind! Only one kind of daughter can live in this house. Obedient daughter!" H

H THEME

The title of this story gives you a clue to the story's theme. The title comes from the argument between Jing-mei and her mother in lines 356–361. Circle the kind of daughter Jing-mei believes herself to be. Put brackets [ ] around the kind of daughter her mother expects her to be.

"Then I wish I wasn't your daughter. I wish you weren't my mother," I shouted. As I said these things I got scared. It felt like worms and toads and slimy things crawling out of my chest, but it also felt good, as if this awful side of me had surfaced, at last.

"Too late change this," said my mother shrilly.

And I could sense her anger rising to its breaking point. I wanted to see it spill over. And that's when I remembered the babies she had lost in China, the ones we never talked about. "Then I wish I'd never been born!" I shouted. "I wish I were dead! Like them."

IN OTHER WORDS **The argument between Jing-mei and her mother turns physical as Jing-mei's mother drags her to the piano bench.**

► What hateful thing does Jing-mei say to her mother? With a partner, discuss your answer.

Students should discuss how Jing-mei shouts that she wishes she was not her mother's daughter, that her mother was not her mother, and that she'd never been born.

It was as if I had said the magic words. Alakazam!—and her face went blank, her mouth closed, her arms went slack, and she backed out of the room, stunned, as if she were blowing away like a small brown leaf, thin, brittle, lifeless.

It was not the only disappointment my mother felt in me. In the years that followed, I failed her so many times, each time asserting my own will, my right to fall short of expectations. I didn't get straight A's. I didn't become class president. I didn't get into Stanford. I dropped out of college.

For unlike my mother, I did not believe I could be anything I wanted to be. I could only be me.

And for all those years, we never talked about the disaster at the recital or my terrible accusations afterward at the piano bench. All that remained unchecked, like a betrayal that was now unspeakable. So I never found a way to ask her why she had hoped for something so large that failure was inevitable.

And even worse, I never asked her what frightened me the most: Why had she given up hope?

For after our struggle at the piano, she never mentioned my playing again. The lessons stopped. The lid to the piano was closed, shutting out the dust, my misery, and her dreams.

IN OTHER WORDS Jing-mei's mention of the dead children shocks her mother and stops the argument. After that, Jing-mei's mother allows her to quit the piano. As she grows older, Jing-mei wonders about her mother's reasons for having and then giving up on her hopes for Jing-mei's success.

So she surprised me. A few years ago, she offered to give me the piano, for my thirtieth birthday. I had not played in all those years. I saw the offer as a sign of forgiveness, a tremendous burden removed.

"Are you sure?" I asked shyly. "I mean, won't you and Dad miss it?"

"No, this your piano," she said firmly. "Always your piano. You only one can play."

"Well, I probably can't play anymore," I said. "It's been years."

"You pick up fast," said my mother, as if she knew this was certain. "You have natural talent. You could been genius if you want to."

"No I couldn't."

"You just not trying," said my mother. And she was neither angry nor sad. She said it as if to announce a fact that could never be disproved. "Take it," she said. **PAUSE & REFLECT**

PAUSE & REFLECT

Based on lines 393–408, do you think Jing-mei's mother ever completely gave up on Jing-mei? Explain your answer.

Possible answer: No, the mother's attitude has not changed. She continues to believe that Jing-mei could be a genius.

But I didn't at first. It was enough that she had offered it to me. And after that, every time I saw it in my parents' living room, standing in front of the bay windows, it made me feel proud, as if it were a shiny trophy I had won back.

Last week I sent a tuner over to my parents' apartment and had the piano reconditioned, for purely sentimental reasons. My mother had died a few months before and I had been getting things in order for my father, a little bit at a time. I put the jewelry in special silk pouches. The sweaters she had knitted in

Monitor Your Comprehension

yellow, pink, bright orange—all the colors I hated—I put those in mothproof boxes. I found some old Chinese silk dresses, the kind with little slits up the sides. I rubbed the old silk against my skin, then wrapped them in tissue and decided to take them home with me.

After I had the piano tuned, I opened the lid and touched the keys. It sounded even richer than I remembered. Really, it was a very good piano. Inside the bench were the same exercise notes with handwritten scales, the same secondhand music books with their covers held together with yellow tape.

I opened up the Schumann book to the dark little piece I had played at the recital. It was on the left-hand side of the page, "Pleading Child." It looked more difficult than I remembered. I played a few bars, surprised at how easily the notes came back to me.

And for the first time, or so it seemed, I noticed the piece on the right-hand side. It was called "Perfectly Contented." I tried to play this one as well. It had a lighter melody but the same flowing rhythm and turned out to be quite easy. "Pleading Child" was shorter but slower; "Perfectly Contented" was longer, but faster. And after I played them both a few times, I realized they were two halves of the same song. ❶

IN OTHER WORDS On Jing-mei's thirtieth birthday, her mother offers her the old piano. Jing-mei turns it down but sees this as a sign of forgiveness. Years later, Jing-mei's mother dies. Jing-mei helps her father organize things and hires someone to tune the piano. Sitting down at the piano, she practices the piece she had played at the talent show and another piece by the same composer.

► With a partner, discuss what you think Jing-mei feels at the end of this story.

Students should discuss that Jing-mei is happy because she realizes that her mother's gift of the piano is a peace offering and a sign that she loves Jing-mei for who she is.

❶ THEME

Reread lines 428–439. Then, think about the title of this story. What two kinds of children are presented in the songs Jing-mei plays at the end of this story?

Pleading child and perfectly contented child

What do you think might be a possible **theme,** or message about life, in this story? Discuss your answer with a partner.

Possible answer: The story's message is that unrealistic expectations can harm a relationship.

SET A PURPOSE FOR READING
Read this poem to discover the expectations the speaker's mother has for her daughter.

RICE *and* ROSE BOWL BLUES

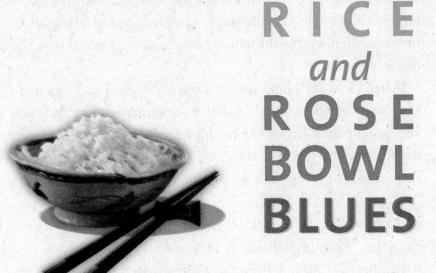

Poem by

DIANE MEI LIN MARK

BACKGROUND The Rose Bowl is an important college football game played every year on New Year's Day. The speaker uses football terms in the poem. A "pass interception" is a throw that is caught by the other team. When the other team is "on our 20" they are 20 yards away from the speaker's team's goal—close to scoring a touchdown.

I remember the day
Mama called me in from
the football game with brothers
and neighbor boys
in our front yard

said it was time
I learned to
wash rice for dinner (J)

glancing out the window
I watched a pass interception

(J) SET A PURPOSE FOR READING
How do you react to what seems to be unfair treatment? Discuss with a partner how you think the speaker might react.
Students should discuss that the speaker may think that she should not be confined to traditional women's tasks.

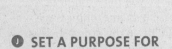

setting the other team up
on our 20
Pour some water
into the pot,
she said pleasantly,
turning on the tap
Rub the rice
between your hands,
pour out the clouds,
fill it again
(I secretly traced
an end run through
the grains in
between pourings)
with the rice
settled into a simmer
I started out the door
but was called back K

IN OTHER WORDS The speaker is playing football with boys when her mother calls her inside to cook rice. She obeys. When the speaker starts to leave the kitchen to return to the game, her mother calls her back.

► Circle the words in lines 9–24 that tell you what the speaker wants to be doing.

the next day
Roland from across the street
sneeringly said he heard
I couldn't play football
anymore

K THEME

What conflict, or struggle, is the speaker of the poem having? Discuss your answer with a partner.

Students should discuss that the speaker's heart is still with the players on the football field, but she hides her true feelings from her mother.

I laughed loudly,
asking him
where
he'd heard
such a thing (L)

IN OTHER WORDS The next day, one of the boys says in a scornful way that he's heard the speaker can no longer play football. The speaker laughs at him.

(L) THEME

What can you tell about the speaker's feelings from her reaction to Roland?

Possible answer: She feels rebellious and angry about the changes in her life; however, she downplays her frustrations by laughing at Roland's unkind words.

After Reading

Text Analysis: Theme Across Genres

Now that you've read both selections, you are ready to identify each writer's theme, or message about life. Fill in the chart below.

For this chart, answers may vary. See samples below.

Points of Comparison	In the Story	In the Poem
What is the main conflict, or struggle?	*Jing-mei's mother wants her to be a prodigy, but Jing-mei rebels.*	*The speaker's mother wants her to learn how to wash rice, but the speaker wants to play football.*
What lesson does the narrator or speaker learn?	*The narrator learns that her mother still loves her despite disappointments.*	*The speaker learns that she can find ways to claim her freedom.*
What do you learn from the title?	*It emphasizes the conflicts between the obedient daughter and the willful daughter.*	*It emphasizes the conflict between traditional female roles and the freedom of childhood.*
What is the theme, or message, of the work?	*Unrealistic expectations can create bitterness.*	*Expectations don't have to stifle treasured freedoms.*

Based on your chart, what is a **theme** of both selections? Try to combine the common ideas in your notes in the chart. Write the theme on the lines below.

Possible answer: People can't always live up to expectations.

Reading Strategy: Set a Purpose for Reading

Think back to the purposes for reading that you discussed with a partner as you read the two selections. In what ways did having a purpose affect the details you noticed in the selections? On the lines below, tell what your purpose for reading each selection was and what it helped you notice.

Answers will vary.

How do EXPECTATIONS affect what we do?

Do you think it's a good idea to set really high expectations for other people? Why or why not?

Answers will vary.

Vocabulary Practice

Circle the part of each sentence that answers each question.

1. Would you describe a **prodigy** as brilliant or average?
2. If you felt someone's **reproach**, would she be blaming you or praising you?
3. Would you describe a **discordant** sound as one that is pleasing to hear or one that is unpleasant?
4. If someone were to **lament** what he did, would he be happy about it or feel regret about it?

Academic Vocabulary in Speaking

The word **context** (KON tekst) is a noun that means *the conditions in which an event or idea happens or exists.*

You misunderstood my comment because you took it out of **context**.

The word **tradition** (truh DISH uhn) is a noun that means *a custom, belief, or practice passed down from one generation to the next.*

My grandfather always gave gifts to others on his birthday, and my family has continued that **tradition**.

TURN AND TALK With a partner, talk about why Jing-mei rebelled against her mother. Consider the **context** of her rebellion and her family's **traditions.** Be sure to use the words **context** and **tradition** in your discussion.

Encourage students to use the Academic Vocabulary words in their discussions.

Assessment Practice

DIRECTIONS Use "Two Kinds" and "Rice and Rose Bowl Blues" to answer questions 1–4.

1 In "Two Kinds" the narrator's mother wants her to become a —

- (A) straight A student
- (B) prodigy
- (C) chess player
- (D) TV star

2 In lines 93–95, the narrator says,

"I had new thoughts . . . filled with lots of won'ts.
I won't let her change me, I promised myself.
I won't be what I'm not."

This statement fits a theme of —

- (A) learning to accept one's limitations
- (B) setting high expectations for oneself
- (C) respecting one's parents
- (D) always being true to oneself

3 At the end of the story, Jing-mei realizes that the two piano pieces, "Pleading Child" and "Perfectly Contented" —

- (A) remind her of the conflict with her mother
- (B) have the same qualities she sees in herself
- (C) bring back the terrible memories of her recital
- (D) mean very little to her

4 In the poem, the mother calls her daughter but not her sons inside to learn to cook, because the mother —

- (A) has different expectations for her daughter than she does for her sons
- (B) thinks her sons should learn to play football better
- (C) thinks girls shouldn't play sports
- (D) thinks all her children should learn to cook

UNIT 5

Ideas Made Visible

AUTHOR'S PURPOSE

Be sure to read the Text Analysis Workshop on pages 552–557 in *Holt McDougal Literature.*

Academic Vocabulary for Unit 5

You will see these Academic Vocabulary words as you work through this book. You will also be asked to use them as you write and talk about the selections in this unit.

Conclude (kuhn KLOOD) is a verb that means *to decide by reasoning*.
The falling rocks made me **conclude** that the cave was not safe.

How do you **conclude** which classes to take? ______

Answers will vary.

Construct (kuhn STRUHKT) is a verb that means *to build or put parts together*.
Marco could **construct** an engine out of almost anything.

What supplies could you use to **construct** a shelter in the wilderness? ______

Answers will vary.

Implicit (im PLIS it) is an adjective that means *not actually said but hinted at instead*.
They did not know the **implicit** meaning of the movie until later.

What is an example of an **implicit** agreement with someone? ______

Answers will vary.

Primary (PRY mehr ee) is an adjective that means *first* or *most important*.
The **primary** point of the story was that nature is a powerful force.

Describe your **primary** goal at school: ______

Answers will vary.

Specific (spih SIF ik) is an adjective that means *definite* or *exact*.
With my short dark hair, I needed a **specific** wig for the play.

Name one **specific** thing you enjoy about your favorite after-school activity:

Answers will vary.

Who Killed the Iceman?

Based on the magazine article

Skeletal Sculptures

Process description by Donna M. Jackson

How do scientists UNLOCK the past?

Have you ever watched a television show about criminal investigations? If so, you probably know that many crimes are solved not only by police investigation but also by the study of human remains. Scientists can learn a lot about a person's life—and death—by studying even very old bones.

TURN AND TALK What do you already know about criminal or scientific investigations? With a partner, discuss the different methods, such as fingerprinting, that you know detectives and scientists use to investigate crimes.

Answers will vary.

Text Analysis: Text Features

Many nonfiction articles, such as those in magazines and newspapers and on Web sites, include **text features** that help organize and highlight key information. You can also use these special design elements to preview an article and learn what information is in it. Here are several commonly used text features:

- **Subheadings** signal the beginning of a new topic or section and identify the subject of the text to follow.
- **Graphic aids,** such as maps and photographs, present information visually. Photographs usually include **captions,** written descriptions that explain the images.
- **Numbered lists** often show steps in a process. The numbers show the order in which the steps are performed.

Reading Strategy: Take Notes

A good way to make sure you understand what you read is to **take notes.** Simply write down the main ideas in a way that is easy for you to understand. As you read "Who Killed the Iceman?" and "Skeletal Sculptures," write down each subheading or process step in your notes. Then, write down the main ideas included under each subheading or step number. The examples below show how you can organize your notes.

"Who Killed the Iceman?"
Background
- *He was frozen for 5,000 years.*
- ____________________

"Skeletal Sculptures"
1. *Cut rubber pegs to different lengths.*
2. ____________________

Vocabulary in Context

Note: Words are listed in the order in which they appear in the selections.

Refute (rih FYOOT) is a verb that means *to prove false by argument or evidence.*

The scientists who disagreed could not **refute** his point.

Compile (kuhm PYL) is a verb that means *to put together by gathering from many sources.*

The scientists got together to **compile** their evidence.

Presumed (prih ZOOMD) is an adjective or verb that means *thought to be true.*

Police say it is **presumed** that the victim was a man.

Vocabulary Practice

Review the words and sample sentences above. Based on these Vocabulary words, what do you think the selections will be about? Discuss your prediction with a classmate.

Encourage students to use the Vocabulary words in their predictions.

SET A PURPOSE FOR READING
Read this article to learn about a 5,000-year-old mummy found frozen in an Italian glacier.

WHO KILLED THE ICEMAN?

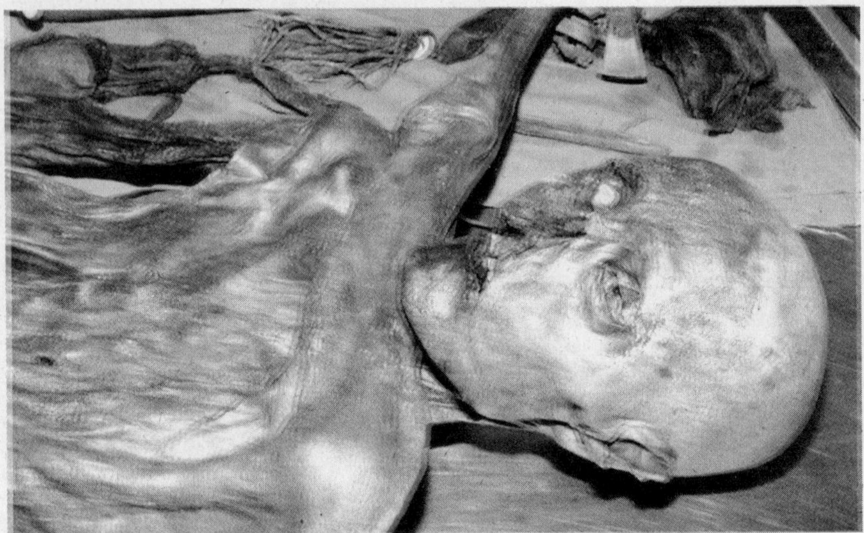

Based on an article from NATIONAL GEOGRAPHIC MAGAZINE

BACKGROUND "Who Killed the Iceman?" discusses some of the ideas people have about a man who died around 3000 B.C. The "Iceman" is the oldest frozen mummy ever found. He was discovered when German hikers in the Alps saw a body covered in ice. The hikers thought they had found a dead mountain climber. Instead, they had discovered the remains of a man who died 5,000 years ago. Today, the Iceman is kept at a museum in Italy.

Background

For 5,000 years, the Iceman lay frozen in a mountain glacier. Then, in 1991, passing hikers discovered him. Today he is kept in a refrigerated room at a museum in Italy, so that his body will remain in good condition. Since his discovery, the Iceman mummy has been closely examined. This past summer, researchers noticed something new and important:

"Ötzi," (ERT zee) as he came to be called, didn't freeze to death in a sudden snowstorm. Instead he was killed. He was a victim of war, murder, or human sacrifice.

Clues Discovered

X-rays reveal an arrowhead buried in the Iceman's left shoulder. This discovery led researchers to decide that the Iceman had been killed. The wound could be seen as a small, dark smudge on the mummy's skin. It had been missed in all earlier studies. This wound shows that the Iceman was shot with an arrow in the back. But who did it? And why? (A)

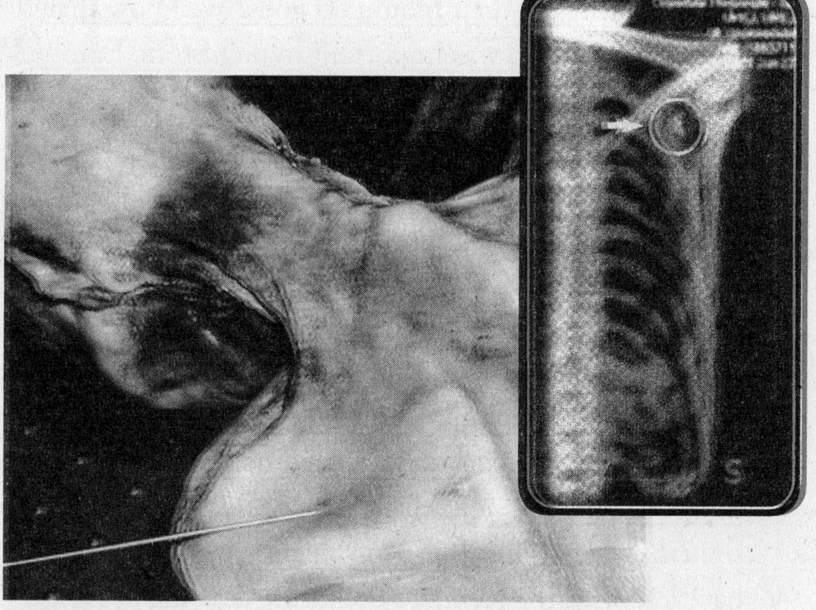

X-Ray Vision When scientists gave the Iceman an X-ray, they saw the arrowhead buried in his shoulder. (B)

IN OTHER WORDS Ötzi, the Iceman, had been buried for 5,000 years. After hikers discovered his body in 1991, scientists began examining him. Recently, they found an arrowhead buried in his shoulder.

(A) TAKE NOTES

The second subheading in this article is "Clues Discovered." In the box below, write the main idea from this section.

Clues Discovered
Possible answer: Because of an arrowhead found in the Iceman's left shoulder, researchers decided that the Iceman had been killed.

(B) TEXT FEATURES

Look at the photograph and caption. What information does the caption provide that the photograph does not?

Possible answer: The caption tells you that the circled smudge is an arrowhead.

Differing Theories

"There's no way anyone can really know," says Johan Reinhard, a National Geographic Society explorer. "It might have been murder. Or it might have been ritual sacrifice."

Reinhard knows a lot about mummies. In 1995, he discovered a 500-year-old mummy known as the "ice maiden." The girl was a victim of sacrifice in the mountains of Peru. Based on his studies, Reinhard believes that the Iceman's death was not a chance killing.

"Look at where he died," Reinhard says, noting the importance of the mountain pass. "It's the kind of place where people from mountain cultures have traditionally made offerings to their mountain gods. We know that mountain worship was important in prehistoric Europe."

Reinhard's view seems to answer questions about the mummy's **artifacts**. Many of the things found with the Iceman have puzzled experts. For example, scientists found broken arrows near him. Breaking objects in ceremonies was a common practice around 4000 B.C. **C** Also, the Iceman's copper ax is the oldest complete ax ever found in Europe. Its copper must have been mined from a mountain. Reinhard explains that mountains were worshiped by people all over the world. "This helps explain why the ax was left with the body after the killing." Murderers would likely have taken something so useful. But people performing a ritual might have left it for the Iceman's use in the next life.

IN OTHER WORDS Johan Reinhard believes that Ötzi's wound came from a ritual sacrifice, a ceremony in which a person or animal is killed to please the gods.

► Reread lines 24–40. Underline the evidence that Reinhard uses to explain why he thinks Ötzi was a victim of ritual sacrifice.

VISUAL VOCABULARY
An **artifact** is something created by humans, usually for a practical purpose. The knife and knife sheath, or cover, shown above are artifacts that were found with the Iceman.

C LANGUAGE COACH
In line 33, the writer refers to the date 4000 B.C. The letters *B.C.* are an **abbreviation** for "Before Christ." In the dating system most widely used throughout the world, B.C. refers to the years before the birth of Jesus Christ. Dates labeled *B.C.* count backward, so that 400 B.C. is closer to today than 4000 B.C. is. The years after Jesus's birth are noted as *A.D.*, which is an abbreviation for the Latin words *Anno Domini* ("In the year of our Lord").

Where Ötzi Died

Ötzi was found at a height of 10,500 feet in the Ötztal Alps between Austria and Italy. After examining him, researchers realized they had found a 5,300-year-old mummy.

Another clue: The Iceman's body was found in a trench, or shallow ditch. At first, scientists thought he had taken shelter there from a storm. "But the trench is not deep," explains Reinhard, so it would have been a poor place to hide from a storm. Instead, the Iceman may have been buried there by whoever killed him. That would explain why his body has not decayed. D

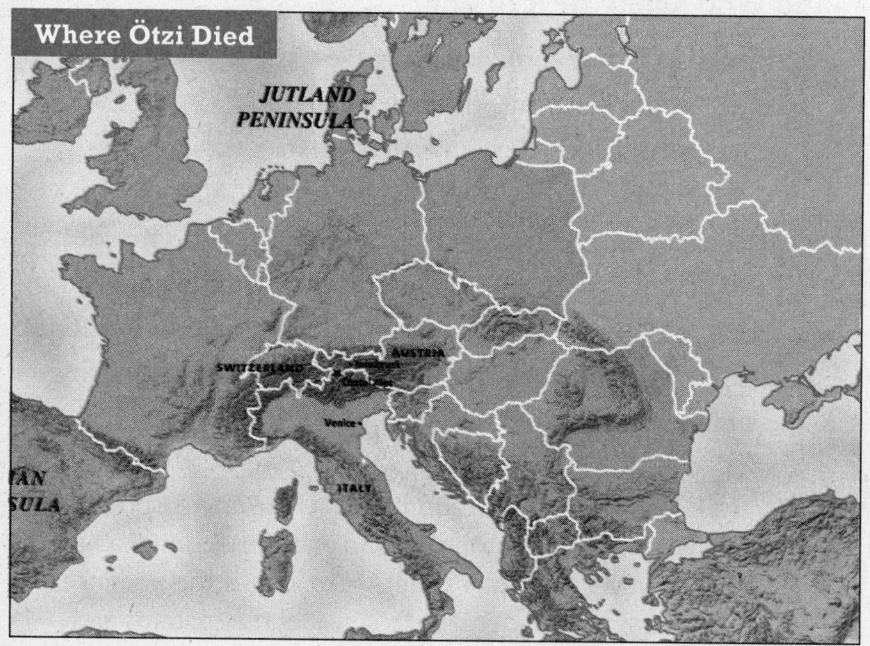

Where Ötzi Died

Reinhard's ideas have not convinced European experts. The mummy's caretaker at the museum, Eduard Egarter Vigl, believes that Ötzi may have been running from an attacker. He says, "The Iceman was hit by an arrow from behind." Others argue that arrows aren't the best weapons

D TAKE NOTES

The subheading "Where Ötzi Died" tells you the main idea of the section that follows. Underline the sentences that tell where Ötzi died.

for ritual killing. They also state that there is no evidence of other sacrifices from the same time period in Europe.

PAUSE & REFLECT

PAUSE & REFLECT

Reread lines 54–56. Why might some scientists think arrows aren't good weapons for ritual killing? Discuss your thoughts with a partner.

Students should discuss that arrow wounds may not always cause death.

IN OTHER WORDS At first, scientists believed that Ötzi was trying to take shelter from a storm. Reinhard argues that the ditch would not have provided shelter. Instead, he believes Ötzi was buried there by the person who killed him.

► With a partner, discuss how some scientists disagree with Reinhard's view.

Students should discuss the other scientists' views.

So Who Killed the Iceman?

Reinhard says that some scientists view the idea of human sacrifice as too startling. "But they can't **refute** what I've pointed out, and I believe my theory better explains the facts," he says.

Reinhard admits that people can disagree with his idea. "But it's time to **compile** all the evidence" and look at it from a different point of view. He says that we should look at these artifacts based on what might have been happening during the time when the Iceman lived.

VOCABULARY

The word **refute** (rih FYOOT) is a verb that means *to prove false by argument or evidence.*

Reread lines 59–61. Then, underline the idea that Reinhard says scientists can't refute.

VOCABULARY

The word **compile** (kuhm PYL) is a verb that means *to put together by gathering from many sources.*

IN OTHER WORDS Reinhard admits that there are reasons to disagree with his idea that the Iceman was the victim of a human sacrifice. However, he wants scientists to look at the evidence again. Reinhard wants scientists to consider the customs and ways of life that existed in Ötzi's society as they look at the evidence.

Skeletal SCULPTURES

Process description by

DONNA M. JACKSON

BACKGROUND "Skeletal Sculptures" describes how scientists help police solve crimes. These scientists help identify a victim's age, sex, race, and physical traits. They also find the likely cause of death.

SET A PURPOSE FOR READING
Read this process description to learn how scientists help detectives identify human remains.

Dr. Michael Charney is an expert in forensic anthropology[1]. His expertise has enabled him to take a few pieces of a skeleton found in Missouri and compile a portrait of a five-foot, 120-pound Asian woman in her mid-twenties. Still, that isn't enough to identify her.

The dead woman's "face" needs to be brought back to life.

Reconstructing the likeness of a person in clay, using the skull as a guide, is a last resort at identification, Dr. Charney says. It gives police a new lead to follow, a visual clue that can be photographed and displayed in the media.

Facial reconstruction is not an identifying tool, he warns. The goal is to trigger someone to recognize the model and to identify the person through scientific means. (E)

"All that's needed is a general recognition that it looks like so-and-so," he says.

Before re-creating a face, Dr. Charney and forensic sculptor Nita Bitner search the skull for signs of disease, injury, and structural defects.

"We look for things that shouldn't be there," Bitner says. "Sometimes we find broken noses, cuts, or dentures." These affect the face's appearance and aid in the identification process. If the nose bone is curved to one side, for example, it's important to show it in the face because it's a distinguishing feature.

(E) TAKE NOTES
Reread lines 11–13. Underline the goal of facial reconstruction.

1. **forensic anthropology** (fuh REN sik an thruh PAHL uh gee): the scientific study of human remains for the purpose of criminal investigation.

"We have to be careful, however, not to include anything that happened at the time of death," Bitner notes, "because it wouldn't be recognizable to others."

Age also influences how a face is built. Wrinkled skin, which might help illustrate an older person, is often incorporated into a sculpture for accuracy.

After studying the Missouri woman's skull, Bitner makes a latex mold and pours a plaster cast. Now she's ready to sculpt the face. **F**

IN OTHER WORDS Dr. Charney can use a few pieces of a skeleton to identify key facts about a person. However, a clay sculpture of the person's face is needed to get a recognizable image of who the person was. Nita Bitner, a sculptor, and Dr. Charney examine the skull for unique features that could help in identifying the person.

F TAKE NOTES
According to this article, what does Nita Bitner do after examining the skull? Put brackets [ ] around the text that answers the question.

G TEXT FEATURES
How does the image at right add to your understanding of step 1?

The image shows the different lengths of rubber pegs.

G

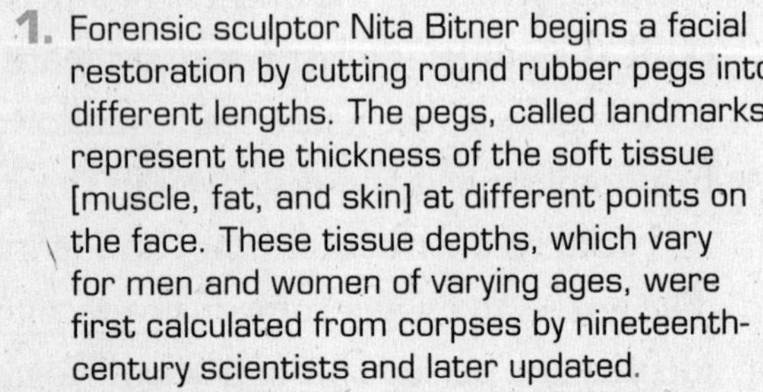

1. Forensic sculptor Nita Bitner begins a facial restoration by cutting round rubber pegs into different lengths. The pegs, called landmarks, represent the thickness of the soft tissue [muscle, fat, and skin] at different points on the face. These tissue depths, which vary for men and women of varying ages, were first calculated from corpses by nineteenth-century scientists and later updated.

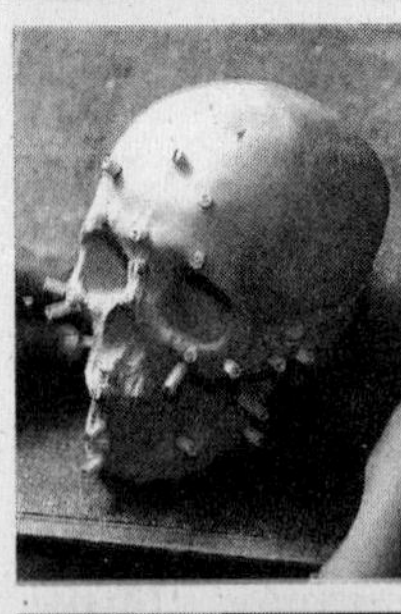

2. She then glues the rubber pegs to the skull cast.

3. Bitner "connects the dots" with strips of modeling clay. When attaching the strips of clay, she begins at the forehead and works her way down to the cheekbones, nasal area, chin, and mouth.

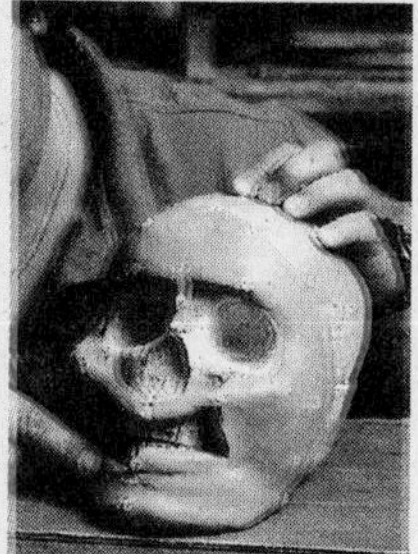

4. Once the dots are connected, Bitner fills in the spaces with clay and fleshes out the face. Now the prominent cheekbones of the Missouri woman become strikingly clear. Suddenly her broad face and delicate nose emerge. (H)

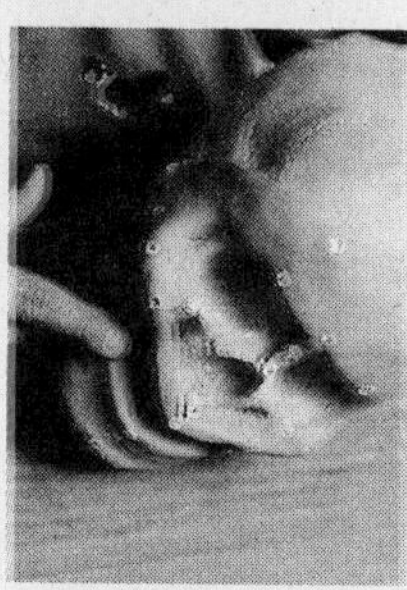

5. As Bitner smooths the clay with her thumb and fingers, the face develops like a photograph. (I)

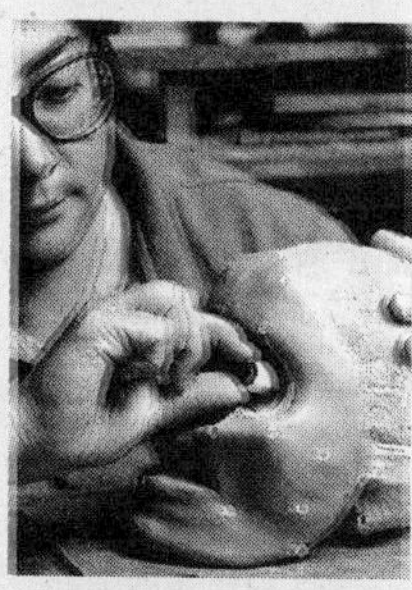

6. Bitner sets the plastic brown eyes in their sockets.

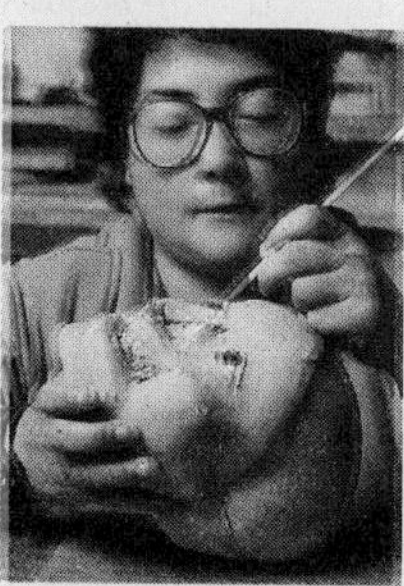

7. Next come the eyelids.

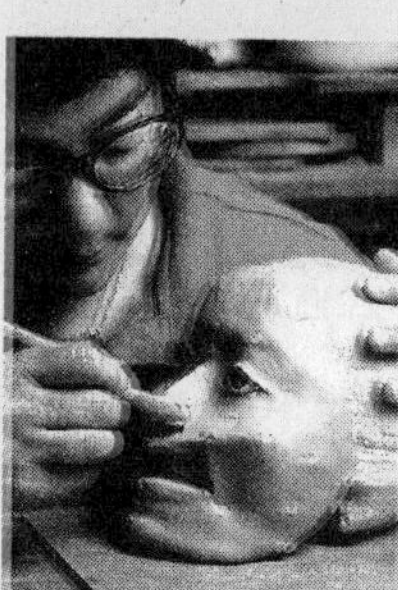

8. Bitner then sculpts the sides of the nose.

(H) TAKE NOTES

Reread step 4. On the lines below, write the main idea expressed in this step.

Possible answer: As Bitner fills in the spaces between the dots, the woman's features begin to emerge.

(I) TEXT FEATURES

What do the numbers before each caption tell the reader? Discuss your answer with a partner.

Students should discuss that the numbers give the order of each step in the process.

J TEXT FEATURES
Look back through the images to this point. Would you understand what was going on if the images did not have captions? Explain.

Possible answer: No, because the captions explain things in the image that a person might not recognize.

VOCABULARY
The word **presumed** (prih ZOOMD) is an adjective or verb. that means *thought to be true.*

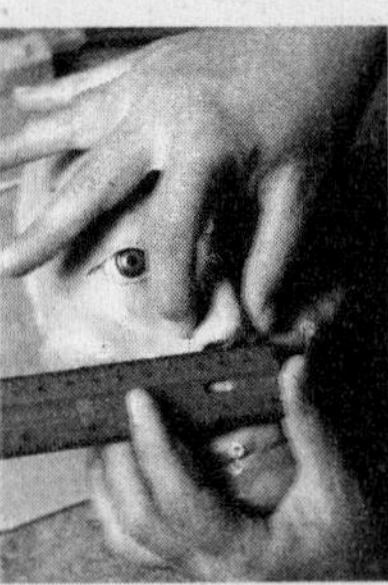

9. She measures the nose with a ruler to ensure it is the correct width. J

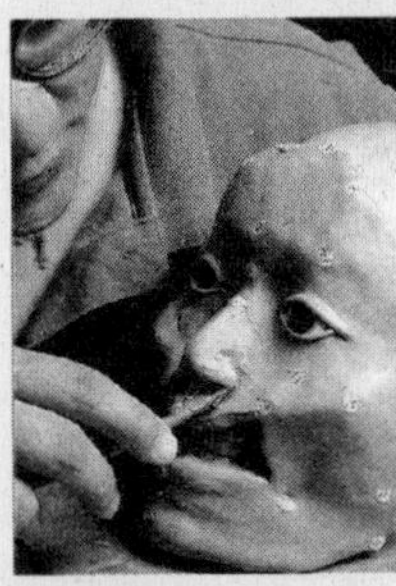

10. Now it's time to mold the upper lip.

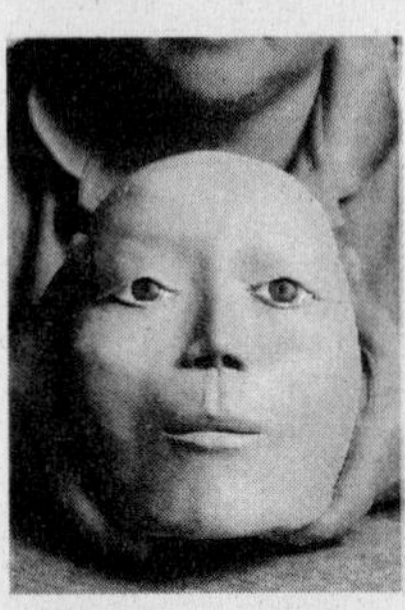

11. The face is nearly complete. Because the Missouri woman is **presumed** to be Asian, Bitner will add a black wig. She will then add a scarf for a finishing touch.

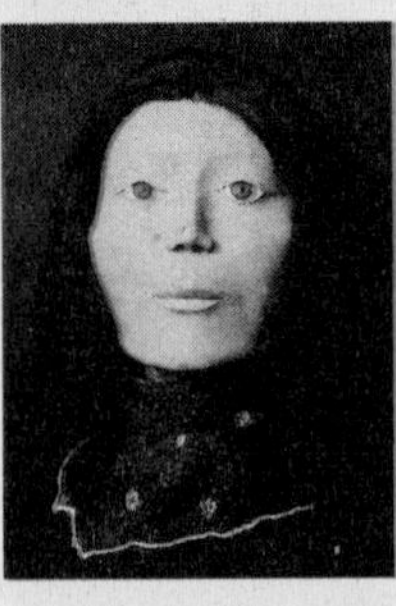

12. The model is now ready to be photographed and publicized in the media so that millions of amateur detectives can help solve the riddle of her identity.

IN OTHER WORDS Bitner attaches pegs to the skull to indicate skin thickness on various parts of the face. Next, she fills in the spaces between the pegs and smooths out the clay. Finally, she adds eyes and sculpts the nose and lips.

► Reread step 12. With a partner, discuss how the finished image will be used.

Students should discuss that the finished image will be shown on the Internet and on television so that people can try to identify the person.

Text Analysis: Text Features

Make sure you can identify the text features used in the articles you just read. In the chart below, fill in the titles and subheadings from "Who Killed the Iceman?" and "Skeletal Sculptures." Then complete the chart by briefly describing the visuals from each selection and telling what kind of information the captions provide.

For this chart, answers may vary. See samples below.

	"Who Killed the Iceman?"	"Skeletal Structures"
Title	*Who Killed the Iceman?*	*Skeletal Sculptures*
Subheads	*"Background," "Clues Discovered," "Differing Theories," "Where Ötzi Died," "So Who Killed the Iceman?"*	*No subheads, numbered steps*
Visuals	*Visuals show the Iceman when he's first discovered, a map of where he's discovered, and an x-ray of his shoulder.*	*Visuals show the steps of recreating a face.*
Captions	*Captions describe the x-ray and where the Iceman was found.*	*Descriptions of steps serve as captions.*

How did the text features in "Who Killed the Iceman?" and "Skeletal Structures" increase your understanding of the ideas presented?

Answers will vary.

Reading Strategy: Take Notes

Look back at the notes that you took as you read. Review each article, and make sure the main ideas are included in your notes. Then, fill in the main ideas for the remaining subheading and process step listed below. The main ideas for the first two subheadings and process steps are completed for you.

For this chart, answers may vary. See samples below.

"Who Killed the Iceman?"

Background

- He was frozen for 5,000 years.

Clues Discovered

- X-rays showed an arrowhead in his shoulder.

Differing Theories

- *One scientist believes that the Iceman may have been killed in a ritual human sacrifice.*

"Skeletal Sculptures"

1. Cut rubber pegs to different lengths.
2. Glue rubber pegs to skull cast.
3. *Use clay strips to connect the pegs.*

How do scientists UNLOCK the past?

How does learning about the past help us understand our own lives and current events? Discuss with a classmate why the kinds of research explained in these articles might be important to us today.

Students should discuss how research can help solve crimes today.

Vocabulary Practice

Write *true* or *false* next to each statement.

true 1. If I **refute** an argument, I make a convincing case against it.

true 2. To write a good report, you should **compile** information from several sources.

false 3. Someone **presumed** to be innocent has already proved that he or she is not guilty.

Academic Vocabulary in Speaking

The word **conclude** (kuhn KLOOD) means *to decide by reasoning.*

Gwen's bright red shoulders made it easy to **conclude** that she had been out in the sun too long.

The word **construct** (kuhn STRUKT) means *to build or put parts together.*

It was impossible to **construct** the model bridge without the missing support columns.

TURN AND TALK What do you think scientists can **conclude** by **constructing** a skeletal sculpture? Discuss your thoughts with a partner, and be sure to use the words **conclude** and **construct** in your discussion.

Encourage students to use the Academic Vocabulary words in their discussions.

Assessment Practice

DIRECTIONS Use "Who Killed the Iceman?" and "Skeletal Sculptures" to answer questions 1–6.

1 What is Johan Reinhard's theory about how the Iceman died?

- (A) He was killed by other hunters.
- (B) He was killed in a ritual sacrifice.
- (C) He was killed by animals.
- (D) He bled to death.

2 What evidence led scientists to conclude that the Iceman had been killed?

- (A) A sheath and dagger
- (B) Hair on his clothes
- (C) A copper ax
- (D) An arrowhead in his shoulder

3 According to "Skeletal Sculptures," facial reconstruction is used for —

- (A) showing how a person might age
- (B) determining a skeleton's age
- (C) triggering recognition of skeletal remains
- (D) repairing a facial injury

4 Subheads are used for all of the following reasons *except* —

- (A) to preview the following text
- (B) to signal a new topic or idea
- (C) to visually break up the text
- (D) to explain the main idea of the article

5 "Who Killed the Iceman?" contains all of the following text features *except* —

- (A) captions
- (B) subheads
- (C) numbered lists
- (D) images

6 According to "Skeletal Sculptures," what do forensic sculptors use as a guide to facial reconstruction?

- (A) Crime scene photographs
- (B) The victim's skull
- (C) Descriptions from the victim's friends
- (D) X-ray images

The Lost Boys

Based on the magazine article by **Sara Corbett**

How far would you go to find **FREEDOM?**

Most of us can't imagine what it would be like to live as a refugee—someone who has to leave his or her home country to escape danger or gain freedom. What would it take to make you leave your home and live in a strange new place?

CHART IT In the chart at left, list what you would miss most about each part of your life if you suddenly became a refugee.

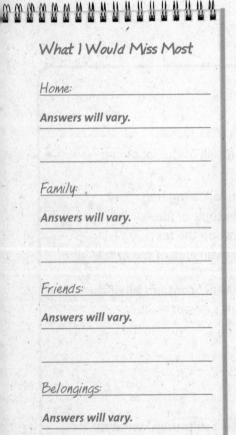

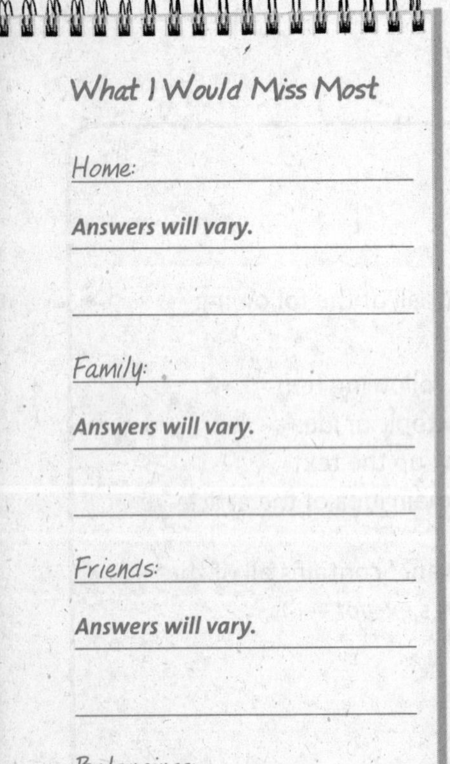

What I Would Miss Most
Home:
Answers will vary.
Family:
Answers will vary.
Friends:
Answers will vary.
Belongings:
Answers will vary.

Text Analysis: Author's Purpose

An **author's purpose** is what the writer hopes to achieve by writing a particular work. An author's purpose may be to inform or explain, to persuade, to entertain, or to express thoughts and feelings. The chart below lists clues to help you identify an author's purpose.

AUTHOR'S PURPOSE	CLUES IN THE WRITING
TO INFORM OR EXPLAIN **Examples:** magazine articles, instruction manuals	Facts and statistics, directions, steps in a process
TO PERSUADE **Examples:** editorials, advertisements, speeches	Opinion statements, appeals to emotion, calls to action
TO ENTERTAIN **Examples:** short stories, novels, plays, movies	Suspenseful situations, funny details, interesting characters
TO EXPRESS THOUGHTS OR FEELINGS **Examples:** essays, poems, diaries, journals	Thoughtful descriptions, insightful observations, the writer's personal feelings

Reading Skill: Interpret Graphic Aids

Magazine articles often include **graphic aids**, such as charts, maps, and photographs, to present important information. Here are some tips to help you get the most from graphic aids.

- Look closely at **photographs** that go with the article. What information do they provide that is not in the text?
- Study any **maps** or **charts** in the article, and note the information they provide. How does the map or chart help you understand the article?

Vocabulary in Context

Note: Words are listed in the order in which they appear in the article.

Exodus (EKS uh duhs) is a noun that means *an event in which a large group of people leaves a place.*

Threats from bandits caused an **exodus** among villagers, who left their homeland to go to safer places.

Marauding (muh RAWD ing) is an adjective that means *roaming in order to steal and destroy property.*

The **marauding** men set fire to the villagers' homes after taking everything of value.

Subsist (suhb SIST) is a verb that means *to support oneself just enough to survive.*

We had no food, so we had to **subsist** on gifts of rice.

Boon (boon) is a noun that means *a benefit* or *blessing.*

Help from aid workers was a **boon** for which the refugees were very thankful.

Vocabulary Practice

Review the words and sample sentences above. Then, with a partner, discuss what you think this article will be about. Use the Vocabulary words in your discussion. Finally, write your thoughts on the lines below.

Students should use the Vocabulary words in their discussions and written responses.

SET A PURPOSE FOR READING
Read this magazine article to learn about the hardships faced by refugees from Sudan.

THE LOST BOYS

Based on the magazine article by
SARA CORBETT

BACKGROUND The boys in this article are from Sudan (soo DAN), the largest country in Africa. For many years, Sudan has been torn apart by a civil war. Over 4 million Sudanese people have become refugees: they have been driven from their homes. Two million have died, and thousands more have been forced into slavery. In May 2004, peace talks brought about a decrease in the fighting, but war soon broke out again in western Sudan.

Three brothers survived lions, crocodiles, and starvation. Now they're starting life over in America.

One January evening, Peter Dut leads his two teenage brothers through the Minneapolis airport. The brothers are African refugees. Two days earlier they had learned about light switches and stairs for the first time. Now they are alone in Minneapolis.

Finally, a traveler asks, "Where are you headed?" Peter answers in careful English. A few days earlier, they left a mud **hut** in an African refugee camp where they had lived as orphans for nine years. Without parents, the boys had escaped their war-torn country and walked hundreds of miles to the camp. Now

VISUAL VOCABULARY
A **hut** is a small house with a simple design, often built out of local, natural materials. The boys' hut was built out of dried mud.

they are headed to Fargo, North Dakota. "You're joking!" the traveler replies.

The brothers are part of a group of refugees called the Lost Boys of Sudan. This group of around 10,000 boys arrived in Kenya in 1992. They were seeking a safe place away from their country's war.

Almost 17,000 boys were separated from their families. They fled their homes in an **exodus** in 1987. They walked about 1,000 miles from Sudan to Kenya. Most of the boys were between the ages of 8 and 18.

They endured attacks from **marauding** bandits and lions, and they suffered from a lack of food and water. Some boys drowned or were eaten by crocodiles.

The Lost Boys have spent nine years **subsisting** on simple meals and living with very little adult supervision. They've been pretty much on their own. Now, they are coming to America. Because they learned English at the refugee camp, the boys will start school at a grade level normal for their age. Eventually, they can become American citizens.

IN OTHER WORDS Peter Dut and his two younger brothers are African refugees—people who have nowhere to live because disasters or warfare have destroyed their homes. The Lost Boys faced many dangers as they traveled hundreds of miles to a refugee camp. In America, they must learn a new way of life.

Nighttime in America?

Peter and his brothers arrive in Fargo. Snow falls around the airport. The younger brothers, Maduk, 17, and Riak, 15, look frightened. Peter studies the night. "Excuse me," he says worriedly. "Please, is it now night or day?"

The brothers' new home is a two-bedroom apartment. Rent is $445 a month. Food and other necessary items have been donated by local churches and businesses. A

VOCABULARY

The word **exodus** (EKS uh duhs) is a noun that means *an event in which a large group of people leaves a place.*

Circle the phrase in line 18 that helps you understand the word's meaning.

The word **marauding** (muh RAWD ing) is an adjective that means *roaming in order to steal and destroy property.*

The word **subsist** (suhb SIST) is a verb that means *to support oneself just enough to survive.*

A AUTHOR'S PURPOSE

Reread lines 30–36. Then, draw a check mark ✔ next to the paragraph that the author is using "to entertain." Draw a circle around the paragraph that the author is using "to inform."

Monitor Your Comprehension

A social worker empties a bag of donated clothing. The clothes look like they'd belonged to an elderly man. I know how lucky the boys are: War, lack of food, and disease in their country have killed more than 2 million people, but these three boys are still alive. Still, I hate to think of the boys showing up for school in these clothes, which their classmates may laugh at.

The next day I check on the boys at noon. They are very hungry. "What about your food?" I ask. I point to the bread and the box of cereal.

Peter grins in embarrassment. I realize they have never opened a box. And so I show them how. We open a can of beans and a loaf of bread. Soon, the boys are eating a hot meal. B

IN OTHER WORDS The boys have an apartment, food, and clothing provided for them. However, they still have trouble knowing what to do and how to deal with everyday items that are unfamiliar to them.

► Underline the sentence that explains why the boys are hungry.

B AUTHOR'S PURPOSE

Reread lines 43–48. Is the author's purpose here to inform or to express thoughts and feelings? Explain.

Possible answer: The author's purpose is to inform readers. The anecdote shows how unfamiliar the boys are with some of the ordinary features of American life. The author's purpose may also be to entertain because the scene is somewhat humorous.

C

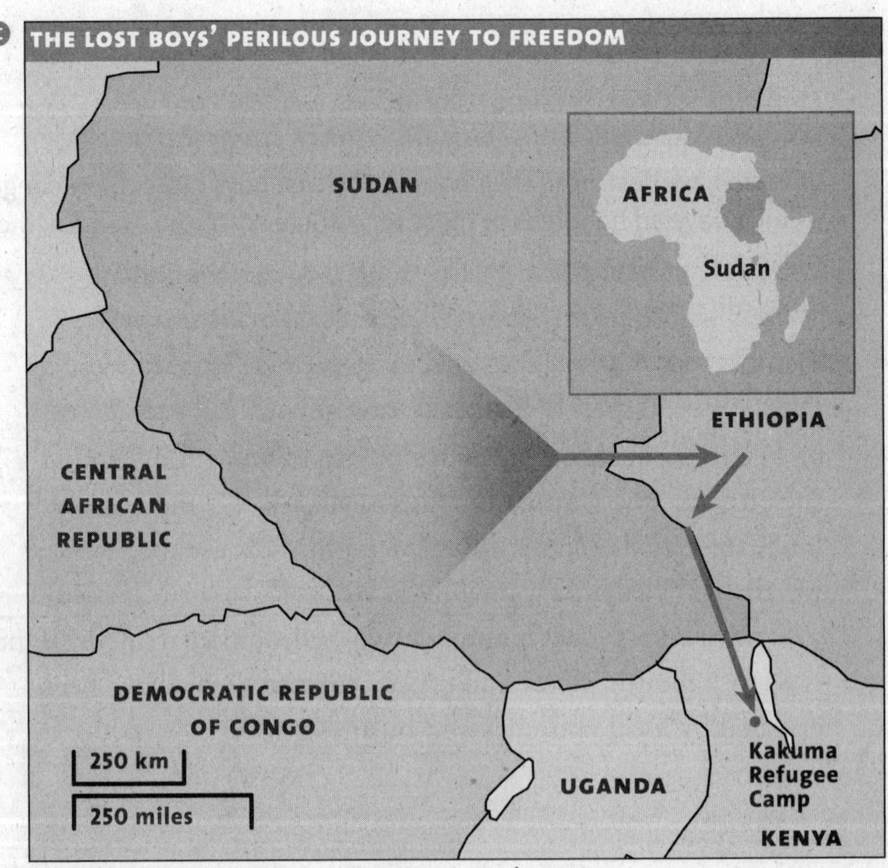

C GRAPHIC AIDS

List two details included on this map that are not provided in the article. How does this map help you understand the boys' experience?

Possible answer: The map gives information about what countries border Sudan and where Sudan is located in Africa. The map also allows the reader to better visualize the Lost Boys' difficult trek.

Monitor Your Comprehension

Living on Leaves and Berries

The three brothers have traveled a long way since fleeing their home. Their parents and three sisters were killed by soldiers. The Lost Boys first survived a 6- to 10-week walk to Ethiopia. Often they ate leaves and berries and, once in a while, the **boon** of a dead wild pig. Many boys fell behind and died.

They lived for three years in Ethiopia. Then, the Lost Boys were forced back into Sudan by the Ethiopian government. Somehow, more than 10,000 of the boys made it to Kenya's refugee camps in 1992.

Within weeks, Riak is placed in a local junior high. Maduk starts high school classes, and Peter begins adult-education classes.

VOCABULARY
The word **boon** (boon) is a noun that means *a benefit* or *blessing*.

IN OTHER WORDS The Lost Boys left their homes because of war. They walked to a refugee camp in Ethiopia. Then, the Ethiopian government sent them back to Sudan. About 10,000 boys walked to another refugee camp in Kenya. Soon after they arrive in America, the brothers in the story start going to school.

Refugee Blues

Five weeks later, Riak listens quietly in his history class. He is ignored by the white students around him. At a nearby high school, Maduk is often alone as well.

Peter worries about money. The three brothers spend most of the money they receive each month on rent and utility bills. PAUSE & REFLECT

Social workers say the brothers are going through normal adjustments, just as many other refugees do. The first three months are always the toughest.

PAUSE & REFLECT
Reread lines 61–66. Think about how the boys must feel in their new life. Then with a partner, discuss some things that you think they might miss about their old life in Sudan.

Possible answer: I think the boys miss being surrounded by other Sudanese people who share their experiences and culture. They must feel lonely. However, they probably also realize that they are safer in America.

The Lost Boys can only hope so. A return to Africa could kill them. "There is nothing left for The Lost Boys to go home to—it's a war zone," says a relief worker whose job is to help refugees.

Getting used to American life is hard, but the boys also experience joyful moments.

On a quiet Friday night, the boys make dinner. Peter changes into a finely woven African outfit.

Then, the doorbell rings unexpectedly. D Four Sudanese boys crowd into the apartment. They have been in America for several years. I watch as one wraps his arms around Peter. "It's a hard life here," he whispers to the older boy, "but it's a free life, too."

D LANGUAGE COACH

The word *unexpectedly* in line 78 is a **derivation** (der uh VAY shuhn) of, or comes from, the adjective *unexpected*. The *-ly* at the end changes the adjective to an adverb that tells *how* the doorbell rang.

IN OTHER WORDS Getting used to their new lives is difficult. Peter and his brothers cannot go back to Africa. One day four other Sudanese boys visit.

► Reread lines 78–82. With a partner, discuss why the other boys think that moving to America has been a good thing.

Possible answer: The boys who have been in America longer know that they have a level of freedom and security here that they would not have back in the camps or in Sudan.

Text Analysis: Author's Purpose

"The Lost Boys" includes passages that inform, that persuade, that entertain, and that express thoughts and feelings. To determine the author's *main* purpose for writing, you must decide which purpose *most* of the clues in the article support. Look back at the article for evidence that supports each purpose listed in the chart below, and write your notes in the chart. The row with the most clues listed will be the author's main purpose. Some clues are filled in for you.

For this chart, answers will vary. See samples below.

Author's Purpose	Clues in the Writing
To inform or explain (Clues: facts and statistics, directions, steps in a process)	*Almost 17,000 boys left Sudan in 1987 to escape war.* ***War, lack of food, and disease in Sudan have killed more than 2 million people. More than 10,000 Sudanese boys made it to Kenya's refugee camps in 1992.***
To persuade (Clues: opinion statements, appeals to emotion, calls to action)	***"The Lost Boys can only hope so. A return to Africa could kill them. 'There is nothing left for The Lost Boys to go home to—it's a war zone,' says a relief worker whose job is to help refugees."***
To entertain (Clues: suspenseful situations, funny details, interesting characters)	*The boys have never opened a box.* ***"'Where are you headed?' ... Fargo, North Dakota. 'You're joking!' the traveler replies."***
To express thoughts and feelings (Clues: thoughtful descriptions, insightful observations, the writer's personal feelings)	***"I know how lucky the boys are ... Still, I hate to think of the boys showing up for school in these clothes."***

Reading Skill: Interpret Graphic Aids

This article includes graphic aids, such as photographs and a map. Use the chart below to identify how graphic aids add to your understanding of the topic of the Lost Boys of Sudan.

For this chart, answers will vary. See samples below.

Type of Graphic Aid	What It Shows	How It Adds to What I Know
The photograph of a boy at the beginning of the selection on page 252.	*It shows a Sudanese boy in Africa.*	*It helps me visualize what life was like in Sudan for the Lost Boys before they came to the United States.*
The map of Sudan	*It shows the location of Sudan and illustrates the Lost Boys' march to Kenya.*	*This map give me more detailed geographical information and helps me visualize the Lost Boys' march; it shows me how far they traveled.*

How far would you go to find FREEDOM?

What did the Lost Boys sacrifice for their freedom? Do you think what they have gained is worth what they have given up? Discuss your ideas with a partner. *Answers will vary.*

Vocabulary Practice

In each group of four words, circle the word that is most different in meaning from the others.

1. (a) compassion (b) escape (c) **exodus** (d) migration
2. (a) **boon** (b) gift (c) sacrifice (d) surprise
3. (a) destroying (b) inspiring (c) **marauding** (d) stealing
4. (a) manage (b) reconsider (c) **subsist** (d) survive

Academic Vocabulary in Writing

The word **implicit** (im PLIS it) means *not actually said but hinted at instead.*

Elena's strong interest in seeing the movie was **implicit** in her excited talk about the actors and the story.

WRITE IT "The Lost Boys" describes many hardships that the boys faced on their journey from Sudan to the United States. What is **implicit** in these descriptions about the kinds of people the boys are? Write your response on the lines below, making sure to use the word **implicit**.

Possible answer: Implicit in all of the descriptions of the Lost Boys is the idea that they are still gentle and kind young men even after the terrible things they've experienced.

Assessment Practice

DIRECTIONS Use "The Lost Boys" to answer questions 1–4.

1 The author begins the article with the brothers' arrival at the airport to —

- (A) introduce a funny story about them
- (B) show that the boys are unhappy
- (C) emphasize the differences in weather that the boys experience
- (D) highlight the difference between where the boys left and their new home

2 What is the main reason the Lost Boys are unable to return to Sudan?

- (A) There is nothing left for them in Sudan.
- (B) The Sudanese government will not let them return.
- (C) They don't have enough money.
- (D) The United States will not let them go back.

3 The author includes the information about clothing in lines 37–42 to —

- (A) gain readers' sympathy for the boys
- (B) share her own feelings about how the boys were treated by the Americans
- (C) argue that the boys should have been given new clothes
- (D) make the article more entertaining

4 Why did the Lost Boys leave Ethiopia?

- (A) They wanted to go back home to Sudan.
- (B) The Ethiopian government forced them out.
- (C) They were chased by lions.
- (D) Relief workers at the refugee camp told them it was safe.

Consumer Documents: From the Manufacturer to You

Based on Product Information, Safety Information, and Warranty Documents

Why are **PROCEDURAL** texts necessary?

Have you ever started reading a manual and found yourself confused after just a few sentences? **Procedural** (pruh SEED yuhr uhl) **texts** give instructions or other detailed, step-by-step information. You will need to read them slowly and pay attention to details to gather the information you need from them.

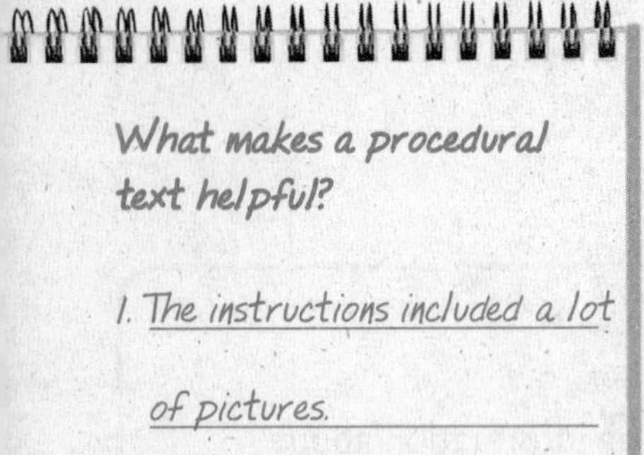

What makes a procedural text helpful?
1. The instructions included a lot of pictures.
Answers will vary.

WRITE IT Think of a procedural text that you have read recently. It might have been a manual for a cell phone or instructions on how to install some software. Were the instructions helpful? Why or why not? Record your thoughts on the lines at left.

Text Analysis: Consumer Documents

A **consumer** is someone who uses a product or service. Many of the things you buy—a cell phone, a game, or even a backpack—come with **consumer documents.** These might be instructions for how to put something together or warranty information that tells you what rights you have if there is a problem with the item.

All good consumer documents have a clear **purpose,** or objective. For example, they might describe how to put something together correctly, or they might describe a product in great detail, so that you know everything the product can do. Writers of consumer documents try to organize information to make it clear and easy to follow. Here are some of the features, or elements, that often appear in consumer documents:

Common Features in Consumer Documents

- Charts
- **Boldface** text
- Bulleted lists (like this one)
- Numbered lists
- Section headings
- Pictures or diagrams

Reading Strategy: Adjust Reading Rate

When you read an email from a friend or a magazine article on your favorite subject, you might read fairly quickly. But when you read a consumer document, your **reading rate**—the speed at which you read the text—might slow down at times. You may have to pause more often and think about what you've read or reread sections of the text. Adjusting your reading rate is something good readers do all the time. They speed up when reading about something that is familiar and easy. They slow down when a text becomes complex and detailed.

As you read the documents that follow, you will be asked to take notes about your reading rate. Use the suggestions in the chart below to help guide your reading.

Feature	Characteristics	Reading Rate
Introduction	easy-to-read prose	fast
Bulleted list	clear parts of a topic	medium
Table or chart	lots of information in categories	slow
Numbered list	steps in sequence	medium to slow
Dense text	long and complicated sentences	slow

SET A PURPOSE FOR READING
Test your knowledge of consumer documents by reading the following selections.

CONSUMER DOCUMENTS:

From the Manufacturer to You

Based on Product Information, Safety Information, and Warranty Documents

BACKGROUND The three consumer documents you are about to read are what you might expect to get with a new game system. As you read the documents, think about other kinds of consumer documents you have seen.

Imagine that you have just bought a new computer game system. In your hurry to get the product out of the box, you drop some papers on the floor. You might throw away the papers by accident, along with the box and packing materials. However, it is important that you keep the papers and read them carefully. These consumer documents can make a big difference in how much you enjoy your new game system. Ⓐ

Ⓐ LANGUAGE COACH
In some English words, a pair of the same consonant can appear in a word. An example of this spelling pattern is found in line 2: "hurry." The word *hurry* is pronounced (HUR ee). Underline other examples of doubled consonants in the first paragraph. Practice pronouncing them, using a dictionary to check your pronunciation.

Elements and Features of Consumer Documents

Here are some types of consumer documents and the kinds of information that each document provides:

- **product information**—a description of what the product will do
- **instruction manual**—information on how to use the product, including safety information and any directions you may need to install it or put it together
- **warranty**—information about what the product's maker promises to do for you if the product does not work (B)

IN OTHER WORDS It's important to keep documents that come with a product you buy. Consumer documents include helpful information, instructions, and details about what the company that made the item will do if the product does not work.

Consumer documents often give you a list of details about a product. Here is an example from an electronic game system.

Product Information

WYSIWYGAME ARTS

CPU	800MHz
Video card	250 MHz GPU
Resolution	1920 × 1080 maximum
Memory	128 MB
Storage	Memory Card—Hard Drive
Sound card	64 Channels
DVD	Yes
Media	12 × DVD-ROM 6.2 GB Capacity
Hard drive	8 GB
Modem	Yes
Ethernet port	Yes
Controllers	4

(C)

(B) ADJUST READING RATE

Reread lines 8–16. Underline the key ideas in these lines. What elements or features do you see in this section of text?

bullets, boldface text

Did these features make you read quickly or slowly? Why?

They help me read more quickly because they help organize the information.

(C) CONSUMER DOCUMENTS

Reread the Product Information chart. Then answer the questions below.

What kind of information is presented in this document?

information about an electronic game system

What feature is used to organize the information? How does organizing information in this way help readers?

It is a chart that is organized by feature, which can help readers easily locate different featues of the game.

VISUAL VOCABULARY

Air vents are openings that allow air to flow out of a space or a box. They keep things cool.

Safety Information

Please follow these safety measures when you install and use your game system:

1. When installing your console, the main control unit of the system, make sure you leave enough air space around it so that it stays cool and doesn't overheat. Never block or cover the console's **air vents** with objects such as cloth, books, or magazines.
2. Do not place your game console in a closed bookcase or cabinet where it could overheat.
3. Do not place the game console in direct sunlight or near something hot.
4. Do not set the game console on a soft surface, such as a bed, sofa, or rug.
5. If any of the following occurs, unplug the game console and contact the service department:
   a. The power-supply cord or plug is damaged.
   b. Liquid is spilled on, or objects fall into, the game console.
   c. The game console gets wet.
   d. The game console does not work properly.
   e. The game console is dropped, or the outer covering is damaged.
   f. The way the game works suddenly changes.

Do not try to repair this product yourself. Opening or removing the outside cover may cause serious injury. All service must be done by an approved service person. (D)

(D) CONSUMER DOCUMENTS

Reread the Safety Information document. Then, fill in the chart below.

What kind of information is presented in this document?

safety information about the game system

↓

How is the information organized? List three features of this document.

It is organized by number and letter, and important information is placed in italics.

IN OTHER WORDS Product information lists details about the product. Safety information tells you how to install or use a product safely.

► What is one main safety concern with this game system? Draw brackets [ ] around all information that talks about that safety concern.

Possible answer: Overheating is a main safety concern.

Limited Warranty

WYSIWYGame Arts makes the following warranties. These warranties are for the person who buys the product or for anyone who receives this product bought new as a gift.

Limited Ninety [90] Day Warranty

WYSIWYGame Arts guarantees this product and its parts against defects in materials and workmanship for ninety [90] days after purchase. During this time, WYSIWYGame Arts will replace any defective product or part at no cost to you. To get a new system or part, you must take the entire product back to the place where it was bought. PAUSE & REFLECT

Limited One [1] Year Warranty of Parts

WYSIWYGame Arts further guarantees the parts of this product against defects in materials or workmanship for a period of one [1] year after the date of purchase. During this time, WYSIWYGame Arts will replace a defective part. If a defective part is replaced after ninety [90] days from the date the system was bought, you will have to pay to have someone install the new part. You must deliver the entire product to a WYSIWYGame Arts service station. You pay all charges for getting the product to and from the service station. E

Owner's Manual and Warranty Registration

Read the owner's manual carefully before using this product. WYSIWYGame Arts does not take responsibility

PAUSE & REFLECT

In this paragraph (and throughout this document) the writer has included numbers in [brackets]. Circle each example of this in the document. Why do you think the writer chose to include these numbers? What purpose do they serve?

Possible answer: Since this is a legal document, the company wants to make sure that there is no confusion about the time periods.

E ADJUST READING RATE

Slowly reread this paragraph. Underline details that help you understand what you will have to pay for if a part breaks after 90 days.

for any defect caused by improper or incorrect installation or use. Complete and mail the attached registration card within fourteen [14] days. The warranty is effective only if your name, address, and the date the system was bought are on file and you are listed as the new owner of a WYSIWYGame Arts product. F

F CONSUMER DOCUMENTS

Reread this document. Then, fill in the chart below.

What kind of information is presented in this document?
warranty information about the consumer's rights

↓

What features are used to organize the information?
section headings, paragraphs, numbers placed in brackets

IN OTHER WORDS The warranty tells you what the maker of the product will do if your product doesn't work properly, either because something was wrong with the materials or because it was made incorrectly.

► What does the limited warranty cover if you buy it used from a friend? Underline the details that help you answer this question.

You are not covered if you buy it used from a friend.

Text Analysis: Consumer Documents

Evaluate the organization of the consumer documents you just read. To do this, think about the type of information that is included in each document and how that information is organized. Remember that the features used to organize information can include charts, boldface text, bulleted or numbered lists, section headings, and pictures or diagrams. Use the following chart to record your responses.

For this chart, answers will vary. See samples below.

Document	Type of Information Presented	Features Used to Organize the Information
Product Information	*information on the features and performance of the game system*	*chart organized by feature*
Safety Information	*information on how to safely use the system*	*numbered and lettered lists, use of italics for emphasis*
Warranty	*information on the rights of the buyer should the device break*	*section headings*

Consumer documents are written for the purpose of informing, instructing, or educating readers. How effective do you think these documents were in achieving that purpose? Which features helped the documents communicate information clearly? Are there any features that would have made the documents more helpful?

Answers will vary.

Reading Strategy: Adjust Reading Rate

Think about how you adjusted your reading rate as you read the three consumer documents. For each type of feature listed in the chart below, label the rate at which you read: fast, medium, or slow. Then identify how well you understood the information that was presented in each type of feature: a lot, a little, or not much.

Answers will vary.

Feature	Reading Rate	Level of Understanding
Introduction		
Bulleted list		
Table or chart		
Numbered list		
Dense text		

What connection do you see between your reading rate and your level of understanding? Explain.

Answers will vary.

Why are **PROCEDURAL** texts necessary?

Imagine what life would be like without procedural texts. What kinds of documents would we no longer have? Without procedural texts, what kinds of things would be more difficult to do? Write your response below.

Answers will vary. Students will likely realize that procedural texts are an important part of everyday life. Without them we wouldn't have cookbooks or instructions on how to assemble products we buy. We would also not have forms, driving directions, or legal documents.

Academic Vocabulary in Speaking

The word **primary** (PRY mehr ee) is an adjective that means *first* or *most important*.

The **primary** focus of our experiment is to determine what caused the chemical reaction.

The word **specific** (spih SIF ik) is an adjective that means *definite* or *exact*.

So that I can figure out what the problem is, you will need to give me some **specific** examples of what you saw.

TURN AND TALK With a partner, discuss some of the important features of procedural documents. Be sure to use the words **primary** and **specific** in your conversation.

Encourage students to use the Academic Vocabulary words in their discussions.

Assessment Practice

DIRECTIONS Use "Consumer Documents" to answer questions 1–4.

1 According to the Product Information, you would not want to purchase this product if you were looking for a product with —

- (A) more than 4 controllers
- (B) more than 6 GB of hard drive space
- (C) a modem and an ethernet port
- (D) a memory card

2 According to the Safety Information on page 264, what should you do if the product does not work correctly?

- (A) Return the product to the nearest store.
- (B) Try to repair the product yourself.
- (C) Call the product manufacturer.
- (D) Unplug the product and contact a service person.

3 To organize information, the Limited Warranty includes —

- (A) boldface headings
- (B) charts
- (C) graphic illustrations
- (D) numbered steps

4 The purpose of a warranty is to provide —

- (A) information about what to do if a product is defective
- (B) a list of the product's safety hazards
- (C) directions for operating a product
- (D) a lifetime guarantee that a product will always work as it is supposed to

UNIT 6

Taking Sides

ARGUMENT AND PERSUASION

Be sure to read the Text Analysis Workshop on pages 654–659 in *Holt McDougal Literature*.

Academic Vocabulary for Unit 6

You will see these Academic Vocabulary words as you work through this book. You will also be asked to use them as you write and talk about the selections in this unit.

Coherent (koh HIR uhnt) is an adjective that means *connected or logical, making sense.*
George's argument in debate class was **coherent** and convincing.

What does it mean if your essay is **coherent**? ____________

Answers will vary.

Differentiate (dif uh REN shee ayt) is a verb that means *to be aware of or point out a difference between two or more things.*
Some students couldn't **differentiate** between facts and opinions.

How do you **differentiate** between ripe and unripe fruit? ____________

Answers will vary.

Evident (EV ih duhnt) is an adjective that means *easy to see or understand.*
It was **evident** that the geometry quiz would not be difficult.

Name something that is **evident** to you but not to others: ____________

Answers will vary.

Relevant (REL uh vuhnt) is an adjective that means *having to do with the subject being discussed.*
Jean thought the nutrition lesson before lunch was **relevant.**

Which school subject do you feel is the most **relevant** to your life? ____________

Answers will vary.

Technique (tek NEEK) is a noun that means *a special way of doing something.*
I developed my own **technique** for playing the guitar.

Describe a **technique** you use to stay calm when giving a speech:

Answers will vary.

I Have a Dream

Adapted from the speech by **Dr. Martin Luther King Jr.**

Can a **DREAM** change the world?

Many people have dreamed of how to make the world a better place. Powerful words—words that inspire others to find ways to improve our lives—can help turn a person's dream into reality. In the speech you are about to read, Dr. Martin Luther King Jr. shares his dream for a better world.

TURN AND TALK What is your dream for a better world? Write a list of changes you would like to see to make a better world. With a partner, discuss the reasons each of these changes is necessary.

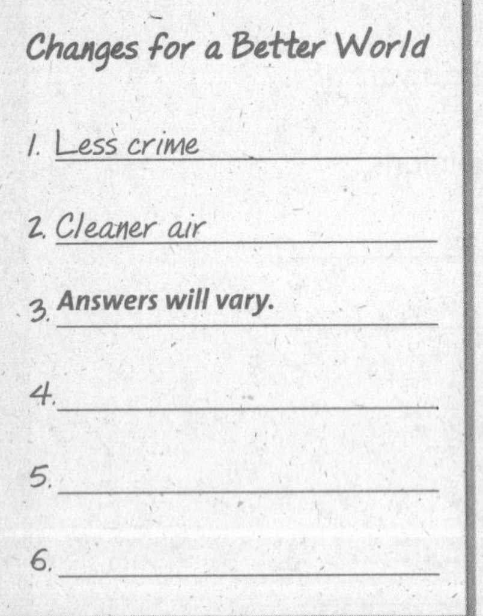

Changes for a Better World
1. Less crime
2. Cleaner air
3. Answers will vary.
4.
5.
6.

Text Analysis: Argument

You may think of an argument as an angry discussion. In formal speaking and writing, however, an argument expresses a position on an issue and supports the position with reasons and evidence. A strong argument includes these elements:

- **claim**—the writer or speaker's position on an issue
- **support**—the reasons and evidence that support this claim

King argues that in his time African Americans do not have freedom and equality in America and that their situation must change. As you read, you will record in a chart like this one King's claims and the support he provides for them in the form of reasons and evidence.

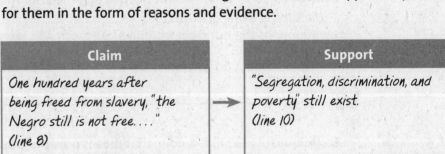

Claim		Support
One hundred years after being freed from slavery, "the Negro still is not free. . . ." (line 8)	→	*"Segregation, discrimination, and poverty" still exist. (line 10)*

Reading Skill: Understand Rhetorical Devices

To persuade readers and listeners, writers and speakers use words in ways that make their arguments more memorable and powerful. As you read his speech, notice how the wording King uses makes his message more memorable and powerful.

Repetition is the repeated use of the same words and phrases for emphasis.
We will try again and again until we achieve our goal.

Parallelism is the use of similar grammatical structures, such as phrases or sentences, to link ideas together.

We will not, cannot, and should not wait until it is too late to decide.

Analogy compares two subjects point by point.

I might have been talking to a wall, they ignored me so completely.

Vocabulary in Context

Note: Words are listed in the order in which they appear in the speech.

Momentous (moh MEN tuhs) is an adjective that means *of great importance.*
Lincoln's action to free the slaves was **momentous.**

Default (dih FAWLT) is a verb that means *to fail to keep a promise* or *to fail to pay a debt.*
King argued that America seemed to **default** on its promise of equality for all.

Inextricably (in EK strih kuh blee) is an adverb that means *in a way impossible to untangle.*
King believed the lives of all Americans are **inextricably** linked.

Vocabulary Practice

With a partner, discuss answers to the following questions, using the Vocabulary words in your discussion.

Encourage students to use the Vocabulary words in their answers.

1. What is a **momentous** event you have seen or heard about?
2. Why is it wrong to **default** on something you owe?
3. What are two things in school that are **inextricably** linked?

SET A PURPOSE FOR READING
Read "I Have a Dream" to find out what Dr. Martin Luther King Jr. says life is like for African Americans 100 years after slavery ended and why their situation should change.

I Have a Dream

Based on the speech by
DR. MARTIN LUTHER KING JR.

BACKGROUND On August 28, 1963, over 200,000 people had gathered in Washington, D.C. They wanted Congress to pass a civil rights bill, a law that would give equal rights to all Americans. The crowd stood in front of the Lincoln Memorial as Dr. Martin Luther King Jr., an African American minister, spoke directly from his heart to the crowd about his dream of freedom, equality, and unity.

I am happy to join with you today in what will go down in history as the greatest demonstration for freedom in the history of our nation.

Five score[1] years ago, Abraham Lincoln signed the Emancipation Proclamation[2]. This **momentous** decree gave hope to millions of Negroes who had faced withering, devastating injustice as slaves.

VOCABULARY
The word **momentous** (moh MEN tuhs) is an adjective that means *of great importance.*

But one hundred years later, the Negro still is not free; one hundred years later, the Negro is still sadly crippled by

1. **five score:** 100; *score* means "twenty." (King's use of the phrase is a reminder of the beginning of Abraham Lincoln's Gettysburg Address: "Four score and seven years ago. . . .")
2. **Emancipation Proclamation** (ih man suh PAY shuhn prok luh MAY shuhn): a document signed by President Lincoln in 1863, during the Civil War. It declared that all slaves in states still at war with the Union were free.

segregation,[3] discrimination, and poverty; one hundred years later, the Negro still finds himself in exile[4] in his own land.

When the creators of our nation wrote the Constitution and the Declaration of Independence, they made the promise that all men, yes, black men as well as white men, would be guaranteed the unalienable[5] rights of life, liberty, and the pursuit of happiness. **A**

[It is obvious today that America has **defaulted** on this promise] where her citizens of color are concerned. We have come here to demand the riches of freedom and the security of justice promised to us. **B**

We have also come here to remind America of how important it is to act now. Now is the time to make the promises of democracy real; now is the time to move from segregation to racial justice; now is the time to make justice a reality for all of God's children. It would be fatal for the nation to overlook this.

Nineteen sixty-three is not an end, but a beginning. There will be no rest in America until the Negro is granted his citizenship rights and justice is achieved. **PAUSE & REFLECT**

IN OTHER WORDS King says that the Emancipation Proclamation, the Constitution, and the Declaration of Independence promise equality to all Americans. But in 1963, African Americans still face inequality. They are segregated, or separated, from white Americans. They are not treated as equals under the law and, as a result, many live in poverty. King demands immediate justice; if it does not happen, he says, protests will continue.

But in the process of gaining our rightful place we must not be guilty of doing wrong, or of bitterness and hatred. We must forever conduct our struggle with dignity. We must not allow our protests to sink to physical violence. Again and again we

3. **segregation** (seg rih GAY shuhn): the separation of one racial group from another, especially in public places.
4. **exile:** the act of forcing a person to leave home or country, often as a punishment.
5. **unalienable** (uhn AYL yuh nuh buhl) **rights:** rights that cannot be taken away.

Monitor Your Comprehension

A ARGUMENT

Underline the **evidence** King presents in lines 12–16 to support his **claim** that "black men as well as white men" should have freedom.

VOCABULARY

The word **default** (dih FAWLT) is a verb that means *to fail to keep a promise* or *to fail to pay a debt.*

B RHETORICAL DEVICES

In lines 17–20, King uses an **analogy** as a rhetorical device. Bracket [ ] the words that show the comparison King makes in these lines. To what does King compare America's failure to establish racial equality and justice?

a defaulted promise

PAUSE & REFLECT

With a partner, discuss what King means when he says, "Nineteen sixty-three is not an end, but a beginning."

Students should discuss that African Americans will continue to protest inequality.

must meet physical force with soul force. Our anger must not lead us to distrust all white people. Many of our white brothers, as we can see by their presence here today, realize that their destiny[6] is tied up with our destiny. And they realize that their freedom is **inextricably** bound to our freedom. We cannot walk alone. And as we walk, we must make the pledge that we shall always march ahead. We cannot turn back. (C)

There are some who are asking those who want civil rights, "When will you be satisfied?" We are not satisfied, and we will not be satisfied until we have justice.

I know that some of you have experienced great suffering. Some of you have faced brutal, unfair treatment by the police. Continue to work with the faith that this undeserved suffering will help set you free. Return home knowing that somehow this situation can and will be changed. Do not give up hope.

IN OTHER WORDS King tells people who protest and demonstrate for civil rights to stay away from physical violence and hatred. He points out that some white people have joined the fight to gain civil rights for all. He also encourages people who have been treated unfairly by the police to have faith that things will get better.

► What does King mean when he tells listeners to "meet physical force with soul force"? Discuss your answer with a classmate.

Students should discuss how African Americans should counter physical force with strength of character.

6. **destiny** (DES tuh nee): what becomes of a person or thing.

Monitor Your Comprehension

VOCABULARY

The word inextricably (in EK strih kuh blee) is an adverb that means *in a way impossible to untangle.*

(C) ARGUMENT

Reread lines 29–39. Identify the **reasons** King provides for his claim that physical violence should not be used as a form of protest. Write those reasons in the box below.

Claim
Physical violence should not be used to protest racial inequality.

Reasons
Possible answer: King notes that they must not be guilty of doing wrong and that they must conduct their struggle with dignity.

My friends, even though we face these difficulties, I still have a dream. It is a dream deeply rooted in the American dream. I have a dream that one day this nation will live out the true meaning of "We hold these truths to be self-evident; that all men are created equal." I have a dream that one day the sons of former slaves and the sons of former slave owners will sit down together at the table of brotherhood. I have a dream that my children will one day live in a nation where they will not be judged by the color of their skin, but by the content of their character. Ⓓ

I have a dream today!

I have a dream that one day down in Alabama[7] little black boys and black girls will be able to join hands with little white boys and white girls as sisters and brothers.

I have a dream today!

I return with this faith to the South. With this faith we will be able to work together, to pray together, to struggle together, to go to jail together, to stand up for freedom together, knowing that we will be free one day. Ⓔ This will be the day when all of God's children will be able to sing with new meaning, "My country 'tis of thee, sweet land of liberty, of thee I sing. Land where my fathers died, land of the pilgrims' pride, from every mountainside, let freedom ring." And if America is to be a great nation, this must become true. Ⓕ

So let freedom ring from the hilltops of New Hampshire; let freedom ring from the mighty mountains of New York; let freedom ring from the snow-topped mountains of Colorado; let freedom ring from the peaks of California. But not only that. Let freedom ring from Stone Mountain of Georgia; let freedom ring from Lookout Mountain of Tennessee; let freedom ring from every hill of Mississippi. "From every mountainside, let freedom ring." Ⓖ

7. **Alabama:** In 1963, George Wallace, governor of Alabama, tried to keep African Americans from going to the same schools as white students. Separating black people from white people in schools and other public places was common in the American South.

Monitor Your Comprehension

Ⓓ RHETORICAL DEVICES

King uses **repetition** in lines 48–57. Underline the phrase he repeats. With a partner, discuss what kind of emotions repeating this phrase might inspire in King's audience.

Students should discuss how repeating the phrase could inspire hope and determination.

Ⓔ LANGUAGE COACH

An **idiom** is an expression with a special meaning different from the combined literal, or normal, meanings of its words. The phrase *stand up* usually means "to rise from a seated position." But as an idiom it can also mean "to insist upon." Reread line 65. What does King ask his listeners to insist upon? Circle the answer.

Ⓕ ARGUMENT

Reread lines 70–71. What does King **claim** will happen to America if there is not freedom for all? Write your answer on the lines below.

Possible answer: America will not be a great nation.

Ⓖ RHETORICAL DEVICES

In lines 72–79, King uses **parallelism.** He structures a series of sentences this way: "Let freedom ring from . . . ." With a partner, discuss the effect King's use of parallelism creates.

Students should discuss how parallelism makes King's ideas more vivid and compelling.

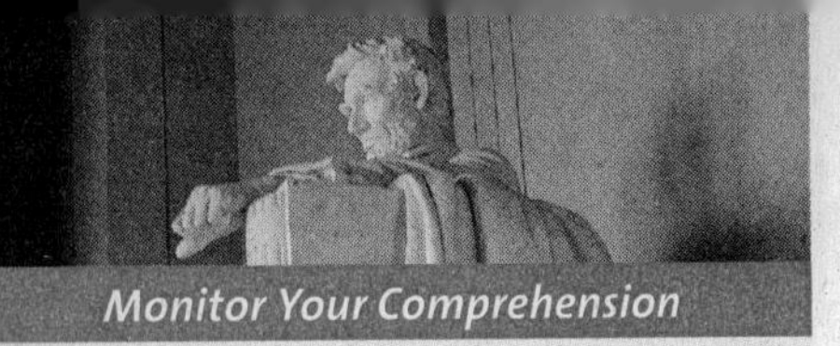

And when we allow freedom to ring everywhere, we speed up that day when all of God's children—black men and white men, Jews and Gentiles,[8] Protestants and Catholics—will be able to join hands and sing in the words of the old Negro spiritual,[9] "Free at last. Free at last. Thank God Almighty, we are free at last."

IN OTHER WORDS Dr. King shares his dream of a united America, no longer divided by differences in race or religion, but with equal rights for all, in every part of the country.

8. **Gentiles** (JEN tylz): people who are not Jews.
9. **spiritual:** a religious song developed by African Americans in the South.

After Reading

Text Analysis: Argument

In his speech, King argues for freedom and equality for all Americans. Complete the chart with additional reasons and evidence King provides to support his claim that freedom and equality do not exist for African Americans and that their situation must change.

For this chart, answers will vary. See samples below.

Claim
One hundred years after being freed from slavery, "the Negro still is not free. ..." (line 8)

↓

Support (Reasons/Evidence)
1. "Segregation, discrimination, and poverty" still exist. (line 10)
2. brutal, unfair treatment by the police
3.

Review your notes on "I Have a Dream" and your completed chart. Then, write a summary of King's argument about the need for freedom and equality for African Americans.

Possible answer: King argues that America has promised certain rights to all but has not honored that promise for African Americans. He has faith that wrongs can be made right and that all people can be free.

After Reading

Reading Skill: Understand Rhetorical Devices

King uses **repetition, parallelism,** and **analogy** to persuade his audience about his point of view by making it memorable and powerful. Which of these rhetorical devices do you think is the most persuasive? List it in the chart below.

For this chart, answers will vary. See samples below.

Rhetorical Device: *repetition*
Examples: *I have a dream, let freedom ring*
Effect on Audience: *King's use of repetition gives the audience hope and also makes his ideas more vivid and compelling.*

Explain why you think this is the strongest rhetorical device King uses to communicate his ideas.

Answers will vary.

Can a **DREAM** change the world?

With a partner, discuss what you think is the single *most* important change that is needed in the world today.

Encourage students to discuss how the change will affect their own lives.

Vocabulary Practice

Circle the answer to each question to show your understanding of the Vocabulary words.

1. Which would be more **momentous**? the birth of a baby / the first snow of the season
2. What does it mean to **default** on a loan? sign up to borrow money / fail to make a payment
3. Which of these are more likely to be **inextricably** linked? shoppers in a drugstore / players on a football team

Academic Vocabulary in Speaking

The word **technique** (tek NEEK) is a noun that means *a special way of doing something.*

I learned a new **technique** for throwing the ball so I could score more points in the game.

TURN AND TALK King is considered one of the most accomplished American speakers in history. With a partner, discuss which **technique** he uses in this speech that you would like to try using yourself. How could this way of speaking help you persuade others? Be sure to use the word **technique** in your discussion.

Encourage students to use the Academic Vocabulary word in their discussions.

Assessment Practice

DIRECTIONS Use "I Have a Dream" to answer questions 1–6.

1 Why does King refer to the Emancipation Proclamation at the start of his speech?

- (A) He is at the march to celebrate the end of slavery.
- (B) He wants people to remember how shameful slavery was.
- (C) He plans to explain that African Americans are still not free.
- (D) He is honoring President Lincoln for signing the document.

2 In lines 17–18, what does King mean when he says that America "defaulted" on its promise?

- (A) It failed to support racial equality.
- (B) It prevented banks from insuring funds.
- (C) It continued to allow slavery in the South.
- (D) It broke its promise of economic support.

3 Which of the following facts supports King's argument that African Americans are not free?

- (A) Many African Americans live in poverty.
- (B) Slavery was outlawed but still continues.
- (C) Unalienable rights restrict African Americans.
- (D) The Constitution only gives citizenship rights to white people.

4 In lines 41–42, how does King's repetition of the word "satisfied" support his argument?

- (A) He appeals to his audience's sense of guilt.
- (B) He emphasizes the need to continue the fight for equality.
- (C) He provides examples of injustice each time he uses the word.
- (D) He makes the speech memorable by adding rhyme to it.

5 Why does King refer to many different parts of the country in his speech?

- (A) To emphasize that freedom should extend across the nation
- (B) To point out that segregation is limited to certain areas
- (C) To express sorrow that injustices exist in so many places
- (D) To acknowledge that people traveled great distances to attend the march

6 Which emotion or idea is expressed in lines 80–84 of "I Have a Dream"?

- (A) Unity
- (B) Persistence
- (C) Anger
- (D) Sorrow

Before Reading

Testimony Before the Senate

Based on the speech by **Michael J. Fox**

How do you **SELL AN IDEA?**

You've probably seen hundreds of ads that try to sell you something. But did you know that many organizations work hard to "sell" people and ideas, too?

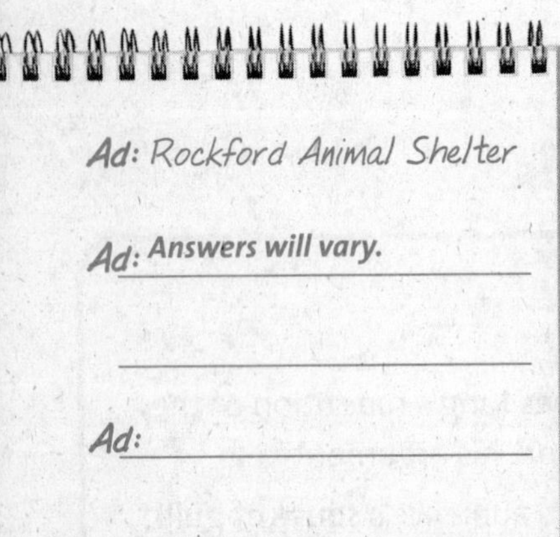

Ad: Rockford Animal Shelter
Ad: Answers will vary.
Ad:

TURN AND TALK First, think of advertisements you've seen recently. Write down two examples on the lines at left. Then, with a partner, answer these questions: What did each ad want you to buy, do, or think? How did the ad try to persuade you to take action?

Text Analysis: Persuasive Techniques

Writers and speakers use **persuasive techniques** to try to convince people. Persuasive techniques are messages and language that appeal to people's emotions, values, and desires. One type of persuasive technique is the emotional appeal—an attempt to persuade the audience by stirring up strong feelings. Here are some ways writers and speakers use emotional appeals to persuade:

- **Appeals to compassion or pity** try to make the audience feel sorry for the subject.

For just one dollar a day, you can give a stray pet a second chance.

- **Loaded language** uses words with strongly negative or positive connotations.

To force these poor animals to suffer at shelters is beyond cruel.

- **Ethical appeals** point out what is the moral or right action to take.

Rescuing these animals is the right thing for our community to do.

As you read Michael J. Fox's speech, pay attention to the persuasive techniques he uses and how they help him to convince his listeners to take action.

Reading Strategy: Summarize

A **summary** is a brief retelling of the main ideas, or most important points, of a text. When you **summarize,** use your own words to restate the main ideas. As you read this speech, you will fill in a chart like the one below.

Paragraph/Section 1
Main Idea: *Michael J. Fox actively supports Parkinson's research.*
Important Details:

↓

Paragraph/Section 2
Main Idea:
Important Details:

Vocabulary in Context

Note: Words are listed in the order in which they appear in the speech.

Meager (MEE ger) is an adjective that means *small in amount* or *poor in quality.*

*We hoped our **meager** supply of food would last for the entire camping trip.*

Neurological (nur uh LOJ ih kuhl) is an adjective that means *having to do with the nervous system.*

*Brain surgery can give patients with **neurological** problems hope.*

Eradicate (ih RAD ih kayt) is a verb that means *to do away with completely.*

*That group of scientists is working to **eradicate** the flu virus.*

Vocabulary Practice

Identify each statement below as *True* or *False.*

1. *false* A **meager** meal is filling and includes several types of food.

2. *true* A head injury might cause **neurological** problems.

3. *false* To **eradicate** a certain type of plant from your yard, you should feed and water it with care.

SET A PURPOSE FOR READING
Read this speech to find out why Michael J. Fox decided to speak before the Senate about Parkinson's disease.

Testimony Before the Senate

Based on the speech by Michael J. Fox

PARKINSON'S DISEASE RESEARCH AND TREATMENT

HEARING

BEFORE A

SUBCOMMITTEE OF THE

COMMITTEE ON APPROPRIATIONS

UNITED STATES SENATE

ONE HUNDRED SIXTH CONGRESS

FIRST SESSION

SPECIAL HEARING

Printed for the use of the Committee on Appropriations

Senator SPECTER. We have with us today Mr. Michael J. Fox, a successful actor for many years. Michael was found to have Parkinson's disease in 1991, at the age of 30.

He has become very active in supporting Parkinson's research. When someone like Michael J. Fox steps forward, it makes the problem very personal. It also focuses our attention on an issue and the need to help. So we thank you for being here, Michael J. Fox, and look forward to hearing you speak.

Mr. FOX. Mr. Chairman and members of the Subcommittee—thank you for inviting me to speak about the need for more money to pay for Parkinson's research.

Perhaps most of you are familiar with me from 20 years of work in film and television. What I wish to speak to you about today has little to do with being famous.

The first time I spoke about my 8 years of experience with Parkinson's, many people were surprised. I had hidden my struggles well.

IN OTHER WORDS Michael J. Fox, a famous actor, speaks at a special meeting being held by a committee of the U.S. Senate that recommends how taxpayers' money should be spent. After he is introduced, he talks about the time he first told others about his battle with Parkinson's disease.

The changes in my life were huge and growing. But I kept them to myself because of fear and denial. I also felt that it was important for me to quietly "soldier on"—to keep going.

When I did share my story, the response was amazing and deeply inspiring. I heard from thousands of Americans with Parkinson's. They spoke of pain, frustration, fear, and hope. Always hope. (A)

What I understood from them is that the time for quietly "soldiering on" is over. The war against Parkinson's can be won, and I want to play a role in that victory.

Being a movie star has given me the chance to raise awareness of Parkinson's

(A) SUMMARIZE

In the first box below, list the important details in lines 16–26. In the second box, use your own words to restate the main idea of the passage.

Important Details

Possible answers: Most people were surprised when they found out that Fox had Parkinson's because he had hidden his struggles. Fox was inspired by the responses he received from the thousands of Americans who also have the disease.

↓

Main Idea

Possible answer: Fox lived with Parkinson's for eight years before sharing his disease with the world. When he did, others with the disease responded with hope.

disease and the need to find more money for research]. While I can do what I love best right now, others can't. Many people with Parkinson's cannot work, provide for their families, and live out their dreams. B

The one million Americans with Parkinson's want to beat this disease. So do the millions of Americans who have family members with the disease. But it won't happen until Congress provides more money for Parkinson's research.

IN OTHER WORDS **Fox uses examples from his own life to describe the difficulties faced by people with Parkinson's. He talks about other sufferers and their problems.**

► Place brackets [ ] around the phrase that explains what Fox is able to do *because* he is a movie star.

Many people with Parkinson's find that managing their disease is a full-time job. Taking too little medicine leads to shaking and stiffness. Too much medicine leads to uncontrollable movement and slurred, indistinct speech. New treatments have helped some people like me control my symptoms. But in the end, the medicines stop working. C

For people living with Parkinson's, the way things are now isn't good enough.

As I looked at the promise of research for the future, I became hopeful. Perhaps I won't face the terrible suffering so many with Parkinson's endure. But I was surprised and frustrated to learn that the amount of money for Parkinson's research is so **meager**. Far less money is provided for Parkinson's research than for other diseases.

B PERSUASIVE TECHNIQUES

Reread lines 33–39. Which type of emotional appeal listed on page 282 is Fox making in these lines? Discuss your answer with a partner.

Students should discuss that Fox is making an appeal to compassion.

C PERSUASIVE TECHNIQUES

Sometimes speakers strengthen their emotional appeal by repeating important words. Circle the words that Fox repeats in lines 44–49. What affect does this repetition have on you?

Possible answer: It makes clear the delicate balance required to manage the disease.

VOCABULARY

The word **meager** (MEE ger) is an adjective that means *small in amount* or *poor in quality.*

Why does Fox think the money being spent on Parkinson's is *meager*? Underline the sentence that tells you.

In a country with $15 billion in funding for medical research, we can and we must do better. D

At present, Parkinson's research is given very little money. This leads to a lack of helpful treatments and slow progress in understanding the cause of the disease. Ultimately, it means little chance of a cure any time soon. I applaud the steps we are taking, but we must be clear—we aren't there yet.

IN OTHER WORDS Fox talks about the difficulties Parkinson's sufferers undergo. Taking care of their health is a full-time job, and in time their medicines quit working. The amount of money spent on research of the disease is much smaller than the amount spent on other diseases. Fox asks Congress to spend more money on Parkinson's research.

► Circle the total amount of money the government provides for medical research.

However, if more money is available, there is hope. Scientists believe that more funding will bring about new discoveries and better treatments. Many believe that Parkinson's is a **neurological** disorder that can be cured—possibly by the end of the next decade. That is, if research dollars are available.

The members of the Subcommittee have done much to increase the funding for medical research in this country. Thank you.

The Parkinson's community strongly supports your efforts to double funding for medical research. At the same time, I beg you to do more for people with Parkinson's. Increase

D PERSUASIVE TECHNIQUES

Read lines 52–59 again. Which type of appeal listed on page 282 is Fox making here?

Possible answer: Fox is making an ethical appeal to the senators' sense of fairness and justice.

VOCABULARY

The word **neurological** (nur uh LOJ ih kuhl) is an adjective that means *having to do with the nervous system.*

funding for Parkinson's research by $75 million, and make it a goal to fully fund Parkinson's research. **E**

Today you will hear from experts in many fields. I am an expert in only one—what it is like to be a young man, husband, and father with Parkinson's disease. Currently, I can still perform my job and can help out at home. But that will change. One day I will become easily exhausted. I will have increased stiffness and shaking, and I won't be able to control my body. But with your help, we can eradicate this disease. If we do, [in my 50s I'll be dancing at my children's weddings]. And mine will be just one of millions of happy stories. **F**

Thank you again for your time and attention.

Senator SPECTER. Thank you very much, Mr. Fox, for those very profound and moving words.

IN OTHER WORDS Fox is hopeful that additional government money will bring about a cure for Parkinson's disease. He ends with an appeal to Congress and a personal account of what his life would be like if he were cured.

E SUMMARIZE

Read lines 74–78 again. Then, write the main idea below.

Main Idea

Possible answer: Although the steps that are being taken for Parkinson's research are good, much more money is needed.

VOCABULARY

The word **eradicate** (ih RAD ih kayt) is a verb that means *to do away with completely.*

F PERSUASIVE TECHNIQUES

In lines 79–88, what does Fox say is possible if more money is given to fund Parkinson's research? Put brackets [ ] around the words that tell you this. Which type of emotional appeal is he using here?

appeal to compassion

Text Analysis: Persuasive Techniques

Look back at the speech and find at least one example of each type of appeal listed on page 282.

For this chart, answers will vary. See samples below.

Persuasive Technique	Example from Speech
Appeal to Compassion or Pity	*"While I can do what I love best right now, others can't."*
Loaded Language	*"terrible suffering"; "meager"*
Ethical Appeal	*"Far less money is provided for Parkinson's research than for other diseases."*

How do you **SELL AN IDEA?**

Of the persuasive techniques you noticed in Fox's speech, which did you find the most persuasive? Explain your answer.

Answers will vary.

Vocabulary Practice

Using context clues, decide which Vocabulary word (**meager, neurological,** or **eradicate**) best completes each sentence. Write the word in the blank. On the line following each sentence, write a definition of the word.

1. The doctor told my uncle that he had a *neurological* disease, a disorder of the nervous system.

   Possible answer: Neurological means having to do with the nervous system.

2. The tomato crop was *meager* this year because squirrels ate most of the tomatoes.

   Possible answer: Meager means a small, or poor, amount.

3. The goal of the company is to *eradicate* fire ants in Texas by 2025.

   Possible answer: Eradicate means to make something completely disappear.

Reading Strategy: Summarize

In a persuasive speech, the speaker's claim is the main idea of his or her argument. Look at the notes you made while reading Michael J. Fox's speech. Then, in the organizer below, list three important ideas that support his claim.

Claim: *Congress must provide more funding for Parkinson's research.*

Supporting Idea: *Far less money is provided for Parkinson's research than for other diseases.*

Supporting Idea: *In a country with $15 billion in funding for medical research, we can and we must do better.*

Supporting Idea: *Scientists believe that more funding will bring about new discoveries and better treatments.*

Write a summary of Michael J. Fox's speech. Remember, a summary includes only important ideas and key details.

Possible answer: Fox urges an increase in federal funding of Parkinson's disease research. Fox describes his expectation that a cure could be found soon—if the research were better funded.

Academic Vocabulary in Speaking

The word **evident** (EV ih duhnt) is an adjective that means *easy to see or understand.*

Her huge smile made it **evident** that she was happy about winning second place.

The word **relevant** (REL uh vuhnt) is an adjective that means *having to do with the subject being discussed.*

After searching the library, Dennis found only two books that were **relevant** to his research topic.

TURN AND TALK With a partner, discuss whether you think the U.S. government should provide more money for Parkinson's research. Consider the facts that are clear (**evident**) and important (**relevant**) based on Michael J. Fox's speech. Be sure to use the words **evident** and **relevant** in your discussion.

Encourage students to use the Academic Vocabulary words in their discussions.

Assessment Practice

DIRECTIONS Use "Testimony Before the Senate" to answer questions 1–4.

1 What does Michael J. Fox want to persuade the senators to do?
- (A) Increase funding for Parkinson's research
- (B) Forget that he is a celebrity
- (C) Feel sorry for people with neurological disorders
- (D) Double the funding for the National Institutes of Health

2 Which of these is the best summary of lines 44–49?
- (A) Shaking and stiffness are side effects of taking too little medicine.
- (B) It can take a long time for medicines to start working.
- (C) Medicating Parkinson's patients is difficult, and in time the medicines stop working.
- (D) Parkinson's symptoms can be controlled with the right medications.

3 Fox makes an appeal to pity when he —
- (A) asks the Senate to increase funding by $75 million
- (B) describes the suffering of Parkinson's patients
- (C) mentions his career as a famous movie actor
- (D) praises the senators for supporting medical research

4 When Fox mentions "dancing at my children's weddings," he is looking forward to a time when —
- (A) he learns to control his shaking and stiffness
- (B) his children no longer have to take care of him
- (C) people have more sympathy for Parkinson's patients
- (D) Parkinson's disease has been cured

Before Reading

How Private Is Your Private Life?

Based on the magazine article by **Andrea Rock**

The Privacy Debate: One Size Doesn't Fit All

Based on the newspaper editorial by **Arthur M. Ahalt**

Is PRIVACY an illusion?

Your phone number appears in a hundred databases. Your favorite Web site keeps track of every click you make. How comfortable are you with having this kind of information available to people you don't know? Do you think there are more problems or more benefits to your information being public?

Privacy at Risk?

1. *Privacy is something that* ______ *people* ______
Answers will vary. ______

2. *Privacy needs to be* ______ ______

3. ______ ______

4. ______ ______

5. ______ ______

TURN AND TALK Do you think your privacy is at risk in today's society? Write notes in the notepad at the left to use in a debate about personal privacy in today's society. Then debate your ideas with a partner who has chosen the opposite answer to the question.

Text Analysis: Fact and Opinion

Most nonfiction writers use a mix of facts and opinions to support a **claim,** or position on a topic. To evaluate a work of nonfiction, you need to know the difference between a fact and an opinion.

- A **fact** is a statement that can be proved with evidence.
- An **opinion** is a statement that cannot be proved because it expresses a belief, feeling, or thought.

Not all opinions, however, are equal. Opinions that come from respected experts are often very reliable. But some opinions are just personal preferences. As you read these two selections, you will evaluate whether statements are facts or opinions as shown below.

Example	Can It Be Proved?	Fact or Opinion?
"Technology has made it easier for others to find out personal information about us."	*Yes; you could compare what information was easy to get 30 years ago with now.*	*Fact*

Reading Skill: Recognize Bias

Bias (BY uhs) is a strong preference either for something or against something. For example, some people are biased against vegetables or cats. Some writers are unfairly biased in favor of certain ideas or arguments. To recognize biased arguments, look for

- arguments in which the writer presents **evidence to support only one side**
- the presence of **loaded language**—words that create very positive or negative impressions
- **opinions stated as if they were facts** with no supporting evidence
- **vague language** and **oversimplified descriptions**

As you read these selections, you will identify whether the authors show bias in their arguments.

Vocabulary in Context

Note: Words are listed in the order in which they appear in the selections.

Pervasive (puhr VAY sihv) is an adjective that means *spreading everywhere.*
The stealing of personal data is a **pervasive** problem; it happens every day to thousands of people.

Surveillance (suhr VAY luhns) is an adjective that means *watching closely from a distance.*
Surveillance cameras are all around us, watching and recording every move we make.

Anonymity (an uh NIM ih tee) is a noun that means *the condition of being unknown.*
It is difficult to achieve **anonymity** in a small community.

Vocabulary Practice

Review the words and sample sentences above. Then, with a partner, discuss why privacy is important. Try to use each Vocabulary word in your discussion of privacy in the electronic age.

Encourage students to use the Vocabulary words in their discussions.

SET A PURPOSE FOR READING
Read "How Private Is Your Private Life?" to find out what kind of threats there are to your privacy.

How Private Is Your Private Life?

ANDREA ROCK

Based on the magazine article by
ANDREA ROCK

BACKGROUND Many Americans are concerned that the benefits of technology have meant a loss of personal privacy. Some Americans want Congress to pass stronger privacy laws.

When you use a computer online or eat out, you reveal personal information to strangers. Here's what you need to know about who's watching you—and how to protect yourself.

Technology has made it easier for others to find out personal information about us. In 1999, loss of privacy was one of Americans' top concerns.

Lawmakers and people who make rules for businesses to follow have suggested ways to keep our private lives safe. However, many business owners disagree with these suggestions. The people who run these businesses want to collect information about our personal lifestyles. They can make money by selling this personal information to others.

I set out to find out how **pervasive** the system really is—how often our private information is used. I was surprised by what I learned:

9:00 A.M.

I use a discount card at the grocery store. Later, I discover that this card keeps track of what I've bought, how much money I spent, and how often I shop at this store. "When people use these cards, they are selling their privacy," says Ari Schwartz, an expert on the matter. Ⓐ

9:25 A.M.

I stop to mail a medical insurance form. The data on the form, information in my medical records, is not protected. By signing the form, I allow doctors to give information about me to others. In many states, this is information I wouldn't be allowed to see myself.

IN OTHER WORDS Some people want personal information to be guarded. Others want to gather this information to help their businesses make money. The writer decides to see how much of her personal information is available to others. She discovers that a discount card and a medical insurance form both make her personal information available to people she doesn't know.

10:00 A.M.

I call the car dealer about the car I just bought there. If I own a car or apply for a driver's license in New York, my personal information and the details about my car can be sold to others. However, the Driver's Privacy Protection Act of 1994 allows me to block the release of information taken from driver's licenses and documents that show ownership.

VOCABULARY

The word **pervasive** (puhr VAY siv) is an adjective that means *spreading everywhere.*

Ⓐ FACT AND OPINION

Underline the quotation in lines 18–20. Is this statement a fact that can be proved or just one person's opinion? Explain.

Possible answer: This statement is an opinion, on a topic that people disagree about.

10:20 A.M.

On my way into New York City, I pay a road toll with my E-Z Pass. This is a tag that subtracts the money for the toll, a fee charged for driving on certain roads, from my account. [Using the pass allows a record of my travels to be kept. This kind of information can help police track down criminals.] [But it can also be used to collect personal information about people who have done nothing wrong.]

IN OTHER WORDS In some states, businesses can buy information about the cars people own and the information on their driver's licenses.

▶ What are two ways that information taken from toll road tags can be used? Put brackets [ ] around the sentences that tell you.

11:30 A.M.

As I cross the corner of 45th Street and Fifth Avenue, I'm being filmed by a hidden video camera. It sends the images to an Internet site. This camera is used for advertising and entertainment. But **surveillance** cameras also are being used by police and businesses to fight crime.

According to John Pike, who analyzes security policy, soon most public places will have surveillance cameras connected to a computer. The computer will compare the faces on the camera with faces of people wanted by the police. B

NOON

My friend Diane joins me at a restaurant. Tiny cameras in the ceiling allow the chefs in the kitchen to watch diners eating. The chefs can then send out food at just the right time. The food is delicious, but it's troubling knowing that every bite I take is being watched. C

VOCABULARY

The word **surveillance** (suhr VAY luhns) is an adjective that means *watching closely from a distance.* Circle the phrase in this paragraph that is a synonym for "surveillance cameras."

B FACT AND OPINION

Who is John Pike? Why might we trust what he says?

John Pike is a security specialist.

He is a professional, so his words

carry more weight.

C RECOGNIZE BIAS

Circle the word *troubling* and the clause *every bite I take is being watched.* Are these examples of loaded language? Explain.

Possible answer: Both are examples of loaded language because they have strong negative associations. They are not neutral and are meant to sway readers through emotion.

Diane tells me that a friend of hers received a ticket by mail for driving through an intersection after the traffic light had turned red. A police surveillance camera photographed the license plate of her friend's rental car. Then, the police used the information to find her friend's name and address. (D)

IN OTHER WORDS Surveillance cameras record people on streets and in businesses. This information is sometimes sent to the Internet and can be available to others. Also, surveillance cameras are used to watch people eat and to catch people breaking traffic laws.

1:30 P.M.

I use Diane's cell phone to leave a message for a friend. I'm aware that what I say could be heard by someone with a radio receiver. Pike says that if you are discussing something that you wouldn't want others to know, you shouldn't talk about it on a cell phone. PAUSE & REFLECT

4:00 P.M.

After I check my e-mail at home, my son uses the Internet to research his fifth-grade science project. A new law says that Web sites cannot collect personal information from children under thirteen unless their parents agree to it.

6:11 P.M.

Back on the computer, I go to my online bank to check my account. When I first signed up for this service, I had to use my Social Security number. I avoid giving out that number when possible, but I had no choice. The bank protects my account information from others. But the bank does share information about me with its inside affiliates,[1]

1. **affiliates** (uh FIL ee its): people or groups closely connected to another group.

(D) RECOGNIZE BIAS

Notice the way the writer relates the events described in lines 53–57. Is her language emotional and opinionated, or is it clear and factual? On the lines below, explain why this paragraph does or does not show bias.

Possible answers: The author's tone is mostly neutral. She does not use loaded language. But some students might feel that the author's suggestion that her example is a privacy violation is a matter of opinion more than fact, which may represent a bias.

PAUSE & REFLECT

Does knowing this information change the way you feel about using cell phones? Discuss your response with a partner.

Answers will vary. Some students may be surprised that cell phone calls might not be private. Other students may already know that there are security concerns with cell phones but may still choose to use them.

such as its partners who manage the money people invest in stocks.

IN OTHER WORDS Personal information can accidentally be made public when people talk on cell phones, and many Web sites record personal information about adults.

► When might a bank give out personal information to a partner company? Circle the statement that tells you this.

9:35 P.M.

I go to *Amazon.com* to get information about a book. A message says that the Web site is trying to place a "cookie," a tag that identifies me on the Internet. Normally, computer users don't receive this alert, but I've learned how to make my computer show it. It warns me every time a cookie is about to be placed. I can choose to accept the cookie or not.

Cookies can give you more than you wanted. A Web site may share your information with an ad network that places ads on Web sites. An online profile with information about you is created. This profile keeps track of the sites you visit and can be sold to anyone without your knowing or agreeing. (E)

E FACT AND OPINION

Reread lines 71–75. Which information in this paragraph can be proved? Underline the facts that the writer shares about "cookies."

10:45 P.M.

Finally, I return to my computer home page to read my horoscope. "Your home is your castle," it says, "and you are the supreme ruler within its walls." After today, I'm not so sure.

IN OTHER WORDS Unless blocked, Web sites send "cookies" to computers and record information about the users. This information is shared without your knowing it or agreeing to allow it to be shared.

► Reread lines 71–78. With a partner, discuss how the author feels about her information being shared.

Students should discuss that the author feels uncomfortable about her information being shared.

SET A PURPOSE FOR READING
Read "The Privacy Debate" for a different perspective on the issue of privacy.

The Privacy Debate

One Size Doesn't Fit All

Based on the newspaper editorial by
ARTHUR M. AHALT

BACKGROUND The U.S. Constitution does not actually say Americans have a right to privacy. Although the Supreme Court has ruled on many privacy issues, privacy remains difficult to define and protect. This article explores the current debate over privacy issues.

The current debate over privacy rarely shows both sides of the issue. Instead, we are often told that there should be no debate over the need for privacy.

This article will show the benefit of having access to public records.

I am a retired judge who spent 17 years in the courtroom. I've seen the benefits of open access to public records.

(F) RECOGNIZE BIAS

Reread lines 1–9. Circle the sentence that describes the aim of this article. How might the writer's background as a judge affect his views on the privacy debate?

Possible answer: As the judge, the writer should know more about the practical benefits of having information available to law enforcement.

VOCABULARY

The word **anonymity** (an uh NIM ih tee) is a noun that means the condition of being unknown.

(G) FACT AND OPINION

Reread lines 11–14. Underline a fact and circle an opinion in this paragraph.

Unfortunately, too many Americans want to reduce this access for the sake of privacy. (F)

Why is privacy such an issue today?

Maybe it comes from the disconnected nature of today's society and the global economy. These things make us wish for more **anonymity**. There are now 280 million Americans. We no longer do business with people who know our names. (G)

Maybe technology is to blame. The use of credit cards and electronic information makes people's personal information available to others.

IN OTHER WORDS The writer was a judge for many years. He argues that some private information needs to be available to the public. He says that privacy may be such a concern to people because people feel cut off from others. He also thinks that people don't like the idea of technology that stores private information.

Maybe it's because some politicians or people in the media scare people about privacy.

Privacy is also a nonpartisan[2] concern. Both Republicans and Democrats often work on the same privacy issues. Media stories about privacy issues are often written to attract an audience. Research groups and people who collect private information report stories about privacy to the press, increasing people's fears.

Confusion, fear, and concern replace a balanced view of the privacy issue. People see only one side of it.

Politicians and the media say that polls, or surveys, show that 93 percent of people are concerned about privacy.

---

2. **nonpartisan** (non PAHR tih zuhn): not supported by just one political party.

However, those polls don't ask questions such as "Do you want your bank loan approved in three days or three months?" Most people expect to get loans quickly. **H**

Instant loans and credit happen because information is available right away. It's the reason we can buy and sell property in just weeks, not months or years.

PAUSE & REFLECT

IN OTHER WORDS The writer argues that politicians and media sources often frighten people about privacy issues. He says that this fear gives people unreasonable worries about their private information. He points out that people expect to be able to buy things through loans and credit quickly, which can only happen if information is easy to get.

Openness also provides other benefits. It makes it possible to find people and to get child support payments from parents trying to avoiding paying them. Access to private information helps keep dangerous people from getting certain kinds of jobs. It also helps connect people with money they have inherited and prevents identity theft. **I**

There are real problems that affect real people in privacy matters. But often, all people hear is the bad side of the news.

Each day, billions of business deals occur in America. Do some go awry? Of course, but it is a small percentage. Unfortunately, no one wants to read a headline that says, "Today 299,999,033 Americans Did Not Suffer Privacy-Related Problems." **J**

H FACT AND OPINION

Underline a fact that can be proved in lines 28–32. Circle the writer's response to that fact. Is his response a fact or an opinion? Explain.

Possible answer: The writer's response is a fact. It could be proved by seeing the questions used in the polls and by surveying people about what they expect.

PAUSE & REFLECT

What are the benefits of instant loans and credit? Is there a bad side to them as well? Discuss this with a partner.

Answers will vary.

I FACT AND OPINION

Could the details in this paragraph be proved? Identify each as a fact or an opinion.

Possible answer: All the examples the writer gives on the benefits of openness could be proved with evidence. They are facts.

J LANGUAGE COACH

Some English spellings can be confusing. *No one* (line 46), meaning "not one person," is often misspelled *noone* or *no-one*. And the word *nobody,* which also means "not one person," is sometimes misspelled *no body*. Remember: You can always use a dictionary to confirm the correct spelling of a word.

K RECOGNIZE BIAS

Compare the ideas in this paragraph to "How Private is Your Private Life?" Do you think Ahalt's claim is correct, or does it show his bias?

Possible answer: Ahalt thinks that sharing some private information is beneficial for society. The other article, however, focuses mainly on the problems of identity theft and on the hazards of near-constant surveillance. Because of Ahalt's background and the reasons he cites, I think his claim is probably correct, but he offers very little evidence.

There is also a need to divide the issue of privacy into several different parts. Each part should be thought about differently.

Tracking Internet surfing and purchases is different from identity theft. Using information to make phone calls trying to sell things is different from allowing access to public records.

Privacy supporters would have us believe that "one size fits all" when it comes to addressing matters of privacy. I am concerned about the need for access to public records and their contents. K

When you hear people talk about the need to keep information hidden, remember this: "for every problem, there is a simple solution, which is usually wrong."

IN OTHER WORDS The writer points out that access to private information is necessary and usually good. He also says that the many parts of the issue of privacy require different approaches.

► Reread the last sentence of the essay. With a partner, put the idea the writer expresses in that sentence into your own words.

Possible answer: There are no simple solutions when debating issues such as privacy.

Text Analysis: Fact and Opinion

Complete the chart below with two facts and two opinions from each article that provide support for the authors' positions. One has already been filled in for you.

For this chart, answers will vary. See samples below.

Example	Can It Be Proved?	Fact or Opinion?
"How Private Is Your Private Life?"		
"Technology has made it easier for others to find out personal information about us."	Yes; you could compare what information was easy to get 30 years ago with now.	Fact
"A new law says that Web sites cannot collect personal information from children under thirteen unless their parents agree to it."	*Yes; you could look this up to see whether there is such a law.*	*Fact*
"'When people use these cards, they are selling their privacy,' says Ari Schwartz, an expert on the matter."	*No; this is too general a statement to be proved.*	*Opinion*
"But it can also be used to collect personal information about people who have done nothing wrong."	*Yes; you could research whether this was legal in your state.*	*Fact*
"The Privacy Debate"		
"Instant loans and credit happen because information is available right away."	*Yes; this statement could be proved.*	*Fact*
"[Openness] makes it possible to find people and to get child support payments from parents trying to avoid paying them."	*Yes; this statement could be proved with some research.*	*Fact*
"Media stories about privacy issues are often written to attract an audience."	*No; the writer provides no evidence to support this and it would be difficult to prove*	*Opinion*
"Most people expect to get loans quickly."	*Yes; you could take a survey to determine what most people expect.*	*Fact*

Which article do you think provides better support for its main position or claim? Explain your choice.

Answers will vary.

After Reading

Reading Skill: Recognize Bias

Complete the chart below with examples of bias from both articles. Identify each example as loaded language, unbalanced evidence for an argument, vague and oversimplified language, or an opinion stated as a fact.

For this chart, answers will vary. See samples below.

Example from Article	Explanation of Bias
"Your home is your castle" (Rock)	loaded language
"it's troubling knowing that every bite I take is being watched." (Rock)	*loaded language*
"Confusion, fear, and concern replace a balanced view of the privacy issue." (Ahalt)	*opinion stated as fact*
"Unfortunately, no one wants to read a headline that says, 'Today 299,999,033 Americans Did Not Suffer Privacy-Related Problems.'" (Ahalt)	*opinion stated as fact*

Is PRIVACY an illusion?

What steps can you take to protect your privacy?

Answers will vary.

Vocabulary Practice

Working with a partner, discuss and answer each of the following questions.

Encourage students to use the Vocabulary words in their answers.

1. Why do banks need **surveillance** cameras?
2. Why might a famous person wish for **anonymity**?
3. What is something that is **pervasive** in your home?

Academic Vocabulary in Writing

The word **coherent** (koh HIR uhnt) means *connected or logical, making sense.*

We were all persuaded by Eva's **coherent** presentation.

The word **differentiate** (dif uh REN shee ayt) means *to be aware of or point out a difference between two or more things.*

To be a successful chemist, you must be able to **differentiate** among many chemicals to use the correct one.

WRITE IT Does either author make a **coherent** argument about what people should do to protect themselves? Do the authors give guidance on how to **differentiate** between real threats and non-threats to our security? Explain, using both boldfaced words.

Possible answer: Neither article provides coherent solutions for avoiding identity theft. Also, neither article provides guidance on how to differentiate between risky and non-risky behavior.

Assessment Practice

DIRECTIONS: Use "How Private Is Your Private Life?" and "The Privacy Debate" to answer questions 1–4.

1 In "How Private Is Your Private Life?" the author says that supermarket discount cards —

(A) help customers share common interests
(B) let businesses track shopping choices
(C) gather information on people's medical history
(D) give away people's social security numbers

2 Writers use loaded language in order to persuade readers with —

(A) phrases using faulty reasoning
(B) arguments that give stronger evidence for one side than the other
(C) opinions stated as if they were facts
(D) words that create very positive or negative impressions

3 Which fact from the selections supports the idea that privacy is threatened?

(A) *The current debate over privacy rarely shows both sides of the issue.*
(B) *This profile keeps track of the sites you visit and can be sold to anyone without your knowing or agreeing.*
(C) *Access to private information helps keep dangerous people from getting certain kinds of jobs.*
(D) *We no longer do business with people who know our names.*

4 Ahalt's article is persuasive because —

(A) he presents only one side of the issue
(B) his argument focuses only on opinions, not on facts
(C) as a former judge, he has direct experience with the topic
(D) he emphasizes the use of loaded language

UNIT 7

Special Effects

THE LANGUAGE OF POETRY

Be sure to read the Text Analysis Workshop on pages 740–747 in *Holt McDougal Literature.*

Academic Vocabulary for Unit 7

You will see these Academic Vocabulary words as you work through this book. You will also be asked to use them as you write and talk about the selections in this unit.

Conventional (kuhn VEN shuh nuhl) is an adjective that means *in keeping with traditional ideas or ways of doing things.*
The pirate theme at last year's prom was not at all **conventional**.

Do you dress in a **conventional** way? Why or why not? *Answers will vary.*

Effect (ih FEKT) is a noun that means *the result of an event or of an action taken by someone.* It can also mean *the overall impression created by an artistic work.*
The soggy carpet was just one **effect** of the flood at school.

What is one **effect** of studying for an important test? *Answers will vary.*

Evoke (ih VOHK) is a verb that means *to bring out or produce.*
Maria's poems **evoke** a sense of excitement in her classmates.

What souvenirs or photos **evoke** memories of your childhood?
Answers will vary.

Before Reading

Spring is like a perhaps hand

Poem by E. E. Cummings

Elegy for the Giant Tortoises

Poem by Margaret Atwood

Today

Poem by Billy Collins

New Tool

Answers will vary.

What it will do: ________

How it will work: ________

Can you think OUT OF THE BOX?

Many of the things you enjoy every day were once new and original ideas. Inventions, stories, games—everything was a new idea once, and creative new ideas can make life both easier and more interesting. New ideas are important in poetry, too. A good poet always looks at things in a new and creative way.

TURN AND TALK With a partner, plan a design for a new tool. You might want to create a tool to help with a chore you don't like, such as cleaning your room or mowing the yard. Record ideas from your discussion on the lines at left.

Text Analysis: Diction

Poets are known for their careful use of language. When you read poetry, pay special attention to the poet's **diction**, or choice of words, and the effects that the diction creates. For example, Billy Collins chooses his words carefully in these lines from "Today":

Diction	Effects
"it made you want to throw open all the windows in the house"	creates a sense of joy, freedom, and movement

This use of words has more of an impact on the reader than if Collins had simply said he felt like opening a window. Like any good poet, Collins has chosen his words carefully to create a specific effect. As you read the poems in this lesson, you will be asked to find effective or unusual examples of diction.

Reading Skill: Paraphrase

Sometimes poems can be difficult to understand because of their unusual structure. When you **paraphrase** a poem, you put the poet's words into your own words. To paraphrase, you should:

- find the main ideas and important details
- think of simpler or more familiar ways of saying what the writer has written
- rewrite sentences in standard subject-verb order

As you read each of the poems that follow, you will be asked to paraphrase difficult passages in a chart like the one below.

"Elegy for the Giant Tortoises"		
Original Wording		*Paraphrase*
"on the road where I stand they will materialize, / plodding past me in a straggling line / awkward without water"	⟷	*They [the tortoises] will appear on the road where I stand, walking slowly by in a scattered line, looking clumsy because they are not in the water.*

Monitor Your Comprehension

SET A PURPOSE FOR READING

Read "Spring is like a perhaps hand" to discover the speaker's ideas about the change in seasons.

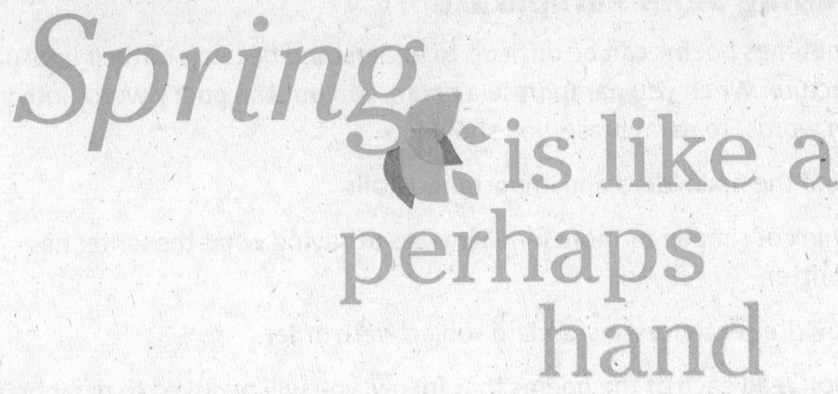

Spring is like a perhaps hand

Poem by

E. E. CUMMINGS

BACKGROUND The poet E. E. Cummings is known for using unusual style elements in his poetry. In this poem, he uses parentheses and capitalization to emphasize important words. He also leaves out some punctuation. This poem describes the surprises in nature that come during springtime.

Ⓐ PARAPHRASE

Reread lines 1–9. Underline words and phrases that describe how spring is like a hand arranging a window. Then restate these lines in your own words on the lines below.

Possible answer: Like a hand, Spring comes from nowhere to carefully arrange and change things while people watch.

Spring is like a perhaps hand
(which comes carefully
out of Nowhere) arranging
a window, into which people look (while
people stare
arranging and changing placing
carefully there a strange
thing and a known thing here) and

changing everything carefully Ⓐ

spring is like a perhaps
Hand in a window
(carefully to
and fro moving New and
Old things, while
people stare carefully
moving a perhaps
fraction of flower here placing
an inch of air there) and

without breaking anything. B

IN OTHER WORDS The speaker says that when spring arrives, it is like watching someone carefully rearranging a window display.

► With a partner, discuss the types of changes Cummings hints at in his poem.

Students should discuss that Cummings hints at the very subtle changes of spring, such as a slight change in temperature or the slow growth of a flower, and how, added together, those changes transform our environment.

Monitor Your Comprehension

B **DICTION**

Notice Cummings's choice of words, or **diction**, in lines 16–19. Circle the words used as measurements. What do these words suggest about the speaker's idea of spring?

Possible answer: The speaker thinks that spring's changes come quite slowly yet in measurable increments. These small changes make everything look new and different.

SET A PURPOSE FOR READING
Read this poem to discover how the speaker feels about giant tortoises becoming extinct.

Elegy for the GIANT TORTOISES

Poem by
MARGARET ATWOOD

BACKGROUND Some animals, such as passenger pigeons and dodo birds, are extinct; they no longer exist. Many other animals, such as whooping cranes and giant tortoises—large turtles—are endangered and nearing extinction. This elegy, or poem in which the speaker thinks about death, honors the giant tortoises.

Let others pray for the passenger pigeon
the dodo, the whooping crane, the eskimo:
everyone must specialize

I will confine myself to a meditation[1]
upon the giant tortoises
withering finally on a remote island. C

I concentrate in subway stations,
in parks, I can't quite see them,
they move to the peripheries[2] of my eyes

C DICTION
Reread line 6. *Withering* means " becoming dry and lifeless." Why does Atwood use this word instead of *dying*? What effect does this word have on the reader?

Possible answer: To the reader, the word withering *implies that the turtles' death is long and drawn out.*

IN OTHER WORDS The speaker thinks about the giant tortoises as they slowly die out. She tries to picture them, but because she is in the city, she can barely glimpse them in her mind.

1. **meditation:** thoughtful consideration.
2. **peripheries** (puh RIF uh reez): outside edges

but on the last day they will be there;
already the event
like a wave travelling shapes vision:

on the road where I stand they will materialize,
plodding past me in a straggling line
awkward without water

their small heads pondering
from side to side, their useless armour
sadder than tanks and history,

in their closed gaze ocean and sunlight paralysed,
lumbering up the steps, under the archways
toward the square glass altars

where the brittle gods are kept,
the relics[3] of what we have destroyed,
our holy and obsolete[4] symbols. (D)

IN OTHER WORDS The speaker imagines seeing the tortoises traveling toward extinction. They are encased in museums instead of living in nature.

► Underline the words Atwood uses to describe how the tortoises look and move.

---

3. **relics** (REL iks): things left from the past, kept as a memorial.
4. **obsolete:** out of date, no longer in use.

Monitor Your Comprehension

(D) PARAPHRASE

Use the chart to **paraphrase** lines 13–24. In the first box, list synonyms for each word from the poem. Then use the synonyms to help you restate the passage in your own words.

Words From the Poem:

materialize (line 13):

appear

pondering (line 16):

thinking carefully

lumbering (line 20):

moving slowly

↓

Paraphrase:

Possible answer: The turtles appear and slowly walk past. They think about their movement. Their shells cannot protect them. The turtles climb the steps of the museum to see the remains of their ancestors who were destroyed by humans.

SET A PURPOSE FOR READING
Read "Today" to find out how the speaker describes a spring day.

Today

Poem by
BILLY COLLINS

BACKGROUND In this poem, the speaker describes the wonder of a perfect spring day. The poet uses a few violent words, like *throw* and *rip,* to create images that jolt readers into thinking about the excitement of spring.

If ever there were a spring day so perfect,
so uplifted by a warm intermittent[5] breeze

that it made you want to throw
open all the windows in the house

and unlatch the door to the canary's cage,
indeed, rip the little door from its jamb,

a day when the cool brick paths
and the garden bursting with peonies (E)

seemed so etched in sunlight
that you felt like taking

(E) DICTION
Reread lines 3–8. Underline phrases that suggest quick actions. What is the effect of these words on the poem's meaning?

Possible answer: The words create a sense of urgency and a need to physically act out and change one's environment.

5. **intermittent** (in tuhr MIT uhnt): stopping and starting again.

a hammer to the glass paperweight
on the living room end table,

releasing the inhabitants
from their snow-covered cottage

so they could walk out,
holding hands and squinting (F)

into this larger dome of blue and white,
well, today is just that kind of day. PAUSE & REFLECT

IN OTHER WORDS The speaker asks if you have ever experienced a spring day that made you want to open all the windows or set a captive bird free. The speaker then asks if spring makes you want to breathe life and freedom into something lifeless, like a snow globe paperweight.

► With a partner, discuss Collins's description of the paperweight. What does it contain? Why would someone want to smash it?

Students should discuss that the paperweight is like a prison, confining the people within it and keeping them from experiencing life. Someone might want to smash it to release the people within and allow them to be out in the world.

Monitor Your Comprehension

(F) DICTION

Reread lines 15–16. Circle the words the speaker uses to describe those who live in the glass paperweight. What sense or feeling is created by this language?

Possible answer: The reader senses that these people are innocent, inexperienced, and sheltered in the paperweight. As they leave it behind, they are experiencing a whole new world.

PAUSE & REFLECT

With a partner, discuss why this poem is more effective than if Collins had simply said "Today is a beautiful spring day."

Students should discuss how the images of people acting in unconventional ways on a beautiful spring day make the poem effective.

Text Analysis: Diction

The poets in this lesson have chosen their words carefully to communicate certain ideas. Use this chart to list unusual or effective examples of diction from each poem. Then describe the effect each choice of words has on you.

For this chart, answers will vary. See samples below.

"Spring is like a perhaps hand"
Words and Phrases: *"inch of air" (line 18)*
Effects: *The line helps the reader understand that spring's changes may be small but are transforming.*
"Elegy for the Giant Tortoises"
Words and Phrases: *"their useless armour sadder than tanks and history" (lines 17–18)*
Effects: *The line helps the reader understand that the turtles' shells are outdated, providing them with little protection in today's world.*
"Today"
Words and Phrases: *"taking a hammer to the glass paperweight" (lines 10–11)*
Effects: *The line helps the reader understand the forceful and sudden changes about to take place.*

Reading Skill: Paraphrase

Review some of the paraphrases you made as you read each poem. Then read aloud one of your paraphrases and the original passage. Which one has the stronger impact? Explain.

Answers will vary but should show an understanding of the passage's meaning.

Can you think OUT OF THE BOX?

Why are new ideas and new ways of thinking so important?

Possible answer: Innovative thinking breeds creativity and problem solving.

Academic Vocabulary in Speaking

The word **conventional** (kuhn VEN shuhn uhl) is an adjective that means *in keeping with traditional ideas or ways of doing things.*

The **conventional** Thanksgiving dinner includes turkey and dressing.

The word **effect** (uh FEKT) is a noun that means *the result of an event or of an action taken by someone.* It can also mean *the overall impression created by an artistic work.*

One **effect** that good writing produces is to make the reader think.

The word **evoke** (ih VOHK) is a verb that means *to bring out or produce.*

What feelings does looking at photos of your childhood **evoke** in you?

TURN AND TALK With a partner, discuss how poetry is able to express everyday ideas in a fresh and interesting way. Use at least two Academic Vocabulary words in your discussion.
Encourage students to use the Academic Vocabulary words in their discussions.

Assessment Practice

DIRECTIONS Use the three poems you have just read to answer questions 1–4.

1 What words might the speaker in "Spring is like a perhaps hand" use to describe spring?

(A) Fun and exciting
(B) Delicate and surprising
(C) Weak and hesitant
(D) Intense and bold

2 "Their useless armour" in line 17 of "Elegy for the Giant Tortoises" describes defenseless —

(A) army tanks
(B) tortoise shells
(C) immune systems
(D) animal protection laws

3 What does "this larger dome" refer to in line 17 of "Today"?

(A) The roof of the canary cage
(B) The sky above the real world
(C) The top of the glass paperweight
(D) The blooming flowers in the garden

4 The speaker of "Elegy for the Giant Tortoises" would prefer that —

(A) people see the tortoises in museums
(B) actions be taken to save the tortoises
(C) the tortoises be honored in art and literature
(D) other extinct or threatened creatures also be honored

UNIT 8

A Way with Words

AUTHOR'S STYLE AND VOICE

Be sure to read the Text Analysis Workshop on pages 820–825 in *Holt McDougal Literature*.

Academic Vocabulary for Unit 8

You will see these Academic Vocabulary words as you work through this book. You will also be asked to use them as you write and talk about the selections in this unit.

Appreciate (uh PREE shee ayt) is a verb that means *to recognize the value of something.*
Madison should **appreciate** the money I loaned her for lunch.

What is something about your friends that you appreciate? *Answers will vary.* ______

______

Attribute (AT ruh byoot) is a noun that means *a quality or feature of someone or something.*
From a sense of humor to a willingness to help others, Michelle has every **attribute** we value in our neighbors.

What is your best attribute? *Answers will vary.* ______

______

Indicate (IN dih kayt) is a verb that means *to point out or show.*
The principal did not **indicate** which parking lot would be paved.

What is one way to indicate that you are in a hurry? *Answers will vary.* ______

______

Unique (yoo NEEK) is an adjective that describes something that is *the only one of its kind and is not like any other.*
The red and purple sweater Carol made was **unique**.

What is a unique idea you've had recently? *Answers will vary.* ______

______

Vary (VAIR ee) is a verb that means *to change or become different in some way.*
The cheerleaders had to **vary** their routine for each football game.

How do you vary your clothes each day? *Answers will vary.* ______

______

Before Reading

Where Have You Gone, Charming Billy?

Based on the short story by Tim O'Brien

Tim O'Brien: The Naked Soldier

Based on the interview from *Verbicide magazine*

Is FEAR our worst enemy?

Your heart pounds. Your hands shake. You're afraid, and the way you react is as unique as you are. In "Where Have You Gone, Charming Billy?" a young soldier struggles against his growing fear during his first night in Vietnam.

TURN AND TALK On the lines at left, list several things or situations that cause people to be afraid. Then share your list with a small group of classmates. Discuss this question: Is fear always a problem, or are there times when it is smart to be afraid?

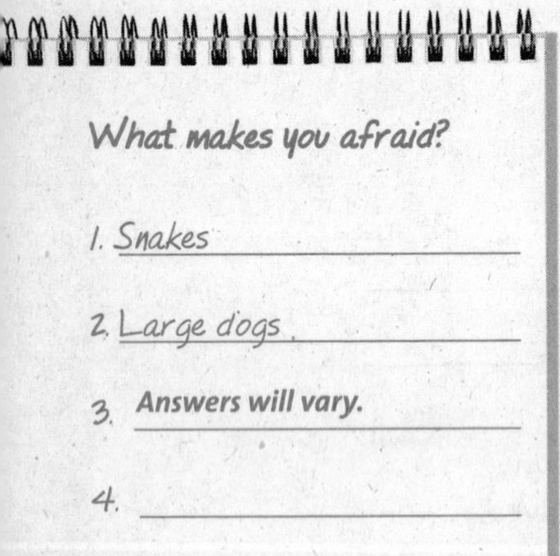

Text Analysis: Realism

A writer's **style** is the unique way he or she communicates ideas. In "Where Have You Gone, Charming Billy?" Tim O'Brien uses the style of **realism** to show the horrors of combat as seen through the eyes of a young soldier. The chart below describes two elements of O'Brien's realistic style.

Element of O'Brien's Style	Example
Dialogue that sounds natural, like actual speech	*"Hey!" a shadow whispered, "We're moving. . . . Get up."* *"Okay," said PFC Berlin.*
Vivid, realistic descriptions of what the soldiers see or do	*Next to the watery field, they squatted down in the shadows in the quiet stealth of warfare.*

As you read, think about the way the characters talk to each other, and consider O'Brien's word choice and sentence structure. Note passages that seem very realistic to you.

Reading Skill: Analyze Sequence

The **sequence** of a story is the order in which events take place. Sometimes a writer interrupts the normal flow of time with a **flashback,** or a description of events that happened before the start of the story's action. A flashback provides more background information about the story and helps the reader understand what's going on. To identify flashbacks, look for sudden changes in scene. As you read this story, you will keep track of its sequence of events by filling in a sequence chain like the one below.

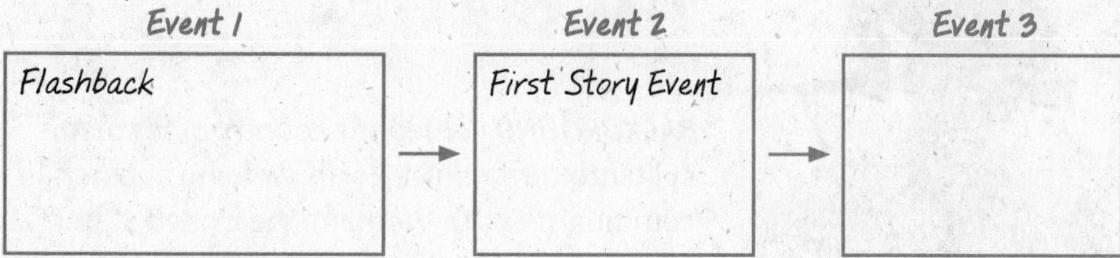

Vocabulary in Context

Note: Words are listed in the order in which they appear in the story.

Stealth (stelth) is a noun that means *cautious or secret action or movement.*
Because of the soldiers' **stealth,** the enemy didn't hear them.

Fecund (FEE kuhnd) is an adjective that means *producing much growth.*
Dense plants made walking through the **fecund** field difficult.

Diffuse (dih FYOOS) is an adjective that means *unfocused.*
After the terrible incident, the soldier's mind was fuzzy and confused and his thoughts **diffuse.**

Inertia (ih NER shuh) is a noun that means *a feeling of not wanting to change what one is doing.*
The soldiers fought **inertia,** trying to get up and march.

Vocabulary Practice

Review the meanings of the Vocabulary words. How might each word relate to a story about a soldier's experience in combat? Write a short paragraph that describes what a soldier might do, see, think, or feel. Be sure to use all of the Vocabulary words in your paragraph.

Encourage students to use the Vocabulary words in their paragraphs.

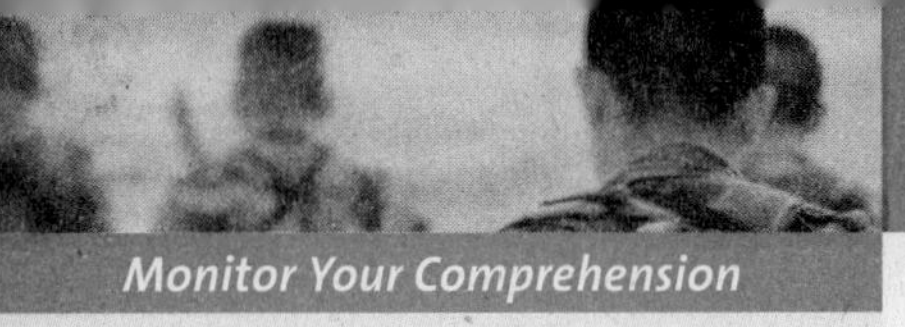

SET A PURPOSE FOR READING

Read "Where Have You Gone, Charming Billy?" to find out why the main character, Paul Berlin, is so afraid.

Where Have You Gone, Charming Billy?

Based on the short story by

TIM O'BRIEN

BACKGROUND When the country of Vietnam split into communist North Vietnam and non-communist South Vietnam, the United States supported South Vietnam. In 1965, President Lyndon Johnson sent the first U.S. troops to the region. By 1969, 540,000 American troops were in Vietnam. Ground troops, like the men in this story, fought communist soldiers who were in South Vietnam. The story's author spent two years as a soldier in Vietnam.

VOCABULARY

The word **stealth** (stelth) is a noun that means *cautious or secret action or movement.*

Circle some of the words in the first paragraph that reveal the soldiers' **stealth**.

A REALISM

Reread lines 10–11. Is this dialogue realistic? Does it sound like something two soldiers would say to each other? Explain.

Possible answer: The dialogue sounds realistic because it is said quietly to not reveal the soldiers' position, it is brief and to the point, and it is an order from a superior officer for the PFC to follow.

VOCABULARY

The word **fecund** (FEE kuhnd) is an adjective that means *producing much growth.*

The twenty-six silent soldiers moved slowly in the dark. One by one they stopped at the rice paddy. Next to the watery field, they squatted down in the shadows in the quiet **stealth** of warfare. At the rear, Private First Class Paul Berlin was pretending he was not in the war, pretending he had not watched Billy Boy Watkins die of a heart attack that afternoon.

In the morning, when they reached the sea, PFC Berlin would forget how frightened he had been on his first day at the war. The second day would not be so bad.

"Hey!" a shadow whispered, "We're *moving*. . . . Get up."

"Okay," said PFC Berlin. A

It was a dark, clear night. Wading through the **fecund** warmth of the field, he tried not to think. He now knew that fear came in many kinds. In the hot afternoon the fear had been

bundled and tight as he crawled like an ant escaping a giant's footsteps, watching Billy Boy Watkins die. Now his fear was **diffuse**—unfocused. But then he felt the fear of being afraid again.

To keep from thinking, he counted his steps. He also sang songs to himself as he walked toward the sea, *Where have you gone, Billy Boy, Billy Boy, oh, where have you gone, charming Billy? I have gone to seek a wife, she's the joy of my life, but she's a young thing and cannot leave her mother.*

When he reached the sea, he would dig a deep hole in the sand, and he would sleep, and he would not be afraid any more.

IN OTHER WORDS A group of soldiers is walking through a rice paddy. Private First Class (PFC) Paul Berlin is thinking about Billy Watkins, who died earlier that day. Berlin is afraid that his own fear will get to him. He sings the children's song "Where Have You Gone, Charming Billy?" to help him forget his fear.

The moon came out, pale and small.

He walked carefully, remembering what he'd been taught. Stay off the center of the path, where the land mines and booby traps[1] were planted. Stay alert. Better alert than inert. But he could not remember how to stop being afraid.

Stretching ahead of him, the string of nameless shadow soldiers moved with the slow grace of drifting smoke. Mostly the soldiers were quiet and hidden and seemed far away. He kept moving, feeling pulled along by **inertia**.

So he counted his steps. When he had reached 3,485, the column stopped.

One by one the soldiers knelt or squatted down.

PFC Berlin lay back. He might have slept. "I *wasn't* afraid," he was screaming or dreaming, facing his father's stern eyes. When he opened his eyes, a soldier was beside him, chewing a stick of gum. (B)

---

1. **land mines and booby traps:** land mines are explosive devices used to harm enemy soldiers or damage equipment; they are often buried just below the surface of the ground; booby traps are devices used to capture people unaware.

Monitor Your Comprehension

VOCABULARY
The word **diffuse** (dih FYOOS) is an adjective that means *unfocused.*

VOCABULARY
The word **inertia** (in NER shuh) is a noun that means *a feeling of not wanting to change what one is doing.*

(B) ANALYZE SEQUENCE
Reread lines 1–41. In the boxes below, briefly describe the major events in the story so far. Focus on the things Paul does, thinks about, or remembers.

Event 1
Paul Berlin stops in a rice paddy and tries to forget about the death of Billy Boy.

↓

Event 2
Possible answer: To help him forget his fear, Paul sings the children's song "Where Have You Gone, Charming Billy?"

↓

Event 3
Possible answer: Paul walks carefully and remembers what he has been taught about marching. He thinks about how important it is to stay alert.

↓

Event 4
Possible answer: As Paul marches with the other soldiers, he counts his steps until the group stops.

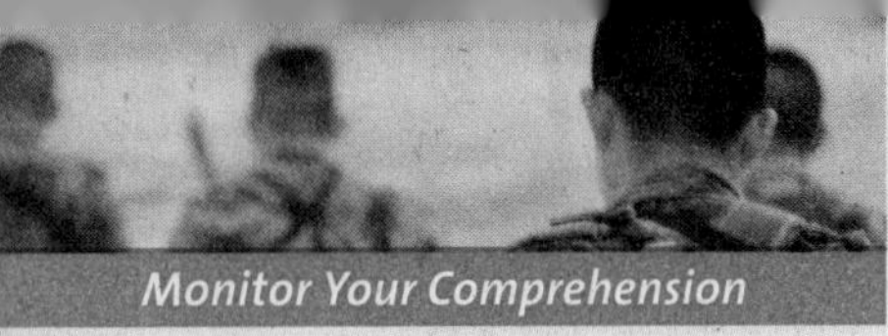

Monitor Your Comprehension

"You sleepin'?" the soldier whispered.

"No," said PFC Berlin.

The soldier took a swallow of water from his **canteen** and handed it through the dark. "You're the new guy?"

"Yes." He did not want to admit to being new to the war.

The soldier handed him a stick of gum. "Chew it quiet—OK?"

They chewed the gum until all the sugars were gone; then the soldier said, "Bad day today, buddy."

PFC Berlin nodded but did not speak. C

IN OTHER WORDS As the soldiers walk, PFC Berlin reminds himself of the survival skills he's been taught. Finally, the group stops for a rest. Berlin falls asleep and has a nightmare. A friendly soldier starts talking to Berlin.

"It's not always so bad," the soldier whispered. "You get used to it. "What's your name, buddy?"

"Paul."

"Nice to meet ya. Mine's Toby. Everybody calls me Buffalo, though."

The moon was high and bright, and they were waiting for cloud cover to dim its light. The soldier suddenly snorted. "Can't get over old Billy Boy dying from a lousy heart attack. . . . Ever hear of such a thing?"

"Not till now," said PFC Berlin.

"Tough as nails. . . . And what happens? A heart attack. Can you imagine it?" D

PFC Berlin wanted to laugh. "I can imagine it." He giggled. He imagined Billy's father opening the telegram: SORRY TO INFORM YOU THAT YOUR SON BILLY BOY WAS YESTERDAY SCARED TO DEATH IN ACTION IN THE REPUBLIC OF VIETNAM. . . . Berlin's body shook with giggles. E

VISUAL VOCABULARY
A **canteen** (kan TEEN) is a small water bottle used by soldiers or campers.

C REALISM
Reread lines 42–51. Underline the words, phrases, and details that make the story seem realistic.

D LANGUAGE COACH
The phrase *tough as nails* (line 62) is an **idiom**, or an expression that cannot be understood word-for-word. The idiom *tough as nails* means "strong and determined." Where do you think this expression comes from? Discuss your ideas with a partner.

Students should discuss that the idiom may have come from the fact that nails themselves are hard, durable items. When paired with the word "tough" their strength is reinforced as is the meaning of the two words together.

E ANALYZE SEQUENCE
Circle the event that Paul imagines happening in the future.

Monitor Your Comprehension

IN OTHER WORDS Berlin and Buffalo talk about the unusual way Billy died—from a heart attack. Suddenly, Berlin understands the irony of Billy's death: Billy, a brave soldier, had died of a heart attack, perhaps out of fear.

► With a partner, discuss Berlin's response to Billy's death.

Students should discuss that Berlin is saddened by Billy's death until he sees the irony in it and laughs at the idea that such a seemingly strong soldier would have been scared to death in Vietnam.

The big soldier hissed at him to shut up, but he could not stop giggling and remembering the hot afternoon, and how they'd started on the day's march, and how a little while later poor Billy Boy stepped on the mine, and how it made a tiny little "poof," and how Billy Boy stood there with his mouth wide open, looking down at where his foot had been blown off.

"War's over, Billy," the men had said, but Billy Boy got scared and started crying and said he was about to die. "Nonsense," the medic[2] said, but Billy Boy kept bawling. His face went pale and his veins popped out—he was scared stiff. Even when Doc Peret stuck him with morphine to kill the pain, Billy Boy kept crying.

"Shut up!" the big soldier hissed, but PFC Berlin could not stop giggling, the same way Billy Boy could not stop bawling that afternoon.

Afterward Doc Peret had explained: "You see, Billy Boy was scared he was gonna die—so scared he had himself a heart attack—and that's what really killed him." F

F ANALYZE SEQUENCE
Reread lines 70–86. Underline the events that took place before the start of the story's action.

IN OTHER WORDS Berlin cannot stop giggling. He thinks about how Billy had stepped on a mine and lost his foot. Although a doctor had tried to calm Billy down, he had died of a heart attack. Buffalo tries to quiet PFC Berlin's laughter. The sound might alert the enemy to the soldiers' location.

So they wrapped Billy in a plastic poncho,[3] eyes still wide open and scared stiff. They carried him over the meadow to a rice paddy. And then the mortar rounds[4] were falling everywhere. They loaded Billy's body into a rescue helicopter,

2. **medic:** a soldier or sailor trained to provide first aid.
3. **poncho:** waterproof cape with a central slit through which the head can pass.
4. **mortar rounds:** artillery shells fired from short cannons that can be taken apart and carried by soldiers.

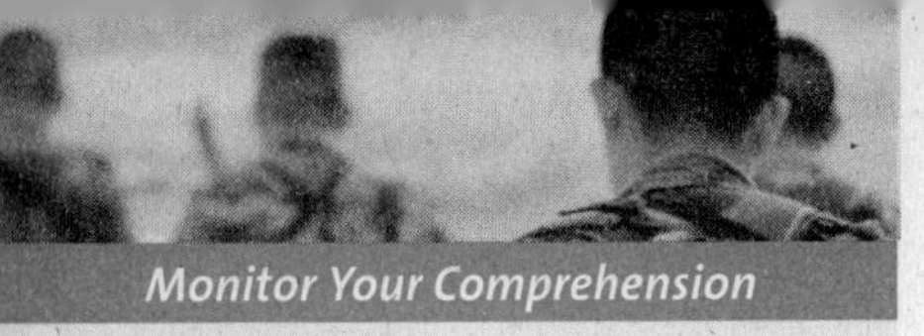

Monitor Your Comprehension

G REALISM

Reread lines 90–97. Do you think the details about the body falling out of the helicopter and the soldiers singing are realistic? Why?
Possible answer: I think that the body could have fallen from the helicopter if the soldiers were in a rush to take off and had not carefully secured it. I think the singing is realistic as well—the soldiers are exhausted and on the verge of hysteria. As they look for the body, they sing to keep from thinking about their own fears much as Berlin did earlier in the story.

H ANALYZE SEQUENCE

Reread lines 98–115. Briefly describe the final events in the story.

Event 1

Possible answer: Once Berlin begins to laugh at the idea of Billy being scared to death, he cannot stop. Buffalo covers Berlin's mouth to make him stop giggling.

↓

Event 2

Possible answer: Berlin finally calms down and joins the other soldiers as they march through the night.

↓

Event 3

Possible answer: Berlin tells himself that he will be calmer once he reaches the sea; however, he cannot suppress his fears.

PAUSE & REFLECT

Has Berlin grown as a character during this story? With a partner, discuss how has he changed.
Possible answer: While Berlin still cannot stop being afraid, he has changed because he can see the irony in the war. Additionally, he continues to try to remain calm.

but when the helicopter pulled upward, Billy Boy came tumbling out, falling slowly and then faster, and the paddy water sprayed up when he landed.

Later they waded in after him, using the ends of their rifles to look for Billy Boy lying under the stinking paddy water, singing—some of them—*Where have you gone, Billy Boy, Billy Boy, Oh, where have you gone, charming Billy?* G

"Shut up!" the soldier said loudly, shaking him.

But PFC Berlin could not stop. The giggles were caught in his throat, drowning him in his own laughter: scared to death like Billy Boy. A fine war story. He would tell his father how Billy Boy had been scared to death, never letting on. . . . He could not stop.

The soldier smothered him. PFC Berlin tried to fight back, but he was weak from the giggles.

IN OTHER WORDS PFC Berlin remembers how Billy's body had been loaded onto a rescue helicopter. The body had fallen out into a rice paddy. Soldiers looked for his body, and some of them sang the song, "Where Have You Gone, Charming Billy?" Berlin continues giggling. Buffalo covers his mouth to make him stop laughing.

The moon was under the clouds and the column was moving. The soldier helped him up. "You OK now, buddy?"

"You got to stay calm, buddy." The soldier handed him his rifle. "You'll get better at it."

He turned away, and still shivering, PFC Berlin hurried after him.

He would do better once he reached the sea. A funny war story that he would tell to his father, how Billy Boy Watkins was scared to death. A good joke. But even when he smelled salt and heard the sea, he could not stop being afraid. H

PAUSE & REFLECT

IN OTHER WORDS PFC Berlin's nervous laughter finally ends. Buffalo tells him he must stay calm. Berlin vows to handle himself better once the group reaches the sea. However, he is still afraid.

SET A PURPOSE FOR READING
Read this interview to learn more about Tim O'Brien's experiences as a soldier and writer.

Tim O'Brien: **The Naked Soldier**

Based on the interview from *Verbicide* magazine

BACKGROUND In this interview with editors from *Verbicide* magazine, Tim O'Brien talks about two kinds of bravery: the courage it took to decide to go to Vietnam, as well as the courage it took to avoid the war by moving to Canada.

Verbicide Would you have become a writer if you hadn't gone to Vietnam?

O'Brien Probably. It probably would've been something different. If I'd gone to Canada I'd be writing about that. Life gives you plenty of material, with girlfriends or whatever.

Verbicide Do you think you romanticize, or deal unrealistically, with Vietnam at all?

O'Brien No. I think a lot of veterans think I haven't done that enough, but I refuse to do it.

Verbicide Is there a reason they think it should be romanticized?

O'Brien Yeah, they look back on it as more heroic, and with nostalgia, a kind of longing. They talk about the friendship among men, and there's some truth to that. But it's fake; it comes from need. Even if you don't like someone, you've got to trust them at night when they're on guard and you're sleeping. And you learn who to trust and who not to trust. You bond that way. But I never found it very heroic. I just found it to be got to stay alive stuff. And that's all there was to it. PAUSE & REFLECT

PAUSE & REFLECT

O'Brien notes that some veterans wish he had presented a more nostalgic, or romantic, view of the war, but he refuses to do it. Why? Explain.

Possible answer: O'Brien does not want to present the war in a heroic, romanticized manner because he believes that many of the friendships formed there were fake and need-based. While O'Brien notes that bonding did exist, he states that it was not heroic in foundation but based on a desire to stay alive.

IN OTHER WORDS O'Brien says he would have been a writer even if he had never gone to Vietnam. He also says that he refuses to make the war look more glamorous than it was. Some veterans remember the war and wartime friendships with wistful affection, but he doesn't share those feelings.

► With a partner, discuss O'Brien's view of wartime friendship. Underline the sentences that explain why friendships exist in wartime, according to O'Brien.

Verbicide Are soldiers heroes?

O'Brien In some ways. It's heroic just not to stop. Physically, there are always other options; I mean, just stop walking. What can they do? Court martial[1] you, but they're not gonna kill you. It looks pretty attractive, especially in bad days when guys have been dropping like flies. . . . You just

1. **court martial:** to try soldiers and sailors accused of certain crimes in a military court of law.

keep going. There's a weird heroism in that. An uninteresting kind of bravery to just keep going, knowing you might die with every step, and just keep walking. (I)

Verbicide Is the heroism there in your books to be discovered if the reader wants it, or is it directly implied?

O'Brien I remember one part in *The Things They Carried* when I was talking about going on and just taking one step after the next. At one point I called it a kind of courage, which it is, just to keep your legs moving. I'm kind of clear about that kind of courage, but there are other kinds of courage just like there are kinds of truth. It took a lot of guts, for example, to go to Canada. Your whole hometown is going to think of you as a sissy or a coward, even though it's totally honorable. So I admire the heroism and courage it took. I didn't have the guts to do it, to cross over the border. (J)

Verbicide Do you still regret that?

O'Brien Yeah, you can't live your life over, but it would have been the right thing to do. I mean, think how hard it would be, even now it would be hard and I'm grown up. It was the thing that was worse than anything about the war, just going to it. Once you're in the war, it's pretty much what you'd expect. But, boy, making that decision, because you're in control of things. You can go in

(I) LANGUAGE COACH
The phrase *dropping like files* (line 26) is an **idiom,** or an expression that cannot be taken word-for-word, that means "falling ill or dead in large numbers." Like many idioms, its origin is unclear. But it seems to relate to the fact that insects don't live very long.

(J) REALISM
Reread lines 22–41. Underline some of the words or descriptions that remind you of Paul Berlin. What do these details suggest to you about the realism of "Where Have You Gone, Charming Billy?"

Possible answer: The details suggest that O'Brien based the story on his personal experiences in Vietnam and support its realistic tone.

the army, or you can go to Canada. I never actually made that drive and went to the Rainy River.[2] That's invented, made up. But it did happen in my head all summer long. I thought about driving to Canada.

PAUSE & REFLECT

PAUSE & REFLECT

What kind of courage would it take to go to Canada to escape the draft? What things might prevent someone from doing that? Discuss these ideas with a partner.

Possible answer: It took courage to go to Canada because your friends and family might have disapproved of your decision, calling you a coward or a sissy. It would also take courage to leave your friends and family behind and begin a new life in a new country.

IN OTHER WORDS O'Brien talks about heroism. He says that soldiers are heroic simply because they keep going when they're tempted to stop. He says that people who moved to Canada to avoid the draft—to avoid being forced to join the military—also were heroic. He thought about avoiding the draft, but he didn't. O'Brien now regrets that decision.

2. **Rainy River:** a river on the U.S.–Canadian border. In O'Brien's short story "On the Rainy River," the main character drives to the river and thinks about crossing into Canada to escape the draft.

After Reading

Text Analysis: Realism

In "Where Have You Gone, Charming Billy?" Tim O'Brien uses the style of **realism** to bring his main character's experiences to life for the reader. Complete the chart by finding two examples in the text that illustrate these elements of O'Brien's style.

For this chart, answers will vary. See samples below.

Element of O'Brien's Style	Example
Dialogue that sounds natural, like actual speech	*"It's not always so bad," the soldier whispered. "You get used to it. "What's your name, buddy?" "Paul." "Nice to meet ya. Mine's Toby. Everybody calls me Buffalo, though." "Can't get over old Billy Boy dying from a lousy heart attack. . . . Ever hear of such a thing?" "Not till now," said PFC Berlin. "Tough as nails. . . . And what happens? A heart attack. Can you imagine it?" (lines 52–56; 58–63)*
Vivid, realistic descriptions of what Paul sees and does	*To keep from thinking, he counted his steps. He also sang songs to himself as he walked toward the sea, Where have you gone, Billy Boy, Billy Boy, oh, where have you gone, charming Billy? I have gone to seek a wife, she's the joy of my life, but she's a young thing and cannot leave her mother. When he reached the sea, he would dig a deep hole in the sand, and he would sleep, and he would not be afraid any more. (lines 19–25)*

Why does it matter that this war story is written using realism? How does the realism make the story more powerful? Write your response on the lines below.

Possible answer: The story is about a historical event so using realism makes the events in the story believable, as if they might have really happened. O'Brien is able to draw from his personal experiences in writing the story, again, making the events in the story read as if they really took place.

After Reading

Reading Skill: Analyze Sequence

Some of the events described in "Where Have You Gone, Charming Billy?" take place before the start of the story's action. And some take place in the future, as Paul Berlin imagines them happening. Using the notes you made as you read, fill in the chart below.

For this chart, answers will vary. See samples below.

What happened before the story begins?
1. *Billy stepped on a mine that blew his foot off.*
2. *Billy had a heart attack and died.*
3. *The soldiers wrapped Billy's body in a poncho and loaded it onto a rescue helicopter.*
What happens during the story?
4. *Paul counts his steps and sings songs to keep himself from thinking about how afraid he is of the war.*
5. *Paul and Toby (Buffalo) talk about the day's events. Toby tells Paul that he will get used to things and that not every day is as bad as that day was.*
6. *Once Paul sees the irony in Billy's death, he cannot stop giggling as he remembers what has taken place.*
What events does Paul imagine happening in the future?
7. *Billy's father opens a telegram telling him his son has died.*
8. *Paul imagines telling his father the funny war story of how Billy was scared to death.*

Is FEAR our worst enemy?

How does fear affect, or influence, what Paul Berlin does in this story? How do his actions put him in danger?

Answers will vary but should reflect an understanding of the story's events.

Vocabulary Practice

Working with a partner, answer each question, giving reasons for your response. *Encourage students to use the Vocabulary words in their answers.*

1. What is an animal that needs to act with **stealth**?
2. What does it mean to say that someone has a **fecund** mind?
3. What kind of lamp might produce a **diffuse** light?
4. How might a feeling of **inertia** affect your weekend plans?

Academic Vocabulary in Speaking

The word **indicate** (IN dih kayt) is a verb that means *to point out or show.*

Sally says that yellow leaves on a plant might ***indicate*** that you're watering too often.

The word **vary** (VAIR ee) is a verb that means *to change or become different in some way.*

The temperature of the ocean can ***vary*** based on changes in weather or ocean currents.

TURN AND TALK In "Where Have You Gone, Charming Billy?" one of Paul Berlin's responses to fear is laughing (lines 64–69). What does this **indicate** about him? How might responses to fear **vary** from one person to another? Discuss these questions with a partner, using **indicate** and **vary** in your conversation.

Encourage students to use the Academic Vocabulary words in their discussions.

Assessment Practice

DIRECTIONS Use "Where Have You Gone, Charming Billy?" and "Tim O'Brien: Naked Soldier" to answer questions 1–6.

1 The death of Billy Boy Watkins takes place —

(A) in Paul's fevered imagination
(B) after the platoon reaches the sea
(C) shortly before the main action of the story
(D) about a year before Paul arrives in Vietnam

2 Why does Paul imagine telling his father that he was not scared in Vietnam?

(A) His father was a brave soldier.
(B) He thinks his father will enjoy the joke.
(C) He knows that none of the other soldiers are scared.
(D) He is trying to convince himself that he is not scared.

3 One element that gives this story a realistic style is —

(A) dialogue that reflects the way people actually talk
(B) a flashback to an event that happened at a different time
(C) a narrator who is outside the story
(D) its setting in a country far from the United States

4 The author uses a flashback to show —

(A) why Billy Boy and Paul were close friends
(B) why Paul is afraid of being overcome by his own fear
(C) Paul's sense of humor about death
(D) that soldiers have nothing to fear as long as they remain calm

5 Paul cannot stop giggling because —

(A) he remembers a joke his father told him
(B) he thinks Billy Boy's death was funny
(C) his fear of dying causes him to lose control
(D) Toby is shaking him in a way that tickles

6 What does the interview with Tim O'Brien reveal about the story?

(A) The story draws upon O'Brien's actual experiences in Vietnam.
(B) O'Brien does not think Paul is a courageous character.
(C) O'Brien wanted his story to romanticize the Vietnam War.
(D) The story shows how O'Brien wishes he had acted in the war.

A Few Words

Based on the essay by Mary Oliver

Is "CUTE" a compliment?

Before you answer, think about it. What does *cute* really mean? Can you be cute and still be taken seriously? In this essay, Mary Oliver has a few words to say about what happens when we label something as being cute.

WRITE IT Use the notepad at left to write down what comes to mind when you think of something cute. Would you want to be described that way? Why or why not?

What does it mean to be cute?

Answers will vary.

Is "cute" a compliment? Why or why not?

Answers will vary.

Text Analysis: Tone

A writer's **tone** is his or her attitude toward a subject, expressed through word choice and details. Sometimes a writer's tone isn't clear or obvious right away, but sometimes you can identify it in the first paragraph. To identify a writer's tone, look carefully at his or her choice of words and details. For example, notice the opening sentence of Mary Oliver's essay:

Nothing in the forest is charming.

What is Oliver's tone in this opening statement?
challenging

How do you know?
She starts with a statement that challenges a common idea people have about the forest and the things that live in it.

As you read "A Few Words," note vivid words, details, and images that Oliver uses, and consider the tone they communicate.

Reading Skill: Paraphrase

To understand difficult passages or sentences when you read, it is sometimes helpful to **paraphrase,** or restate the writer's ideas in your own words. When you paraphrase, you include the main idea and all of the key details in a passage.

As you read "A Few Words," you will be asked to paraphrase some passages. See the chart below for an example.

Passage	My Paraphrase
When we see something as "cute," "charming," or "adorable," that thing is stripped of its dignity and power. Instead it becomes entertainment, something that can be replaced.	*Calling something "cute," "charming," or "adorable" makes it seem small and weak. The thing becomes like a toy that is there only to entertain or amuse us.*

Vocabulary in Context

Note: Words are listed in the order in which they appear in the selection.

Stalk (stawk) is a noun that means *a stem of a plant.*

She picked the flower at the bottom of its long **stalk** so she could put it in a tall vase.

Diminutive (dih MIN yuh tiv) is an adjective that means *very small.*

The **diminutive** ant was so tiny that I could barely see it.

Valorous (VAL uhr uhs) is an adjective that means *brave.*

Facing down a bear might be a **valorous** act—but it would be smarter to run away.

Vocabulary Practice

Review the Vocabulary words and think about their meanings. Then use the words in a paragraph about a walk in the forest.

Encourage students to use the Vocabulary words in their paragraphs.

SET A PURPOSE FOR READING
Read this essay to find out why Oliver believes we shouldn't view the natural world as "cute."

A Few Words

Based on the essay by
MARY OLIVER

BACKGROUND We may think baby animals are "cute." But as Mary Oliver reminds us, we should remember that they have sharp teeth. In this essay, Oliver suggests that nature is not as cute or charming as we might want to believe. Instead, Oliver argues, nature is a powerful force we should respect.

Nothing in the forest is charming. Gardens are charming and so are some farm scenes—orderly rows of crops or lazy herds of animals or neatly gathered **stalks** after the harvest.[1]

And nothing in the forest is cute. The dog fox is not cute, nor the little foxes. I watch them as they run up and down. One carries the dirty wing of a bird. The others grab onto it and pull. They dart in and out of the grasses, their small teeth snapping. They are not adorable, or charming, or cute.

The owl is not cute. The snake is not cute, nor the spider in its web, nor the fish. Neither is the skunk. Its name is not "Flower." Nor is there a rabbit in the forest whose name is "Thumper."[2] Ⓐ

Toys are cute. But animals are not toys. Neither are trees, rivers, oceans, swamps, mountains, the mockingbird singing all night in a thorn bush, the snapping turtle, or the mushroom.

VOCABULARY
The word **stalk** (stawk) is a noun meaning *the stem of a plant.*

Ⓐ TONE
Reread lines 1–12. How would you describe Oliver's **tone**, or attitude toward her subject? Underline words and phrases the author uses to create this tone.
Possible answer: Oliver's tone can be described as direct, brisk, and forceful. She creates this tone through the strong and repeated use of the negative. She also uses strong, sometimes disturbing images. Oliver also uses many short, declarative sentences.

1. **harvest** (HAHR vist): the gathering of a crop when it reaches maturity.
2. **Flower** and **Thumper:** cute cartoon skunk and rabbit appearing in the Walt Disney movie *Bambi.*

Words like "cute," "charming," and "adorable" are wrong. When we see something as "cute," "charming," or "adorable," that thing is stripped of its dignity and power. Instead, it becomes entertainment, something that can be replaced. The words lead us and we follow: what is cute is **diminutive** and powerless; it is a small thing that can be captured and trained. And it is ours. This view is a mistake. At our feet are the ferns. Savage and stubborn, they grew in the frightening waters of the first oceans, long before humans existed. Now we find them pretty, delicate, and charming. We carry them home to add to our gardens.

This is how we imagine ourselves to be the masters of nature. If nature is full of adorable and charming, diminutive and powerless things, then who is in the position of power? We are! We are in control. This idea makes us see the world as a playground and laboratory—a weak and incomplete way to look at it. Our point of view seems so harmless, so responsible. But it is neither. B

IN OTHER WORDS The author lists animals, plants, and other features of nature that we mistakenly think are cute or charming. When we call them cute, charming, or adorable, we feel superior to them.

► Reread Oliver's description of ferns. Circle the words and phrases that show that ferns are *not* cute.

This mistaken idea about nature also makes the other view of nature impossible, that nature is sacred and complex, as well as powerful. We are just a single part of it. Nature is the wheel

Monitor Your Comprehension

VOCABULARY

The word **diminutive** (dih MIN yuh tiv) is an adjective meaning *very small.*

B PARAPHRASE

Reread lines 27–33. What is Oliver saying about human attitudes toward nature? Restate her ideas in your own words.

Possible answer: While humans believe that their attitude about nature is harmless and even responsible, Oliver states that it is in fact neither. She also states that our view of the world as a laboratory and a playground is a weak, incomplete way of looking at the world.

Monitor Your Comprehension

PAUSE & REFLECT
Reread lines 34–40. Why does Oliver believe that those who try to "run the world" will have no joy or pleasure in it? Discuss this idea with a partner.

Possible answer: To Oliver, the people who try to run the world will become stuck in an endless cycle, which will have few positive results.

VISUAL VOCABULARY
Niagara Falls is a large waterfall on the border between the United States and Canada.

Ⓒ PARAPHRASE
Paraphrase the ideas in lines 41–50.

Possible answer: People are more like plants and animals than they realize. We all try to improve our lives while alive, and we all die, too. We all occupy the same place and environment and need to embrace our surroundings as part of us instead of trying to get control over them.

VOCABULARY
The word **valorous** (VAL uhr uhs) is an adjective meaning *brave*.

that drives our world. Those who choose to ride this wheel might discover a dazzling, even spiritual, peace. People who say that we must run the world for our own benefit will be dragged round and round on the wheel. They will gather dust but no joy. **PAUSE & REFLECT**

Humans or tigers, tigers or tiger lilies[3]– how different and yet alike they are! Don't we all try to use our physical and mental skills to improve our condition while we're alive? And don't we then fall back into the grass, into death? What is cute or charming as it rises, as it falls? Life is **Niagara**, or nothing. I do not want to be master of a single blade of grass. I want to be its sister. I put my face close to the lily and give it a good greeting from the stem of my heart. We live, I am sure, in the same country, in the same household. We are all wild, **valorous**, amazing. We are, none of us, cute. Ⓒ

IN OTHER WORDS The author suggests that nature is complex and powerful, not cute. She says that we should try not to rule nature, but should see ourselves as part of it.

3. **tiger lilies:** a type of orange flower with black spots.

After Reading

Text Analysis: Tone

"A Few Words" expresses a clear tone. Fill in the chart below to understand how Oliver establishes, or sets, her tone. In the Example column, list words, details, and images that contribute to the tone. Then, in the Tone column, describe the tone that each example communicates.

For this chart, answers will vary. See samples below.

Example	Tone
"Toys are cute. But animals are not toys. Neither are trees, rivers, oceans, swamps, mountains, the mockingbird singing all night in a thorn bush, the snapping turtle, or the mushroom." (lines 13–15)	*Oliver's tone is direct and brisk.*
"When we see something as 'cute,' 'charming,' or 'adorable,' that thing is stripped of its dignity and power. Instead, it becomes entertainment, something that can be replaced." (lines 16–19)	*Oliver's tone is angry and frustrated.*
"nature is sacred and complex, as well as powerful. We are just a single part of it. Nature is the wheel that drives our world." (lines 35–37)	*Oliver's tone is admiring and reverent.*
"I do not want to be master of a single blade of grass. I want to be its sister. I put my face close to the lily and give it a good greeting from the stem of my heart. (lines 46–48)	*Oliver's tone reveals her great respect for nature, noting that it is not to be controlled or undervalued.*

Review your notes for "A Few Words" and your completed chart. What is the overall tone of this essay?

Possible answer: Oliver's overall tone can be described as forceful and impassioned. She wants to persuade the reader of nature's value as a stunning and powerful part of the world with which we should co-exist rather than try to control.

Is "CUTE" a compliment?

Did reading "A Few Words" change how you think of the word *cute*? Explain.

Possible answer: Having read Oliver's essay I now think that the word cute is somewhat demeaning and is not really a compliment because it is misused.

Reading Skill: Paraphrase

Look back at the paraphrases you made as you read "A Few Words." Using your chart, summarize the main idea of this essay in your own words. Then list the details that support the main idea.

For this chart, answers will vary. See samples below.

Main Idea:
Nothing in nature is cute or adorable. Humans need to stop trying to control it and stop viewing it as entertainment. Humans, animals, and plants are all interconnected and deserve respect.

Detail:	Detail:	Detail:
Nothing in the forest is cute—a thing that is cute is small and powerless and capable of being captured and trained.	*Humans are not the masters of nature—our view of it is both harmful and irresponsible.*	*Humans should co-exist with the plants, such as grasses and lilies that surround them.*

Vocabulary Practice

In which situation might you use each vocabulary word? Circle the correct answers.

1. **diminutive:** **(a)** describing a miniature poodle, **(b)** listing the pros and cons of a school rule, **(c)** explaining how to draw trees
2. **stalk:** **(a)** explaining how to paint a chair, **(b)** describing a field of corn, **(c)** listing the reasons you like bungee jumping
3. **valorous:** **(a)** telling about a peaceful day in the country, **(b)** describing how the hero of a movie saved the day, **(c)** explaining how to build a brick sidewalk

Academic Vocabulary in Writing

The word **appreciate** (uh PREE shee ayt) is a verb that means *to recognize the value of something.*

After working outside in the summer heat, you might **appreciate** shade and a cold drink.

The word **unique** (yoo NEEK) is an adjective that describes something that is *the only one of its kind and is not like any other.*

Each person's fingerprints are **unique**—no two people have exactly the same patterns.

WRITE IT Mary Oliver discusses two very different ways of looking at nature. In a few sentences, explain which view you agree with more, and why. Be sure to use the words **appreciate** and **unique** in your response.

Encourage students to use the Academic Vocabulary words in their responses.

Assessment Practice

DIRECTIONS Use "A Few Words" to answer questions 1–4.

1 The image of the foxes in lines 4–8 is used in contrast with the idea that —

- (A) nature has order
- (B) animals are cute and adorable
- (C) animals should kill other animals
- (D) animals are easier to tame than plants

2 The tone of lines 9–12 is —

- (A) forceful
- (B) peaceful
- (C) playful
- (D) thoughtful

3 Oliver says that viewing humans as being in a position of power is harmful because it —

- (A) takes away a person's dignity
- (B) suggests that people can be replaced
- (C) keeps people from being creative
- (D) fails to recognize the power of nature

4 Which of these best describes who Oliver means by the pronoun "we" in lines 41–50?

- (A) All humans
- (B) All animals
- (C) Everything in nature
- (D) Everyone in this country

Before Reading

The Sneeze

from *The Good Doctor,* a play by **Neil Simon**

Based on a short story by **Anton Chekhov**

Who makes you LAUGH?

Can your best friend or a favorite comedian make you laugh every time? What's so funny about this person? If you enjoy ridiculous characters and their out-of-control bodies, you'll like "The Sneeze."

LIST IT Think about the last time you laughed so hard you couldn't stop. On the lines at left, create your own top-five list of the things and people you find funniest.

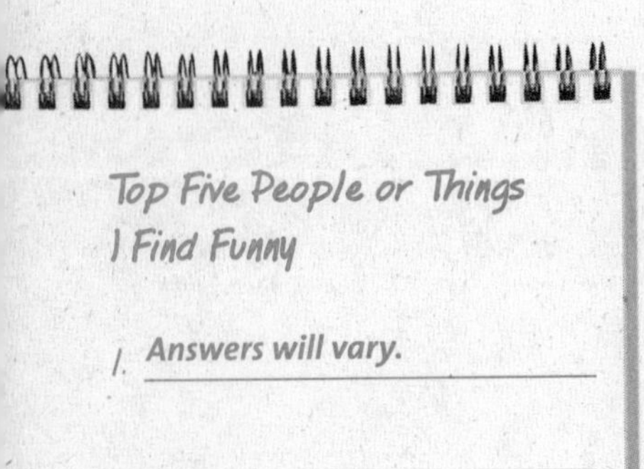

Top Five People or Things I Find Funny
1. Answers will vary.
2. Answers will vary.
3. Answers will vary.
4. Answers will vary.
5. Answers will vary.

Text Analysis: Farce

A **farce** is a humorous play that presents ridiculous situations, comic dialogue, and physical humor, such as one character sneezing all over another. In some cases, the writer of a farce might want to make fun of someone or something in particular. To recognize a farce, look for the following

Elements of a Farce	Examples
A ridiculous plot driven by a humorous conflict	The main character, Cherdyakov, can't stop apologizing to a man for having accidentally sneezed on him.
Behavior and language that exaggerates for humorous effect by making events seem more important than they really are	After sneezing, Cherdyakov says, "It's unpardonable. It was monstrous of me—"
Physical comedy: makes jokes using the body	Cherdyakov sneezes in an exaggerated way, leaning his head back and then snapping it forward.

Reading Strategy: Visualize

When you **visualize,** you use details, descriptions, and dialogue to create pictures in your mind of what you read. Visualizing this play can help you monitor your understanding of it and enjoy its humor. Try the following:

- Read the stage directions so you can picture the characters, what they do, and where the play takes place.
- One character, called the Writer, serves as a narrator in this play. Pay attention to this character's descriptions of the other characters.
- Pay attention to how characters react to each other to picture how each character looks and behaves.

As you read, you will list the details that help you visualize the play in a chart like the one below.

Details from the Text	My Visualization
"He is in his mid-thirties, quiet and unassuming." (lines 3–4)	*I picture a nervous-looking, boring man with a pale face and a worried expression.*

Monitor Your Comprehension

SET A PURPOSE FOR READING
Read this play to determine which character, Cherdyakov or the general, deserves more sympathy.

THE SNEEZE

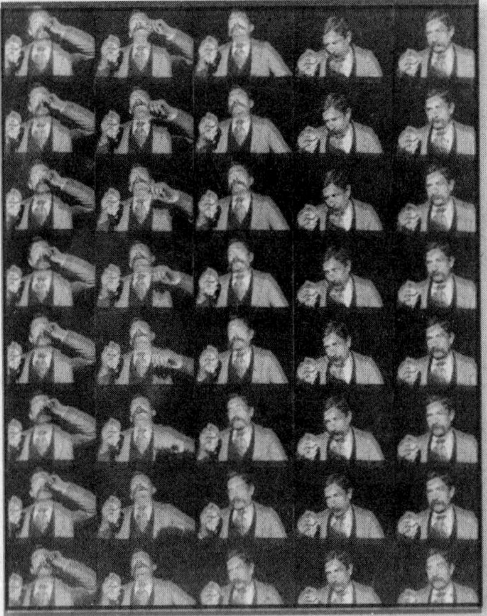

Drama by
NEIL SIMON
Based on a story by
ANTON CHEKHOV

BACKGROUND This dramatic sketch, or short play, was meant to be performed on stage. In this dramatic sketch, a character called the Writer shares a story idea with the play's audience. This makes the Writer the narrator of the story's events, as well as one of the story's characters.

CHARACTERS

Writer

Cherdyakov, Ivan Ilyitch (CHERD yuh kuhv, ee VAHN il YEECH)

General, Mikhail Brassilhov (mee kah EEL BRAHS il uhv)

Wife, Cherdyakov's wife

Madame Brassilhov, the General's wife

Writer. If Ivan Ilyitch Cherdyakov, a civil servant, a clerk in the Ministry of Public Parks, had any passion in life at all, it was the theater. (*Enter* Ivan Cherdyakov *and his* Wife. *He is in his mid-thirties, mild-mannered and unassuming. He and his* Wife *are dressed in their best, but are certainly no match for the grandeur around them. They are clearly out of their element here. They move into their seats. As his* Wife *peruses*[1] *her program,* Cherdyakov *is beaming with happiness as he looks around and in back at the theater and its esteemed audience. He is a happy man tonight.*) **A** He certainly had hopes and ambitions for higher office and had dedicated his life to hard work, zeal and patience. Still, he would not deny himself his one great pleasure. So he purchased two tickets in the very best section of the theater for the opening night performance of Rostov's *The Bearded Countess.*[2] (*A splendidly uniformed* General *and his* Wife *enter, looking for their seats.*) As fortune would have it, into the theater that night came His Respected Superior, General Mikhail Brassilhov, the Minister of Public Parks himself.

(*The* General *and his* Wife *take their seats in the first row, the* General *directly in front of* Cherdyakov.)

Cherdyakov (*leans over to the* General). Good evening, General.

General (*turns, looks at* Cherdyakov *coldly*). Hmm? . . . What? Oh, yes. Yes. Good evening.

(*The* General *turns front again, looks at his program.*)

Cherdyakov. Permit me, sir. I am Cherdyakov . . . Ivan Ilyitch. This is a great honor for me, sir.

General (*turns; coldly*). Yes.

Cherdyakov. Like yourself, dear General, I too serve the Ministry of Public Parks . . . That is to say, I serve *you*, who is indeed *himself* the Minister of Public Parks. I am the Assistant Chief Clerk in the Department of Trees and Bushes.

General. Ahh, yes. Keep up the good work . . . Lovely trees and bushes this year. Very nice.

1. **peruses** (puh ROOZ iz): reads carefully.
2. **Rostov's *The Bearded Countess:*** a made-up author and play.

Monitor Your Comprehension

A VISUALIZE

Reread lines 1–9. In the chart below, record the details in these lines that help you **visualize** the setting and characters based on the Writer's comments.

Details from the Text

Setting:
A grandly decorated theater filled with a respected audience.

Cherdyakov/Wife:
Cherdyakov is in his mid-thirties, happy to be attending the theater, and dressed in his best clothes. His wife is dressed in her best clothes, too.

↓

My Visualization

I picture Cherdyakov and his wife as a plain, unassuming couple who arrive at the theater dressed in their best clothes. In spite of their efforts, they are still out of place in their lavish surroundings. Cherdyakov is visibly excited to be at the theater.

Monitor Your Comprehension

(*The* General *turns back.* Cherdyakov *sits back, happy, grinning like a cat. The* General's Wife *whispers to him and he shrugs back. Suddenly the unseen curtain rises on the play and they all applaud.* Cherdyakov *leans forward again.*)

Cherdyakov. My wife would like very much to say hello, General. This is she. My wife, Madame Cherdyakov.

Wife (*smiles*). How do you do?

General. My pleasure.

Wife. *My* pleasure, General.

General. How do you do?

(*He turns front, flustered.* Cherdyakov *beams at his* Wife; *then*)

Cherdyakov (*to the* General's Wife). Madame Brassilhov—my wife, Madame Cherdyakov.

Wife. How do you do, Madame Brassilhov?

Madame Brassilhov (*coldly*). How do you do?

Wife. I just had the pleasure of meeting your husband.

Cherdyakov (*to* Madame Brassilhov). And I am my wife's husband. How do you do, Madame Brassilhov?

(*The* Writer *"shushes" them.*)

General (*to the* Writer). Sorry. Terribly sorry.

(*The* General *tries to control his anger as they all go back to watching the play.*) PAUSE & REFLECT

PAUSE & REFLECT

With a partner, discuss why you think Cherdyakov and his wife are happier to meet the general and his wife than the general and his wife are to meet them.

Students should discuss that Cherdyakov and his wife are in a lower social class than the general and his wife. As a result, they are excited and impressed by meeting the general and his wife. Additionally, Cherdyakov and his wife continue to talk to the general and his wife after the curtain has risen on the play, indicating it is going to begin.

IN OTHER WORDS The Writer explains that Cherdyakov and his wife have come to a theater to see a play. Cherdyakov buys expensive theater seats, although he is an ordinary worker. He and his wife don't fit in with the wealthier audience members. The general and his wife sit down in front of them. The general runs the government office where Cherdyakov works, so Cherdyakov repeatedly introduces himself and his wife. The general and his wife are annoyed. Finally, the Writer tells them to be quiet.

Cherdyakov. I hope you enjoy the play, sir.

General. I will if I can watch it.

(*He is getting hot under the collar. They all go back to watching the performance.*)

Writer. Feeling quite pleased with himself for having made the most of this golden opportunity, Ivan Ilyitch Cherdyakov sat back to enjoy *The Bearded Countess.* He was no longer a stranger to the Minister of Public Parks. They had become, if one wanted to be generous about the matter, familiar with each other . . . And then, quite suddenly, without any warning, like a bolt from a gray thundering sky, Ivan Ilyitch Cherdyakov reared his head back, and—

Cherdyakov. AHHHHHHHH—CHOOOOOOOO!!! (Cherdyakov *unleashes a monstrous sneeze, his head snapping forward. The main blow of the sneeze discharges on the back of the* General's *completely bald head. The* General *winces and his hand immediately goes to his now-dampened head.*) Ohhh, my goodness, I'm *sorry*, your Excellency! I'm so terribly sorry!

(*The* General *takes out his handkerchief and wipes his head.*)

General. Never mind. It's all right.

Cherdyakov. *All right?* . . . It certainly is *not* all right! It's unpardonable. It was monstrous of me—

General. You make too much of the matter. Let it rest.

(*He puts away his handkerchief.*)

Cherdyakov (*quickly takes out his own handkerchief*). How can I let it rest? It was inexcusable. Permit me to wipe your neck, General. It's the least I can do. B

(*He starts to wipe the* General's *head. The* General *pushes his hand away.*)

General. Leave it be! It's all right, I say.

Cherdyakov. But I splattered you, sir. Your complete head is splattered. It was an accident, I assure you—but it's *disgusting!*

B FARCE

Lines 67–81 include **exaggerated language.** Reread these lines and bracket [ ] the words and phrases that exaggerate Cherdyakov's sneeze.

Writer. Shhhh!

General. I'm sorry. My apologies.

IN OTHER WORDS The characters begin watching the play. Suddenly, Cherdyakov sneezes on the general's bald head. He tells the general that he's sorry, and the general wipes his head with a handkerchief.

► How does the general react to Cherdyakov's repeated apologies? Put a check mark (✔) next to each line that tells you.

Cherdyakov. The thing is, your Excellency, it came completely without warning. It was out of my nose before I could stifle it.

Madame Brassilhov. Shhh!

Cherdyakov. Shhh, yes, certainly. I'm sorry . . . (*He sits back, nervously. He blows his nose with his handkerchief. Then* Cherdyakov *leans forward.*) It's not a cold, if that's what you were worrying about, sir. Probably a particle of dust in the nostril—

General. Shhh! PAUSE & REFLECT

PAUSE & REFLECT

With a partner, discuss whether you think Cherdyakov's apologies after the sneeze make the situation better or worse. Explain.

Students should discuss that with each apology Cherdyakov makes, he makes the situation worse and further irritates the general.

(*They watch the play in silence, and* Cherdyakov *sits back, unhappy with himself.*)

Writer. But try as he might, Cherdyakov could not put the incident out of his mind. The sneeze, no more than an innocent anatomical accident,[3] grew out of all proportion in his mind, until it resembled the angry roar of a cannon aimed squarely at the enemy camp. He played the incident back in his mind, slowing the procedure down so he could view again in horror the infamous deed.

(Cherdyakov, *in slow motion, repeats the sneeze again, but slowed down so that it appears to us as one frame at a time. It also seems to be three times as great in intensity as the original sneeze. The* General, *also in slow motion, reacts as though he has just taken a fifty-pound hammer blow at the base of his skull. They all go with the slow motion*

3. **innocent anatomical** (an uh TOM ih kuhl) accident: an action by the body that cannot be controlled.

of the "sneeze" until it is completed, when the unseen curtain falls and they applaud. They all rise and begin to file out of the theater, chattering about the lovely evening they have just spent.) (C)

General. Charming . . . Charming.

Madame Brassilhov. Yes, charming.

General. Charming . . . Simply charming. Wasn't it charming, my dear?

Madame Brassilhov. I found it utterly charming.

(Cherdyakov *stands behind them tapping the* General.)

Writer. I was completely charmed by it.

Cherdyakov (*still tapping away at the* General). Excuse me, Excellency—

General. Who's tapping? Somebody's tapping me. Who's that tapping?

Cherdyakov. I'm tapping, sir. I'm the tapper . . . Cherdyakov.

Madame Brassilhov (*quickly pulls the* General *back*). Stand back, dear, it's the sneezer.

Cherdyakov. No, no, it's all right. I'm all sneezed out . . . I was just concerned about your going out into the night air with a damp head.

General. Oh, that. It was a trifle. A mere faux pas.[4] Forget it, young man. Amusing play, don't you think? Did you find it amusing?

Cherdyakov. Amusing? Oh, my goodness, yes. Ha, ha. So true. Ha, ha. I haven't laughed as much in years. Ha, ha, ha . . .

General. Which part interested you the most?

Cherdyakov. The sneeze. When I sneezed on you. It was unforgivable, sir.

General. Forget it, young man. Come, my dear. It looks like rain. I don't want to get my head wet again.

Madame Brassilhov. You shouldn't let people sneeze on you, dear. You're not to be sneezed at. (D)

4. **faux pas** (foh PAH): an embarrassing but unimportant mistake.

Monitor Your Comprehension

(C) VISUALIZE

In lines 106–113, underline details that help you visualize the way Cherdyakov remembers his sneeze. With a partner, discuss the difference between what really happened and the **exaggerated language** that describes how Cherdyakov remembers it.

Students should discuss that while the original event took place quite quickly, Cherdyakov recalls that the sneeze took much longer to complete. Additionally, he recalls it having three times the intensity of the original sneeze.

(D) LANGUAGE COACH

When the general's wife tells her husband, "You shouldn't let people sneeze on you," she actually means that people should not sneeze on him, as Cherdyakov did. But when she tells him, "You're not to be sneezed at" in line 142, she is using an **idiom**, an expression in which the word *sneezed* means something different from its usual meaning. "You're not to be sneezed at" is an idiomatic (id ee uh MAT ik) expression meaning "No one should treat you as if you are not important." What is the event she refers to with this comment?

Possible answer: the persistent pestering from Cherdyakov

Monitor Your Comprehension

IN OTHER WORDS Cherdyakov again tries to apologize to the general. The Writer explains that Cherdyakov cannot forget about the sneeze. As Cherdyakov replays the sneeze in his mind, he imagines what happened as being much worse than what really occurred. After the play they've been watching ends, the characters leave the theater. Cherdyakov continues to annoy the general by talking about the sneeze, although the general tells him not to worry about it.

(*They are gone.*)

Cherdyakov. I'm ruined! Ruined! He'll have me fired from Trees and Bushes. They'll send me down to Branches and Twigs.

Wife. Come, Ivan.

Cherdyakov. What?

Wife. You mustn't let it concern you. It was just a harmless little sneeze. The General's probably forgotten it already.

Cherdyakov. Do you really think so?

Wife. No! I'm scared, Ivan.

Writer. And so they walked home in despair.

Cherdyakov. Perhaps I should send him a nice gift. Maybe some Turkish towels.

Writer. Cherdyakov's once-promising career had literally been blown away.

Cherdyakov (*as they arrive home*). Why did this happen to me? Why did I go to the theater at all? Why didn't I sit in the balcony with people of our own class? They love sneezing on each other. E

E FARCE
With a partner, discuss why Cherdyakov believes that sitting in a different part of the theater would have prevented his **humorous conflict** with the general.

Students should discuss that Cherdyakov thinks that sitting elsewhere would have removed him from being so close to the general, and, therefore, he would have avoided contact with him entirely and directed his sneeze elsewhere.

Wife. Come to bed, Ivan.

Cherdyakov. Perhaps if I were to call on the General and explain matters again, but in such a charming, honest and self-effacing[5] manner, he would have no choice but to forgive me . . .

Wife. Maybe it's best not to remind him, Ivan.

Cherdyakov. No, no. If I ever expect to become a gentleman, I must behave like one.

5. **self-effacing** (self ih FAY sing): humble.

Writer. And so the morning came. It so happened this was the day the General listened to petitions, and since there were fifty or sixty petitions ahead of Cherdyakov, he waited from morning till late, late afternoon . . .

IN OTHER WORDS **Cherdyakov worries that the general will move him to a less important job. The next day, Cherdyakov waits in line with people who have come to the general with requests or complaints.**

(Cherdyakov *moves into the office set.*)

General. Next! . . . NEXT!

Cherdyakov. I'm not next, your Excellency . . . I'm last.

General. Very well, then . . . Last!

Cherdyakov. That's me, sir.

General. Well, what is your petition?

Cherdyakov. I have no petition, sir. I'm not a petitioner.

General. Then you waste my time.

Cherdyakov. Do you not recognize me, sir? We met last night under rather "explosive" circumstances . . . I am the splatterer. F

General. The what?

Cherdyakov. The sneezer. The one who sneezed. The sneezing splatterer.

General. Indeed? And what is it you want now? A *Gesundheit?*[6]

Cherdyakov. No, Excellency . . . Your forgiveness. I just wanted to point out there was no political or antisocial motivation behind my sneeze. It was a nonpartisan,[7] nonviolent act of God. I curse the day the protuberance[8] formed itself on my face. It's a hateful nose, sir, and I am not responsible for its indiscretions . . .

6. **Gesundheit** (guh ZUNT hyt): a German word meaning "good health"; often used after someone sneezes.
7. **nonpartisan** (non PAR tih zuhn): not strongly supportive of any one political party, cause, or person.
8. **protuberance** (proh TOO ber uhns): something that sticks out, such as a nose.

Monitor Your Comprehension

F LANGUAGE COACH

Reread lines 179–180. In a farce, characters often make **puns,** verbal jokes that use two different meanings of the same word at the same time. Cherdyakov puns on two different meanings of the word *explosive* in this line. He refers to the explosive power of his sneeze. What other meaning does Cherdyakov's choice of the word *explosive* suggest?

Possible answer: Cherdyakov is referring to the way in which the general and his wife reacted to his repeated apologies.

Monitor Your Comprehension

G VISUALIZE

Reread lines 181–192. Based on what the characters say to each other, how do you picture the facial expressions and actions of Cherdyakov and the general during this scene?

Possible answer: At first, the general looks confused because he does not understand to what Cherdyakov is referring. Then, he looks annoyed at Cherdyakov for continuing to pursue the matter. Cherdyakov looks apologetic as well as disgusted at his own nose, grabbing it for emphasis.

(*grabbing his own nose*) Punish that which committed the crime, but absolve the innocent body behind it. Exile my nose, but forgive me, your kindship. Forgive me. G

General. My dear young man, I'm not angry with your nose. I'm too busy to have time for your nasal problems. I suggest you go home and take a hot bath—or a cold one—take *something*, but don't bother me with this silly business again . . . Gibber, gibber gibber, that's all I've heard all day. (*going offstage*) Gibber, gibber, gibber, gibber . . .

(Cherdyakov *stands alone in the office sobbing.*)

Cherdyakov. Thank you, sir. God bless you and your wife and your household. May your days be sweet and may your nights be better than your days.

Writer. The feeling of relief that came over Cherdyakov was enormous . . .

Cherdyakov. May the birds sing in the morning at your window and may the coffee in your cup be strong and hot . . .

Writer. The weight of the burden that was lifted was inestimable . . .

Cherdyakov. I worship the chair you sit on and the uniform you wear that sits on the chair that I worship . . .

Writer. He walked home, singing and whistling like a lark. Life was surely a marvel, a joy, a heavenly paradise . . .

Cherdyakov. Oh, God, I am happy!

IN OTHER WORDS Cherdyakov waits his turn to see the general. He begs the general to forgive him for the sneeze, and the general tells Cherdyakov that he is not angry.

► How does Cherdyakov feel after talking with the general? With a partner, discuss Cherdyakov's reaction.

Students should discuss that Cherdyakov feels great relief and is quite happy at the outcome of their conversation.

Writer. And yet—

Cherdyakov. And yet—

Writer. When he arrived home, he began to think . . .

Monitor Your Comprehension

Cherdyakov. Have I been the butt of a cruel and thoughtless joke?

Writer. Had the Minister toyed with him?

Cherdyakov. If he had no intention of punishing me, why did he torment me so unmercifully?

Writer. If the sneeze meant so little to the Minister, why did he deliberately cause Cherdyakov to writhe in his bed?

Cherdyakov. . . . to twist in agony the entire night?

Writer. Cherdyakov was furious!

Cherdyakov. I AM FURIOUS! **PAUSE & REFLECT**

Writer. He foamed and fumed and paced the night through, and in the morning he called out to his wife, "SONYA!"

Cherdyakov. SONYA! (*She rushes in.*) I have been humiliated.

Wife. *You*, Ivan? Who would humiliate *you?* You're such a kind and generous person.

Cherdyakov. Who? I'll tell you who! General Brassilhov, the Minister of Public Parks.

Wife. What did he do?

Cherdyakov. The swine! I was humiliated in such subtle fashion, it was almost indiscernible. The man's cunning is equal only to his cruelty. He practically forced me to come to his office to grovel and beg on my knees. I was reduced to a gibbering idiot. **H**

Wife. You were that reduced?

Cherdyakov. I must go back and tell him what I think of him. The lower classes must speak up . . . (*He is at the door.*) The world must be made safe so that men of all nations and creeds, regardless of color or religion, will be free to sneeze on their superiors! It is *he* who will be humiliated by *I!*

Writer. And so, the next morning, Cherdyakov came to humiliate *he.*[9]

(*Lights up on the* General *at his desk.*)

---

9. **humiliated by *I* . . . humiliate *he*:** Cherdyakov uses an incorrect pronoun (*I* rather than *me*), and the Writer makes fun of him by repeating a similar error (*he* rather than *him*).

PAUSE & REFLECT

Reread lines 215–224. With a partner, discuss why Cherdyakov goes from being so happy to being so angry in such a short period of time.

Students should discuss that Cherdyakov second-guesses his initial happiness, suspecting the general is playing a cruel joke on him. Once again, his uncertainty leads him to convince himself that the general is seeking revenge on him and he becomes quite angry as a result.

H FARCE

Reread lines 227–236. Do you think there is any truth to Cherdyakov's conclusion that the general meant to humiliate him, or is his anger an example of **exaggerated behavior**? Explain your answer.

Possible answer: I think that Cherdyakov's response is an example of exaggerated behavior. He has let his own insecurities and concerns create a situation that does not exist between him and the general.

IN OTHER WORDS Cherdyakov begins to think that the general had really wanted him to worry about the sneeze. He decides that the general has tricked him into begging for forgiveness. Cherdyakov becomes angry. He decides to go back to the general so that he can complain about how poorly the general has treated him.

General. Last! (Cherdyakov *goes to the* General's *desk. He stands there glaring down at the* General *with a faint trace of a smile on his lips. The* General *looks up.*) Well?

Cherdyakov (*smiles*). Well? Well, you say? . . . Do you not recognize me, your Excellency? Look at my face . . . Yes. You're quite correct. It is I once again.

General (*looks at him, puzzled*). It is you once again who?

Cherdyakov (*confidentially*). Cherdyakov, Excellency. I have returned, having taken neither a hot bath nor a cold one.

General. Who let this filthy man in? What is it?

Cherdyakov (*on top of the situation now*). What is it? . . . What is it, you ask? You sit there behind your desk and ask, What is it? You sit there in your lofty position as General and Minister of Public Parks, a member in high standing among the upper class and ask me, a lowly civil servant, What is it? You sit there with

full knowledge that there is no equality in this life, that there are those of us who serve and those that are served, those of us that obey and those that are obeyed, those of us who bow and those that are bowed to, that in this life certain events take place that cause some of us to be humiliated and those that are the cause of that humiliation . . . and still you ask, "WHAT IS IT?"!

PAUSE & REFLECT

Students should discuss that Cherdyakov's comments are insulting because he attacks the general's social status as well as professional status.

General (*angrily*). *What is it?* Don't stand there gibbering like an idiot! What is it you want?

Cherdyakov. *I'll tell you what I want!* . . . I wanted to apologize again for sneezing on you . . . I wasn't sure I made it clear. It was an accident, an accident, I assure you . . . (I)

General (*stands and screams out*). *Out! Out, you idiot!* Fool! Imbecile! Get out of my sight! I never want to see you again. If you ever cross my line of vision I'll have you exiled forever . . . WHAT'S YOUR NAME?

Cherdyakov. Ch—Cherdyakov!

(*It comes out as a sneeze in the* General's *face.*)

General (*wiping himself*). You germ spreader! You maggot! You insect! You are lower than an insect. You are the second cousin to a cockroach! The son-in-law of a bed bug! You are the nephew of a *ringworm!* You are nothing, nothing, do you hear me? . . . *NOTHING!* (J)

(Cherdyakov *backs away, and returns home.*)

Writer. At that moment, something broke loose inside of Cherdyakov . . . Something so deep and vital, so organic, that the damage that was done seemed irreparable . . . Something drained from him that can only be described as the very life force itself . . . (Cherdyakov *takes off his coat. He sits on the sofa, head in hands.*) The matter was over, for once, for all, forever. What happened next was quite simple . . . (Cherdyakov *lies back on the sofa.*) Ivan Ilyitch Cherdyakov arrived at home . . . removed his coat . . . lay down on the sofa—and died! (Cherdyakov's *head drops and his hand falls to the floor.*) (K)

Blackout

Monitor Your Comprehension

PAUSE & REFLECT

With a partner, discuss why Cherdyakov's comments might be insulting to the general.

(I) FARCE

Reread lines 256–271. Why is it ridiculous for Cherdyakov to make an apology at this point in the play?

At this point an apology for the sneeze is ridiculous because Cherdyakov's behavior toward the general has become increasingly hostile and insulting.

(J) FARCE

Farce often includes **physical comedy** that adds to the the plot's ridiculous events. Why does the general finally lose his temper when Cherdyakov sneezes on him this time?

Possible answer: The general finally loses his temper with Cherdyakov because of all of the time he has wasted apologizing for what was an accidental, insignificant act. In the process, Cherdyakov has managed to irritate the general with his persistent, annoying attempts at apology.

(K) FARCE

Reread the Writer's comments in lines 284–293. What characteristics of farce—humorous conflict, exaggerated behavior or language, physical comedy—do these lines include?

Possible answer: Cherdyakov's lying down on the sofa and dying is an example of physical comedy.

Monitor Your Comprehension

IN OTHER WORDS Cherdyakov goes to see the general again. He complains that the lower classes—people like himself—are treated poorly by the upper classes—people like the general. The general angrily asks Cherdyakov what he wants. Cherdyakov starts to yell, but—surprisingly—he announces that he wants to apologize for the sneeze again. The general yells at Cherdyakov, and Cherdyakov sneezes his own name into the general's face.

► The second sneeze is more than the general can take. How does the general's reaction affect Cherdyakov? Discuss your answer with a partner.

Students should discuss that the general's reaction upsets Cherdyakov terribly, leaving him feeling beyond repair.

Text Analysis: Farce

Use the chart below to record examples of ridiculous or humorous conflict, exaggerated behavior or language, and physical comedy that appear in "The Sneeze." Refer to the notes you took while reading to help you identify three examples you can add to each column of this chart.

For this chart, answers will vary. See samples below.

Humorous Conflict	Exaggerated Behavior or Language	Physical Comedy
Cherdyakov's excessive apologies to the general (lines 72–96; lines 179–192); Cherdyakov's slow-motion reenactment of the sneeze (lines 99–113)	*Cherdyakov and his wife's overly-polite introduction at the theater (lines 24–56); the description of the first sneeze (lines 64–70); the general's abusive outburst (lines 272–275; lines 278–282)*	*the first sneeze (lines 64–70); Cherdyakov's slow-motion reenactment of the sneeze (lines 106–113); the second sneeze (lines 276–277); Cherdyakov's sudden death (lines 290–293)*

The playwright, Neil Simon, uses the characteristics of farce to make fun of something. What exactly does he seem to be mocking?

Possible answer: Simon uses farce to mock the human tendencies to blow events out of proportion and to misinterpret other people.

Reading Strategy: Visualize

Which scenes or characters in the play were you able to visualize most clearly? Think about how you might update this play for an audience today. Use your visualization skills to help you fill out the chart below.

For this chart, answers will vary. See samples below.

Elements of the Play	Visualizing an Update
Setting: *Where could the opening of the play be set, other than in the theater?*	***The opening could be set at a movie premiere in Hollywood.***
Main characters: *What kinds of jobs, costumes, and personalities would the general, Cherdyakov, the Writer, and the wives have today?*	***The general could be the director of the movie, Cherdyakov could be the assistant to the assistant to the director, the Writer could be the writer of the movie, and the wives could be professionals, such as doctors or teachers.***
Conflict: *How would you update the play to show a conflict between two different groups in today's society?*	***The language of the characters could be updated so that they use today's language. The conflict could be something as simple as the Cherdyakov character on accident parking his car in the general/director's parking space.***

Who makes you **LAUGH?**

What did you find funniest about "The Sneeze"? Why?

Answers will vary but should be supported by the text.

Academic Vocabulary in Writing

The word **attribute** (AT ruh byoot) is a noun that means *a quality or feature of someone or something.*

His loyalty to his friends was one of his best **attributes.**

WRITE IT Write a few sentences about the different **attributes** of Cherdyakov and the general. How do their personalities differ? Be sure to use the word **attribute** in your response.

Encourage students to use the Academic Vocabulary word in their responses.

Assessment Practice

DIRECTIONS Use "The Sneeze" to answer questions 1–6.

1 Cherdyakov's great passion in life is —

- (A) caring for trees and bushes
- (B) going to the theater
- (C) advancing his social position
- (D) sneezing on other people

2 Cherdyakov's sneeze creates a conflict because —

- (A) he is thrown out of the theater
- (B) the general refuses to forgive him
- (C) his wife fears he will lose his job
- (D) he cannot stop apologizing for it

3 Which element of farce is strongest in the stage directions that describe Cherdyakov's actions?

- (A) Physical comedy
- (B) Clever dialogue
- (C) Exaggerated language
- (D) Humorous conflict

4 Which of the following is an example of humorous exaggeration?

- (A) *This is a great honor for me, sir.* (line 25)
- (B) *I'm* sorry, *your Excellency! I'm so terribly sorry!* (line 72)
- (C) *The sneezer. The one who sneezed. The sneezing splatterer.* (lines 182–183)
- (D) *The [General's] cunning is equal only to his cruelty.* (lines 234–235)

5 Why does Cherdyakov return to the general's office a second time?

- (A) To invite the general and his wife to a play
- (B) To express his anger at being made a fool of by the general
- (C) To ask for a promotion in the Ministry of Public Parks
- (D) To apologize for sneezing on the general

6 The ending of the play is appropriate for a farce because —

- (A) the Writer tells the audience what happens
- (B) the main character loses his job
- (C) Cherdyakov's death is an exaggerated reaction
- (D) the conflict is not fully resolved

UNIT 9 Putting It in Context

HISTORY, CULTURE, AND THE AUTHOR

Be sure to read the Text Analysis Workshop on pages 918–923 in *Holt McDougal Literature*.

Academic Vocabulary for Unit 9

You will see these Academic Vocabulary words as you work through this book. You will also be asked to use them as you write and talk about the selections in this unit.

Contrast (kuhn TRAST) is a verb that means *to show differences between two things.*

Stephanie didn't want people to **contrast** her with her sister.

Name two colors that contrast with each other: *Answers will vary.* ______

______

Environment (en VY ruhn muhnt) is a noun that means *the conditions in which something exists.*

The cold **environment** in the lab helped preserve the samples.

Describe the natural environment of polar bears: *Answers will vary.* ______

______

Factor (FAK tuhr) is a noun that means *a thing or condition that helps produce a result.*

One **factor** in my decision to take Spanish was my upcoming trip to Mexico.

What is one factor that helps you decide whether to take a class? ______

Answers will vary. ______

Incorporate (in KOR puh rayt) is a verb that means *to take in or include as a part of something bigger.*

Mrs. Keller will **incorporate** fun games into her journalism class.

How can you incorporate new words into your vocabulary? *Answers will vary.*

______

Predominant (prih DOM uh nuhnt) is an adjective that means *most important* or *occurring most often.*

The **predominant** color of our plaid school uniform is red.

What is the predominant musical instrument in your favorite song? ______

Answers will vary. ______

Before Reading

from Angela's Ashes

Based on the memoir by Frank McCourt

How does FRIENDSHIP begin?

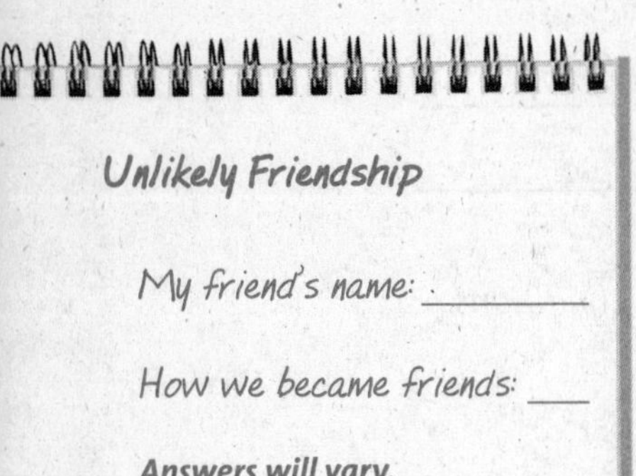

What makes two people connect? Something special often happens to turn a mere acquaintance into a friend. In his memoir *Angela's Ashes,* Frank McCourt describes two friendships that develop in an unusual situation.

WRITE IT Have you ever formed an unlikely friendship? Maybe it was with someone much older or much younger than you or just someone very different from you. Using the notepad on the left, write notes about your friend and how the friendship formed.

Text Analysis: Memoir

A **memoir** is a form of nonfiction writing. Memoir writers share their ideas about people and events from their own lives. Often, memoirs also show readers the influence of history and culture in people's lives. The chart below lists examples of historical and cultural factors that can affect a writer's work.

Historical Influences	
Politics • the Vietnam War	**Social Trends** • the women's movement
Economics • the Great Depression	**Environmental Change** • effects of pollution
Cultural Influences	
Ethnicity • being Mexican American	**Values/Beliefs** • following the Jewish faith
Technology • invention of the computer	**Arts/Entertainment** • country music

In this selection, McCourt recalls being hospitalized as a child. He suffered from typhoid (TY foyd), a life-threatening illness that was common in Ireland at the time. As you read, think about the impact of McCourt's hospital stay on his life. In addition, note what you learn about Irish history and culture.

Reading Skill: Use Allusions to Make Inferences

An **allusion** (uh LOO zhuhn) is a reference to a well-known person, place, event, or literary work. For example, a writer might refer to a strong character as having the strength of Hercules (HUR kyuh leez), a Greek hero famous for his strength. Writers use allusions

- to help characterize, or describe, people or situations
- to create ideas or feelings in the reader's mind
- to clarify or highlight important ideas, including the theme

As you read, you will be asked to notice allusions and make **inferences** (IN fuhr uhns iz), or guesses, about what they mean. See the chart below for an example.

Allusion	Significance	Inference
"It includes the first bit of Shakespeare I ever read. . . . it's like having jewels in my mouth when I say the lovely words." (lines 42–47)	Refers to William Shakespeare, famous English poet and playwright who lived around 400 years ago	Frank loves language and poetry.

Vocabulary in Context

Relapse (REE laps) is a noun that means *a worsening or new period of illness after some improvement.*

After Frank begins to recover, the nurse worries about a **relapse.**

Torrent (TAWR uhnt) is a noun that means *a sudden rush like a stream of water.*

Frank holds back his urge to cry a **torrent** of tears.

Perfidy (PUR fih dee) is a noun that means *disloyalty.*

Seamus earns Frank's trust and never shows **perfidy.**

Vocabulary Practice

Review the words and sample sentences above. Then, circle the word that is most nearly *opposite* in meaning to the given Vocabulary word.

1. **relapse:** (recovery) regret setback
2. **torrent:** river tornado (trickle)
3. **perfidy:** theft (faithfulness) anger

SET A PURPOSE FOR READING

Read this excerpt from *Angela's Ashes* to find out how a special friendship makes Frank McCourt's hospital stay more bearable.

Angela's Ashes

Based on the memoir by

FRANK McCOURT

BACKGROUND Frank McCourt grew up in a crowded Irish slum where serious diseases like typhoid fever and diphtheria (dif THIR ee uh) were common. Both diseases are easy to catch. In 1940s Ireland, sick people were kept in "fever hospitals," away from healthy people. The Roman Catholic Church ran most of these hospitals, and nuns cared for patients. McCourt caught typhoid fever when he was ten years old and was sent to a fever hospital.

Mam, my mother, comes with the doctor, and he examines me. When he's done, he picks me up and runs to his car. Mam runs after us. He tells her I have typhoid fever. Then, he rushes me to the Fever Hospital. I sleep a lot, and they stick tubes into my ankles and the back of my hand. Then they use the tubes to give me blood.

At first, everyone thinks I'm going to die, so they let Mam sit with me. The priest, Father Gorey, prays over me, and I sleep and sleep. Finally, Sister Rita smiles at me. "Oh," she says, "we're awake, are we? You've come through the worst. Our prayers are answered." Ⓐ

The room next to me is empty till one morning a girl's voice says, "Yoo hoo, boy with the typhoid, are you awake?"

"I am."

Ⓐ MEMOIR

McCourt chose to share this experience in a **memoir** because his illness and hospital stay were very important in his early life. What information is revealed in lines 1–11 that shows the seriousness of McCourt's illness? Underline the information.

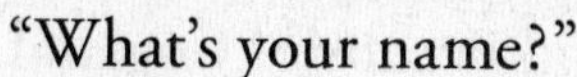

"What's your name?"

"Frank."

"My name is Patricia Madigan. How old are you?"

"Ten."

"Oh." She sounds disappointed.

"But I'll be eleven next month."

"Well, that's better than ten. I'll be fourteen in September." She tells me she is in the Fever Hospital with diphtheria and "something else," nobody knows what.

Soon Sister Rita lectures us about not talking between rooms. She says we should be saying the **rosary** and giving thanks for our recoveries.

She leaves and Patricia whispers, "Give thanks, Francis, and say your rosary." I laugh so hard the stern nurse runs in to see if I'm all right. She's not smiling. She scolds me for laughing and says, "No laughing because you'll damage your internal apparatus!"[1]

After she slowly plods out, Patricia whispers again in a heavy accent, "No laughing, Francis, and pray for your internal apparatus." PAUSE & REFLECT

IN OTHER WORDS The doctor examines Frank at home and then rushes him to the hospital. At first, everyone thinks Frank will die, but he starts to get better. One day, an older girl named Patricia starts talking with Frank. A stern nurse overhears them and tries to make them quit talking. Patricia makes fun of the nurse.

Mam visits me on Thursdays. She says my father is back at work at Rank's Flour Mills and "if it please God, this job will last a while with the war on and the English desperate for flour."

Patricia gives Seamus[2], the man who mops the floors, a book for me. It's a short history of England. Seamus tries to sing me a song, but the nurse makes him stop. "You know singing could lead to a **relapse**."

1. **internal apparatus** (ap uh RAT uhs): body organs, such as the heart and lungs.
2. **Seamus** (SHAY muhs).

Monitor Your Comprehension

VISUAL VOCABULARY
The **rosary** (ROH zuh ree) is a series of prayers repeated by Roman Catholics, usually counted off on a special string of beads as they are said. The word *rosary* also refers to the special string of beads itself.

PAUSE & REFLECT
Why do you think Sister Rita objects to Frank and Patricia talking to each other?

Possible answer: Sister Rita wants the children to focus on healing and on saying the rosary to give thanks for their recoveries.

VOCABULARY
The word **relapse** (REE laps) is a noun that means *a worsening or new period of illness after some improvement.*

Monitor Your Comprehension

VOCABULARY

The word **torrent** (TAWR uhnt) is a noun that means *a sudden rush like a stream of water.*

B ALLUSIONS

"The Highwayman" is a romantic, action-packed poem written by Alfred Noyes (noyz) in the early 20th century. Based on McCourt's allusion to this poem, what can you infer about how Patricia and Frank feel about being in the hospital? Write your inference in the third box below.

Allusion

"Patricia reads to me from 'The Highwayman' every day."

↓

Significance

"The Highwayman" is a romantic, action-packed poem.

↓

Inference

Possible answer: Patricia and Frank are bored during their hospital stay and look forward to the diversion and escape offered by the poetry and books that she reads aloud.

The book tells about the kings and queens of England. It includes the first bit of Shakespeare I ever read:

I do believe, induced by potent circumstances
That thou art mine enemy.

I don't know what it means, but it's like having jewels in my mouth when I say the lovely words.

Patricia reads to me from "The Highwayman" every day:

The wind was a ***torrent*** *of darkness among the gusty trees,*
The moon was a ghostly galleon tossed upon cloudy seas, . . .

I can't wait to learn what happens to the highwayman and the landlord's red-lipped daughter. I love the poem because it's exciting and almost as good as my two lines of Shakespeare. **B**

Patricia's ready to read the last few verses when in comes the nurse shouting at us. "I told ye there was to be no talking between rooms. Diphtheria is never allowed to talk to typhoid and visa versa." And she makes Seamus take me upstairs.

IN OTHER WORDS Patricia gets Seamus to deliver a book to Frank. She begins reading him the "The Highwayman," a poem about two doomed lovers—a robber and an innkeeper's daughter.

► Underline the sentences that tell you why Patricia is not able to finish reading the poem to Frank.

Seamus whispers, "I'm sorry, Frankie," as he hides the book under my shirt and lifts me from the bed.

Sister Rita stops us to say I'm a great disappointment to her and that I'll have plenty of time to think about my sins in the big ward upstairs and I should beg God's forgiveness for my disobedience reciting a pagan English poem about a thief on a horse when I could have been praying.

There are twenty beds in the ward, all white, all empty. The nurse tells Seamus to put me at the far end of the ward to make sure I don't talk to anyone, which is very unlikely since there isn't another soul on this whole floor. She tells me this was the fever ward during the Great Famine[3] long ago. She says,

3. **Great Famine:** a time when potato crops failed in 1845–1847. About one million people in Ireland starved to death as a result.

Monitor Your Comprehension

"'Twould break your heart to think of what the English did to us, no pity at all for the little children with their mouths all green from trying to eat the grass, God bless us and save us." (C)

The nurse takes my temperature. "'Tis up a bit. Have a good sleep for yourself now that you're away from the chatter with Patricia Madigan below who will never know a gray hair." (D)

Nurses and nuns never think you know what they're talking about. You can't show you understood that Patricia is going to die. You can't show you want to cry over this girl who taught you a lovely poem which the nun says is bad.

IN OTHER WORDS In the upstairs ward, Frank is alone in a large room. The nun Sister Rita tells him he should be sorry for his sin of talking to Patricia. Then, she says that Patricia will never grow old enough to have gray hair. Frank knows that she means Patricia is going to die.

Seamus tells me the nurse is a right ol' witch for running to Sister Rita and telling her about the poem going between the two rooms. "Anyway, Frankie, you'll be outa here one of these fine days," he says, "and you can read all the poetry you want though I don't know about Patricia below, I don't know about Patricia. . . ."

He knows about Patricia in two days because she collapsed and died in the bathroom. There are tears on his cheeks when he says, "She told me she was sorry she had you reciting that poem and getting you shifted from the room, Frankie. She said 'twas all her fault."

"It wasn't, Seamus."

"I know and didn't I tell her that."

Patricia is gone and now I'll never know what happened to the highwayman and Bess, the landlord's daughter. Seamus encourages me to read my history of the English and learn about their **perfidy**. But neither of us knows what that word really means. He says he'll ask the men in his local pub about the poem, and he'll bring it back to me.

I can't sleep because I imagine people in the other beds all dying and green around their mouths and moaning for soup, any soup. I cover my face with the pillow hoping they won't come and stand around the bed howling for bits of my chocolate bar.

(C) MEMOIR

Reread lines 65–72. What do the nurse's comments tell you about the Great Famine? What do they tell you about Ireland's relationship with England? Share your thoughts with a partner.

Students should discuss that her comments tell the reader that during the Great Famine many people in Ireland went hungry and became sick. Her comments also indicate that the Irish and the English did not have a good relationship at the time as the English did not help feed the Irish, even when young children went hungry.

(D) LANGUAGE COACH

People from different regions and social groups have their own **dialect,** or way of speaking, that includes the words they use and how they pronounce them. In lines 70 and 73, the nurse uses the contractions *'twould*, meaning "it would," and *'tis*, meaning "it is." These contractions are not common in U.S. English, but they are part of the nurse's Irish dialect. You'll come across a similar contraction in Seamus's speech in lines 82–89. When you do, circle it.

VOCABULARY

The word **perfidy** (PUR fih dee) is a noun that means *disloyalty.*

Why do you think Seamus would accuse the English of *perfidy* without knowing exactly what the word means?

Possible answer: Seamus may know that the word has a negative connotation, which is enough for him to apply it to the English since the Irish and the English have a hostile relationship.

Monitor Your Comprehension

I can't have any more visitors. Sister Rita says that after my bad behavior with Patricia and that poem I can't have the privilege anymore. She says I'll be going home in a few weeks and I must think only about getting better.

I don't want to be in this empty ward with ghosts of children and no Patricia and no highwayman and no red-lipped landlord's daughter. (E)

(E) ALLUSIONS
The "ghosts of children" mentioned in lines 106–107 are the starving famine victims that McCourt imagines. Why do you think McCourt included allusions to the Great Famine?

Possible answer: McCourt includes allusions to the Great Famine to show that these events haunted him as a child and continued to affect Ireland during his childhood.

IN OTHER WORDS Two days later, Frank hears that Patricia has died. Before she dies, she apologizes for getting Frank in trouble. Frank has a hard time sleeping in the big empty room that was once full of starving people. He wonders what happens at the end of "The Highwayman."

Seamus says he knows a man who knows all the verses of the highwayman poem. [Seamus can't read, so he has carried me the poem in his head. He stands in the middle of the ward leaning on his mop. Seamus recites how Bess warned the highwayman by shooting herself dead with a redcoat's musket and how the highwayman returns for revenge only to be shot down by the redcoats.]

Blood-red were his spurs in the golden noon; wine-red was his velvet coat,
When they shot him down on the highway,
Down like a dog on the highway,
And he lay in his blood on the highway, with a bunch of lace at his throat.

Seamus wipes his sleeve across his face and sniffles. He says, "'Tis a very sad story and when I said it to my wife she cried all evening. Now if you want to know any more poems, Frankie, tell me and I'll get them from the pub and bring 'em back in my head." (F)

(F) MEMOIR
With a partner, discuss the relationship that Frank and Seamus have formed. Why, looking back years later, would McCourt write about the man who cleaned the floors at the hospital?

Students should discuss that McCourt remembers Seamus because they became friends while McCourt was in the hospital. Seamus would bring things, such as books, to McCourt from Patricia. Also, since McCourt was forbidden to have visitors by Sister Rita, Seamus was likely the only contact he had with people aside from the nurses during the end of his stay.

IN OTHER WORDS Seamus says that someone he knows told him the end of the poem "The Highwayman."

► How does Frank finally hear the end of the poem? Put brackets [ ] around the sentences that tell you.

Text Analysis: Memoir

In *Angela's Ashes*, Frank McCourt shares personal experiences from his youth. These experiences and his thoughts about them were influenced by history and culture. Fill in the chart below with historical and cultural events and ideas that influenced McCourt. Look back at the chart on page 362 for examples. Note: If you think there is no information from the selection to add to a box, explain your thinking.

For this chart, answers will vary. See samples below.

Historical Influences	
Politics • *the Great Famine*	**Social Trends** • *keeping people sick with typhoid fever and diphtheria in "fever hospitals"*
Economics • *growing up in a crowded Irish slum*	**Environmental Change** • *no information from the selection—The selection does not discuss the effects of environmental changes on Ireland or McCourt.*
Cultural Influences	
Ethnicity • *no information from the selection—The selection does not discuss the ethnicity of McCourt or the other people he describes.*	**Values/Beliefs** • *being Roman Catholic*
Technology • *no information from the selection—The selection does not discuss technology.*	**Arts/Entertainment** • *reading books about the history of England and poetry by Alfred Noyes ("The Highwayman")*

Review your completed chart and the notes you took while reading. Then, with a classmate or in a small group, talk about how McCourt's hospital stay may have affected his life. Finally, discuss what you learned about Irish history and culture.

After Reading

Reading Skill: Use Allusions to Make Inferences

In the chart below, list three allusions to Catholicism, such as Catholic religious practices or the beliefs and behaviors of priests or nuns, that appear in the selection. What do you think is McCourt's view of the Catholic Church and its influence on Irish society in the 1940s? Explain your answer.

For this chart, answers will vary. See samples below.

Allusions		McCourt's View of Church Influence
1. *"The priest, Father Gorey, prays over me ... Finally, Sister Rita smiles at me. ... You've come through the worst. Our prayers are answered." (lines 8–11)*	→	*McCourt implies that people are both nourished and confined by the Church, especially by the authoritative nuns.*
2. *"Soon Sister Rita lectures us about not talking between rooms. She says we should be saying the rosary and giving thanks for our recoveries." (lines 24–26)*	→	
3. *"Sister Rita stops us to say ... I should beg God's forgiveness for my disobedience reciting a pagan English poem ... when I could have been praying." (lines 60–64)*	→	

How does FRIENDSHIP begin?

How can a friendship end? List some possible ways below.

Answers will vary, but students may recognize that many friendships end when people are separated by circumstances.

Vocabulary Practice

Place brackets [ ] around the answer that best completes each sentence.

1. Experiencing a **relapse** of the flu usually means that [(a)] you will be sick for a little longer, **(b)** you have caught the measles, **(c)** it is time to go back to school.
2. A **torrent** of water would most likely be produced by **(a)** a leaky faucet, [(b)] a large rain cloud, **(c)** a spray bottle.
3. A friend's **perfidy** might make you **(a)** invite the friend to a party, [(b)] feel angry and betrayed, **(c)** read a comic book.

Academic Vocabulary in Speaking

The word **predominant** (prih DOM uh nuhnt) is an adjective that means *most important* or *occurring most often.*

When everyone saw Leslie after she got her waist-length hair cut very short, "Wow!" was the **predominant** reaction.

TURN AND TALK With a partner, discuss the "fever hospital" where Frank stayed. What are its characteristics? What are the **predominant** differences between it and hospitals in the United States today? Be sure to use the word **predominant** in your conversation.

Encourage students to use the Academic Vocabulary word in their discussions.

Assessment Practice

DIRECTIONS Use the excerpt from *Angela's Ashes* to answer questions 1–6.

1 Why does Father Gorey pray over Frank at the beginning of the excerpt?

- (A) Because Frank is not Catholic
- (B) Because Mam asked him to
- (C) Because Frank is not expected to live
- (D) Because Father Gorey wants to keep an eye on the tubes giving Frank blood

2 The tone of lines 32–34 is —

- (A) serious because Frank needs to be reminded of the rules
- (B) boring because Patricia is just repeating Sister Rita's words
- (C) confusing because laughing usually helps sick people
- (D) humorous because Patricia is mimicking Sister Rita

3 What can the reader infer about Frank's father from lines 35–37?

- (A) He does not always work regularly.
- (B) He is an expert flour miller.
- (C) He will soon be volunteering for military duty.
- (D) He is an Englishman.

4 The reference to Shakespeare in lines 42–47 is an allusion because it —

- (A) helps the reader understand the kings and queens of England
- (B) helps Frank remember who wrote "The Highwayman"
- (C) includes two lines that do not rhyme
- (D) refers to a well-known English writer

5 What effect did the friendship with Patricia have on Frank's life?

- (A) It brought excitement into Frank's lonely world.
- (B) It taught him how important it was to obey the nuns.
- (C) It meant that he wasn't afraid of dying.
- (D) It kept him from being bored even though he wasn't interested in poetry.

6 The poem "The Highwayman" is similar to this excerpt in that —

- (A) both are sad because of unfortunate deaths
- (B) both are poems that tell a story
- (C) both were written in the 1940s
- (D) both deal with Irish history

American History

Based on the short story by **Judith Ortiz Cofer**

When do **WORLD EVENTS** hit home?

Once in a while, something tragic happens that makes people stop everything. The following story takes place on November 22, 1963, when the assassination, or murder, of President John F. Kennedy stunned an entire nation.

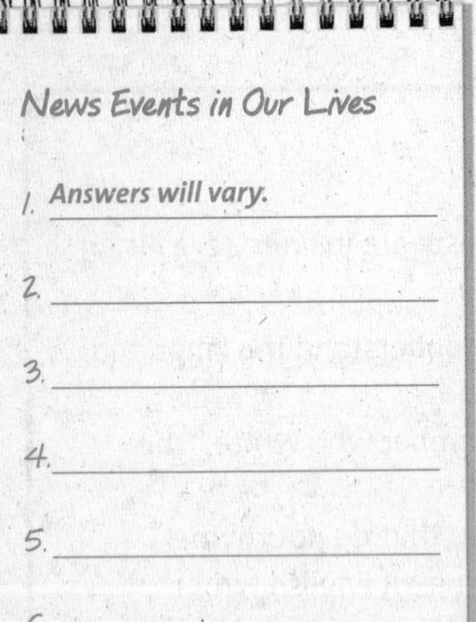

WRITE IT What news story really shocked you when you first heard it? Survey five classmates to find out what news event stands out most clearly in their memories. Record your results at left. What kinds of events have the strongest effect on people? Write your response on the lines below.

Answers will vary.

Text Analysis: Influence of Author's Background

An **author's background**—that is, the writer's life experiences and culture—shapes his or her perspective on the world and influences what he or she writes. For example, Judith Ortiz Cofer was born in Puerto Rico but moved at a young age to Paterson, New Jersey. There, her family lived in a large apartment building known by its residents as *El Building*. However, when her father was on active duty with the U.S. Navy, her mother would take the family back to Puerto Rico to live with their grandmother. Her father wanted her to adopt American ways, while her mother tried to get her to hold on to Puerto Rican customs. As you read the story, look for the following details:

- references to places Cofer probably lived or visited
- characters whose beliefs, values, or heritage remind you of this description of Cofer's background
- events and circumstances that are similar to Cofer's own life experiences described above

Reading Strategy: Connect

Good readers **connect** what they know from their own experience to what they are reading in order to better understand the text. As you read "American History," connect your own life experiences to what you find in the story—the characters' situations, actions, and feelings. Here is an example:

Detail from Story	Connection	Better Understanding
Elena is called "Skinny Bones." (lines 2–4)	*I've been called names sometimes. It made me unhappy and depressed.*	*I know that Elena feels sad and picked on.*

Vocabulary in Context

Note: Words are listed in the order in which they appear in the story.

Maneuvering (muh NOO ver ing) is a noun that means *acting carefully to achieve a goal.*

Because of her planning and **maneuvering,** Elena managed to catch a glimpse of Eugene walking to school.

Distraught (dis TRAWT) is an adjective that means *very upset.*

Many people in the country were **distraught** when they heard about the death of President Kennedy.

Resigned (rih ZYND) is an adjective that means *accepting something that cannot be avoided.*

Elena's mother was **resigned** about Elena's plans and decided to let her daughter go out anyway.

Dilapidated (dih LAP ih day tid) is an adjective that means *broken down and shabby.*

The neighborhood, which was filled with old, abandoned buildings, was **dilapidated** and run-down.

Vocabulary Practice

Circle the choice that best fits each Vocabulary word's meaning.

1. **maneuvering** **a.** walking on a path **b.** skating through a crowd
2. **distraught** **a.** losing a beloved pet **b.** missing a favorite show
3. **resigned** **a.** shrugging sadly **b.** protesting angrily
4. **dilapidated** **a.** an elegant new mansion **b.** an old shack

SET A PURPOSE FOR READING
Read "American History" to learn how a young girl's life is changed by an important event in American history.

American History

Based on the short story by
JUDITH ORTIZ COFER

BACKGROUND In this story, fourteen-year-old Elena describes her experiences on the day President John F. Kennedy was killed. As the author did in real life, Elena and her family live in El Building, a large, noisy apartment building filled with other Puerto Rican families. John Fitzgerald Kennedy (1917–1963) was shot to death on November 22, 1963, after less than three years in office.

It was a cold gray day in Paterson, New Jersey, and I was at P.E., feeling miserable and cold. "Hey, Skinny Bones, pump it, girl," Gail yelled. "Didn't you eat your rice and beans and pork chops for breakfast today?"

I could not manage to twirl my end of the jump rope in time with Gail. The chill was entering my bones, making me cry, humiliating and shaming me. I hated the city, especially in winter. I hated Public School Number 13, and I hated my skinny, flat-chested body.

Seeing Eugene was the one source of beauty and light that school year. In August, Eugene and his family had moved into the only house on the block that had a yard. I could see into their kitchen and backyard from my window in El Building. Eugene was tall and blond, and he wore glasses. I liked him right away because he sat at the kitchen table and read books for hours. (A)

Once school started, I looked for him in all my classes, but P.S. 13 was a huge, crowded place. It took me days to find out

(A) AUTHOR'S BACKGROUND
Reread the first three paragraphs of this story. Underline the words, phrases, or sentences that remind you of Cofer's own life.

that Eugene was in honors classes. I was a straight-A student, but I couldn't take honors classes because English was not my first language. After much **maneuvering**, planning and trying out various routes from one place to another, I managed to "run into him" in the hallway, but we never spoke. Finally, on the way home one day, I blurted out, "You're Eugene. Right?" I was scared, but he smiled and nodded. In the following weeks, we walked home together.

IN OTHER WORDS Elena is unhappy about a lot of things. The one thing that makes her happy is watching her neighbor, Eugene. She has a crush on him and soon finds a way to talk to him.

My father had a good job at the blue jeans factory in a nearby town. Soon, he kept telling us, we would move to a house there. Every Sunday we drove out of the city to the suburbs where children made snowmen from pure white snow. It wasn't like the gray slush of Paterson, which seemed to fall from the sky in that color. I listened to my parents' dreams, spoken in Spanish, like their stories about life in Puerto Rico before I was born. My dreams were about going to college and becoming a teacher. B

Eugene's family had come from Georgia. The kids at school called him "the Hick" and made fun of the way he talked. "Skinny Bones and the Hick" was what they called us when we were together.

On the day that President Kennedy was shot, Mr. DePalma asked us to line up in front of him. He was the science teacher and PE coach, and he handled the school's troublemakers. We were shocked to see he was crying. Someone giggled behind me.

"Listen," Mr. DePalma said. His voice broke, and he covered his face with his hands. "Listen," he repeated, "something awful has happened." He turned and spat on the cement. There was a lot of laughter. "The president is dead, you idiots. I should have known that wouldn't mean anything to a bunch of losers like you kids." He shrieked, "Go home." No one moved for a minute; then we all scrambled to get out of there. PAUSE & REFLECT

VOCABULARY

The word **maneuvering** (muh NOO ver ing) is a noun that means *acting carefully to achieve a goal.*

Underline the clues in the text that hint at the meaning of the word *maneuvering.*

B AUTHOR'S BACKGROUND

Reread lines 26–33. Underline the words, phrases, or sentences that remind you of Cofer's own life.

PAUSE & REFLECT

Do you think Mr. DePalma is too hard on his students? Do you think the students react in a proper way? Discuss these questions with a partner.

Students may discuss that while Mr. DePalma's behavior is not acceptable, he is clearly upset by the news of the president's death. The students do not know how to respond to seeing Mr. DePalma crying.

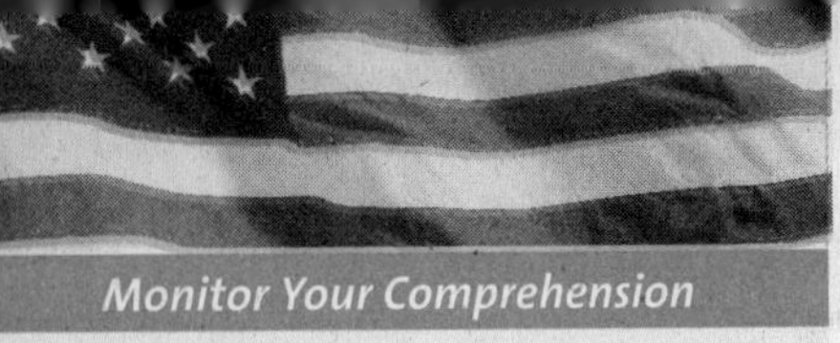

Monitor Your Comprehension

CONNECT

Reread lines 38–53. Then think of some personal experiences that connect to these events. How do your experiences help you better understand the text?

Connection
Answers will vary.

↓

Better Understanding
Answers will vary.

VOCABULARY

The word **distraught** (dis TRAWT) is an adjective that means *very upset.*

Circle the words or phrases that tell you Elena's mother is *distraught.*

VOCABULARY

The word **resigned** (rih ZYND) is an adjective that means *accepting something that cannot be avoided.*

VOCABULARY

The word **dilapidated** (dih LAP ih day tid) is an adjective that means *broken down and shabby.*

As I headed home there was an eerie, strange feeling on the streets. There were no horns blasting that day. There was silence in El Building. No music came from open doors. I found my mother sitting in front of our television. She looked at me with a tear-streaked face and said: "Dios mio."[1] I went into my room.

IN OTHER WORDS **The president of the United States is shot and killed. Mr. DePalma tries to announce the news, but he has trouble telling students that the president is dead. Not knowing what has happened, the students laugh. Finally, Mr. DePalma shouts that the president is dead and sends them home.**

► Underline the sentence that shows how Elena's mother responds to the news about the president.

I wanted to feel the right thing about President Kennedy's death, but I felt happy because I was going to visit Eugene. He had asked me to study for an American history test with him.

I got my books together. When I went in to tell my mother that I was going to a friend's house to study, I did not expect her reaction.

"You are going out *today?* The president has been killed. We must show respect. He was a great man. Come to church with me tonight." I wanted to comfort her because she seemed so **distraught**, so upset, but I had to meet Eugene.

"I have a test to study for, Mama. I will be home by eight," I said.

"You are forgetting who you are," Mama said. "I have seen you staring down at that boy's house. You are heading for humiliation and pain." She spoke in Spanish in a **resigned** tone that surprised me. It was as if she had given up and did not plan to stop me from "heading for humiliation and pain."

I walked around the chain-link fence that separated our shabby, **dilapidated** apartment building from Eugene's house. His door was painted deep green, *verde*—the color of hope. Moments after my knock, the door opened and the red, swollen

1. ***Dios mio*** (DEE os MEE oh): Spanish for "my God."

face of a woman appeared. She had a **halo** of red hair floating over a delicate white face. PAUSE & REFLECT

IN OTHER WORDS Elena wants to feel sad about the president's death, but Eugene has asked her to study with him. She tells her mother that she's going, but her mother asks her to go to church instead. Elena goes to Eugene's house anyway.

"What do you want?" The woman's voice sounded sweet, like a little girl's, but her tone was not friendly.

"I'm Eugene's friend. He asked me over. To study." I said.

"You live there?" She pointed up to El Building, which looked like a gray prison.

"Yes. I do."

She looked at me for a couple of heartbeats, then said, as if to herself, "I don't know how you people do it." Then directly to me she said, "Listen. Honey. Eugene doesn't want to study with you. He is a smart boy. Doesn't need help. You understand me. I am truly sorry if he said you could come over. He cannot study with you. It's nothing personal. You understand? We won't be in this place much longer, no need for him to get close to people. It'll just make it harder for him later. Run back home now."

I stood there in shock, unable to move.

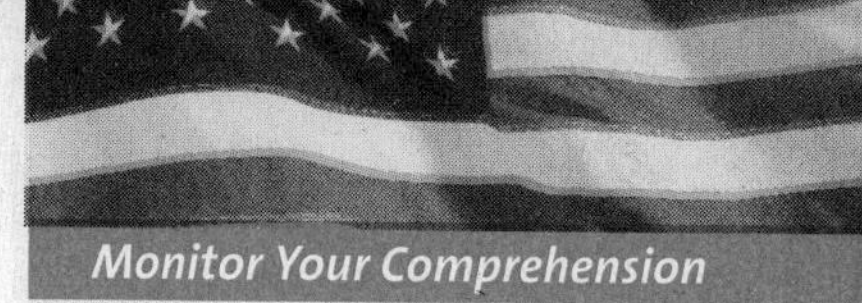

Monitor Your Comprehension

VISUAL VOCABULARY

A **halo** (HAY loh) is a circle of light around someone's head. In religious images, angels and saints are often given halos.

PAUSE & REFLECT

Why are Eugene's mother's eyes red and her face swollen?

Possible answer: She has been crying over the news about President Kennedy.

Monitor Your Comprehension

E LANGUAGE COACH
Working with a partner, reread lines 83–94 aloud. Focus especially on the punctuation and **dialogue,** or the words that Eugene's mother speaks. Practice reading it aloud to each other until you feel that your **tone,** or expression, and **pace,** or speed, are correct.

F CONNECT
Reread lines 77–100. Then think of some personal experiences that connect to these events. How do your experiences help you better understand the text?

Connection

Possible answer: I have been caught off guard by an adult I do not know well and told that my behavior was inappropriate.

↓

Better Understanding

Possible answer: I understand the shock and frustration that Elena feels having been in a similar, seemingly innocent, situation.

"Didn't you hear what I said?" She seemed very angry, and I finally snapped out of my trance. As I turned away from the green door I heard her close it gently. E

That night I lay in my bed trying to feel the right thing for our dead president, but my tears were only for me. Sometime during the night, I went to my window and pressed my face to the glass. Looking up at the streetlight, I could see the white snow falling like a lace veil over its face. I did not look down to see it turning gray as it touched the ground below. F

IN OTHER WORDS Eugene's mother finds out that Elena lives in El Building. She says that Eugene doesn't want to study with her and that he doesn't need help with school. Elena is stunned. She goes home and cries.

► Circle the words that give you some clues about how Elena feels at the end of the story.

Text Analysis: Influence of Author's Background

Review the background information about Judith Ortiz Cofer on pages 372 and 374. Then review the notes you took while reading "American History." In the chart, list three facts from Cofer's background and some specific details from the story that reflect those facts.

For this chart, answers will vary. See samples below.

Fact from the Author's Background	Story Detail(s) That Reflect This Fact
Cofer moved with her family from Puerto Rico to Paterson, New Jersey.	*The story is set on a winter's day in Paterson, New Jersey.*
Cofer's family lived in an apartment building known as El Building.	*The main character, Elena, lives in an apartment building called* El Building.
Cofer's mother wanted to hold onto Puerto Rican customs.	*In the story, Elena's mother speaks Spanish to her.*

Why do you think Judith Ortiz Cofer decided to include some personal experiences and details in her short story?

Possible answer: Cofer included details from her own background to help shape the perspective of the main character Elena.

When do WORLD EVENTS hit home?

Think about the title of this story: "American History." Some history has little or nothing to do with our lives. But some events touch our lives and change our world. In this story, how does the killing of President Kennedy affect Elena's life? If the president hadn't been killed, do you think her day would have ended differently? Explain.

Answers will vary but should reflect an understanding of the events described in the selection.

After Reading

Reading Strategy: Connect

Recall the connections you made while reading this story. What were some of your strongest connections, and how did they help you understand the story better? Use the chart to record your responses.

For this chart, answers will vary. See samples below.

Details from the Story
President Kennedy was shot and killed on November 22, 1963.

Connections to My Own Experiences
Answers will vary.

My Better Understanding of the Story Based on Those Experiences
Answers will vary.

Vocabulary Practice

Based on your knowledge of the blue Vocabulary words, answer the following questions. Work with a partner, and explain each of your responses.

Encourage students to use the Vocabulary words in their responses.

1. Why would you not want to own a **dilapidated** car?
2. What kind of **maneuvering** would a driver do to fit a large car into a small parking space?
3. How might a **resigned** person sit in a chair?
4. What kind of experience might make a person feel **distraught**?

Academic Vocabulary in Speaking

The word **environment** (en VY ruhn muhnt) is a noun that means *the conditions in which something exists.*

Changes to the **environment** have had a major effect on the birds and animals in this forest.

The word **incorporate** (in KOR puh rayt) is a verb that means *to take in or include as a part of something bigger.*

The club organizers decided to **incorporate** all of the school groups that were doing volunteer work.

TURN AND TALK How does the **environment** in which this story takes place—Paterson, New Jersey—influence the plot of "American History"? Did Cofer's decision to **incorporate** details about her community into the story make her writing more effective? Discuss these questions with a partner.

Encourage students to use the Academic Vocabulary words in their discussions.

Assessment Practice

DIRECTIONS Use "American History" to answer questions 1–4.

1 Which of the following reflects the author's background?

- (A) Eugene speaks with a Southern accent.
- (B) Elena's family is from Puerto Rico.
- (C) Elena puts on pink lipstick.
- (D) Eugene's mother is a nurse.

2 Elena's "one source of beauty and light" is —

- (A) jumping rope on the school playground
- (B) reading books by the window
- (C) watching television with her mother
- (D) watching Eugene at his kitchen table

3 Why does it take Elena days to find Eugene at school?

- (A) Eugene is in honors classes, unlike Elena.
- (B) Eugene doesn't attend the same school.
- (C) Eugene is so shy that he has been hiding.
- (D) Eugene is in a different grade than Elena.

4 Which aspect of Puerto Rican culture is expressed in the story?

- (A) Deep respect for the dead
- (B) Belief in an afterlife
- (C) Love of flowers and gardens
- (D) Children's obedience to elders

Special Report

Magazine Article

Background

This article, written 40 years after President John F. Kennedy was killed, discusses the nation's feelings about Kennedy and his death. Many people today still have strong memories of his time as president and the shock of his assassination.

Standards Focus: Identify Controlling Idea

The **controlling idea** of an expository text determines the information the writer includes and how the writer develops and organizes details. For the reader, the controlling idea is the text's most important point.

Here are some tips to help you identify the controlling idea of a magazine article:

- Preview the first paragraph or two of the article. Sometimes the controlling idea will be stated at the beginning. More often, though it will be revealed over the course of the article.
- Identify which details in each paragraph are more important and which are less important.
- Try to state the key idea of each paragraph in your own words. When you consider the key ideas together, they should suggest the controlling idea of the article as a whole.

As you read, you can keep track of details and key ideas in a chart like the one below.

Paragraph	Important Details	Key Idea
1	*After 9/11, many Americans visited the JFK Library and Museum . . .*	*Kennedy was a strong and skillful leader during difficult times.*

SET A PURPOSE FOR READING

Read the article to learn more about how the death of President John F. Kennedy affected the nation.

BY KENNETH T. WALSH

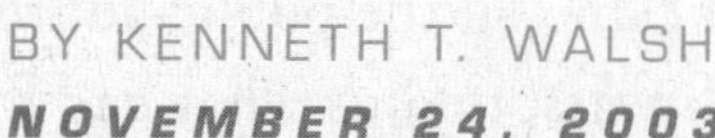

In the days immediately after 9/11,[1] Americans in large numbers showed up at the John F. Kennedy Library and Museum in Boston, apparently looking for strength and hope at a time of national peril and sorrow. They were drawn in particular to a film recounting the Cuban missile crisis, when Kennedy guided the nation through a confrontation[2] with the Soviet Union that could easily have led to nuclear war. Many visitors seemed comforted by the idea that prudent leadership and common sense could make all the difference, even in the worst of times.

1. **9/11:** This date refers to terrorist attacks on the United States on September 11, 2001.
2. **confrontation** (kon fruhn TAY shuhn): an open or direct clash between two forces or ideas.

The fact that Kennedy still has such a hold on America's imagination comes as no surprise to historians and other observers of popular culture. This connection will become even more apparent in the coming weeks as the nation marks the 40th anniversary of his assassination, on Nov. 22, 1963. (A)

Yet the reasons for his mystique[3] are less clear. The fact that he was assassinated in the prime of life goes only so far in explaining it. President William McKinley, another popular leader, was murdered in 1901, but his death generated no vast outpouring of emotion and no enduring sense of a lost legacy. In contrast, millions of Americans still recall where they were when they heard that Kennedy had been shot. (I was attending history class at St. Rose High School in Belmar, N.J., when the principal came on the public-address system and, choking back tears, told us what had happened. Everyone marched to our nearby church, and we spent the next few hours praying for the president's survival and, a bit later, his soul.) (B)

We all seem to have vivid memories of his funeral, carried on live television, with those unforgettable images of his grieving widow and his young son saluting smartly when his father's **cortege** passed by.

"Kennedy is frozen in our memory at age 46," says historian Robert Dallek, author of *An Unfinished Life: John F. Kennedy 1917–1963*. "People don't realize that this past May 29 he would have been 86 years of age."

3. **mystique** (mis TEEK): air of reverence surrounding someone or something.

(A) CONTROLLING IDEA
Reread lines 11–16. Based on these lines, what can you guess will be the **controlling idea** of this article?

Possible answer: The continued hold that Kennedy has on the American imagination.

(B) CONTROLLING IDEA
Reread lines 17–30. Circle the sentence in this paragraph that states the paragraph's topic. How would you rewrite the sentence as a question?

Possible answer: Why has Kennedy continued to be so popular with Americans?

As you continue reading, look for the answer to the question and consider how it relates to the article's controlling idea.

VISUAL VOCABULARY
A **cortege** (kor TEZJH) is a line of people or vehicles moving in a formal procession, such as for a funeral.

IN OTHER WORDS Although he has been dead for many years, President Kennedy still appeals to many Americans. After 9/11, many people remembered his leadership. Many people still think of Kennedy as a young man; his image as a young man is frozen in time.

▶ With a partner, discuss why President Kennedy is still so popular, according to the article.

Students should discuss that Kennedy continues to be so popular, in part, because he was killed during the prime of his life. Additionally, his funeral was broadcast live on television.

Some deft PR by the White House helped to create his charismatic aura in the first place. He and his advisers quickly grasped the power of the new medium of television, and the handsome, eloquent young leader quickly mastered it and went on to convey an image of optimism and charm that still surrounds him today. His performances at live press conferences are remembered as tours de force.[4] His speeches are used as brilliant examples of political communication. And if his legislative record fell short, his ideas about ending the Cold War and achieving racial equality at home, at least under the law, eventually took root and became reality. Ⓒ

Further, his glamorous wife, Jacqueline, reinforced the exciting image of Camelot, especially in contrast to his solid but dull predecessor, Dwight Eisenhower. Ike had been the oldest man to serve as president up until that time; Kennedy was the youngest ever elected to the office. The White House never let anyone forget it.

"One of the things President Kennedy did was instill in the American people the idea they could make a difference," says Deborah Leff, director of the Kennedy Library and Museum. ". . . It was a time when you saw America striving to be its best."

4. **tours de force** (toor duh FORS): a French term meaning feats of unusual skill.

Ⓒ CONTROLLING IDEA
Reread lines 39–50. What does the author say about the relationship between Kennedy and television? Write your answers in the chart below.

IMPORTANT DETAILS:
Possible answer: the handsome, eloquent young leader quickly mastered the television; Kennedy's performances at live press conferences are remembered as tours de force; Kennedy's speeches are used as examples of political communication

↓

KEY IDEA:
Possible answer: Kennedy used television as a powerful medium through which to communicate with the American people; it communicated a sense of optimism and charm about him.

D CONTROLLING IDEA
How do the quotations in lines 57–66 support the controlling idea of the article?

Possible answer: The quotations support the controlling idea of Kennedy's hold on the American people. They demonstrate that Kennedy convinced Americans that they could make a difference during an era when the country was striving to be its best.

For his part, Kennedy said in one of his famous speeches, at American University on June 10, 1963: "No problem of human destiny is beyond human beings. Man's reason and spirit have often solved the seemingly unsolvable—and we believe they can do it again." D

The tragic Kennedy mythology was reinforced when his brother Robert was assassinated in 1968 and, later, when his son, John F. Kennedy Jr., died in a plane crash in 1999. All of this perpetuated the idea that the Kennedys, despite all their advantages, were not immune from life's calamities. This deepened their connection to the rest of us.

Yet Kennedy governed prior to the age of cynicism[5] brought on by the Vietnam War, the Watergate scandal, and the wrenching social changes of the past four decades (including, of course, his own assassination). Perhaps not even Kennedy could have emerged from this era unscathed[6] had he lived and remained in public life.

5. **cynicism** (SIN ih siz uhm): a negative attitude; a general distrust of what others say or believe.
6. **unscathed** (un SKAYTHD): unharmed.

"The sudden end to Kennedy's life and presidency has left us with tantalizing 'might have beens,'" Dallek writes. "Yet even setting these aside and acknowledging some missed opportunities and false steps, it must be acknowledged that the Kennedy thousand days spoke to the country's better angels,[7] inspired visions of a less divisive nation and world, and demonstrated that America was still the last best hope of mankind." It is a legacy any president would be proud of. PAUSE & REFLECT

PAUSE & REFLECT
What does this article add to your understanding of how the death of President Kennedy affected the nation? Explain.

Possible answer: Kennedy's death, like that of his brother and son, deepened a connection with regular Americans, reminding us that in spite of their privileges, the Kennedy family was not safe from life's calamities. Additionally, the abrupt end to JFK's life left many wondering what he might have accomplished.

IN OTHER WORDS Kennedy knew how to make himself look good to Americans. He was a talented speaker and had ideas that people respected. The Kennedy family's tragedies reminded people that in some ways the Kennedys were just like everyone else. But people today are more critical of their elected officials and other leaders. Kennedy might not be admired as much if he'd lived through the last four decades. Even so, his legacy lives on.

7. **spoke to the country's better angels**: appealed to Americans' good and moral side.

Practicing Your Skills: Identify Controlling Idea

Look back at the notes you made as you read "Special Report." Fill in the chart below, and then use the chart to help you complete the sentence starter.

For this chart, answers will vary. See samples below.

Paragraph	Important Details	Key Idea
1	After 9/11, many Americans visited the JFK Library and Museum . . .	Kennedy was a strong and skillful leader during difficult times.
2–3	*Kennedy's influence on the American people will be evident during the weeks marking the 40th anniversary of his death.*	*Kennedy continues to impact the American imagination.*
4–5	*People clearly remember images from his funeral—his grieving widow and his son saluting his casket.*	*The nation's memory of Kennedy is frozen in time.*
6	*Through his televised speeches, Kennedy conveyed a sense of optimism and charm.*	*Kennedy wisely mastered the powerful medium of television.*
7–9	*In a speech on June 10, 1963, Kennedy noted that "No problem of human destiny is beyond human beings..."*	*Kennedy instilled Americans with the idea that they could achieve anything.*
10	*Kennedy's son, John, died in a plane crash in 1999.*	*Like other Americans, the Kennedy family was not immune to life's calamities.*
11–12	*Kennedy led the country before the Vietnam War and the Watergate scandal.*	*Kennedy governed during an idyllic time in the United States.*

The controlling idea of this article is that

Possible answer: Kennedy continues to attract us because he represents America's promise.

Academic Vocabulary in Speaking

The word **contrast** (kuhn TRAST) is a verb that means to *show differences between two things.*

If you **contrast** my lab results with my partner's, the first thing you will see is that my mixture is red while hers is green.

The word **factor** (FAK tuhr) is a noun that means *a thing or condition that helps produce a result.*

One **factor** in the push for American independence was that Great Britain taxed the American colonies but didn't give them a voice in government.

TURN AND TALK According to the author, how are the other tragedies that happened to the Kennedy family a **factor**, or influence, on people's feelings about President Kennedy? **Contrast** this with how attitudes might be different if these tragedies had not happened. Discuss this question with a partner, using **contrast** and **factor** in your conversation.
Encourage students to use the Academic Vocabulary words in their discussions.

Assessment Practice

DIRECTIONS Use "Special Report" to answer questions 1–4.

1 Many people who visited the John F. Kennedy Library after 9/11 were looking for —

(A) information about what happened
(B) someone to blame
(C) reassurance and comfort
(D) a safe place

2 In lines 21–22, the writer says that there was "no enduring sense of a lost legacy" after President McKinley's assassination in order to —

(A) present a reminder that presidents are not always important
(B) tell the reader that assassination is common in the United States
(C) give the reader additional information about President McKinley
(D) emphasize the sorrow of the people after Kennedy's assassination

3 In line 45, what does the writer's use of the expression "tours de force," meaning "feats of unusual skill," tell you about Kennedy's press conferences?

(A) Kennedy toured the country for press conferences.
(B) Kennedy used press conferences to speak French.
(C) Kennedy handled press conferences skillfully.
(D) Kennedy's press conferences were unappreciated.

4 What is the most important reason that the subject of President John F. Kennedy continues to interest people?

(A) He represented America's huge potential to do great things.
(B) He was elected at a young age.
(C) He was able to speak well on television.
(D) He failed to encourage people to make a difference.

UNIT 10

Shakespearean Drama

THE TRAGEDY OF ROMEO AND JULIET

Be sure to read the Historical Background and the Text Analysis Workshop on pages 1022–1033 in *Holt McDougal Literature*.

Academic Vocabulary for Unit 10

You will see these Academic Vocabulary words as you work through this book. You will also be asked to use them as you write and talk about the selections in this unit.

Characteristic (kair uhk tuh RIS tik) is a noun that means *a feature or key detail about a person or thing.*

My favorite **characteristic** of plums is their sweetness.

Name one **characteristic** of your favorite athlete: *Answers will vary.* ______

______

Critical (KRIT uh kuhl) is an adjective that means *having to do with making judgments based on strengths and weaknesses.*

Maria examined her latest painting with a **critical** eye.

When are you **critical** of the way people drive? *Answers will vary.* ______

______

Influence (IN floo uhns) is a noun that means *the power of a person or thing to affect others.* It can also be a verb that means *to have an effect on.*

Mrs. Coyne's **influence** finally got me to read Shakespeare.

How has your **influence** changed someone's mind? *Answers will vary.* ______

______

Motivate (MOH tuh vayt) is a verb that means *to cause someone to take action.*

My dad let me borrow the car to **motivate** me to earn my license.

What is one way teachers can **motivate** students to get better grades?

Answers will vary. ______

Resolve (rih ZOLV) is a verb that means *to figure out, solve, or make clear.*

Evan could not **resolve** the difficult puzzle without help from Ali.

How do you **resolve** a disagreement with a friend? *Answers will vary.* ______

______

The Tragedy of Romeo and Juliet

Drama by William Shakespeare

Is LOVE stronger than HATE?

What happens when two teenagers fall in love even though their families hate each other? What love can—and cannot—overcome is at the heart of *The Tragedy of Romeo and Juliet.*

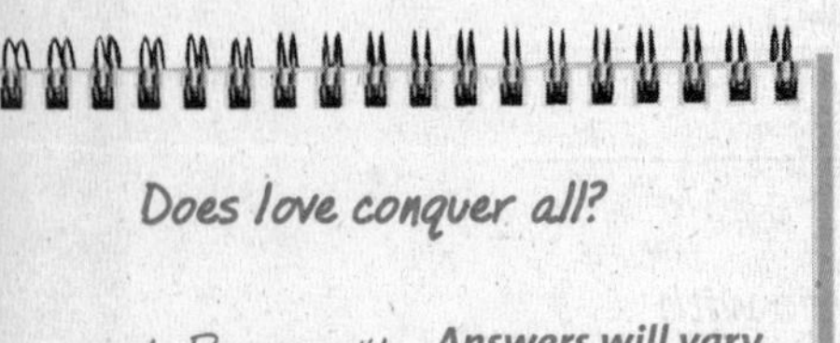

Does love conquer all?
1. Reason #1: Answers will vary.
2. Reason #2: Answers will vary.

LIST IT When people say that love conquers all, they mean that love should be strong enough to overcome any problem. Is this true? In the chart at the left, list two reasons why you think this is true or two reasons you think it is not true

Text Analysis: Shakespearean Drama

A **tragedy** is not going to end with the words "and they all lived happily ever after." Shakespearean tragedies are dramas that end in disaster—most often death—for the main characters. This tragic end may be caused by the actions of the characters, by fate, or by a combination of both.

Playwrights rely on conventions—techniques familiar to audiences that may not be realistic but that communicate important ideas. As you read *Romeo and Juliet,* pay attention to these dramatic conventions that Shakespeare uses to develop the tragedy of Romeo and Juliet's love.

Figurative Language: language that communicates beyond the literal meaning of words to convey emotion and emphasize ideas.

Dramatic Irony: when the audience knows more than the characters. Dramatic irony adds an extra layer of meaning to a character's words and actions.

Soliloquy (suh LIL uh kwee): a long speech given by a character alone on stage. It lets the audience, but not the other characters, know what the character is thinking or feeling.

Reading Strategy: Reading Shakespearean Drama

Shakespeare's English is sometimes hard for today's readers to understand. Use the following strategies to help you read the excerpt from the play:

- Read the background notes and the summary notes to get important information about the structure and main conflict in the play.
- Use the footnotes to understand the meanings of unfamiliar words and unusual sentence structures.
- Restate in your own words lines from an individual character or a dialogue between characters.
- Keep track of major events or changes in the plot in the order in which they take place in each scene.

As you read, you will use a chart like this one to help you keep track of any major events or changes in this scene from the play.

Major Events/Changes in the Plot

Romeo hides in the Capulets' orchard to see Juliet, who is on her balcony. She cannot see or hear him. He declares his love for her to himself. (lines 2–25)
↓
Juliet declares her love for Romeo to herself. She wishes their families were not enemies. (lines 33–49)
↓

Monitor Your Comprehension

SET A PURPOSE FOR READING

Read the Prologue to see how the tragedy is introduced to the audience. Then, read one of the most famous scenes in all of Shakespeare's works.

THE TRAGEDY OF

Romeo & Juliet

Prologue and Act 2, Scene 2

Drama by

WILLIAM SHAKESPEARE

BACKGROUND *The Tragedy of Romeo and Juliet* is a play about two teenagers who fall in love, although their families hate each other. The passages you are about to read include the Prologue, or introduction, and a famous scene from Act 2. In the Prologue, the "Chorus" is one actor who serves as narrator. Act 2, Scene 2, is the balcony scene in which Romeo and Juliet promise their love to each other.

TIME

The 14th century

PLACE

Verona (vuh ROH nuh) and Mantua (MAN choo uh) in northern Italy

CAST

Chorus, the narrator

Romeo, boy from the Montague family (MAHN tuh gyoo)

Juliet, girl from the Capulet family (CAP yoo let)

Nurse, Juliet's personal servant

Prologue

[*Enter* Chorus.]

Chorus. Two households, both alike in dignity,
In fair Verona, where we lay our scene,
From ancient grudge break to new mutiny,
Where civil blood makes civil hands unclean.[1]
From forth the fatal loins of these two foes,
A pair of star-crossed[2] lovers take their life,
Whose misadventured[3] piteous overthrows
Doth with their death bury their parents' strife.
The fearful passage of their death-marked love,
And the continuance of their parents' rage,
Which, but their children's end, naught[4] could remove,
Is now the two hours' traffic of our stage,[5]
The which if you with patient ears attend,
What here shall miss, our toil shall strive to mend.[6]

[*Exit.*]

IN OTHER WORDS The Chorus, or narrator, tells the audience that two families in Verona (a town in Italy) have been fighting each other. Each family has a child, and the two children will fall in love. Their deaths will end the fighting between the families. The narrator then explains that the play will last two hours and asks the audience to wait patiently for events to unfold.

► According to the Prologue, how will Romeo and Juliet die? Underline the phrase that tells you.

1. **ancient . . . unclean:** Fighting (**mutiny**) between families has caused the people of Verona to have one another's blood on their hands.
2. **star-crossed:** doomed. The position of the stars when the lovers were born was not favorable. In Shakespeare's day, people looked for signs in the stars.
3. **misadventured:** unlucky.
4. **but:** except for; **naught:** nothing.
5. **the two hours' . . . stage:** what will be shown on the stage in the next two hours.
6. **what . . . mend:** The play will fill in the details not mentioned in the prologue.

What Happens Next

Romeo, a boy from the Montague family, is sad because he loves a girl named Rosaline, who doesn't love him. His friends try to cheer him up by taking him to a party at the home of the Capulets, his family's enemy. There, Romeo falls in love with Juliet, a Capulet, and Juliet falls in love with him. The two are upset when they realize that they are from enemy families. After the party, Romeo's friends tease him about being in love with Rosaline. They don't understand that he's now in love with Juliet. He goes to Juliet's house and hides in the orchard, hoping to see her again.

As Act 2, Scene 2, begins, Juliet walks out onto her **balcony**. Romeo is in the orchard, a garden of fruit trees below her balcony. Juliet does not know that Romeo can see and hear her. (A)

Act 2

SCENE 2 *Capulet's orchard.*

[*Enter* Romeo.]

Romeo. He jests at scars that never felt a wound.[7]

[*Enter* Juliet *above at a window.*]

But soft! What light through yonder window breaks?
It is the East, and Juliet is the sun!
Arise, fair sun, and kill the envious moon,
Who is already sick and pale with grief
That thou her maid art far more fair than she. (B)
Be not her maid, since she is envious;
Her vestal livery is but sick and green,
And none but fools do wear it; cast it off.[8]
It is my lady; O, it is my love!
O that she knew she were!
She speaks, yet she says nothing. What of that? (C)

7. **He jests . . . wound:** At the end of Scene 1, Romeo's friends tease him about being in love. Here, Romeo comments that one of those friends makes fun of love because he has never been wounded by it.
8. **But soft . . . cast it off:** Romeo sees Juliet at the window. For a moment he is speechless (**soft**: be still), but then he praises her beauty.

Monitor Your Comprehension

VISUAL VOCABULARY

A **balcony** is a platform high on a wall, surrounded by a railing.

(A) SHAKESPEAREAN DRAMA

Reread the Background note and What Happens Next. Underline the reason Romeo has gone to Capulet's orchard.

(B) SHAKESPEAREAN DRAMA

Reread lines 3–6. Circle what Romeo compares Juliet to in these lines. Why does he think the moon is envious, or jealous, of Juliet?

Possible answer: The moon is jealous because Juliet, the sun, is more beautiful than it is.

(C) SHAKESPEAREAN DRAMA

Romeo declares his love for Juliet in a **soliloquy**, a speech he makes to himself on stage that Juliet cannot hear. With a partner, discuss why Romeo may choose to do this instead of directly telling Juliet how he feels about her.

Students may discuss that Romeo may be afraid to admit his feelings for Juliet since they are from enemy families or he may be too shy to tell her, fearing rejection.

Monitor Your Comprehension

Her eye discourses; I will answer it.
I am too bold; 'tis not to me she speaks.[9]
Two of the fairest stars in all the heaven,
Having some business, do entreat her eyes
To twinkle in their spheres till they return.
What if her eyes were there, they in her head?
The brightness of her cheek would shame those stars
As daylight doth a lamp; her eyes in heaven
Would through the airy region stream so bright
That birds would sing and think it were not night.[10] D
See how she leans her cheek upon her hand!
O that I were a glove upon that hand,
That I might touch that cheek!

IN OTHER WORDS Romeo is talking to himself. Then, he sees a light through Juliet's window. He describes Juliet's beauty as being like the sun. He sees Juliet speak, but he can't hear her. He starts to say something but decides not to speak.

► Reread lines 23–25. Why does Romeo wish he were a glove? Circle the words that tell you.

Juliet. Ay me!

Romeo. She speaks.
O, speak again, bright angel! for thou art
As glorious to this night, being o'er my head,
As is a winged messenger of heaven
Unto the white-upturned wond'ring eyes
Of mortals that fall back to gaze on him
When he bestrides the lazy-pacing clouds
And sails upon the bosom of the air.[11] PAUSE & REFLECT

D SHAKESPEAREAN DRAMA

Reread lines 15–22. Underline the words and phrases Romeo uses to compare Juliet's eyes to stars. What does this **figurative language** tell you about how Romeo feels about Juliet? Write your answer on the lines below.

Possible answer: Romeo compares Juliet's eyes to the stars in the sky in order to emphasize their brightness. His comparison tells the reader that he feels very strongly about Juliet, comparing her to the heavens.

PAUSE & REFLECT

Romeo has only met her a few hours before, but he compares Juliet to an angel. With a partner, discuss whether you think this response is appropriate.

Students may discuss that Romeo's response to Juliet is one of love at first sight— and his emotional descriptions of her mirror his reaction to seeing her.

9. **Her eye . . . speaks:** Romeo shifts back and forth between wanting to speak to Juliet and being afraid.
10. **Two of . . . not night:** Romeo compares Juliet's eyes to stars in the sky.
11. **thou art . . . of the air:** He compares Juliet to an angel (**winged messenger of heaven**) who stands on (**bestrides**) the clouds.

Monitor Your Comprehension

Juliet. O Romeo, Romeo! wherefore art thou Romeo?[12]
Deny thy father and refuse thy name!
Or, if thou wilt not, be but sworn my love,
And I'll no longer be a Capulet.

Romeo [*aside*]. Shall I hear more, or shall I speak at this?

Juliet. 'Tis but thy name that is my enemy.
Thou art thyself, though not a Montague.
What's Montague? It is nor hand, nor foot,
Nor arm, nor face, nor any other part
Belonging to a man. O, be some other name!
What's in a name? That which we call a rose
By any other name would smell as sweet.
So Romeo would, were he not Romeo called,
Retain that dear perfection which he owes
✔ Without that title. Romeo, doff thy name;
And for that name, which is no part of thee,
Take all myself.[13] E

E SHAKESPEAREAN DRAMA

Reread lines 47–49. Place a check mark ✔ next to the line that tells you what Juliet wants Romeo to do to win her love. With a partner, discuss why Juliet wants him to do this.

Possible answer: Students should discuss that Juliet wants Romeo to abandon his name to distance himself from his allegiance to the Montague family, which is a rival to her own family—the Capulets.

IN OTHER WORDS Romeo hears Juliet talking about him to herself. She seems upset that he is a Montague, a member of an enemy family.

► With a partner, discuss why Juliet says names are not important in lines 40–44.

Students should discuss that Juliet says names are not important but are artificial labels that do not reveal the true nature of things.

Romeo. I take thee at thy word.
Call me but love, and I'll be new baptized;
Henceforth I never will be Romeo.

Juliet. What man art thou that, thus bescreened in night,
So stumblest on my counsel?[14]

Romeo. By a name
I know not how to tell thee who I am.
My name, dear saint, is hateful to myself,

12. **wherefore**: why. Juliet asks why Romeo has to be from her enemy's family.
13. Juliet tries to convince herself that a name is just a meaningless word. She asks Romeo to get rid of (**doff**) his name.
14. Juliet is startled that someone hiding (**bescreened**) nearby hears her private thoughts (**counsel**).

Monitor Your Comprehension

(F) LANGUAGE COACH

Shakespeare sometimes inverts, or reverses, the usual order in which words in sentences appear. Find the words that are reversed in line 57 and place them in the order you would normally expect.

The expected order of "Had I it written" is "If I had it written" (If I had it in writing).

(G) LANGUAGE COACH

Shakespeare is famous for using words and phrases that have two or more meanings at the same time. The phrase "stony limits" in line 67 has more than one meaning. "Stony limits" refers to the actual stone wall Romeo must climb in order to visit Juliet. It also refers to the families' hatred of each another that gets in the way of his and Juliet's romance.

(H) SHAKESPEAREAN DRAMA

Reread lines 62–69. Restate the dialogue between Romeo and Juliet in your own words.

Juliet (lines 62–65) :
Possible answer: Romeo, please tell me how and why you are here. The walls are too high to climb, and you are putting your life at risk if any of my relatives find you here.

Romeo (lines 66–69):

Possible answer: I climbed the wall with love's help. Neither the walls nor your relatives can keep us apart.

Because it is an enemy to thee.
Had I it written, I would tear the word. (F)

Juliet. My ears have yet not drunk a hundred words
Of that tongue's utterance, yet I know the sound.
Art thou not Romeo, and a Montague?

Romeo. Neither, fair saint, if either thee dislike.

Juliet. How camest thou hither, tell me, and wherefore?
The orchard walls are high and hard to climb,
And the place death, considering who thou art,
If any of my kinsmen find thee here.

Romeo. With love's light wings did I o'erperch these walls;
For stony limits cannot hold love out, (G)
And what love can do, that dares love attempt.
Therefore thy kinsmen are no let to me.[15] (H)

Juliet. If they do see thee, they will murder thee.

Romeo. Alack, there lies more peril in thine eye
Than twenty of their swords! Look thou but sweet,
And I am proof against their enmity.[16]

Juliet. I would not for the world they saw thee here.

Romeo. I have night's cloak to hide me from their sight;
And but thou love me, let them find me here.
My life were better ended by their hate
Than death prorogued, wanting of thy love.[17]

Juliet. By whose direction foundst thou out this place?

Romeo. By love, that first did prompt me to enquire.
He lent me counsel, and I lent him eyes.
I am no pilot, yet, wert thou as far
As that vast shore washed with the farthest sea,
I would adventure for such merchandise.

---

15. **With . . . me:** Love helped me climb (**o'erperch**) the walls. Neither walls nor your relatives are an obstacle (**let**) to me.
16. **Look . . . enmity:** Smile on me, and I will be defended against my enemies' hatred (**enmity**).
17. **than death . . . love:** than my death postponed (**prorogued**) if you don't love me.

Monitor Your Comprehension

IN OTHER WORDS Romeo speaks to Juliet. He says he will change his name if she will love him. Juliet recognizes Romeo's voice. She asks him how and why he has come to her house, and Romeo says that love has brought him. Juliet tells him that her family will kill him if they see him. Romeo says that he would rather die than live without her love.

Juliet. Thou knowest the mask of night is on my face;
Else would a maiden blush bepaint my cheek
For that which thou hast heard me speak tonight.
Fain would I dwell on form—fain, fain deny
What I have spoke; but farewell compliment![18]
Dost thou love me? I know thou wilt say "Ay";
And I will take thy word. Yet, if thou swearst,
Thou mayst prove false. At lovers' perjuries,
They say Jove laughs.[19] O gentle Romeo,
If thou dost love, pronounce it faithfully. ❶
Or if thou thinkst I am too quickly won,
I'll frown, and be perverse, and say thee nay,
So thou wilt woo; but else, not for the world.
In truth, fair Montague, I am too fond,
And therefore thou mayst think my 'havior light;
But trust me, gentleman, I'll prove more true
Than those that have more cunning to be strange.[20]
I should have been more strange, I must confess,
But that thou overheardst, ere I was ware,
My true love's passion. Therefore pardon me,
And not impute this yielding to light love,
Which the dark night hath so discovered. **PAUSE & REFLECT**

❶ SHAKESPEAREAN DRAMA

Reread lines 90–94. What worries Juliet in these lines? Restate what she says in your own words.

Possible answer: I know you say that you love me, and I believe you. However, you may not be telling me the truth.

PAUSE & REFLECT

With a partner, discuss how Juliet describes her feelings for Romeo in this speech. How serious are her feelings for him?

Students should discuss that Juliet is very much in love with Romeo and hopes that he feels the same way about her.

18. **Thou . . . compliment:** If I had known you were listening, I would have gladly (**fain**) behaved more properly, but now it's too late for good manners (**farewell compliment**).
19. **At . . . laughs:** Jove, the king of the gods, laughs at lovers who lie to each other.
20. **Or if . . . strange:** You might think I've fallen in love too easily and that I should not tell you right away that I love you. But I'll be truer to you than those who play games to hide their real feelings (**be strange**).

Monitor Your Comprehension

Romeo. Lady, by yonder blessed moon I swear,
That tips with silver all these fruit-tree tops—

Juliet. O, swear not by the moon, the inconstant moon,
That monthly changes in her circled orb,
Lest that thy love prove likewise variable.

Romeo. What shall I swear by?

Juliet. Do not swear at all;
Or if thou wilt, swear by thy gracious self,
Which is the god of my idolatry,
And I'll believe thee.

Romeo. If my heart's dear love—

Juliet. Well, do not swear. Although I joy in thee,
I have no joy of this contract[21] tonight.
It is too rash, too unadvised, too sudden;
Too like the lightning, which doth cease to be
Ere one can say "It lightens." Sweet, good night!
This bud of love, by summer's ripening breath,
May prove a beauteous flow'r when next we meet.
Good night, good night! As sweet repose and rest
Come to thy heart as that within my breast! J

Romeo. O, wilt thou leave me so unsatisfied?

Juliet. What satisfaction canst thou have tonight?

Romeo. The exchange of thy love's faithful vow for mine.

Juliet. I gave thee mine before thou didst request it;
And yet I would it were to give again.

Romeo. Wouldst thou withdraw it? For what purpose, love?

Juliet. But to be frank and give it thee again.
And yet I wish but for the thing I have.
My bounty is as boundless as the sea,
My love as deep; the more I give to thee,
The more I have, for both are infinite.
I hear some noise within. Dear love, adieu!

[Nurse *calls within.*]

J SHAKESPEAREAN DRAMA

Reread lines 116–124. Juliet asks Romeo not to swear, or take an oath, that he loves her. Fill in the lines below with two examples of the **figurative language** Juliet uses to express her concerns about her relationship with Romeo.

Figurative Language
1. Juliet compares Romeo swearing his love to *lightning, which ceases to be.*
2. Juliet compares their new love to *the bud of a flower, which will bloom and grow over time.*

21. **I have . . . contract:** I am concerned about this promise of love (**contract**).

Anon,[22] good nurse! Sweet Montague, be true.
Stay but a little, I will come again.

[*Exit.*]

Romeo. O blessed, blessed night! I am afeard,
Being in night, all this is but a dream,
Too flattering-sweet to be substantial.

[*Re-enter* Juliet, *above.*]

Juliet. Three words, dear Romeo, and good night indeed.
If that thy bent of love be honorable,
Thy purpose marriage, send me word tomorrow,
By one that I'll procure to come to thee,
Where and what time thou wilt perform the rite;[23]
And all my fortunes at thy foot I'll lay
And follow thee my lord throughout the world. (K)

Nurse [*within*]. Madam!

Juliet. I come, anon.—But if thou meanst not well,
I do beseech thee—

Nurse [*within*]. Madam!

Juliet. By-and-by I come.—
To cease thy suit and leave me to my grief.[24]
Tomorrow will I send.

Romeo. So thrive my soul—

Juliet. A thousand times good night! [*Exit.*] (L)

IN OTHER WORDS Juliet asks Romeo if he loves her. She worries that Romeo might not think her love is true because she has been so quick to show her love. Romeo tries to swear his love, but Juliet stops him each time. She says they have been too quick to promise their love.

Romeo. A thousand times the worse, to want thy light!
Love goes toward love as schoolboys from their books;

22. **anon:** right away. Juliet calls to her nurse but asks Romeo to wait.
23. **If that . . . rite:** I'll send a messenger to you tomorrow. If you want to marry me, tell the messenger where and when.
24. **But if . . . grief:** Juliet begs (**beseech**) Romeo to leave her alone if he is not serious about his love for her.

Monitor Your Comprehension

(K) SHAKESPEAREAN DRAMA

Reread lines 143–148. Juliet changes her mind and makes an important decision. If Romeo wants to marry her, what will Juliet do?

Events/Changes in the Plot

Possible answer: If Romeo sends word of where and when they will marry, Juliet will agree to marry him and follow him wherever life takes them.

(L) SHAKESPEAREAN DRAMA

We know what will happen to Romeo and Juliet by the end of the play. How are the lovers' plans an example of **dramatic irony**?

Possible answer: Since the reader knows that Romeo and Juliet will die by the end of the play, their plans for the future are useless.

Monitor Your Comprehension

SHAKESPEAREAN DRAMA

Reread lines 156–157. Romeo uses **figurative language** to describe lovers as they meet ("love goes toward love," line 156) and as they part ("love from love," line 157). To what does he compare each of these situations? Write your answers on the lines below.

"Love goes toward love . . ." (line 156):

Possible answer: Lovers meet as eagerly as schoolboys leave their books.

" . . . love from love . . . (line 157)

Possible answer: Lovers separate with the sadness of boys going to school.

But love from love, towards school with heavy looks.
[*Enter* Juliet *again, above.*]

Juliet. Hist! Romeo, hist! O for a falc'ner's voice
To lure this tassel-gentle back again!
Bondage is hoarse and may not speak aloud;
Else would I tear the cave where Echo lies,
And make her airy tongue more hoarse than mine
With repetition of my Romeo's name.[25]

Romeo!

Romeo. It is my soul that calls upon my name.
How silver-sweet sound lovers' tongues by night,
Like softest music to attending ears!

Juliet. Romeo!

Romeo. My sweet?

Juliet. What o'clock tomorrow
Shall I send to thee?

Romeo. By the hour of nine.

Juliet. I will not fail. 'Tis twenty years till then.
I have forgot why I did call thee back.

Romeo. Let me stand here till thou remember it.

Juliet. I shall forget, to have thee still stand there,
Rememb'ring how I love thy company.

Romeo. And I'll still stay, to have thee still forget,
Forgetting any other home but this.[26]

Juliet. 'Tis almost morning. I would have thee gone—
And yet no farther than a wanton's bird,
That lets it hop a little from her hand,
Like a poor prisoner in his twisted gyves,

25. **Hist . . . name:** Listen, Romeo, I wish I could speak your name as loudly as a falconer calls his falcon (**tassel-gentle**), but because of my parents I must whisper. **Echo** was a nymph in Greek mythology whose unreturned love for Narcissus caused her to waste away till only her voice was left.

26. **What o'clock . . . but this:** The lovers plan to meet the next day. They wish time would pass more quickly and that they could remain together longer.

Monitor Your Comprehension

And with a silk thread plucks it back again,
So loving-jealous of his liberty.[27]

Romeo. I would I were thy bird.

Juliet. Sweet, so would I.
Yet I should kill thee with much cherishing. Ⓝ
Good night, good night! Parting is such sweet sorrow,
That I shall say good night till it be morrow.

[*Exit.*]

Romeo. Sleep dwell upon thine eyes, peace in thy breast!
Would I were sleep and peace, so sweet to rest!
Hence will I to my ghostly father's cell,
His help to crave and my dear hap[28] to tell. PAUSE & REFLECT

[*Exit.*]

IN OTHER WORDS Romeo starts to leave, but Juliet calls him back. She asks what time she should send a messenger to him the next day. Neither of them wants to leave the other, but they finally say "good night."

Final Summary

Romeo and Juliet are married in secret. Later, Juliet's cousin kills one of Romeo's friends, and Romeo kills the cousin. Romeo flees, planning to meet Juliet in another city.

Juliet's parents don't know she has married Romeo. They try to force her to marry another man. She threatens to kill herself, but a friendly priest comes up with a plan: Juliet can take medicine that will make her sleep for two days; her family will think she is dead, and Romeo can rescue her from the family tomb.

27. **I would . . . liberty:** I know you must go, but I want you close to me like a pet bird that a thoughtless child (**wanton**) keeps on a string.
28. **ghostly father:** spiritual adviser or priest; **dear hap:** good fortune.

Ⓝ SHAKESPEAREAN DRAMA

In line 183, Romeo wishes he were Juliet's pet bird. In line 184, Juliet says that if he were her pet, she would give him so much affection that she would love him to death. With a partner, discuss why this is an example of **dramatic irony.**

Students should discuss that the dialogue is an example of dramatic irony because the reader knows that Romeo and Juliet are fated to die whereas the characters do not and they discuss death in their examples as if it is something remote and far away for them.

PAUSE & REFLECT

Romeo and Juliet have met just a few hours before. With a partner, discuss whether their love for each other is real or not.

Students may discuss that their love for one another is not real because they do not know each other well enough for it to have developed and grown over time.

The priest sends Romeo a letter explaining the plan, but Romeo does not get the letter. Instead, he hears that Juliet is dead. He returns to find Juliet in her deathlike sleep. Thinking that she is dead, Romeo drinks poison and dies.

Juliet wakes up from her sleep and finds Romeo dead. Overcome with grief, she takes Romeo's knife and kills herself.

The Montague and Capulet families learn of what has happened, and they agree to end their hatred of each other.

After Reading

Text Analysis: Shakespearean Drama

Shakespeare uses **figurative language, dramatic irony,** and **soliloquy** to tell the tragic tale of Romeo and Juliet. Complete the chart below with examples of each of the dramatic conventions Shakespeare uses to express Romeo and Juliet's passion and its tragic conclusion. Include quotations as examples for figurative language and dramatic irony. Include a brief description of each soliloquy.

For this chart, answers will vary. See samples below.

Dramatic Convention	Examples
Figurative language	*"This bud of love, by summer's ripening breath, May prove a beauteous flow'r when next we meet." (lines 121–122)*
Dramatic irony	*"Romeo. I would I were thy bird. Juliet. Sweet, so would I. Yet I should kill thee with much cherishing." (lines 183–184)*
Soliloquy	*At the beginning of Act 2, Scene 2, Romeo is speaking to himself and verbalizing his thoughts. In this speech, he reveals that he is enraptured by Juliet's beauty, that he idealizes her, that he is unsure of how to communicate with her, and that he wants to touch her.*

Which of these conventions do you think best expresses Romeo and Juliet's tragic love? Explain on the lines below. Use the chart above to gather specific examples as evidence to support your opinion.

Students' answers will vary but should cite examples from the chart above in support of their answers.

Is LOVE stronger than HATE?

Review the reasons you gave for why you think love is or is not stronger than hate. Discuss with a partner what you think makes one of these emotions stronger, or able to overcome, the other.

Students' answers will vary but should cite examples from the chart on page 392.

After Reading

Reading Strategy: Reading Shakespearean Drama

Complete the chart below by summarizing, or briefly stating, the most important events that take place in each part of Act II, Scene 2. Your notes may include the important feelings or thoughts each character expresses, the important decisions he or she makes, and the actions he or she takes.

For this chart, answers will vary. See samples below.

Act II, Scene 2
Romeo's soliloquy about Juliet (lines 1–25): *Romeo declares his love for Juliet.*
Juliet's soliloquy about Romeo (lines 33–49): *Juliet tells herself that names are artificial labels without meaning affixed to things.* *She wishes that Romeo would abandon his own family name.*
Dialogue between Romeo and Juliet about their relationship (lines 52–141): *At first, Romeo and Juliet discuss Romeo's arrival in her family's courtyard and how their warring families cannot keep them apart. Then, they discuss their love, and Juliet worries that they have been too quick to promise their love to each other.*
Dialogue between Romeo and Juliet about their plans for the future (lines 142–190): *Juliet tells Romeo to send word the next day if he wishes to marry her and she will meet him. Both wait impatiently for the long night to end so that they can marry the next day and always be together.*

Academic Vocabulary in Speaking

The word **characteristic** (kair uhk tuh RIS tik) is a noun that means *a feature or key detail about a person or thing.*

His ability to listen is his best **characteristic.**

The word **motivate** (MOH tuh vayt) is a verb that means *to cause someone to take action.*

I **motivate** myself by giving myself a reward when I finish a task.

The word **resolve** (rih ZOLV) is a verb that means *to decide* or *to figure out, solve, or make clear.*

I will **resolve** this problem as soon as possible to avoid a fight.

TURN AND TALK Romeo and Juliet decide to marry only a few hours after meeting for the first time. What **characteristics** do you think **motivate** their actions? How else might they **resolve** the conflict between their families? Discuss your ideas with a partner, using at least two of the Academic Vocabulary words in your conversation.

Encourage students to use the Academic Vocabulary words in their discussions.

Assessment Practice

DIRECTIONS Use *The Tragedy of Romeo and Juliet* to answer questions 1–4.

1 Romeo compares Juliet to —

- (A) a bird
- (B) a lamp
- (C) a schoolboy
- (D) the sun

2 In line 37, Romeo considers —

- (A) leaving the orchard
- (B) revealing his presence
- (C) giving up his family name
- (D) continuing his conversation

3 In line 133, when Juliet says, "My bounty is as boundless as the sea," she means —

- (A) her ability to love Romeo is endless
- (B) her father's fortune is vast like the ocean
- (C) her riches will keep them happy forever
- (D) her love for Romeo will cause unending fighting

4 Romeo and Juliet's wedding plans are ironic because —

- (A) the audience knows they will die
- (B) the arrangements are made in secret
- (C) the scene begins with another celebration
- (D) the union will bring peace to their families

Great Movies: *Romeo and Juliet*

• Critical Review

Background

Romeo and Juliet, one of William Shakespeare's tragic plays, has been made into a movie several times. In this review, movie critic Roger Ebert argues that the best movie version of this play is the one directed by Franco Zeffirelli (FRANK oh zef uh REL ee).

Standards Focus: Analyze a Critical Review

A **critical review** is an essay in which the writer gives his or her opinions about a movie, a play, a book, a TV show, or another work. A critical review typically includes these elements:

- the name of the work and its creator
- a description of the work
- a clearly stated opinion of the work
- reasons that support the opinion
- examples or details that illustrate the reasons

The heart of a review is the writer's opinion and the reasons and examples used to back it up. Opinions that are substantiated, or supported, are more persuasive than those that are simply stated without appropriate support.

You can use a chart like the one shown below to record a writer's opinion and the main reasons and examples that support the opinion.

Ebert's Opinion: *Franco Zeffirelli's 1968 production of Romeo and Juliet is the best film version.*

↓

Reasons	Supporting Examples or Details
Reason 1: *Zeffirelli used actors who were the right age.*	*Olivia Hussey (Juliet) was 16, and Leonard Whiting (Romeo) was 17.*
Reason 2:	
Reason 3:	

GREAT MOVIES

Romeo and Juliet

BY ROGER EBERT

Romeo and Juliet is often said to be the first tragedy that's a love story. But it isn't really a tragedy. It's a terrible misunderstanding. It's not a tragedy because the heroes don't fall as a result of their own weaknesses. Romeo and Juliet have no flaws. They die because their families are fighting. Ⓐ In this play, ordinary people are as important as powerful people. The great tragedies of Shakespeare's time involved people in power—kings, emperors, generals. Here, though, he writes about teenagers in love.

Romeo and Juliet has been filmed many times in many ways. Norma Shearer and Leslie Howard starred in the beloved 1936 Hollywood version. Modern versions include gang wars or forbidden romances between people from

SET A PURPOSE FOR READING

Read this article to learn what one reviewer thinks about film versions of the play *Romeo and Juliet*.

Ⓐ LANGUAGE COACH

In line 1, the phrase "Romeo and Juliet" is set in ***italic type,*** with letters that slant to the right. Italic type is commonly used to set off the titles of plays, movies, and novels. Here, the writer is referring to a play. In line 4, "Romeo and Juliet" refers to the characters in the play, so italic type is not used.

B CRITICAL REVIEW
Reread lines 10–15. Then, circle the sentence that includes the writer's opinion of the work.

different cultures. But the favorite film version is likely to remain Franco Zeffirelli's 1968 production. B

His most important decision was to use actors who were about the right age to play the characters. As the play opens, Juliet is about 14, and Romeo is a little older. Zeffirelli chose Olivia Hussey, a 16-year-old from Argentina, and Leonard Whiting, a British 17-year-old, to play the parts.

IN OTHER WORDS *Romeo and Juliet* is different from other tragedies written by Shakespeare. The main characters aren't people in power. They're teenagers whose lives are under the control of others. Although this play has been made into many films, Roger Ebert believes the 1968 version is the best.

► What decision does Ebert say was important in making Zeffirelli's version a success? Underline the answer.

The two actors certainly look like the characters they play, and they act their parts well. Although neither was a trained actor, both of them mastered Shakespeare's unfamiliar language. Zeffirelli took out about half of the play. But much that needs to be described on the stage can simply be shown onscreen. C

C CRITICAL REVIEW
Reread lines 21–26. Then, with a partner, discuss details that illustrate the writer's first main point of support.

Students should discuss that the actors looked like the characters they were portraying and acted their parts well, too.

What is left is what people love about the play. People love the freshness of the young lovers' passion, the fighting between the young men, and the cruel irony of the deaths of both Romeo and Juliet.

Hussey and Whiting were so good because they didn't know any better. I visited the film set outside Rome when the balcony scene was filmed. Hussey and Whiting were relaxed and easygoing. And when the balcony scene was shot,

I remember the energy that Hussey threw into it. She almost hurled herself off the balcony for kisses. **PAUSE & REFLECT**

Between shots, Zeffirelli strolled around with the composer Nino Rota, who had written the music for many films. Pasqualino De Santis directed his camera crew quietly, urgently. He was trying to be ready for the actors instead of making them wait. Zeffirelli said what everyone could see: The whole movie depended on the balcony and tomb scenes. He felt that his casting decision had proven itself: With these actors, the film would succeed.

IN OTHER WORDS The teen actors looked and acted their parts well. They weren't afraid to tackle a play by Shakespeare, and they did it with energy.

► Circle the two most important scenes in the play according to Zeffirelli.

And the movie did succeed—beyond any other film based on Shakespeare's plays. The movie opened in 1968, a time of unrest around the world. Somehow the story of the ill-fated lovers caught and mirrored the mood of rebellious young people.

Zeffirelli was born in Florence in 1923. He learned the English language early. His most important influence was Laurence Olivier's version of *Henry V* (1945). This movie inspired him to go into a career in performing arts. Before

PAUSE & REFLECT

Reread lines 31–36. What does the writer mean by saying Hussey and Whiting "didn't know any better"? Write your thoughts on the lines below.

Possible answer: I think that the writer means that they didn't know how to not be good, meaning that they didn't know how to fail in their roles as Romeo and Juliet.

he directed *Romeo and Juliet*, he first did Shakespeare's *Taming of the Shrew* (1967). Later he directed Placido Domingo in Verdi's opera *Otello* (1986), and he directed Mel Gibson in *Hamlet* (1990).

Romeo and Juliet remains the high point of his career. It is interesting that Zeffirelli focused on love, while a 1996 version focused on violence. Something basic has changed in films about and for young people. Recent audiences seem shy of sex and love but eager for conflict and action. . . . D

The costumes by Danilo Donati won an award for the film. The nurse (Pat Heywood) is cloaked in heavy fabrics, and Hussey's dresses set off her creamy skin and long hair. Whiting wears his knee-length pants and shirt in a completely natural way. On him they are everyday clothing, not costumes. E

D CRITICAL REVIEW

Reread lines 58–62. Underline the negative statement the writer makes about "recent audiences." Is the writer's opinion substantiated, or supported, in the text? Discuss your answer with a partner.

***Students should discuss that the writer does not support his opinion in the text, focusing his attention on the 1968 version of* Romeo and Juliet.**

E CRITICAL REVIEW

In lines 63–68, what reason does the writer use to support his opinion of the work? Write the reason and supporting details in this chart:

Reason	Supporting Details
The award-winning costumes	*Whiting wears his costume so well that on him it is completely natural and more like everyday clothing; Hussey's dresses complement her skin and hair; the nurse is cloaked in heavy fabrics*

The costumes and everything else in the film are wonderful. However, the two death scenes are too planned out. Their timing is wrong. Yet we overlook the problem because Shakespeare has given us something that is impossible—the experience of two young lovers grieving each others' deaths. The first time Shakespeare's play was seen in London, Shakespeare had the satisfaction of seeing people moved to emotions far beyond anything before known in the theater. Why? Because Romeo and Juliet were not powerful, distant figures. They were not Caesars, Othellos or Macbeths. Instead, they were a couple of kids in love, as everyone in the theater had known, and everyone in the theater had been. **PAUSE & REFLECT**

IN OTHER WORDS Although Zeffirelli directed film versions of many of Shakespeare's plays, *Romeo and Juliet* was his best. Ebert criticizes the death scenes but says that this problem is minor in the context of the story. The play, Ebert says, was a success the first time it was acted in front of an audience because it showed two young people in love—something to which everyone could relate.

PAUSE & REFLECT

In lines 80–82, the writer suggests that audiences relate to Romeo and Juliet because "they were a couple of kids in love." Can you think of other reasons the play might appeal to audiences?

Possible answer: The film explores the topic of rebellion, which many audience members experienced as teenagers.

After Reading

Practicing Your Skills: Analyze a Critical Review

In the critical review you just read, Roger Ebert explains why he thinks Zeffirelli's film production of *Romeo and Juliet* is the best. Look back at the review and at any notes you took as you read. Then, write a brief summary of Ebert's critical review. A **summary** is a brief retelling, in your own words, of the main ideas in a piece of writing.

Summary of Ebert's Review
Possible answer: Ebert thinks Zeffirelli's film will remain a favorite for many years because of the actors' performances, the costumes, the way the movie was shot, and the universal appeal of Shakespeare's play.

What main reasons does Ebert use to substantiate, or support, his opinion of the film?

Students' answers will vary but should use examples from the text that describe how Ebert thinks Zeffirelli's film will remain a favorite for many years.

Academic Vocabulary in Speaking

The word **critical** (KRIT uh kuhl) is an adjective that means *having to do with making judgments based on strengths and weaknesses.*

A **critical** review of our last soccer game showed that our main weakness was poor passing.

The word **influence** (IN floo uhns) is a noun that means *the power of a person or thing to affect others.* It can also be a verb that means *to have an effect on.*

The bad movie review didn't have much **influence** on my friends and me; we thought the movie was great.

TURN AND TALK With a partner, discuss other **critical** reviews you have heard or read. What **influence** did the reviews have on you? Be sure to use the words **critical** and **influence** in your conversation.

Encourage students to use the Academic Vocabulary words in their discussions.

Assessment Practice

DIRECTIONS Use "Great Movies: *Romeo and Juliet*" to answer questions 1–4.

1 Which statement best summarizes the writer's opinion in "Great Movies: *Romeo and Juliet*"?

- (A) No filmmaker has ever created a good version of *Romeo and Juliet.*
- (B) Franco Zeffirelli's 1968 *Romeo and Juliet* will always be thought of as a great movie.
- (C) Costumes are not important in a film version of *Romeo and Juliet.*
- (D) The 1936 Hollywood version of *Romeo and Juliet* is the most enjoyable.

2 In lines 16–20, the writer —

- (A) provides the title of the work and the name of its creator
- (B) describes the original work in detail
- (C) provides a clearly stated opinion of the work
- (D) provides a reason that supports his opinion

3 The writer points out that Zeffirelli's film focuses on love, while a 1996 version focuses on —

- (A) violence
- (B) different cultures
- (C) music
- (D) rebellious young people

4 The writer suggests that the movie succeeded for all of the following reasons *except* —

- (A) the actors were the right age to play the characters
- (B) the story reflected the mood of young people in 1968
- (C) Zeffirelli improved Shakespeare's death scenes
- (D) the costumes looked natural on the actors

UNIT 11

Epic Poetry

THE ODYSSEY

Be sure to read the Text Analysis Workshop on pages 1194–1201 in *Holt McDougal Literature*.

Academic Vocabulary for Unit 11

You will see these Academic Vocabulary words as you work through this book. You will also be asked to use them as you write and talk about the selections in this unit.

Demonstrate (DEM uhn strayt) is a verb that means *to show clearly.*
My high scores **demonstrate** that I'm the best at this video game.

How could you **demonstrate** the best way to play your favorite sport?

Answers will vary.

Emphasis (EM fuh sis) is a noun that means *special attention given to something to show its importance.*
In his speech, the principal put a lot of **emphasis** on test results.

What are some ways to put **emphasis** on an idea when you are talking?

Answers will vary.

Monitor (MON ih tuhr) is a verb that means *to check on* or *to watch.*
We often look at the garden to **monitor** the growth of the flowers.

Why might you want to **monitor** your belongings? *Answers will vary.*

Before Reading

The Cyclops *from the* Odyssey

Epic poem by **Homer**
Translated by **Robert Fitzgerald**

What is a HERO?

When you hear the word *hero*, who comes to mind? Do you think of someone strong, brave, or talented? In Homer's *Odyssey*, you'll meet Odysseus, a legendary hero with some very human flaws.

TURN AND TALK On the lines at the left, list people who are generally thought to be heroes. Then, with a partner, discuss traits—or qualities—that make each person on your list heroic. Which traits seem true of every hero? List those traits.

People Who Are Heroes

1. Martin Luther King Jr.
2. **Answers will vary.**
3.
4.
5.

Essential Traits of a Hero

1. Willing to fight for what's right
2. **Answers will vary.**
3.

Text Analysis: Epic Hero

In literature, an **epic** is a narrative poem that tells the story of an **epic hero**. Epic heroes are larger-than-life characters who go on long and dangerous adventures. The graphic below lists some things that are true of many epic heroes.

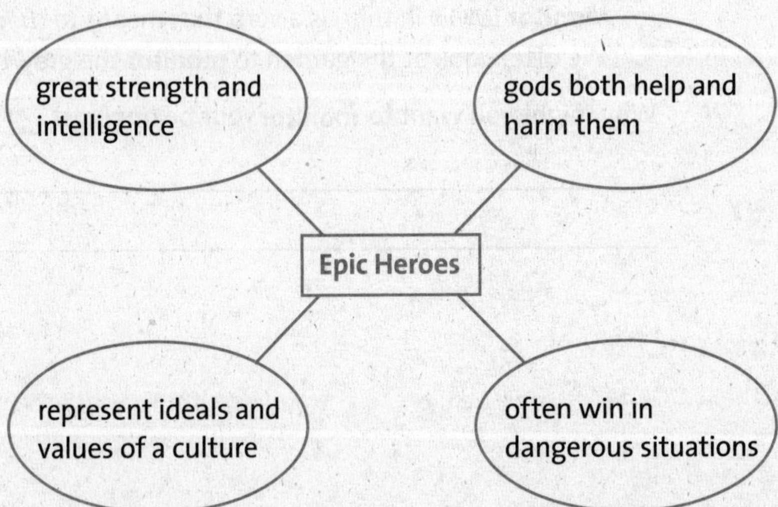

The epic hero Odysseus has helped shape many of our ideas about heroes. Odysseus is brave and self-confident, yet he sometimes ignores warnings. As you read "The Cyclops," pay attention to how Odysseus faces conflicts. What can you tell about his character? How would you describe him to a friend? What does his character show you about qualities the ancient Greeks admired?

Reading Strategy: Reading an Epic Poem

The strategies for reading an epic are very similar to those for reading any narrative poem, or poem that tells a story. As you read—

- keep track of what's happening; list events
- read aloud, especially if something confuses you
- stop and read difficult parts more than once; refer to the footnotes for definitions of unfamiliar words
- pause to visualize **imagery,** or language that appeals to the senses of sight, hearing, touch, smell, and taste
- watch for figurative language, or imaginative comparisons; look for Homer's **epic similes**—long comparisons using *like* or *as*
- note **epithets,** or repeated phrases that are used to describe certain people and things

Vocabulary in Context

Note: Words are listed in the order in which they appear in the epic.

Ponderous (PON duhr uhs) is an adjective that means *heavy and sometimes clumsy.*

The monster's **ponderous** door was too heavy for them to open.

Profusion (pruh FYOO zhuhn) is a noun that means *large quantity* or *abundance.*

They hid behind huge piles of garbage, a **profusion** of waste.

Adversary (AD ver sair ee) is a noun that means *opponent* or *enemy.*

As they escaped, they laughed at the monster, their **adversary**.

Vocabulary Practice

Review the words and sample sentences above. Then, think about the challenges an epic hero might face. Write a short paragraph describing a heroic adventure. Use each of the Vocabulary words.

Answers will vary.

SET A PURPOSE FOR READING
Read to learn about the epic hero Odysseus and his adventure with the Cyclops.

THE CYCLOPS

from the ODYSSEY

Epic Poem by
HOMER
Translated by
ROBERT FITZGERALD

BACKGROUND The *Odyssey* (OD ih see)—an epic from ancient Greece—tells of the adventures of the hero Odysseus (oh DIS ee uhs). In this excerpt, Odysseus describes his meeting with a giant one-eyed monster named Polyphemus (pauhl ih FEE mus). Polyphemus is one of the Cyclopes,[1] and he is also the son of Poseidon (poh SY duhn), the Greek god of the sea. Odysseus' curiosity and pride lead him to the Cyclops' empty cave. They also lead him to wait for the monster to come home.

"In the next land we found were **Cyclopes**,
giants, louts, [without a law to bless them].
[In ignorance leaving the fruitage of the earth in mystery
to the immortal gods], they neither plow
nor sow by hand, nor till the ground, though grain—
wild wheat and barley—grows untended, and
wine-grapes, in clusters, ripen in heaven's rain.
Cyclopes [have no muster and no meeting,
no consultation or old tribal ways],
but each one dwells in his own mountain cave

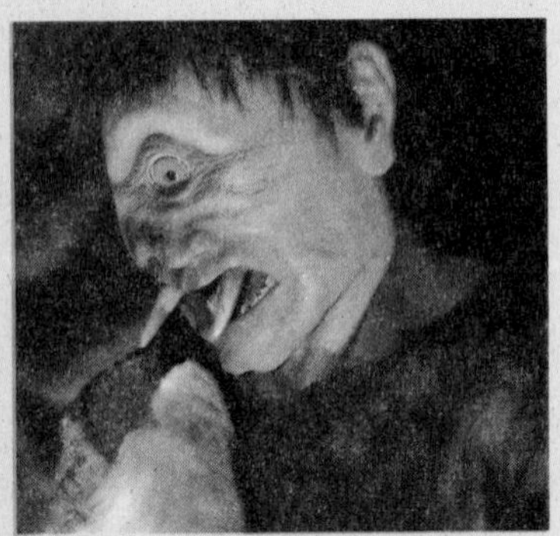

VISUAL VOCABULARY
According to Greek legend, the **Cyclopes** were a race of giants who had one eye in the middle of their foreheads.

1. **Cyclopes (sy CLOH peez)**: refers to the monsters in plural; *Cyclops* (SY clops) is singular.

dealing out rough justice to wife and child,
indifferent to what the others do. . . ." (A)

Across the bay from the land of the Cyclopes was a lush, deserted island. Odysseus and his crew landed on the island in a dense fog and spent days feasting on wine and wild goats and observing the mainland, where the Cyclopes lived. On the third day, Odysseus and his company of men set out to learn if the Cyclopes were friends or foes.

"When the young Dawn with finger tips of rose
came in the east, I called my men together
and made a speech to them: (B)

'Old shipmates, friends,
the rest of you stand by; I'll make the crossing
in my own ship, with my own company,
and find out what the mainland natives are—
for they may be wild savages, and lawless,
or hospitable and god fearing men.'

At this I went aboard, and gave the word
to cast off by the stern.[2] My oarsmen followed,
filing in to their benches by the rowlocks,
and all in line dipped oars in the gray sea.

As we rowed on, and nearer to the mainland,
at one end of the bay, we saw a cavern
yawning above the water, screened with laurel,[3]
and many rams and goats about the place
inside a sheepfold—made from slabs of stone
earthfast between tall trunks of pine and rugged
towering oak trees.

IN OTHER WORDS Odysseus tells his men that he and a small group will explore the island. His shipmates launch his boat, and they row toward the island. As they get close, they see a cave with many sheep and goats nearby.

2. **stern:** the rear part of a ship.
3. **screened with laurel:** partly hidden by laurel trees.

Monitor Your Comprehension

(A) EPIC HERO

In lines 1–12, Odysseus lists at least four reasons he dislikes the Cyclopes. Draw brackets [ ] around each reason.

What does Odysseus' list tell you about the kind of society admired by the ancient Greeks?

Possible answer: The ancient Greeks admired an orderly society administered by laws.

(B) READING AN EPIC POEM

Epithets are short, repeated phrases used to describe particular people or things. One of Homer's most famous epithets describes a sunrise. Reread lines 13–15, and draw a circle around this epithet.

A prodigious man
slept in this cave alone, and took his flocks
to graze afield—remote from all companions,
knowing none but savage ways, a brute
so huge, he seemed no man at all of those
who eat good wheaten bread; but he seemed rather
a shaggy mountain reared in solitude. C
We beached there, and I told the crew
to stand by and keep watch over the ship;
as for myself I took my twelve best fighters
and went ahead. I had a goatskin full
of that sweet liquor that Euanthes' son,
Maron,[4] had given me. He kept Apollo's
holy grove at Ismarus; for kindness
we showed him there, and showed his wife and child,
he gave me seven shining golden talents[5]
perfectly formed, a solid silver winebowl,
and then this liquor—twelve two-handled jars
of brandy, pure and fiery. Not a slave
in Maron's household knew this drink; only
he, his wife and the storeroom mistress knew;
and [they would put one cupful—ruby-colored,
honey-smooth—in twenty more of water]
but still the sweet scent hovered like a fume
over the winebowl. No man turned away
when cups of this came round.

C READING AN EPIC POEM

Reread lines 31–37, and underline **imagery** that helps you visualize, or "see," the Cyclops. In your own words on the lines below, briefly describe how you picture the Cyclops.

Possible answer: I picture the Cyclops as an untidy man who is as large as a mountain.

IN OTHER WORDS Odysseus takes twelve of his best fighting men to explore the cave. They bring along a goatskin container of wine that Odysseus had received as a gift.

► Put brackets [ ] around the words in lines 49–56 that tell you how valuable people think this wine is.

4. **Euanthes** (**yoo AN theez**); **Maron** (**mair AWN**).
5. **talents:** bars of gold or silver used as money.

Monitor Your Comprehension

A wineskin full
I brought along, and victuals[6] in a bag,
for in my bones I knew some towering brute
would be upon us soon—all outward power,
a wild man, ignorant of civility.

We climbed, then, briskly to the cave. But Cyclops
had gone afield, to pasture his fat sheep,
so we looked round at everything inside:
a drying rack that sagged with cheeses, pens
crowded with lambs and kids, each in its class:
firstlings apart from middlings, and the 'dewdrops,'
or newborn lambkins, penned apart from both.
And vessels full of whey[7] were brimming there—
bowls of earthenware and pails for milking.
My men came pressing round me, pleading:
'Why not
take these cheeses, get them stowed, come back,
throw open all the pens, and make a run for it?
We'll drive the kids and lambs aboard. We say
put out again on good salt water!'[8]

IN OTHER WORDS Odysseus and his men find Cyclops gone. They investigate his sheep, his cave, and food. Odysseus' men want to raid the cave and get back to the ship before Cyclops returns.

Ah,
how sound that was! Yet I refused. I wished
to see the caveman, what he had to offer—
no pretty sight, it turned out, for my friends. (D)
We lit a fire, burnt an offering,[9]
and took some cheese to eat; then sat in silence

6. **victuals** (**VIT elz**): food.
7. **whey:** the watery part of milk; during the making of cheese, whey separates from the solid part of milk, the curds.
8. **good salt water:** the open sea.
9. **burnt an offering:** burned a portion of the food as an offering to the gods in the hope that they will be kind. (Such offerings were frequently performed by Greek sailors during difficult journeys.)

(D) EPIC HERO
Reread lines 70–77. Underline the reason Odysseus decides to stay in the cave.

On the lines below, explain what Odysseus' decision shows about his character.

Possible answer: Unlike his men, Odysseus wants to wait for the Cyclops to return. His own curiosity caused him to refuse his men's "sound" request, demonstrating the trait in which an epic hero dismisses danger.

Monitor Your Comprehension

around the embers, waiting. When he came
he had a load of dry boughs on his shoulder
to stoke his fire at suppertime. He dumped it
with a great crash into that hollow cave,
and we all scattered fast to the far wall.
Then over the broad cavern floor he ushered
the ewes he meant to milk. He left his rams
and he-goats in the yard outside, and swung
high overhead a slab of solid rock
to close the cave. Two dozen four-wheeled wagons,
with heaving wagon teams, could not have stirred
the tonnage of that rock from where he wedged it
over the doorsill. Next he took his seat
and milked his bleating ewes. A practiced job
he made of it, giving each ewe her suckling;
thickened his milk, then, into curds and whey,
sieved out the curds to drip in withy baskets,[10]
and poured the whey to stand in bowls
cooling until he drank it for his supper.
When all these chores were done, he poked the fire,
heaping on brushwood. In the glare he saw us.

IN OTHER WORDS Odysseus refuses to leave: he wants to see the monster Cyclops. Cyclops returns, but he moves a huge stone over the opening of the cave, sealing it shut. Then he milks his goats and begins to make cheese. Finally, he notices his visitors when the fire flares up.

'Strangers,' he said, 'who are you? And where from?
What brings you here by sea ways—a fair traffic?[11]
Or are you wandering rogues, who cast your lives
like dice, and ravage other folk by sea?' PAUSE & REFLECT

We felt a pressure on our hearts, in dread
of that deep rumble and that mighty man.

PAUSE & REFLECT

In lines 101–104, Cyclops asks the men four questions. With a partner, talk about the meaning of each question. Then, discuss why Cyclops might be so worried about strangers.

Students should discuss that the Cyclops might worry about strangers because they may be dishonest men who want to steal from him.

10. **withy baskets:** baskets made from twigs.
11. **fair traffic:** honest trading.

Monitor Your Comprehension

But all the same I spoke up in reply:

'We are from Troy, Achaeans, blown off course
by shifting gales on the Great South Sea;
homeward bound, but taking routes and ways
uncommon; so the will of Zeus would have it.
We served under Agamemnon, son of Atreus—
the whole world knows what city
he laid waste, what armies he destroyed. Ⓔ
It was our luck to come here; here we stand,
beholden for your help, or any gifts
you give—as custom is to honor strangers.
We would entreat you, great Sir, have a care
for the gods' courtesy; Zeus will avenge
the unoffending guest.'[12]

IN OTHER WORDS Cyclops asks the men where they are from and why they are on the island. Odysseus does not give clear answers. He asks Cyclops to treat them as honored guests; otherwise, Zeus, the king of the gods, will punish him.

He answered this
from his brute chest, unmoved:

'You are a ninny,
or else you come from the other end of nowhere,
telling me, mind the gods! We Cyclopes
care not a whistle for your thundering Zeus
or all the gods in bliss; we have more force by far.
I would not let you go for fear of Zeus—
you or your friends—unless I had a whim to.
Tell me, where was it, now, you left your ship—
around the point, or down the shore, I wonder?'

Ⓔ EPIC HERO

In lines 108–114, Odysseus tells the story of how the men arrived at the island. Listeners would have known about the war in Troy and King Agamemnon's victory for the Greeks. What does this story help show about the lives of Odysseus and his men?

Possible answer: Odysseus and his men are brave soldiers returning home from war, having served victoriously under Agamemnon. Odysseus is suggesting that he is a great warrior.

12. It was a sacred Greek custom to honor strangers with food and gifts. Odysseus reminds Cyclops that Zeus will punish anyone who mistreats a guest.

Monitor Your Comprehension

He thought he'd find out, but I saw through this,
and answered with a ready lie:

'My ship?
Poseidon Lord, who sets the earth a-tremble,
broke it up on the rocks at your land's end.
A wind from seaward served him, drove us there.
We are survivors, these good men and I.' (F)

Neither reply nor pity came from him,
but in one stride he clutched at my companions
and caught two in his hands like squirming puppies
to beat their brains out, spattering the floor.
Then he dismembered them and made his meal,
gaping and crunching like a mountain lion—
everything: innards, flesh, and marrow bones.
We cried aloud, lifting our hands to Zeus,
powerless, looking on at this, appalled;
but Cyclops went on filling up his belly
with manflesh and great gulps of whey,
then lay down like a mast among his sheep.
My heart beat high now at the chance of action,
and drawing the sharp sword from my hip I went
along his flank to stab him where the midriff
holds the liver. I had touched the spot
when sudden fear stayed me: if I killed him
we perished there as well, for we could never
move his **ponderous** doorway slab aside.

(F) EPIC HERO

In lines 130–135, Odysseus lies to the Cyclops: he says that his ship has been smashed on the rocks.

Which quality of an epic hero is displayed in Odysseus' decision to lie?

Possible answer: In lying to the Cyclops, Odysseus demonstrates great courage and intelligence.

Why do you say so?

Possible answer: Odysseus knows with certainty that the Cyclops has no qualms about mistreating his guests or their property so he lies to protect the ship.

VOCABULARY

The word **ponderous** is an adjective that means *heavy and sometimes clumsy.*

IN OTHER WORDS Cyclops insults the men and tells them he does not fear Zeus. Cyclops asks where their ship is. Odysseus knows the monster will destroy the ship, so he lies, saying that the ship has sunk. Cyclops catches two men and eats them. Then the monster goes to sleep.

► With a partner, discuss why Odysseus does not kill the sleeping monster with his sword.

Students should discuss that Odysseus does not kill the Cyclops because only Polyphemus is strong enough to move the slab that blocks the mouth of the cave.

So we were left to groan and wait for morning.

When the young Dawn with fingertips of rose
lit up the world, the Cyclops built a fire
and milked his handsome ewes, all in due order,
putting the sucklings to the mothers. Then,
his chores being all dispatched, he caught
another brace[13] of men to make his breakfast,
and whisked away his great door slab
to let his sheep go through—but he, behind,
reset the stone as one would cap a quiver.[14]
There was a din of whistling as the Cyclops
rounded his flock to higher ground, then stillness.
And now I pondered how to hurt him worst,
if but Athena granted what I prayed for. G
Here are the means I thought would serve my turn:

a club, or staff, lay there along the fold—
an olive tree, felled green and left to season[15]
for Cyclops' hand. And it was like a mast
a lugger[16] of twenty oars, broad in the beam—
a deep-sea-going craft—might carry:
so long, so big around, it seemed. Now I
chopped out a six foot section of this pole
and set it down before my men, who scraped it;
and when they had it smooth, I hewed again
to make a stake with pointed end. I held this
in the fire's heart and turned it, toughening it,
then hid it, well back in the cavern, under
one of the dung piles in **profusion** there.
Now came the time to toss for it: who ventured
along with me? whose hand could bear to thrust
and grind that spike in Cyclops' eye, when mild
sleep had mastered him? As luck would have it,

G READING AN EPIC POEM
Reread lines 156–168. In your own words on the lines below, list each of the events.

Possible answer: As the day began, the Cyclops built a fire and milked his sheep. When he had finished his chores, he caught two men to have for breakfast. Then, he moved the slab to let his sheep out and reset it behind them. The Cyclops took his sheep to higher ground, whistling as he walked away. Odysseus began to plot how to defeat the Cyclops and escape.

VOCABULARY
The word **profusion** is a noun that means *large quantity* or *abundance.*

13. **brace:** pair.
14. Cyclops moves the massive rock as easily as someone can place the cap on a container of arrows.
15. **left to season:** left to dry out and harden.
16. **lugger:** a small, wide sailing ship.

Monitor Your Comprehension

the men I would have chosen won the toss—
four strong men, and I made five as captain.

IN OTHER WORDS The men spend the night in the cave. The next morning, Cyclops milks his sheep, eats two more men, and leaves the cave. He moves the great stone to block the door. Planning to blind the monster, Odysseus sharpens the end of a long pole. Four men are chosen to help Odysseus use the pole.

At evening came the shepherd with his flock,
his woolly flock. The rams as well, this time,
entered the cave: by some sheep-herding whim—
or a god's bidding—none were left outside.
He hefted his great boulder into place
and sat him down to milk the bleating ewes
in proper order, put the lambs to suck,
and swiftly ran through all his evening chores.
Then he caught two more men and feasted on them.
My moment was at hand, and I went forward
holding an ivy bowl of my dark drink,
looking up, saying:
'Cyclops, try some wine.
Here's liquor to wash down your scraps of men.
Taste it, and see the kind of drink we carried
under our planks. I meant it for an offering
if you would help us home. But you are mad,
unbearable, a bloody monster! After this,
will any other traveller come to see you?'

He seized and drained the bowl, and it went down
so fiery and smooth he called for more:

'Give me another, thank you kindly. Tell me,
how are you called? I'll make a gift will please you.
Even Cyclopes know the wine-grapes grow
out of grassland and loam in heaven's rain,
but here's a bit of nectar and ambrosia!'[17] Ⓗ

17. **nectar (NEK ter) and ambrosia (am BROH zhuh)**: the drink and food of the gods.

Ⓗ **LANGUAGE COACH**

In lines 200–213 Homer uses **dialogue**, or written conversation between characters. Here, dialogue is marked by single quotation marks (' '). Although they are enemies, in this dialogue Odysseus and Cyclops talk as if they are friends. First, circle the quotation marks. Then, with a partner, discuss why Odysseus may have decided to talk with the monster.

Students should discuss that Odysseus talks to the Cyclops in order to offer him wine, which he hopes will cause the Cyclops to fall asleep.

Three bowls I brought him, and he poured them down.
I saw the fuddle and flush[18] come over him,
then I sang out in cordial tones:

IN OTHER WORDS Cyclops returns to his cave in the evening. He finishes his evening chores. Then Odysseus offers him some of the wine he had brought. Cyclops drinks three bowls of wine.

'Cyclops,
you ask my honorable name? Remember
the gift you promised me, and I shall tell you.
My name is Nohbdy: mother, father, and friends,
everyone calls me Nohbdy.'

And he said:
'Nohbdy's my meat, then, after I eat his friends.
Others come first. There's a noble gift, now.' ❶

Even as he spoke, he reeled and tumbled backward,
his great head lolling to one side: and sleep
took him like any creature. Drunk, hiccupping,
he dribbled streams of liquor and bits of men.

Now, by the gods, I drove my big hand spike
deep in the embers, charring it again,
and cheered my men along with battle talk
to keep their courage up: no quitting now.
The pike[19] of olive, green though it had been,
reddened and glowed as if about to catch.
I drew it from the coals and my four fellows
gave me a hand, lugging it near the Cyclops
as more than natural force nerved them; straight
forward they sprinted, lifted it, and rammed it
deep in his crater eye, and I leaned on it
turning it as a shipwright turns a drill

❶ READING AN EPIC POEM
Say the name *Nohbdy* out loud. What word does *Nohbdy* sound like?

Nobody

18. **fuddle and flush:** the state of confusion and redness of the face caused by drinking alcohol.
19. **the pike:** the pointed stake.

in planking, having men below to swing
the two-handled strap that spins it in the groove.
So with our brand we bored that great eye socket
while blood ran out around the red hot bar.
Eyelid and lash were seared; [the pierced ball
hissed broiling], and the roots popped.

IN OTHER WORDS Odysseus tells the monster that his name is "Nohbdy." Drunk with wine, Cyclops goes to sleep. While he's asleep, Odysseus and four of his men heat the sharp pike, or stake, in the fire.

► Underline the sentences that tell you what Odysseus and his men do with the pike.

In a smithy[20]
one sees a white-hot axehead or an adze[21]
plunged and wrung in a cold tub, [screeching steam]—
the way they make soft iron hale and hard—:
just so that eyeball hissed around the spike.
[The Cyclops bellowed and the rock roared] round him,
and we fell back in fear. Clawing his face
he tugged the bloody spike out of his eye,
threw it away, and his wild hands went groping;
then [he set up a howl for Cyclopes]
who lived in caves on windy peaks nearby. J
Some heard him; and they came by divers[22] ways
to clump around outside and call:

'What ails you,
Polyphemus? Why do you cry so sore
in the starry night? You will not let us sleep.
Sure no man's driving off your flock? No man
has tricked you, ruined you?'

J READING AN EPIC POEM
With a partner, read lines 241–254 aloud. As you read, pause to **visualize imagery,** or language that appeals to the senses. Then, draw brackets[ ] around words and phrases that appeal to your sense of hearing.

20. **smithy:** blacksmith's shop.
21. **adze** (**adz**): a sharp tool with a curved blade.
22. **divers:** various.

Out of the cave
the mammoth Polyphemus roared in answer:

'Nohbdy, Nohbdy's tricked me, Nohbdy's ruined me!'

To this rough shout they made a sage[23] reply:

'Ah well, if nobody has played you foul
there in your lonely bed, we are no use in pain
given by great Zeus. Let it be your father,
Poseidon Lord, to whom you pray.' (K)

IN OTHER WORDS Cyclops roars and howls, waking up the other Cyclopes. When the others ask Polyphemus who is bothering him, he tells them that it's "Nohbdy." The others leave, thinking that nothing is wrong.

So saying
they trailed away. And I was filled with laughter
to see how like a charm the name deceived them.
Now Cyclops, wheezing as the pain came on him,
fumbled to wrench away the great doorstone
and squatted in the breach[24] with arms thrown wide
for any silly beast or man who bolted—
hoping somehow I might be such a fool.
But I kept thinking how to win the game:
death sat there huge; how could we slip away?
I drew on all my wits, and ran through tactics,
reasoning as a man will for dear life,
until a trick came—and it pleased me well.
The Cyclops' rams were handsome, fat, with heavy
fleeces, a dark violet. (L)

23. **sage:** wise.
24. **breach:** opening.

Monitor Your Comprehension

(K) EPIC HERO

Reread lines 261–267. Earlier in the story, Odysseus lies about his own name. Circle each time that Polyphemus, the cyclops, says that name. On the lines below, explain why Odysseus lied earlier.

Possible answer: Odysseus lied to Polyphemus about his name in order to conceal his identity. When Polyphemus tries to explain what has happened, the others assume that no one is hurting him.

(L) EPIC HERO

Below are four reasons that Odysseus might be considered an epic hero:

1. He has great strength.
2. He has great intelligence.
3. He is helped by the gods.
4. He is harmed by the gods.

Which of the four choices is best supported by information in lines 268–279? Draw a circle around your answer.

Three abreast
I tied them silently together, twining
cords of willow from the ogre's bed;
then slung a man under each middle one
to ride there safely, shielded left and right.
So three sheep could convey each man. I took
the woolliest ram, the choicest of the flock,
and hung myself under his kinky belly,
pulled up tight, with fingers twisted deep
in sheepskin ringlets for an iron grip.
So, breathing hard, we waited until morning. Ⓜ

Ⓜ READING AN EPIC POEM
Reread lines 281–291. In your own words on the lines below, explain how Odysseus plans to escape from the Cyclops' cave.

Possible answer: To escape from the cave, Odysseus ties together groups of three sheep and then ties each of his men under the middle one so that the man is hidden by the sheep on either side.

When Dawn spread out her finger tips of rose
the rams began to stir, moving for pasture,
and peals of bleating echoed round the pens
where dams with udders full called for a milking.
Blinded, and sick with pain from his head wound,
the master stroked each ram, then let it pass, ✔
but my men riding on the pectoral fleece[25] ✔
the giant's blind hands blundering never found. ✔
Last of them all my ram, the leader, came,
weighted by wool and me with my meditations.
The Cyclops patted him, and then he said:

IN OTHER WORDS Cyclops moves the stone and sits in front of the cave opening so no one can escape. Meanwhile, Odysseus ties the rams together in threes and ties a man under each middle ram. Odysseus himself hangs under one large ram.

► How do the men finally escape the cave? Put a checkmark ✔ **beside** the lines that tell you this.

'Sweet cousin ram, why lag behind the rest
in the night cave? You never linger so,
but graze before them all, and go afar
to crop sweet grass, and take your stately way

25. **pectoral fleece:** the wool covering a sheep's chest.

Monitor Your Comprehension

leading along the streams, until at evening
you run to be the first one in the fold.
Why, now, so far behind? Can you be grieving
over your Master's eye? That carrion rogue
and his accurst companions burnt it out
when he had conquered all my wits with wine.
Nohbdy will not get out alive, I swear.
Oh, had you brain and voice to tell
where he may be now, dodging all my fury!
Bashed by this hand and bashed on this rock wall
his brains would strew the floor, and I should have
rest from the outrage Nohbdy worked upon me.'

He sent us into the open, then. Close by,
I dropped and rolled clear of the ram's belly,
going this way and that to untie the men.
With many glances back, we rounded up
his fat, stiff-legged sheep to take aboard,
and drove them down to where the good ship lay.
We saw, as we came near, our fellows' faces
shining; then we saw them turn to grief
tallying those who had not fled from death.
I hushed them, jerking head and eyebrows up,
and in a low voice told them: 'Load this herd;
move fast, and put the ship's head toward the breakers.'[26]
They all pitched in at loading, then embarked
and struck their oars into the sea. Far out,
as far off shore as shouted words would carry,
I sent a few back to the **adversary**:

'O Cyclops! Would you feast on my companions?
Puny, am I, in a Caveman's hands?
How do you like the beating that we gave you,
you damned cannibal? Eater of guests
under your roof! Zeus and the gods have paid you!'[27]

VOCABULARY
The word **adversary** is a noun that means *opponent* or *enemy.*

---

26. **put . . . the breakers:** turn the ship around so that it is heading toward the waves of the open sea.
27. Odysseus assumes that the gods are on his side.

Monitor Your Comprehension

IN OTHER WORDS Cyclops stops the large ram under which Odysseus is hiding. He wonders why this ram is lagging behind the others. Cyclops lets the ram go, and Odysseus unties his men. They round up the sheep and load them onto the boat.

► With a partner, discuss the meaning of what Odysseus yells at Cyclops.

Students should discuss that Odysseus means to taunt the Cyclops with his words, admonishing him for being beaten by Odysseus and his men and also telling him that the gods are on Odysseus's side.

The blind thing in his doubled fury broke
a hilltop in his hands and heaved it after us.
Ahead of our black prow it struck and sank
whelmed in a spuming geyser, a giant wave
that washed the ship stern foremost back to shore.
I got the longest boathook out and stood
fending us off, with furious nods to all
to put their backs into a racing stroke—
row, row, or perish. So the long oars bent
kicking the foam sternward, making head
until we drew away, and twice as far.
Now when I cupped my hands[28] I heard the crew
in low voices protesting:

'Godsake, Captain!
Why bait the beast again? Let him alone!'

'That tidal wave he made on the first throw
all but beached us.'

'All but stove us in!'
'Give him our bearing with your trumpeting,
he'll get the range and lob a boulder.'

'Aye
He'll smash our timbers and our heads together!' PAUSE & REFLECT

PAUSE & REFLECT
Odysseus insults the Cyclops as he and his men are trying to escape. How do the men react to Odysseus' insults? Why?

Possible answer: Odysseus's men want him to leave the Cyclops alone and are worried that his insults may further anger the Cyclops and lead him to overpower and eventually defeat the men.

28. **cupped my hands:** put his hands on either side of his mouth in order to magnify his voice.

Monitor Your Comprehension

I would not heed them in my glorying spirit,
but let my anger flare and yelled:
'Cyclops,
if ever mortal man inquire
how you were put to shame and blinded, tell him
Odysseus, raider of cities, took your eye:
Laertes' son, whose home's on Ithaca!' (N)

IN OTHER WORDS Polyphemus breaks off the top of a hill and throws it at the boat. It lands in front of the ship, washing the ship back to shore. Odysseus uses a long pole to push the boat away from land. He is about to taunt the monster again when his shipmates beg him to stop. Odysseus continues his insults, this time telling Cyclops his real name.

At this he gave a mighty sob and rumbled:

'Now comes the weird upon me, spoken of old.[29]
A wizard, grand and wondrous, lived here—Telemus,
a son of Eurymus; great length of days
he had in wizardry among the Cyclopes,
and these things he foretold for time to come:
my great eye lost, and at Odysseus' hands.
Always I had in mind some giant, armed
in giant force, would come against me here.
But this, but you—small, pitiful and twiggy—
you put me down with wine, you blinded me. (O)
Come back, Odysseus, and I'll treat you well,
praying the god of earthquake[30] to befriend you—
his son I am, for he by his avowal[31]
fathered me, and, if he will, he may
heal me of this black wound—he and no other
of all the happy gods or mortal men.'

Few words I shouted in reply to him:

29. **Now comes the weird upon me . . . of old:** Now I recall the destiny predicted long ago.
30. **the god of earthquake:** Poseidon, Cyclops' father.
31. **avowal:** an honest admission.

(N) EPIC HERO

Circle the epithet Odysseus uses to refer to himself in lines 360–364. What does Odysseus' use of this epithet show about his character?

Possible answer: This description shows the reader Odysseus's pride in himself.

(O) READING AN EPIC POEM

In lines 365–375 Polyphemus says that a wizard warned him that someone named Odysseus would blind him. Underline the sentence that explains why Polyphemus did not recognize that Odysseus was this man.

'If I could take your life I would and take
your time away, and hurl you down to hell!
The god of earthquake could not heal you there!'

At this he stretched his hands out in his darkness
toward the sky of stars, and prayed Poseidon:
'O hear me, lord, blue girdler of the islands,
if I am thine indeed, and thou art father:
grant that Odysseus, raider of cities, never
see his home: Laertes' son, I mean,
who kept his hall on Ithaca. Should destiny
intend that he shall see his roof again
among his family in his father land,
far be that day, and dark the years between.
Let him lose all companions, and return
under strange sail to bitter days at home.' **P**

P READING AN EPIC POEM

In lines 386–397 Cyclops prays to his father, the god Poseidon. What does Cyclops pray will happen to Odysseus?

Possible answer: The Cyclops prays that Odysseus will never see his home again. However, if the fates decide to permit Odysseus's return, it will be greatly delayed and the years in between will be filled with suffering and sadness. The Cyclops asks for Odysseus to lose all of his men, finally returning home to further unhappiness.

IN OTHER WORDS When Polyphemus hears Odysseus' real name, he remembers a prophecy, a prediction, that Odysseus would one day blind him. Odysseus taunts Cyclops again. Then Polyphemus cries out to his father, the god Poseidon, and curses Odysseus.

In these words he prayed, and the god heard him.
Now he laid hands upon a bigger stone
and wheeled around, titanic for the cast,[32]
to let it fly in the black-prowed vessel's track.
But it fell short, just aft[33] the steering oar,
and whelming seas rose giant above the stone
to bear us onward toward the island.[34]

There
as we ran in we saw the squadron waiting,
the trim ships drawn up side by side, and all

32. **titanic for the cast:** using all of his enormous strength as he prepares to throw.
33. **aft:** behind.
34. **the island:** the deserted island where most of Odysseus' men had stayed behind.

our troubled friends who waited, looking seaward.
We beached her, grinding keel in the soft sand,
and waded in, ourselves, on the sandy beach.
Then we unloaded all the Cyclops' flock
to make division, share and share alike,
only my fighters voted that my ram,
the prize of all, should go to me. I slew him
by the sea side and burnt his long thighbones
to Zeus beyond the stormcloud, Cronus' son,[35]
who rules the world. But Zeus disdained my offering;
destruction for my ships he had in store
and death for those who sailed them, my companions.

Now all day long until the sun went down
we made our feast on mutton and sweet wine,
till after sunset in the gathering dark
we went to sleep above the wash of ripples.

35. **Cronus' son:** Zeus' (**zoos**) father, Cronus (**CROH nuhs**), was a Titan, one of an earlier race of gods.

Monitor Your Comprehension

When the young Dawn with finger tips of rose
touched the world, I roused the men, gave orders
to man the ships, cast off the mooring lines;
and filing in to sit beside the rowlocks
oarsmen in line dipped oars in the gray sea.
So we moved out, sad in the vast offing,[36]
having our precious lives, but not our friends." PAUSE & REFLECT

PAUSE & REFLECT
Reread lines 419–429. With a partner, discuss why Odysseus and his men feel sad as they leave the land of the Cyclopes.

Students should discuss that Odysseus and his men are sad when they leave because they fear the fate awaiting them. Additionally, they are grieving for the men who were killed by the Cyclops.

IN OTHER WORDS Polyphemus throws another stone at the boat. It misses but pushes the boat toward the island where the other men are waiting. Odysseus kills the large ram, hoping to please the god Zeus, but Zeus does not accept the sacrifice. Odysseus predicts he will lose his ships and men before the voyage is over. In the morning, the men leave the island, grieving for their friends who were killed by Cyclops.

---

36. **offing**: the part of the deep sea that can be seen from the shore.

After Reading

Text Analysis: Epic Hero

What makes Odysseus an epic hero? The left column lists things that are true of many epic heroes. In each box in the right column, list an example of Odysseus' words or actions from his adventure with the Cyclops.

For this chart, answers will vary. See samples below.

ODYSSEUS	
Epic Heroes—	**Examples from "The Cyclops"**
have great strength and intelligence	*Odysseus tells the Cyclops that his boat was destroyed in order to protect the boat from harm. (lines 130–135)*
are both helped and harmed by the gods	*Zeus does not accept Odysseus's offering and has plans to destroy Odysseus's ship as well as kill the men onboard it. (lines 416–418)*
represent the ideals and values of their cultures	*Upon reaching the land of the Cyclopes, Odysseus remarks on their lawless and ignorant ways, which reflects the ancient Greeks' love of order. (lines 1–12)*
often win in dangerous situations	*Odysseus and his men fashion a sharp spike from an olive tree branch and use it to blind the Cyclops. (lines 170–244)*

Odysseus has many good qualities, but he's not perfect. Which of Odysseus' personal weaknesses or faults are revealed in the epic?

Possible answer: Odysseus's weaknesses or faults include pride, stubbornness, and an unwillingness to listen to advice from his men.

What is a HERO?

What heroes like Odysseus have you encountered in modern literature, movies, or television shows? Identify one of those heroes, and list the traits he or she has in common with Odysseus.

Students' answers will vary but should name a hero who has the characteristics of an epic hero, such as bravery, determination, and leadership, and explain how their example is similar to Odysseus.

After Reading

Reading Strategy: Reading an Epic Poem

Homer uses epic similes to describe certain events in the story. Remember how the spike in the Cyclops' eye sizzled and steamed *like* a white-hot axe plunged into cold water? Use the chart below to analyze how another epic simile affects you as a reader.

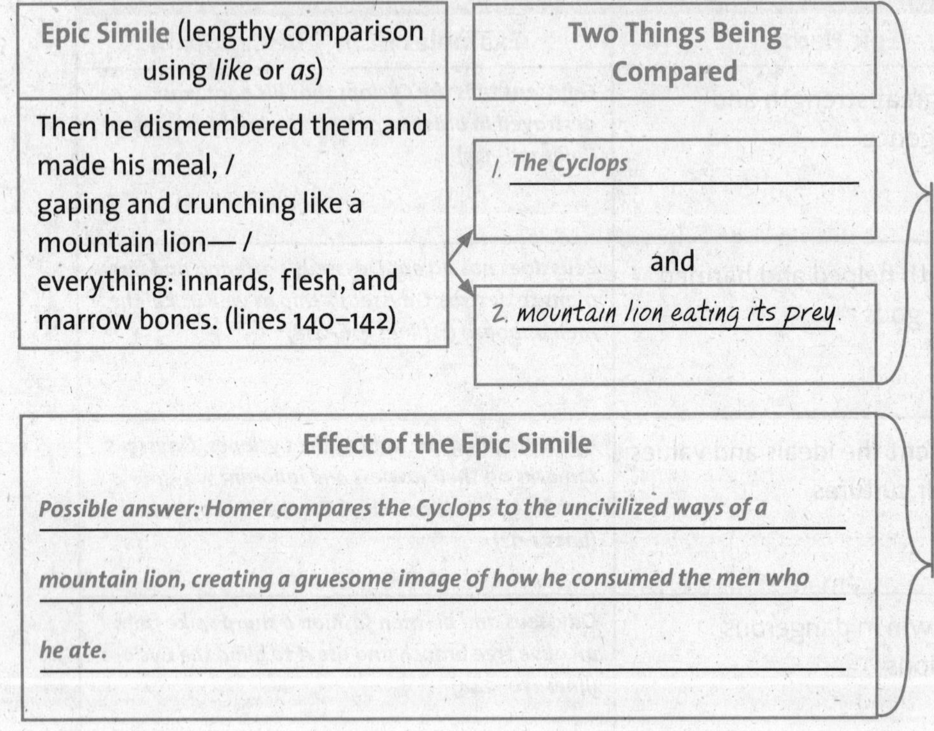

Epic Simile (lengthy comparison using *like* or *as*)
Then he dismembered them and made his meal, / gaping and crunching like a mountain lion— / everything: innards, flesh, and marrow bones. (lines 140–142)
Two Things Being Compared
1. The Cyclops
and
2. mountain lion eating its prey
Effect of the Epic Simile
Possible answer: Homer compares the Cyclops to the uncivilized ways of a mountain lion, creating a gruesome image of how he consumed the men who he ate.

Vocabulary Practice

Answer each of the following questions, using the Vocabulary word to explain your response

1. Why couldn't Odysseus' men move the **ponderous** stone?

Possible answer: The ponderous stone was too heavy and large for the men to move.

2. Why was it easy to hide spears in the **profusion** of garbage?

Possible answer: The profusion of garbage created so much waste that it was easy to hide the spears within it.

3. Why might the Cyclops consider Odysseus an **adversary**?

Possible answer: As an adversary, Odysseus wanted to blind the Cyclops in order to escape from him.

Academic Vocabulary in Speaking

The word **demonstrate** (DEM uhn strayt) is a verb that means *to show clearly.*
To **demonstrate** her strength, she did twenty pull-ups.

The word **emphasis** (EM fuh sis) is a noun that means *special attention given to something to show its importance.*
Vivid language places special **emphasis** on the hero's bravery.

The word **monitor** (MON ih tuhr) is a verb that means to *check on* or *to watch.*
The scientists set up video cameras to **monitor** the volcano.

TURN AND TALK With a partner, select one of the epithets, or descriptive phrases, used for Odysseus in "The Cyclops." Then, discuss what the epithet reveals about Odysseus' character. Use at least two of the Academic Vocabulary words in your discussion.

Encourage students to use the Academic Vocabulary words in their discussions.

Assessment Practice

DIRECTIONS Use "The Cyclops" to answer questions 1–4.

1 The *Odyssey* is an epic poem because it —

- (A) has a main character who is strong and brave
- (B) is a narrative poem that tells about the deeds of a hero
- (C) features a monster that eats human beings
- (D) was written long ago by a famous poet

2 When he first speaks to the Cyclops, Odysseus warns him that —

- (A) the Greeks will kill him
- (B) the Greeks want his land
- (C) Zeus will punish him if he does not treat the Greeks well
- (D) Zeus will kill the Cyclops if he doesn't give the Greeks food and a ship

3 Which of the following is part of an epic simile?

- (A) *young Dawn with finger tips of rose* (line 13)
- (B) *a shaggy mountain reared in solitude* (line 37)
- (C) *caught two in his hands like squirming puppies* (line 138)
- (D) *mother, father, and friends, / everyone calls me Nohbdy* (lines 219–220)

4 Which character trait is revealed in Odysseus' plan to escape the Cyclops?

- (A) Cleverness
- (B) Too much pride
- (C) Respect for the gods
- (D) Courtesy toward strangers

Accurate (AK yuhr it) is an adjective that means *exact* or *correct.*
Preciso es un adjetivo que significa *exacto o correcto.*

Analyze (AN uh lyz) is a verb that means *to examine something by looking critically or closely at it.*
Analizar es un verbo que significa *examinar algo observándolo críticamente o de cerca.*

Appreciate (uh PREE shee ayt) is a verb that means *to recognize the value of something.*
Apreciar es un verbo que significa *reconocer el valor de algo.*

Aspect (AS pekt) is a noun that means *a part or a side of something.*
Aspecto es un sustantivo que significa *parte o lado de algo.*

Attribute (AT ruh byoot) is a noun that means *a quality or feature of someone or something.*
Atributo es un sustantivo que significa *cualidad o característica de alguien o de algo.*

Characteristic (ker uhk tuh RIS tik) is a noun that means *a feature or key detail about a person or thing.*
Característica es un sustantivo que significa *rasgo o detalle clave sobre una persona o cosa.*

Circumstance (SER kuhm stans) is a noun that means *a situation or detail connected with an event.*
Circunstancia es un sustantivo que significa *situación o detalle relacionado con un evento.*

Cite (syt) is a verb that means *to point out or give as an example or proof of something.*
Citar es un verbo que significa *resaltar o dar como ejemplo o prueba de algo.*

Coherent (koh HIR uhnt) is an adjective that means *connected or logical, making sense.*
Coherente es un adjetivo que significa *conectado o lógico, que tiene sentido.*

Complex (kuhm PLEKS) is an adjective that means *made up of two or more parts.* It can also mean *not simple.*
Complejo es un adjetivo que significa *compuesto por dos o más partes.* También puede significar *no simple.*

Conclude (kuhn KLOOD) is a verb that means *to decide by reasoning.*
Concluir es un verbo que significa *decidir por medio del razonamiento.*

Construct (kuhn STRUKT) is a verb that means *to build or put parts together.*
Construir es un verbo que significa *hacer, crear o unir las partes de algo.*

Context (KON tekst) is a noun that means *the conditions in which an event or idea happens or exists.*
Contexto es un sustantivo que significa *condiciones en las que un evento o una idea ocurre o existe.*

Contrast (kuhn TRAST) is a verb that means *to show differences between two things.*
Contrastar es un verbo que significa *mostrar las diferencias entre dos cosas.*

Contribute (kuhn TRIB yoot) is a verb that means *to provide a thing or idea that helps to create a result.*
Contribuir es un verbo que significa *aportar una cosa o idea para alcanzar un resultado.*

Conventional (kuhn VEN shun uhl) is an adjective that means *in keeping with traditional ideas or ways of doing things.*
Convencional es un adjetivo que significa *mantener las ideas o las costumbres tradicionales.*

Critical (KRIT uh kuhl) is an adjective that means *having to do with making judgments based on strengths and weaknesses.*
Crítico es un adjetivo que significa *relacionado con realizar juicios basándose en los puntos fuertes y débiles.*

Demonstrate (DEM uhn strayt) is a verb that means *to show clearly.*
Demostrar es un verbo que significa *mostrar en forma clara.*

Device (dih VYS) is a noun that means *a tool or method used to achieve a specific purpose.*
Dispositivo es un sustantivo que significa *herramienta o método utilizado para alcanzar un propósito específico.*

Differentiate (dif uh REN shee ayt) is a verb that means *to be aware of or point out a difference between two or more things.*
Diferenciar es un verbo que significa *ser consiciente o resaltar la diferencia entre dos o cosas o más.*

Distinct (dih STINGKT) is an adjective that means *separate* or *different*. It can also mean *sharp and clear.*
Distinto es un adjetivo que significa *seprado o diferente*. También puede significar *definido y claro.*

Effect (uh FEKT) is a noun that means *the result of an event or of an action taken by someone.* It can also mean *the overall impression created by an artistic work.*
Efecto es un sustantivo que significa *resultado de un evento o una acción llevada a cabo por alguien.* También puede significar *impresión general creada por una obra de arte.*

Element (EL uh muhnt) is a noun that means *a needed or basic part of something.*
Elemento es un sustantivo que significa *necesidad parte básica de algo.*

Emphasis (EM fuh sis) is a noun that means *special attention given to something to show its importance.*
Énfasis es un sustantivo que significa *atención especial que se da a algo para mostrar que es importante.*

Environment (en VY ruhn muhnt) is a noun that means *the conditions in which something exists.*
Ambiente es un sustantivo que significa *condiciones en las que algo existe.*

Evaluate (ih VAL yoo ayt) is a verb that means *to judge the value or importance of something.*
Evaluar es un verbo que significa *juzgar el valor o la importancia de algo.*

Evident (EV ih duhnt) is an adjective that means *easy to see or understand.*
Evidente es un adjetivo que significa *fácil de ver o comprender.*

Evoke (ih VOHK) is a verb that means *to bring out or produce.*
Evocar es un verbo que significa *traer a la memoria o producir.*

Factor (FAK tuhr) is a noun that means *a cause or condition that helps produce a result.*
Factor es un sustantivo que significa *causa o condición que ayuda a producir un resultado.*

Ideology (eye dee AWL uh jee) is a noun that means *the beliefs and ideas held by a group of people.*
Ideología es un sustantivo que significa *creencias e ideas de un grupo de personas.*

Implicit (im PLIS it) is an adjective that means *not actually said but hinted at instead.*
Implícito es un adjetivo que significa *algo que no se dice pero que se sugiere.*

Incorporate (in KOR puh rayt) is a verb that means *to take in or include as a part of something bigger.*
Incorporar es un verbo que significa *tomar o incluir para formar parte de algo mayor.*

Indicate (IN dih kayt) is a verb that means *to point out or show.*
Indicar es un verbo que significa *señalar o mostrar.*

Infer (in FER) is a verb that means *to make a reasonable guess based on clues or facts.*
Inferir es un verbo que significa *suposición razonable basada en purebas o hechos.*

Influence (IN floo uhns) is a noun that means *the power of a person or thing to affect others.*
Influencia es un sustantivo que significa *el poder de una persona o cosa para afectar a otras.*

Interact (in tuhr AKT) is a verb that means *to act or work together with someone or something.*
Interactuar es un verbo que significa *actuar o trabajar con alguien o algo.*

Interpret (in TER prit) is a verb that means *to explain or make clear the meaning of something.*
Interpretar es un verbo que significa *explicar o aclarar el el significado de algo.*

Investigate (in VES tih gayt) is a verb that means *to search or study carefully for information.*
Investigar es un verbo que significa *buscar o estudiar en detalle para obtener información.*

Monitor (MON ih tuhr) is a verb that means *to check on* or *to watch.*
Supervisar es un verbo que significa *controlar u observar.*

Motivate (MOH tuh vayt) is a verb that means *to cause someone to take action.*
Motivar es un verbo que significa *incitar a alguien para que realice una acción.*

Perceive (puhr SEEV) is a verb that means *to notice or become aware of.*
Percibir es un verbo que significa *notar o tomar conciencia de algo.*

Perspective (puhr SPEK tiv) is a noun that means *point of view* or *a way of looking at things.*
Perspectiva es un sustantivo que significa *punto de vista* o *manera de ver las cosas.*

Predominant (prih DOM uh nuhnt) is an adjective that means *most important* or *occurring most often.*
Predominante es un adjetivo que significa *más importante* o *que ocurre más frecuentemente.*

Primary (PRY mer ee) is an adjective that means *first* or *most important.*
Primario es un adjetivo que significa *primero* o *más importante.*

Relevant (REL uh vuhnt) is an adjective that means *having to do with the subject being discussed.*
Relevante es un adjetivo que significa *relacionado con un tema en cuestión.*

Resolve (rih ZOLV) is a verb that means *to figure out, solve, or make clear.*
Resolver es un verbo que significa *sacar en claro, solucionar o esclarecer.*

Reveal (rih VEEL) is a verb that means *to show* or *make known.*
Revelar es un verbo que significa *mostrar* o *dar a conocer.*

Sequence (SEE kwuhns) is a noun that means *the order in which one thing follows another.*
Secuencia es un sustantivo que significa *orden en el que una cosa sigue a otra.*

Significant (sig NIF ih kuhnt) is an adjective that means *important* or *having meaning.*
Significativo es un adjetivo que significa *importante* o *que tiene sentido.*

Source (sors) is a noun that means *the place where something comes from.* It can sometimes mean *a person or thing that provides information.*
Fuente es un sustantivo que significa *lugar de donde algo proviene.* También puede significar *persona o cosa que proporciona información.*

Specific (spih SIF ik) is an adjective that means *definite* or *exact.*
Específico es un adjetivo que significa *definitivo* o *exacto.*

Structure (STRUK chuhr) is a noun that means *something made of parts put together* or *the way something is put together.*
Estructura es un sustantivo que significa *algo que se construye uniendo diferentes partes* o *manera en la que algo se une.*

Synthesize (SIN thih syz) is a verb that means *to put separate parts together to make a whole.*
Sintetizar es un verbo que significa *unir partes separadas para formar un todo.*

Technique (tek NEEK) is a noun that means *a special way of doing something.*
Técnica es un sustantivo que significa *manera especial de hacer algo.*

Tradition (truh DISH uhn) is a noun that means *a custom, belief, or practice passed down from one generation to the next.*

Tradición es un sustantivo que significa *costumbre, creeencia o práctica que se transmite de generación en generación.*

Undertake (un duhr TAYK) is a verb that means *to agree to do a task* or *to begin that task.*

Asumir es un verbo que significa *aceptar una tarea empezar una tarea.*

Unique (yoo NEEK) is an adjective that describes something that is *the only one of its kind and is not like any other.*

Único es un adjetivo que describe algo que es *solo en sus especie y que no es como ningún otro.*

Vary (VAIR ee) is a verb that means *to change or become different in some way.*

Variar es un verbo que significa *cambiar o ser diferente en cierta manera.*

High-Frequency Word List

Would you like to build your word knowledge? If so, the word lists on the next six pages can help you. These lists contain the 600 most common words in the English language. The most common words are on the First Hundred Words list; the next most common are on the Second Hundred Words list; and so on.

Study tip: Read through these lists starting with the First Hundred Words list. For each word you don't know, make a flash card. Work through the flash cards until you can read each word quickly.

FIRST HUNDRED WORDS			
the	he	go	who
a	I	see	an
is	they	then	their
you	one	us	she
to	good	no	new
and	me	him	said
we	about	by	did
that	had	was	boy
in	if	come	three
not	some	get	down
for	up	or	work
at	her	two	put
with	do	man	were
it	when	little	before
on	so	has	just
can	my	them	long
will	very	how	here
are	all	like	other
of	would	our	old
this	any	what	take
your	been	know	cat
as	out	make	again
but	there	which	give
be	from	much	after
have	day	his	many

SECOND HUNDRED WORDS			
saw	big	may	fan
home	where	let	five
soon	am	use	read
stand	ball	these	over
box	morning	right	such
upon	live	present	way
first	four	tell	too
came	last	next	shall
girl	color	please	own
house	away	leave	most
find	red	hand	sure
because	friend	more	thing
made	pretty	why	only
could	eat	better	near
book	want	under	than
look	year	while	open
mother	white	should	kind
run	got	never	must
school	play	each	high
people	found	best	far
night	left	another	both
into	men	seem	end
say	bring	tree	also
think	wish	name	until
back	black	dear	call

THIRD HUNDRED WORDS			
ask	hat	off	fire
small	car	sister	ten
yellow	write	happy	order
show	try	once	part
goes	myself	didn’t	early
clean	longer	set	fat
buy	those	round	third
thank	hold	dress	same
sleep	full	tell	love
letter	carry	wash	hear
jump	eight	start	eyes
help	sing	always	door
fly	warm	anything	clothes
don’t	sit	around	through
fast	dog	close	o’clock
cold	ride	walk	second
today	hot	money	water
does	grow	turn	town
face	cut	might	took
green	seven	hard	pair
every	woman	along	now
brown	funny	bed	keep
coat	yes	fine	head
six	ate	sat	food
gave	stop	hope	yesterday

FOURTH HUNDRED WORDS			
told	yet	word	airplane
Miss	true	almost	without
father	above	thought	wear
children	still	send	Mr.
land	meet	receive	side
interest	since	pay	poor
feet	number	nothing	lost
garden	state	need	wind
done	matter	mean	Mrs.
country	line	late	learn
different	large	half	held
bad	few	fight	front
across	hit	enough	built
yard	cover	feet	family
winter	window	during	began
table	even	gone	air
story	city	hundred	young
I'm	together	week	ago
tried	sun	between	world
horse	life	change	kill
brought	street	being	ready
shoes	party	care	stay
government	suit	answer	won't
sometimes	remember	course	paper
time	something	against	outside

FIFTH HUNDRED WORDS			
hour	grade	egg	spell
glad	brother	ground	beautiful
follow	remain	afternoon	sick
company	milk	feed	became
believe	several	boat	cry
begin	war	plan	finish
mind	able	question	catch
pass	charge	fish	floor
reach	either	return	stick
month	less	sir	great
point	train	fell	guess
rest	cost	fill	bridge
sent	evening	wood	church
talk	note	add	lady
went	past	ice	tomorrow
bank	room	chair	snow
ship	flew	watch	whom
business	office	alone	women
whole	cow	low	among
short	visit	arm	road
certain	wait	dinner	farm
fair	teacher	hair	cousin
reason	spring	service	bread
summer	picture	class	wrong
fill	bird	quite	age

SIXTH HUNDRED WORDS			
become	themselves	thousand	wife
body	herself	demand	condition
chance	idea	however	aunt
act	drop	figure	system
die	river	case	line
real	smile	increase	cause
speak	son	enjoy	marry
already	bat	rather	possible
doctor	fact	sound	supply
step	sort	eleven	pen
itself	king	music	perhaps
nine	dark	human	produce
baby	whose	court	twelve
minute	study	force	rode
ring	fear	plant	uncle
wrote	move	suppose	labor
happen	stood	law	public
appear	himself	husband	consider
heart	strong	moment	thus
swim	knew	person	least
felt	often	result	power
fourth	toward	continue	mark
I'll	wonder	price	voice
kept	twenty	serve	whether
well	important	national	president

Acknowledgments

Brandt & Hochman Literary Agents: "The Most Dangerous Game" by Richard Connell. Copyright © 1924 by Richard Connell. Copyright renewed © 1952 by Louise Fox Connell. Reprinted by permission of Brandt & Hochman Literary Agents, Inc.

Laura Hillenbrand: Adapted from "Four Good Legs Between Us," from *American Heritage,* July/August 1998, by Laura Hillenbrand. Copyright © 1998 by Laura Hillenbrand. Reprinted by permission of the author.

WGBH/Boston: Adapted from "Timeline: Seabiscuit" from the American Experience/WGBH Educational Foundation © 2009 WGBH/Boston. Used by permission of WGBH/Boston.

NBC News Archives: Adapted from the radio broadcast "Santa Anita Handicap" by Clem McCarthy and Buddy Twist. Copyright © 1937 by NBC News Archives. Reprinted by permission of NBC News Archives.

Alfred A. Knopf: "Incident in a Rose Garden," from *Collected Poems* by Donald Justice. Copyright © 2004 by Donald Justice. Reprinted by permission of Alfred A. Knopf, a division of Random House, Inc.

Houghton Mifflin Harcourt: Adapted from "The Necklace" by Guy de Maupassant from *Adventures in Reading,* Laureate Edition, Grade 9. Copyright © 1963 by Harcourt, Inc., and renewed 1991. Reprinted by permission of the publisher. This material may not be reproduced in any form or by any means without prior written permission of the publisher.

Random House: Excerpt from "Sister Flowers," from *I Know Why the Caged Bird Sings* by Maya Angelou. Copyright © 1969 and renewed © 1997 by Maya Angelou. Used by permission of Random House, Inc.

Penguin Group (USA): Excerpt from "The Bus Boycott" from *Rosa Parks* by Douglas Brinkley. Copyright © 2000 by Douglas Brinkley. Used by permission of Viking Penguin, a division of Penguin Group (USA) Inc.

Rita Dove: "Rosa" by Rita Dove was first published in the Georgia Review, Winter 1998, and subsequently in *On the Bus with Rosa Parks,* published by W.W. Norton. Copyright © 1999 by Rita Dove. Reprinted by permission of the author.

Random House: "A Christmas Memory" by Truman Capote. Copyright © 1956 by Truman Capote. Used by permission of Random House, Inc.

HarperCollins Publishers and Jonathan Clowes: Adapted from "Through the Tunnel," from *The Habit of Loving* by Doris Lessing. Copyright © 1954, 1955 by Doris Lessing, originally appeared in the *New Yorker.* Reprinted by permission of HarperCollins Publishers Inc. and the kind permission of Jonathan Clowes Ltd., London, on behalf of Doris Lessing.

Broadway Books and Doubleday Canada: Excerpt from *A Walk in the Woods* by Bill Bryson. Copyright © 1997 by Bill Bryson. Used by permission of Broadway Books, a division of Random House, Inc., and Doubleday Canada, a division of Random House of Canada Limited.

Doubleday: "Wilderness Letter," from *The Sound of Mountain Water* by Wallace Stegner. Copyright © 1969 by Wallace Stegner. Used by permission of Doubleday, a division of Random House, Inc.

James Hurst: Adapted from "The Scarlet Ibis" by James Hurst. Copyright © 1960 by the *Atlantic Monthly* and renewed 1988 by James Hurst. Reprinted by permission of James Hurst.

Thames & Hudson: "Poem on Returning to Dwell in the Country," from *T'ao the Hermit: Sixty Poems by T'ao Ch'ien* by T'ao Ch'ien, translated by William Acker. Copyright © 1952 by William Acker. Reprinted by kind permission of Thames & Hudson Ltd., London.

Beacon Press: "The Sun," from *New and Selected Poems* by Mary Oliver. Copyright © 1992 by Mary Oliver. Reprinted by permission of Beacon Press, Boston.

G. P. Putnam's and Sons: "Two Kinds," from *The Joy Luck Club* by Amy Tan. Copyright © 1989 by Amy Tan. Used by permission of G. P. Putnam's and Sons, a division of Penguin Group (USA) Inc.

Diane Mei Lin Mark: "Rice and Rose Bowl Blues" by Diane Mei Lin Mark. Copyright © by Diane Mei Lin Mark. Reprinted by permission of the author.

National Geographic Society: Adapted from "Who Killed the Iceman?" *National Geographic,* February 2002. Copyright © 2002 by National Geographic Society. Reprinted by permission of National Geographic Society.

Little, Brown & Company: Excerpt from "Skeletal Sculptures" from *The Bone Detectives* by Donna M. Jackson and Illustrated by Charlie Fellenbaum. Copyright © 1996 by Donna M. Jackson. Photographs copyright © 1996 by Charlie Fellenbaum. By permission of Little, Brown & Company.

Scholastic: Adapted from "The Lost Boys" by Sara Corbett, *New York Times Upfront,* September 3, 2001. Copyright © 2001 by Scholastic Inc. Used by permission.

Writers House: Adapted from "I Have a Dream" speech by Martin Luther King Jr. Copyright © 1963 Martin Luther King Jr., copyright renewed 1991 Coretta Scott King. Reprinted by arrangement with The Heirs to the Estate of Martin Luther King Jr., c/o Writers House as agent for the proprietor, New York, NY.

Andrea Rock: Adapted from "How Private Is Your Private Life?" by Andrea Rock, *Ladies Home Journal,* October 2000. Copyright © 2000 by Andrea Rock. Reprinted with the permission of the author.

Arthur M. Ahalt: Adapted from "The Privacy Debate: One Size Doesn't Fit All" by Arthur M. Ahalt from *The Daily Record,* June 20, 2003. Copyright © 2003 by Arthur M. Ahalt. Reprinted by permission of the author.

Liveright Publishing Corporation: "Spring is like a perhaps hand," from *Complete Poems: 1904–1962* by E. E. Cummings, edited by George J. Firmage. Copyright 1923, 1925, 1951, 1953, © 1991 by the Trustees for the E. E. Cummings Trust. Copyright © 1976 by George James Firmage. Used by permission of Liveright Publishing Corporation.

Houghton Mifflin Harcourt and Larmore Literary Agency: "Elegy for the Giant Tortoises," *Selected Poems 1965–1975* by Margaret Atwood. Copyright © 1976 by Margaret Atwood. Reprinted by permission of Houghton Mifflin Harcourt Publishing Company and Larmore Literary Agency. All rights reserved.

Random House: "Today," by Billy Collins from *Nine Horses.* Copyright © 2002 by Billy Collins. Used by permission of Random House, Inc.

Tim O'Brien: Adapted from "Where Have You Gone, Charming Billy?" by Tim O'Brien, from *Redbook,* May 1975. Copyright © 1975 by Tim O'Brien. Reprinted by permission of the author.

Scissor Press: Adapted from interview with Tim O'Brien by Douglas Novielli, Chris Connal, and Jackson Ellis. From *Verbicide,* Issue 8. Copyright © 2003 by Scissor Press. Reprinted by permission of Scissor Press.

Houghton Mifflin Harcourt: Adapted from "A Few Words," from *Blue Pastures* by Mary Oliver. Copyright © 1995, 1992, 1991 by Mary Oliver. Reprinted by permission of Houghton Mifflin Harcourt Publishing Company. All rights reserved.

Gary N. DaSilva: "The Sneeze" from *The Good Doctor,* by Neil Simon. Copyright © 1974 by Neil Simon, copyright renewed 2004 by Neil Simon. Professionals and amateurs are hereby warned that *The Good Doctor* is fully protected under the Berne Convention and the Universal Copyright Convention and is subject to royalty. All rights, including without limitation professional, amateur, motion picture, television, radio, recitation, lecturing, public reading and foreign translation rights, computer media rights and the right of reproduction, and electronic storage or retrieval, in whole or in part and in any form, are strictly reserved and none of these rights can be exercised or used without written permission from the copyright owner. Inquiries for stock and amateur performances should be addressed to Samuel French, Inc., 45 West 25th Street, New York, NY 10010. All other inquiries should be addressed to Gary N. DaSilva, 111 N. Sepulveda Blvd., Manhattan Beach, CA, 90266-6850.

Simon & Schuster: Adapted with the permission of Scribner, a Division of Simon & Schuster, Inc., from *Angela's Ashes* by Frank McCourt. Copyright © 1996 by Frank McCourt. All rights reserved.

University of Georgia Press: Adapted from "American History," from *The Latin Deli: Prose & Poetry* by Judith Oritz Cofer. Copyright © 1992 by Judith Ortiz Cofer. Reprinted by permission of the University of Georgia Press.

U.S. News & World Report: "Dark Day" by Kenneth T. Walsh from *U.S. News & World Report,* November 24, 2003. Copyright © 2003 by U.S. News & World Report. Reprinted by permission of U.S. News & World Report.

Universal Press Syndicate: Adapted from "Romeo and Juliet" by Roger Ebert, from the *Chicago Sun-Times,* September 17, 2000. Copyright © 2000 by The Ebert Company. Reprinted with permission. All rights reserved.

Farrar, Straus and Giroux: Excerpts from *The Odyssey* by Homer, translated by Robert Fitzgerald. Translation copyright © 1961, 1963 renewed 1989 by Benedict R. C. Fitzgerald on behalf of the Fitzgerald children. This edition © 1998 by Farrar, Straus & Giroux, LLC. Reprinted by permission of Farrar, Straus and Giroux, LLC.

Cover

(tc) Sea World of California/Corbis; (tr) Odysseus Slaying the Suitors (400's B.C.), Penelope Painter. Attic red figure painting on kylix. Height 20 cm. Inv F 2588. Antikensammlung, Staatliche Museen zu Berlin, Berlin. Photo by Juergen Liepe. © Bildarchiv Preussischer Kulturbesitz/Art Resource, New York; (bc) Colin Anderdson/Getty Images; (b) Portrait of William Shakespeare (about 1610), John Taylor. Oil on canvas. National Portrait Gallery, London. © Bridgeman Art Library; (bkgd) © Walter Geiersperger/Corbis; (bl) Ken Kinzie/HMH Publishers.

How to Use the Student Book

xiii *top* © photostogo.com; *center* © DAJ/PunchStock; *bottom* © photostogo.com; **xvi** © photostogo.com.

Unit 1

2 © Firefly Productions/Corbis; **6–32** © AbleStock.com/Jupiterimages Corporation; **6** © Comstock Images/Jupiterimages Corporation; **8** © Bernd Jürgens/Shutterstock; **11** © Luminouslens/ShutterStock; **24** © Cre8tive Images/Shutterstock; **38–42** © photostogo.com; **38** Detail of *Woman at Her Toilette,* Edgar Degas. Pastel on cardboard. State Hermitage Museum, St. Petersburg, Russia. © SuperStock/SuperStock; **40** © Konstantin Reminzov/Shutterstock; **47** © Hulton Archive/Getty Images; **49** © Gergo Orban/Shutterstock; **51** *left* © Bettmann/Corbis; *center* © Keystone/Hulton Archive/Getty Images; *right* © Xavier Marchant/Shutterstock; **58–67** © George Burba/ShutterStock; **58** © IT Stock Free/Jupiterimages Corporation; **60** © Jupiterimages Corporation; **65** © Leonid Kashtalian/istockphoto.com.

Unit 2

70 © Design Pics/Punchstock; **74–78** © photostogo.com; **74** *top* © DAJ/PunchStock; *bottom* © photostogo.com; **84–92** © Digital Vision/PunchStock; **84** © Solus-Veer/Corbis; **86** © Jupiterimages Corporation; **90** © Jerry Zitterman/Shutterstock; **98–104** © Feng Yu/ShutterStock; **98** © Bettmann/Corbis; **102** © CVP/Shutterstock.

Unit 3

108 © Heidi Hart/ShutterStock; **112–126** © Comstock Images/Jupiterimages Corporation; **112** © Edward Charles Le Grice/Hulton Archive/Getty Images; **122** © Jupiterimages Corporation; **132–140** © Comstock Images/Jupiterimages Corporation; **132** © Nathan B. Dappen/ShutterStock; **133** © Dainis Derics/Shutterstock; **146–152** © Digital Archive Japan/PunchStock; **146** San Gennaro Catacombs, Naples, Italy. Photo © Gianni Dagli Orti/The Art Archive; **150** © Jupiterimages Corporation; **158–168** © David Raboin/istockphoto.com; **158** © Comstock Images/Jupiterimages Corporation; **159** © Jim Parkin/Shutterstock; **173** © Photos.com/Jupiterimages Corporation; **177** © Tyler Olson/Shutterstock; **179** © Jupiterimages Corporation.

Unit 4

182 © Design Pics/PunchStock; **186–196** © photostogo.com; **186, 188** © Comstock Images/Jupiterimages Corporation; **202–207** © istockphoto.com; **202, 203** © redchopsticks/PunchStock; **205** © Bill Binzen/Corbis; **206** © EvGraf/ShutterStock; **212–230** © Loke Yek Mang/ShutterStock; **212** © Renars Jurkovskis/ShutterStock; **213** © Purestock/Punchstock; **221** © Gorilla/Shutterstock; **228** © Noam Armonn/ShutterStock.

Unit 5

234 © Lara Jo Regan/Liaison/Getty Images; **238** © Reuters/Corbis; **239** © Regional Hospital of Bolzano/South Tyrol Museum of Archaeology www.iceman.it; **240** © Copper Age/The Bridgeman Art Library/Getty Images; **241** © GeoNova LLC; **244–246** Photos from *The Bone Detective* © Charles Fellenbaum, Boulder, Colorado; **252–256** © Rob Broek/istockphoto.com; **252** *center* © Miroslava Vilimova/Alamy Ltd; *bottom* © Dennis Donohue/Shutterstock; **264** © Stephen Bonk/Shutterstock.

Unit 6

270 Andrew Rullestad/The Ames Tribune/AP/Wide World Photos; **274–278** © Digital Vision/PunchStock; **274** Library of Congress, Prints and Photographs Division [LC–DIG–ppmsc–01269]; **285** © Ron Sachs/CNP/Sygma/Corbis; **294** © Digital Vision/PunchStock; **299, 302** © istockphoto.com.

Unit 7

306 © Saniphoto/ShutterStock; **310–315** © Photos.com/Jupiterimages Corporation; **310** © PhotoDisc/Getty Images; **312** © PhotoObjects.net/Jupiterimages Corporation; **314** © Comstock Images/Jupiterimages Corporation.

Unit 8

318 Detail of *Self Portrait* (1889–1890), Vincent Van Gogh. Oil on canvas. Musée d'Orsay, Paris. © SuperStock/SuperStock; **322–326** © Grant Terry/ShutterStock; **322, 327, 329** © Lukasz Janicki/ShutterStock; **324** © PhotoObjects.net/Jupiterimages Corporation; **336–338** © Karel Broz/ShutterStock; **336** © PhotoDisc/Getty Images; **338** © AbleStock.com/Jupiterimages Corporation; **344–356** © Comstock Images/Jupiterimages Corporation; **344** The Granger Collection, New York.

Art Credits

Unit 9

360 © John Leung/ShutterStock; **364–368** © AbleStock.com/Jupiterimages Corporation; **364** © Corbis Sygma; **365** © Tjerrie Smit/Shutterstock; **374–378** © photostogo.com; **374, 377** © Dubassy/ShutterStock; **377** *right* © Dewayne Flowers/Shutterstock; **383, 387** © photostogo.com; **384** Photograph by Abbie Rowe/National Park Service. Courtesy John F. Kennedy Presidential Library and Museum, Boston.

Unit 10

390 © Mary Evans Picture Library; **394–406** © Comstock Images/Jupiterimages Corporation; **395** *Romeo and Juliet,* 1996. Leonardo Di Caprio and Claire Danes. © 20th Century Fox/Courtesy Everett Collection; **397** © Photos.com/Jupiterimages Corporation; **411** Courtesy Everett Collection; **414** © photostogo.com.

Unit 11

418 © Ruggero Vanni/Corbis; **422–440** © Corbis; **422** © Mary Evans Picture Library; *cyclops* © Chao-Yang Chan/Alamy Ltd.

Index of Authors and Titles